STUDIES IN EARLY MODERN CULTURAL,
POLITICAL AND SOCIAL HISTORY

Volume 4

# HANOVER AND
# THE BRITISH EMPIRE,
# 1700–1837

**Studies in Early Modern Cultural, Political and Social History**

ISSN: 1476–9107

Series editors
David Armitage
Tim Harris
Stephen Taylor

I
Women of Quality
Accepting and Contesting Ideals of Femininity in England, 1690–1760
*Ingrid H. Tague*

II
Restoration Scotland, 1660–1690
Royalist Politics, Religion and Ideas
*Clare Jackson*

III
Britain, Hanover and the Protestant Interest, 1688–1756
*Andrew C. Thompson*

# HANOVER AND THE BRITISH EMPIRE, 1700–1837

*Nick Harding*

THE BOYDELL PRESS

First published 2007
The Boydell Press, Woodbridge


ISBN 978–1–84383–300–0

The Boydell Press is an imprint of Boydell & Brewer Ltd
PO Box 9, Woodbridge, Suffolk IP12 3DF, UK
and of Boydell & Brewer Inc.
668 Mt Hope Avenue, Rochester, NY 14620, USA
website: www.boydellandbrewer.com


A catalogue record for this book is available
from the British Library


This publication is printed on acid-free paper

Typeset by Pru Harrison, Hacheston, Suffolk
Printed in Great Britain by
Antony Rowe Ltd, Chippenham, Wiltshire

# Contents

# Illustrations

# Acknowledgements

I can only hope this book lives up to the collections where it was researched. I am grateful for the permission of Her Majesty Queen Elizabeth II to visit the Royal Archives. My thanks are also due to the registrar at Windsor, Pamela Clark, for her expertise and hospitality. Additionally, I am obliged to dozens of other libraries and archives for their help over the years. In Britain, these included the British Library, the National Archives, Cambridge University Library, and the National Library of Scotland. In Germany, I consulted the Niedersächsische Staats- und Universitätsbibliothek Göttingen, the Gottfried Wilhelm Leibniz Bibliothek in Hannover, the Niedersächsisches Hauptstaatsarchiv, the Herzog August Bibliothek Wolfenbüttel and the Hessisches Staatsarchiv Darmstadt. Finally, I spent a lot of time in American libraries. I owe a lot to the unstinting and enthusiastic assistance of librarians at the Library of Congress and the Folger Shakespeare Library, where I also took advantage of the stimulation afforded by the program of the Folger Institute. I must also thank the library of my graduate school, Columbia University, which possesses a representative sample of Hanoverian publications from the early nineteenth century. Other libraries which enabled me to continue my work stateside were those of the Johns Hopkins University, the University of Pennsylvania, the University of Virginia, and Emory University. Finally, important research was done at my alma mater, Yale University. Yale allowed me to consult the Beinecke Library, and funded a research visit to the Lewis Walpole Library in Farmington, Connecticut. While there, I enjoyed the company of its librarian Richard Williams.

At its best, history is collaborative; I have benefited from the suggestions of several colleagues over the years. I thank my various interlocutors during job interviews and conference panels, although they are too numerous to name here. Nevertheless, two conferences bear mention. Rex Rexheuser kindly invited me to a Dresden conference comparing the dynastic union of Britain and Hanover with that of Saxony and Poland, which the German Historical Institutes of London and Warsaw cosponsored in 1997. Likewise, I wish to thank Brendan Simms and Torsten Riotte for hosting me at their 2004 colloquium on Britain and Hanover in Cambridge. I am also grateful to those historians who have agreed to read various incarnations of my manuscript: Chris Bauermeister, Marcus Collins, Frauke Geyken, Bob Harris, Tim Jenks, Sebastian Küster, John Marshall, and Jonathan Scott. Their input immensely improved my work, although (as the truism goes) they are innocent of any remaining shortcomings.

# ACKNOWLEDGEMENTS

This book originated as a dissertation, and owes most to my college and graduate supervisors. Linda Colley first sparked my interest in eighteenth-century history, and has helped to sustain it over the years. David Underdown broadened my chronological perspective, and Michael Howard convinced me of the European continent's importance to British history. At Columbia, István Deák and Isser Woloch gamely served on my prospectus committee. Volker Berghahn, Christia Mercer, and Deborah Valenze sat on my defense committee; they persuaded me to be less cautious and more ambitious. Hermann Wellenreuther oversaw my work in its early stages, when a DAAD annual grant enabled me to spend a year in Göttingen. One of the best historians of the relationship between Britain and Hanover, his influence on my method and perspective will be evident. David Cannadine was a stimulating and patient dissertation sponsor. Finally, this book is almost as much David Armitage's as it is mine. It was inspired by his tutorial's readings on composite monarchy, and by his willingness to think of state formation in terms of empire. David was always supportive, dispensing encouragement and constructive criticism when appropriate. He disciplined my previously instinctive approach to intellectual history, and engineered a shift from thematic to chronological structure.

David has continued to help me, as one of my series editors for Boydell & Brewer. I must also thank his collaborators, Tim Harris and Stephen Taylor, for their insightful suggestions at every step of the publication process. Peter Sowden, my editor at Boydell, kindly tolerated repeated delays in the delivery of my manuscript.

I have also drawn strength from my friends, both inside and outside of the historical profession. In Britain, I received hospitality from Scott Crawford, Gregory Edelston, Paul Gray, Tori Holt, Sarah Humphries, Robert MacKay, Adam Morris, David Parrott, and Chris Waters. In Germany, I enjoyed the generosity of Norman Brooks, Eva Gorsten, Stefan Kraushaar, Dorin Leder, the Meier family (Horst, Renate, Steffi, and Sven), Ricardo Rosenstiel, Shaun Vargas, and Thorsten Wolf. In the United States, I have relied upon the friendship of Gerard Alexander, Tracey Billado, Kristian Blaich, Karen Bosnos, Jonathyne Briggs, Lori Calbert, Dale Clifford, Charles Closmann, Russell Duke, Andy Eves, Paul Halsall, Darren Kowitt, Debbie Everett-Lane, Hartmut Lehmann, Arielle Masters, Joe Meisel, Jamie Melton, Jacqui Olkin, Dawn Regan, Holley Riley, Trish van der Spuy, Bob Tripp, Eddie Victor, Ted Wallenthin, and Erin Williams. Above all, I have been lucky to have the love and support of Jerry Pumphrey and his family.

Finally, my family has lived with this book since its inception. I am grateful to my extended family, the Owens, the Emmarts, the Goughs, and the Buntings, for their good cheer. I thank my brother Jamie, his wife Loretta, and their children Cary and Sonya for their love and interest in my work. But it is my parents who have made this book possible, by their support both material and moral. I dedicate it to them.

# Note on the text

Unless otherwise indicated, British dates before 1752 conform to the Julian Calendar. Thereafter British dates are in the Gregorian Calendar, as are all German dates. All years are understood to have begun on 1 January. English spelling, capitalization, and punctuation have been updated; all translations are mine. Hanover refers to the German electorate and kingdom, while Hannover refers to the city which served as its capital. The words 'empire', 'emperor', and 'imperial' are not capitalized, except when they refer to the Holy Roman Empire or its ruler.

# Introduction

Tradition holds that Britain's interactions with the outside world have been Janus-faced,[1] distinguishing between transoceanic empire and diplomacy on the European continent.[2] Accordingly, historians have tended to downplay evidence of British empire on the continent. The omission is questionable not merely empirically, but also theoretically, for Europe is geographically and culturally continuous with Asia.[3] Europe is, after all, an Asian subcontinent comparable to India,[4] a familiar subject of British imperial historiography. Including Europe in the history of British empire can solve two stubborn problems. First, it can reduce the cognitive distance between metropolis and periphery that historians of British empire have often regretted.[5] And it will qualify the sense of novelty attending British participation in the European Union, which is itself an empire of sorts.[6] Of course this is opposed by many including John Pocock, who debunks European distinctiveness in order to protect its British equivalent from continental federalism.[7] But for François Guizot and others, European and national exceptionalisms went together.[8] A critique of both enables a truly new

---

[1] For the Janus model, see Timothy Garton Ash, *Free World: America, Europe, and the Surprising Future of the West* (New York, 2004), pp. 13–45.
[2] A rare critique of the distinction between maritime and continental policy can be found in Richard Harding, *Amphibious Warfare in the Eighteenth Century: The British Expedition to the West Indies 1740–1742* (London, 1991), pp. 185–97.
[3] J. G. A. Pocock, 'What Do We Mean by Europe?', *Wilson Quarterly* 21 (1997), pp. 12–29; J. G. A. Pocock, 'Some Europes in Their History', in Anthony Pagden, ed., *The Idea of Europe from Antiquity to the European Union* (Cambridge, 2002), pp. 55–71.
[4] Pocock, 'Some Europes in Their History', p. 58.
[5] J. R. Seeley, *The Expansion of England: Two Courses of Lectures* (Boston, 1883); Eric Stokes, *The English Utilitarians and India* (Oxford, 1959); P. J. Cain and A. G. Hopkins, *British Imperialism 1688–1990* (2 vols., London, 1993); David Armitage, *The Ideological Origins of the British Empire* (Cambridge, 2000); David Cannadine, *Ornamentalism: How the British Saw Their Empire* (Oxford, 2001).
[6] Jan Zielonka, *Europe as Empire: the Nature of the Enlarged European Union* (Oxford, 2006).
[7] J. G. A. Pocock, 'British History: A Plea for a New Subject', *The Journal of Modern History* 47 (1975), pp. 601–28; J. G. A. Pocock, 'The Limits and Divisions of British History: In Search of the Unknown Subject', *The American Historical Review* 87 (1982), pp. 311–36; J. G. A. Pocock, 'History and Sovereignty: The Historiographical Response to Europeanization in Two British Cultures', *Journal of British Studies* 31 (1992), pp. 358–89.
[8] Michael Herzfeld, 'The European Self: Rethinking an Attitude', in Pagden, ed., *The*

1

British history which views political integration with the continent in terms of continuity as well as change.

Both historians and journalists ground British Euroskepticism in the English tradition of unitary sovereignty, dating back at least to the sixteenth century. But at least one country with a similar definition of sovereignty, France, has generally supported European integration. If the argument from sovereignty cannot explain British Euroskepticism, neither can the tradition it seeks to replace. The 'whig interpretation of history', with its celebration of parliamentary liberty over administrative bureaucracy,[9] seems to explain the present-day distrust of continental dirigisme. Although British parliaments arose at the same time as continental estates, whig historians emphasize the partial disappearance of the latter during the early-modern period – and the comparative continuity of British constitutionalism. They explain that Britain's geographic position on an island and naval eminence protected parliamentary and civil liberties, which supposedly suffered more insults from continental governments upon the pretext of greater military vulnerability. This is not so much comparative history as geographical determinism, which leaves out counterexamples such as Ireland (an island without a navy) and the Dutch Netherlands (a continental naval power with strong estates). Indeed the Dutch state launched a successful naval descent upon England in 1688,[10] an event which whig historians had to reinterpret as assistance to internal rebels. The argument from strategic insularity has drawn its fair share of criticism, but has proven more resilient than the purely domestic whig account.[11] Indeed it continues to influence otherwise revisionist historians.[12] But the origins of British Euroskepticism may be more convincingly located in Britons' ambivalence towards empire, their own as well as others'.

If anything belied Britain's insularity it was the empire, in which the sea functioned as a vector for, rather than a barrier to, politics.[13] Yet the whig

---

*Idea of Europe*, p. 162. See also Ariane Chebel d'Appolonia, 'European Nationalism and European Union', in Pagden, ed., *The Idea of Europe*, p. 175.

9  See H. Butterfield, *The Whig Interpretation of History* (London, 1931); H. Butterfield, *The Englishman and His History* (Cambridge, 1944); J. W. Burrow, *A Liberal Descent: Victorian Historians and the English Past* (Cambridge, 1981).

10  Jonathan I. Israel, 'The Dutch Role in the Glorious Revolution', in Jonathan I. Israel, ed., *The Anglo-Dutch Moment: Essays on The Glorious Revolution and Its World Impact* (Cambridge, 1991), pp. 105–62.

11  Michael Bentley, 'The British State and Its Historiography', in Wim Blockmans and Jean-Philippe Genet, eds., *Visions sur le développement des états européens: théories et historiographies de l'état moderne* (Rome, 1993), pp. 156–7.

12  Linda Colley, *Britons: Forging the Nation 1707–1837* (New Haven, 1992), pp. 17, 50; Kidd, *British Identities before Nationalism*, p. 214.

13  This is, of course, also true of the English Channel: John Reeve, 'Britain or Europe? The Context of Early Modern English History: Political and Cultural, Economic and Social, Naval and Military', in Glenn Burgess, ed., *The New British History: Founding a Modern State 1603–1715* (London, 1999), p. 292; Jonathan Scott, *England's Troubles:*

analysis inevitably extended to empire,[14] distinguishing Britain's empire from those of its European neighbors according to the same criteria which supposedly differentiated their respective metropoles. J. R. Seeley's *Expansion of England* (1883) avoided rather than denied the whig inheritance and, *malgré lui*, inaugurated a professional imperial history which saw the empire progressively projecting metropolitan liberties overseas. The whig paradigm flourished as dominions proliferated during the early twentieth century, and then declined as other dependencies achieved outright independence after World War II.[15] Even so, a whig perspective continues to influence much imperial history.[16] And while most imperial historians escaped parliamentarism, they have nonetheless silently respected whig history's anti-continental bias. Beginning in the 1950s, historians used the concept of 'informal' imperialism to extend empire's geographical basis beyond the parts painted red on the map. But they declined to apply their analysis to continental Europe, with the exception of the Ottoman Balkans.[17]

To the extent that the continent has been included in the history of empire, it has been for the pre-modern period. It may be significant that England, the part of Britain presently most resistant to European political integration, is precisely that which has the most historical experience of it.[18] While claims for an ancient, pan-European Celtic empire are more speculative than obvious,[19] the Roman empire established a durable beachhead in England. Imperial contact with the European continent resumed in the eleventh century, when England was conquered by Denmark[20] and

*Seventeenth-Century English Political Instability in European Context* (Cambridge, 2000), p. 10; Armitage, *The Ideological Origins of the British Empire*, p. 15.

[14] Jack P. Greene, 'Empire and Identity from the Glorious Revolution to the American Revolution', in William Roger Louis, ed., *The Oxford History of the British Empire* (5 vols., Oxford, 1998–9), ii, pp. 208–30; Uday Singh Mehta, *Liberalism and Empire: A Study in Nineteenth-Century British Liberal Thought* (Chicago, 1999); Miles Taylor, 'Imperium et Libertas? Rethinking the Radical Critique of Imperialism during the Nineteenth Century', *The Journal of Imperial and Commonwealth History* 19 (1991), pp. 1–23.

[15] William Roger Louis, 'Introduction', in William Roger Louis, ed., *The Oxford History of the British Empire* (5 vols., Oxford, 1998–9), v, pp. 1–42.

[16] Pocock, 'The Limits and Divisions of British History', especially p. 315; Niall Ferguson, *Empire* (London, 2002), p. xxv.

[17] John Gallagher and Ronald Robinson, 'The Imperialism of Free Trade', *The Economic History Review* second series 6 (1953), p. 9.

[18] Scotland's experience of political integration with the continent remained speculative rather than real before 1688. 'The maid of Norway' would not only have unified Scotland to England had she lived to marry Edward II, but might also have inherited Norway from her father. Mary Stuart would have connected Scotland to France had her marriage to François II produced sons.

[19] Peter Beresford Ellis, *The Celtic Empire: The First Millennium of Celtic History c. 1000 BC – 51 AD* (Durham, NC, 1990), p. 1.

[20] Laurence Marcellus Larson, *Canute the Great 995 (circa) – 1035 and the Rise of Danish Imperialism during the Viking Age* (New York, 1912); G. N. Garmonsway, *Canute and His Empire* (London, 1964); Peter Sawyer, 'Cnut's Scandinavian Empire', in Alexander R. Rumble, ed., *The Reign of Cnut: King of England, Denmark and Norway* (London, 1994), pp. 10–26.

Normandy[21] in turn. Henry II inherited the Norman patrimony along with Anjou and Aquitaine, assembling the Angevin empire.[22] This empire's collapse in the early thirteenth century left England with Gascony, which Margaret Wade Labarge memorably called 'England's first colony'.[23] Gascony proved a useful base for England's subsequent conquest of France during the Hundred Years' War. Though Labarge reinforced modern imperial history's anti-continental bias by characterizing the relationship with Gascony as an apprenticeship for a later – exclusively maritime – empire,[24] France did not entirely evict its English adversary during the fifteenth century. England retained Calais, which G. A. C. Sandeman also labeled 'the first English colony'.[25] Henry VIII pursued a policy of naturalization, annexation, and parliamentary union in and near the Calais pale, although he would have also liked to restore his ancestors' dominions in Normandy and Guienne.[26] Another weighty development was Mary I's marriage to Felipe II of Spain, which opened the prospect of political integration during the reigns of their children. Even after the loss of Calais and Mary's childless death in 1558, political integration with the continent remained an option. England pursued union with the United Provinces in the 1650s,[27] and occupied Dunkirk between 1658 and 1662.

Where ancient and medieval historians explored Britain's imperial relations with the European continent, early modernists have been more cautious. Some have called for research into empire's involvement on the European continent.[28] But most have preferred a comparative approach,[29]

---

21 Charles Homer Haskins, *The Normans in European History* (Boston and New York, 1915), pp. 85–115; John Le Patourel, 'Feudal Empires: Norman and Plantagenet', *Les grands empires: Recueils de la Société Jean Bodin pour l'histoire comparative des institutions* 31 (1973), pp. 281–307; John Le Patourel, *The Norman Empire* (Oxford, 1976).

22 Kate Norgate, *England under the Angevin Kings* (2 vols., London, 1887), ii, p. 491; Sir James H. Ramsay of Bamff, *The Angevin Empire, or the Three Reigns of Henry II, Richard I, and John* (London, 1903); Sir Maurice Powicke, *The Loss of Normandy 1189–1204: Studies in the History of the Angevin Empire* (Manchester, 1961); John Gillingham, *The Angevin Empire* (London, 2001).

23 Margaret Wade Labarge, *Gascony, England's First Colony 1204–1453* (London, 1980).

24 Labarge, *Gascony*, pp. 236–7.

25 G. A. C. Sandeman, *Calais under English Rule* (Oxford, 1908), p. 3. See also John Le Patourel, 'L'occupation anglaise de Calais au XIVe siècle', *Revue du Nord* 33 (1951), pp. 228–41.

26 J. J. Scarisbrick, *Henry VIII* (Berkeley, 1968), esp. pp. 21–40; C. G. Cruickshank, *The English Occupation of Tournai 1513–1519* (Oxford, 1971); Steven Gunn, 'The French Wars of Henry VIII', in Jeremy Black, ed., *The Origins of War in Early Modern Europe* (Edinburgh, 1987), pp. 37–9; Thomas F. Mayer, 'On the Road to 1534: The Occupation of Tournai and Henry VIII's Theory of Sovereignty', in Dale Hoak, ed., *Tudor Political Culture* (Cambridge, 1995), pp. 11–30.

27 Steven C. A. Pincus, *Protestantism and Patriotism: Ideologies and the Making of English Foreign Policy, 1650–1668* (Cambridge, 1996).

28 Scott, *England's Troubles*, p. 13; Linda Colley, 'What Is Imperial History Now?', in David Cannadine, ed., *What Is History Now?* (Basingstoke, 2002), p. 140.

*Footnote 29 appears on page 5*

terming Britain a 'composite state' similar to its contemporaries on the European continent.[30] Composite states were systems of systems of legally distinct countries – often with their own representative assemblies – linked by their subjection to a common sovereign.[31] These culturally and linguistically varied assortments have an obvious appeal for those historians sympathetic to present-day political integration across national and cultural boundaries. The composite state model has also influenced histories of Britain's early overseas empire, which was legally diverse in the manner of the European metropolises.[32] But for all that the study of its composite states has resituated Britain in its European context, it has so far overlooked its early-modern unions with continental states. Historians have not absorbed the imperial implications of Jonathan Israel's finding that Dutch state interest drove William III's conquest of Britain in that year.[33] Nor have they evinced much interest in the composite state the king projected in 1701, when his own dynasty's inability to produce a Protestant heir necessitated the extension of England's succession to the elector of Hanover.[34]

[29] For the difference between comparative and transnational analyses, see Reeve, 'Britain or Europe?', p. 288.

[30] Conrad Russell, *The Causes of the English Civil War* (Oxford, 1990), pp. 26–57, 109–30; Conrad Russell, *Unrevolutionary England 1603–1642* (London, 1990), pp. 231–51, 263–79; M. Perceval-Maxwell, 'Ireland and the Monarchy in the Early Stuart Multiple Kingdom', *The Historical Journal* 34 (1991), pp. 279–95; Conrad Russell, *The Fall of the British Monarchies* (Oxford, 1991), pp. 27–70; Jenny Wormald, 'The Creation of Britain: Multiple Kingdoms or Core and Colonies?', *Transactions of the Royal Historical Society* sixth series 2 (1992), pp. 175–94; Ronald Asch, ed., *Three Nations – a Common History?* (Bochum, 1993); Steven G. Ellis and Sarah Barber, eds., *Conquest and Union: Fashioning a British State, 1485–1725* (London, 1995); Alexander Grant and Keith J. Stringer, eds., *Uniting the Kingdom? The Making of British History* (London, 1995); Brendan Bradshaw and John Morrill, eds., *The British Problem, c. 1534–1707: State Formation in the Atlantic Archipelago* (Basingstoke, 1996); Tim Harris, 'Reluctant Revolutionaries? The Scots and the Revolution of 1688–89', in Howard Nenner, ed., *Politics and the Political Imagination in later Stuart Britain* (Rochester, NY, 1997), pp. 97–117; Tim Harris, 'The British Dimension, Religion, and the Shaping of Political Identities during the Reign of Charles II', in Tony Claydon and Ian McBride, eds., *Protestantism and National Identity: Britain and Ireland, c. 1650 – c. 1850* (Cambridge, 1998), pp. 131–56.

[31] H. G. Koenigsberger, '*Dominium regale* or *dominium politicum et regale*: Monarchies and Parliaments in Early Modern Europe', in *Politicians and Virtuosi: Essays in Early Modern History* (London, 1986), pp. 1–25; J. H. Elliott, 'A Europe of Composite Monarchies', *Past and Present* 137 (1992), pp. 48–71; John Robertson, 'Union, State and Empire: The Britain of 1707 in its European Setting', in Lawrence Stone, ed., *An Imperial State at War: Britain from 1689 to 1815* (London, 1994), pp. 224–57.

[32] H. G. Koenigsberger, 'Composite States, Representative Institutions and the American Revolution', *Historical Research* 62 (1989), pp. 135–53; Robertson, 'Union, State and Empire'; J. G. A. Pocock, 'Empire, State and Confederation: The War of American Independence as a Crisis in Multiple Monarchy', in John Robertson, ed., *A Union for Empire: Political Thought and the British Union of 1707* (Cambridge, 1995), pp. 318–48; Armitage, *The Ideological Origins of the British Empire*, p. 23.

[33] Israel, 'The Dutch Role in the Glorious Revolution'.

[34] See Nicholas B. Harding, 'North African Piracy, the Hanoverian Carrying Trade, and

The Hanoverian example challenges the geographic limits of Britain's composite state, causing even Pocock to refer to an 'Anglo-Hanoverian empire between the Elbe and the Ohio'.[35] But Britain's relationship also extended the chronological range of the early-modern British composite state beyond the bounds he once recognized. Although Pocock once declared that 'with the legislative union that created the United Kingdom of Great Britain and Ireland, the early modern period of British history may be said to come to an end',[36] Britain's relationship with Hanover survived the 1801 Act of Union by some thirty-six years. Britain's experience with composite statehood endured until a Hanoverian law barring most instances of female succession favored the claims of the duke of Cumberland over those of Princess Victoria in 1837. Empire's continental component persisted in Gibraltar and in the form of economic penetration of the continent, but there is no question that it assumed a lower profile during the late nineteenth century. Although this retrenchment was relatively new, it influenced the Euroamnesia of the professional history of empire which took off during this period.

Perhaps the recent literature on Britain's composite state has overlooked the relationship with Hanover because the latter has long been subsumed into the older comparative model of diplomatic history.[37] This subdiscipline

the British State, 1728–1828', *The Historical Journal* 43 (2000), pp. 25–47. For treatments which overlook the problem of 'composite statehood', see Ian Campbell, 'From the "Personal Union" between England and Scotland in 1603 to the European Communities Act 1972 and Beyond', in B. S. Jackson and D. McGoldrick, eds., *Legal Visions of the New Europe* (London, 1993), pp. 37–104; Michael John, 'National and Regional Identities and the Dilemmas of Reform in Britain's "Other Province": Hanover, c. 1800 – c. 1850', in Laurence Brockliss and David Eastwood, eds., *A Union of Multiple Identities: The British Isles, c. 1750 – c. 1850* (Manchester, 1997), pp. 179–92.
35  J. G. A. Pocock, 'The Atlantic Archipelago and the War of the Three Kingdoms', in Bradshaw and Morrill, eds., *The British Problem*, p. 175.
36  Pocock, 'The Limits and Divisions of British History', p. 330.
37  See, for example, Günther Lange, 'Die Rolle Englands bei der Wiederherstellung und Vergrößerung Hannovers 1813–1815', *Niedersächsisches Jahrbuch für Landesgeschichte* 28 (1956), pp. 73–178; Gert Brauer, *Die hannoversch-englischen Subsidienverträge 1702–1748* (Aalen, 1962); John J. Murray, *George I, the Baltic and the Whig Split of 1717: A Study in Diplomacy and Propaganda* (London, 1969); W. Mediger, 'Great Britain, Hanover and the Rise of Prussia', in Ragnhild Hatton and M. S. Anderson, eds., *Studies in Diplomatic History: Essays in Memory of David Bayne Horn* (London, 1970), pp. 199–213; T. C. W. Blanning, ' "That Horrid Electorate" or "ma patrie germanique"? George III, Hanover, and the Fürstenbund of 1785', *The Historical Journal* 20 (1977), pp. 311–44; Jeremy Black, *British Foreign Policy in the Age of Walpole* (Edinburgh, 1985), pp. 27–48; Adolf M. Birke and Kurt Kluxen, eds., *England und Hannover* (Munich, 1986), passim; Jeremy Black, ed., *Knights Errant and True Englishmen: British Foreign Policy, 1660–1800* (Edinburgh, 1989), passim; Uta Richter-Uhlig, *Hof und Politik unter den Bedingungen der Personalunion zwischen Hannover und England* (Hannover, 1992); Philip G. Dwyer, 'Prussia and the Armed Neutrality: The Invasion of Hanover in 1801', *International History Review* 15 (1993), pp. 661–87; Brendan Simms, ' "An Odd Question Enough": Charles James Fox, the Crown and British Policy during the Hanoverian Crisis of 1806', *The Historical Journal*

avoids exceptionalism, and examines British history in international context. When hewing to empirical detail, diplomatic historians have been sensitive to the complexities of Hanover's relationship with Britain. Unfortunately, such work is necessarily episodic and does not support extrapolation. Diplomatic historians have therefore borrowed theory from other disciplines including international law. This has promoted the notion that eighteenth-century Britain and Hanover formed a personal union, a category of international law denoting two states which retain their independence under a common ruler.[38] The effect has been to reinforce an insular reading of the British-Hanoverian dynastic union.

The argument for mutual independence rests on two legs, one Hanoverian and one British. Hanover remained a part of the Holy Roman Empire until 1806 and acceded to the German confederation in 1815. Of course, the Empire did not preclude external empire; Austria dominated Hungary while Denmark ruled Schleswig-Holstein. Nor was federal sovereignty a bar to British empire, which first manifested itself in India on a regional basis within the Mughal empire. Arguments for Britain's countervailing independence from Hanover rely upon England's Act of Settlement, the 1701 legislation which imposed various handicaps upon foreign successors in principle and the Hanoverian electoral family in particular. The Act required the successor to be in communion with the Church of England, and

38 (1995), pp. 567–96; Philip G. Dwyer, 'Two Definitions of Neutrality: Prussia, the European States-System, and the French Invasion of Hanover in 1803', *International History Review* 19 (1997), pp. 522–40; Jeremy Black, *The Continental Commitment: Britain, Hanover, and Interventionism 1714–1793* (London, 2005); Rex Rexheuser, ed., *Die Personalunionen von Sachsen-Polen 1697–1763 und Hannover-England 1714–1837: Ein Vergleich* (Wiesbaden, 2005), passim.

38 Ernst von Meier, *Hannoversche Verfassungs- und Verwaltungsgeschichte 1680–1866* (2 vols., Leipzig, 1898), i, pp. 122–3; Adolphus William Ward, *Great Britain and Hanover: Some Aspects of the Personal Union* (Oxford, 1899), pp. 1–2; Karl Bingmann, *Das rechtliche Verhältnis zwischen Großbritannien und Hannover von 1714 bis 1837* (Celle, 1925), pp. 51–2; Kenneth L. Ellis, 'The Administrative Connections between Britain and Hanover', *Journal of the Society of Archivists* 3 (October 1969), p. 548; Georg Schnath, 'Die Personalunion zwischen Großbritannien und Hannover 1714–1837', *Lüneburger Blätter* 20 (1969), pp. 7–8; Waldemar Röhrbein and Alheidis von Rohr, *Hannover im Glanz und Schatten des britischen Weltreiches: Die Auswirkungen der Personalunion auf Hannover von 1714–1837* (Hannover, 1977), p. 20; Ragnhild Hatton, 'The Anglo-Hanoverian Connection 1714–1760' (The Creighton Trust Lecture, London, 1982), pp. 2–3; Sabine Haselau, 'Die Organisation der Personalunion – ihr verfassungsmäßiger Charakter und das rechtliche Verhältnis zwischen Hannover und Großbritannien', in Heide N. Rohloff, ed., *Großbritannien und Hannover: Die Zeit der Personalunion 1714–1837* (Frankfurt am Main, 1989), p. 236; Uriel Dann, *Hanover and Great Britain 1740–1760: Diplomacy and Survival* (Leicester, 1991), p. 137; Philip Konigs, *The Hanoverian Kings and Their Homeland: A Study of the Personal Union 1714–1837* (Sussex, 1993), p. 172; Jeremy Black, *The Hanoverians: The History of a Dynasty* (London, 2004), pp. 21–2; Heide Barmeyer, 'Die Personalunion England-Hannover: Ihre Entstehung, Etablierung und Fortsetzung aus hannoverscher Sicht', in Rexheuser, ed., *Die Personalunionen von Sachsen-Polen 1697–1763 und Hannover-England 1714–1837*, p. 276.

prohibited him or her from leaving England, Scotland, or Ireland without Parliamentary consent. It also submitted military assistance to foreign nations to parliamentary review, and barred foreigners born outside the three kingdoms from public office. Although the Act of Settlement was amended both in law and in practice,[39] supporters of personal union argue it nevertheless set the tone for a high degree of mutual independence between Hanover and Britain. They retained separate laws, governments, churches, and representative assemblies throughout dynastic union, although historians have discovered instances of legal and institutional convergence.[40] British trade with Hanover was dwarfed by that with the neighboring cities of Bremen and Hamburg.[41] Nor was there much of the migration which characterized the early-modern British empire. The apparent absence of material integration has effectively deterred thorough historical study of the British-Hanoverian relationship, despite awareness that contemporaries deemed it important.

One solution to this problem is to shift attention from material structures to ideology, which historians are now taking more seriously. Such an approach immediately raises questions about the use of the term 'personal union', which was invented by the eighteenth-century Hanoverian jurist, Johann Stephan Pütter. Admittedly, he did not apply his neologism to the British-Hanoverian state relationship when introducing it in the *Elementa iuris publici germanici* (Elements of German Public Law) of 1760. Pütter first gave it an entirely German resonance, observing that the duchies of Bremen and Lauenburg were joined to the electorate proper (which was indivisible under German law) 'only in personal unions ("UNIONIS solum PERSONALIS")'.[42] But in 1777 he extended the model to Hanover's dynastic union with Britain in the *Beyträge zum teutschen Staats- und Fürsten-Rechte* (Contributions towards the Law of German States and Princes). It was, Pütter commented, 'only a personal union ("persönliche Vereinigung") [in which] each state remains independent of the other'.[43] He thereby exemplified the Hanoverian 'policy of demarcation, dissociation, and distancing from England' which had predominated since France invaded the electorate in 1757 in response to British provocations in North

---

[39] J. C. D. Clark, *Revolution and Rebellion* (Cambridge, 1986), p. 75.
[40] I. B. Campbell, 'The International and Legal Relations between Great Britain and Hanover 1714–1837' (Ph. D. thesis, Cambridge, 1965); Campbell, 'From the "Personal Union" between England and Scotland in 1603 to the European Communities Act 1972 and Beyond'; Harding, 'North African Piracy, the Hanoverian Carrying Trade, and the British State'.
[41] Klaus Püster, 'Möglichkeiten und Verfehlungen merkantiler Politik im Kurfürstentum Hannover unter Berücksichtigung des Einflusses der Personalunion mit dem Königreich Großbritannien' (Ph. D. dissertation, Hamburg, 1966).
[42] Johann Stephan Pütter, *Elementa iuris publici germanici* (Göttingen, 1760), p. 106.
[43] Johann Stephan Pütter, *Beyträge zum teutschen Staats- und Fürsten-Rechte* (Göttingen, 1777), p. 22.

America.[44] So the term 'personal union' emerged, for all its supposed universality, from the history of the very phenomenon it proposed to classify.

It is possible to overstate Pütter's bias or novelty. His concept simply encapsulated the observations of natural-law theorists such as Hugo Grotius[45] and Samuel Pufendorf,[46] who had not foreseen a dynastic union of Britain and Hanover. For this reason, personal union is a benign anachronism when applied to the early eighteenth-century. Indeed, the personal union idea lasted throughout the eighteenth century, changing according to political circumstances. Just as Pütter sought to emphasize Hanoverian independence, American patriots of the 1760s and 1770s hoped personal union on the Hanoverian model might foil parliamentary sovereignty. But at least from the American perspective, personal union was not incompatible with empire.[47] Indeed, personal union could also bind; supporters of the Hanoverian government in years around 1800 deployed the idea against further disintegration, while Walpolean theorists of the 1730s even used it to argue for greater British obligations to the electorate. But if the concept of personal union is still useful, the recognition of its subjectivity demotes it from its historiographical supremacy to equality with unfamiliar discourses of empire.

Contemporary commentators often preferred to describe Britain and Hanover in more conventionally imperial terms. Although they rarely used the word 'empire', they often compared both countries to familiar colonies. Imperial theorists identified a geographically extensive, culturally heterogeneous entity which relied upon coercion rather than the diplomacy associated with the personal union thesis. But imperial theorists differed over the question of which country profited from this empire. Sometimes circumstances benefited both countries jointly, sometimes they disadvantaged each in equal measure. And if one was able to exploit the other on occasion, circumstances were sure to reverse in the future. Finally, neither Hanoverians nor Britons could agree on their country's international interests at any given time.[48] This indeterminacy belies cost benefit analyses for

---

44 Hermann Wellenreuther, 'Von der Interessenharmonie zur Dissoziation: Kurhannover und England in der Zeit der Personalunion', *Niedersächsisches Jahrbuch für Landesgeschichte* 67 (1995), p. 36.

45 'It happens that several peoples may have the same head, while nevertheless each of them in itself forms a perfect association.' Hugo Grotius, *De jure belli ac pacis libri tres*, trans. Francis W. Kelsey (2 vols., Oxford, 1925), ii, p. 103.

46 'We apprehend that there are two species of systems properly speaking: one where two or more states have one and the same king, the other where two or more states are joined by a pact into one body.' Samuel Pufendorf, *De jure naturae et gentium libri octo*, trans. C. H. and W. A. Oldfather (2 vols., Oxford, 1934), ii, p. 1044.

47 It later characterized the commonwealth of the 1930s and 1940s. I thank David Armitage for reminding me of this.

48 See Jeremy Black, *European International Relations 1648–1815* (Basingstoke, 2002), p. 8.

9

the entire duration of their relationship, such as those offered by Brendan Simms and Jeremy Black (who stress power imbalance, but stop short of describing empire).[49] It is enough to say that Britain's relationship with Hanover was imperial, without generalizing about winners and losers.

Some British contemporaries rallied to defend their nation's sovereignty against Hanoverian empire. British fear of domination from a small continental principality might at first seem strange. But the Dutch conquest of 1688 and the ensuing relationship with the United Provinces under William III raised British suspicions of dynastic unions, even though the Hanoverians could not match Dutch numbers, wealth, or military strength. British republicans distrusted the electoral army, which they believed supported absolute monarchy in Hanover and might do the same at home.[50] Others had hoped the Act of Settlement might forestall Hanoverian ascendancy, but despaired of its integrity. They complained of parliamentary complaisance in approving military aid to the electorate under the Act, and deplored the 1716 repeal of the Act's limitation upon royal travel abroad. Critics interpreted the royal travel expenses or direct military subsidies to Hanover as a kind of imperial tribute. This perspective anticipated later British anxieties respecting federal Europe, albeit on a lesser scale.

Britons were not entirely wrong to detect an imperial motive on the part of Hanover. But the image of a centralized, self-conscious Hanover was a British projection. Britain may have been a new creation, but it was heir to England's unitary ideals. Although it was just as new, the electorate of Hanover was far more comfortable with political diversity; indeed, it hoped to lock Britain into a European system not dissimilar to that of the Holy Roman Empire. Karl Otmar von Aretin has persuasively argued that the Imperial system preserved the German territorial status quo better than the balance of power did on a European level,[51] but Hanoverians did not perceive the difference until the mid-eighteenth century. After Hanoverians lost faith in the balance of power, their political elite maintained its interest in regional expansion. But paradoxically, Hanover expanded after the Congress of Vienna partly by affecting obeisance to Britain.

Some Britons had long expected Hanover's effective or eventual incorporation into their empire. This was not necessarily unrealistic, for dynastic inheritance had already foreshadowed the English parliament's incorporation of its Scottish counterpart in 1707. The argument for British supremacy

---

[49] For an account emphasizing British advantage, see Brendans Simms, 'Hanover in British Policy 1714–1783', in Rexheuser, ed., *Die Personalunionen von Sachsen-Polen 1697–1763 und Hannover-England 1714–1837*, pp. 311–34. For one emphasizing British disadvantage, see Black, *The Continental Commitment*.

[50] Nick Harding, 'Hanover and British Republicanism', in Brendan Simms and Torsten Riotte, eds., *The Hanoverian Dimension in British History, 1714–1837* (Cambridge, 2007), pp. 301–23.

[51] Karl Otmar von Aretin, *Das Reich: Friedensgarantie und europäisches Gleichgewicht 1648–1806* (Stuttgart, 1986), esp. pp. 55–75.

over Hanover had several variants. First, Britain hoped to harness Hanover to its foreign policy. This included maintaining civil and religious liberty in Europe, objectives often referred to as the balance of power and the Protestant interest.[52] Second, Hanover assisted Britain's economic interests by distracting its most formidable commercial rival – France – and by guarding the vital sea-lanes to the Hanseatic cities of northern Germany. Lastly, many Britons believed the Act of Settlement's original limitation upon royal travel abroad guaranteed them imperial tribute, by forcing Hanoverian notables to visit their elector in the expensive capital city of London. Critics accepted that Hanover functioned as a British dependency, but worried that the associated obligations outweighed any advantage.

Some Hanoverians agreed that their electorate was becoming a British dependency. This fear first emerged after 1714 in the circle surrounding George I, who even drafted an abortive scheme to separate the Hanoverian and British inheritances on a future occasion. But it became more widespread after France extended a war against Britain to the electorate in 1757. And it finally went public when France threatened to invade again during the wars of the French Revolution and actually did so in 1803. These repeated invasions ensured that strategic concerns predominated within the Hanoverian analysis of British primacy. Not all Hanoverians condemned the British roots of their vulnerability; others considered Britain an important protector, despite its failure in 1757 and 1803. Hanoverians also detected economic and social elements of British dominance. They feared George III's absence might accelerate cash flows to Britain, a form of imperial tribute. Early-nineteenth-century social reformers also believed the electoral absence had exacerbated aristocratic privilege, although they had once also seen dynastic union as potentially encouraging social mobility on the British model. Without a tradition of unitary sovereignty, Hanoverians were not as overwhelmingly chary of dependence on an external power as their British counterparts. But many were.

Any intellectual history of the relationship between Britain and Hanover runs the risk of excessive literalism. Frauke Geyken has suggested that British debate about Hanover externalized domestic arguments for many reasons, including ignorance of Germany and reluctance to discuss the king's directly.[53] This is only partly true; Britons' and Hanoverians' mutual perceptions also reflected real hopes and fears. Alongside the personal union thesis, imperial perspectives were recognizable traditions upon which political actors could draw. What did change, often quite rapidly, were the circumstances which made one or other of the ideologies more attractive at any given time. Therefore, an intellectual history of Britain's relationship with

---

52 For the linkage of these two concepts, see Andrew C. Thompson, *Britain, Hanover and the Protestant Interest, 1688–1756* (Woodbridge, 2006).
53 Frauke Geyken, *Gentlemen auf Reisen: Das britische Deutschlandbild im 18. Jahrhundert* (Frankfurt, 2002), pp. 131–85.

Hanover is a series of snapshots, organized in chronological order. Context explains fluctuations in the equilibrium of contending views of dynastic union. But it also explains why the public interest in it swung from obsession to relative indifference. If ideologies changed glacially, the frequency with which they were articulated could vary considerably.

Hanoverian ideology did evolve noticeably over time. Monarchism and the balance of power declined as rhetorical forces for union with Britain,[54] while newer arrivals like ancient constitutionalism and egalitarianism tended to corrode it. By contrast British ideology seemed set in aspic, at least as far as Hanover was concerned. As late as the 1830s, Britons were discussing Hanover in terms which their early-eighteenth-century forebears would have recognized; even those who innovated rhetorically in other contexts fell back into older patterns when treating the king's German patrimony. So for Britons, the relationship with Hanover and its intellectual baggage were a significant force for continuity.

In an intellectual history, any source may be valuable – if only to demonstrate what was thinkable at a given conjuncture. But a study of Hanover and Britain in contemporary ideology must privilege printed sources. This is partly because they were more likely to theorize, but also because they more effectively disseminated arguments over a large geographical area. Recent historiography has subsumed the press in the concept of a 'public sphere', which also includes commercial spaces (such as coffeehouses) where printed content might be read aloud to illiterate neighbors. The public sphere represented a new culture which was independent of court patronage. Although there is much debate about periodization, most historians agree that the public sphere developed in Britain before Germany.[55] This lag partly explains why sources related to dynastic union are so lopsided in Britain's favor before 1789. Indeed, the historian of eighteenth-century Hanover has greater resort to archival sources. But it would be a mistake to assume that these always conformed to the obsequious stereotype. Texts destined for the elector could often be impertinent. So there was debate before the public sphere, even if it did not openly announce itself as such.

Britain's cultural advantage doubtless proceeded from its relative afflu-

---

54 Hermann Wellenreuther, 'Göttingen und England im achtzehnten Jahrhundert', *Göttinger Universitätsreden* 75 (1985), pp. 30–63; Hermann Wellenreuther, 'Die Bedeutung des Siebenjährigen Krieges für die englisch-hannoveranischen Beziehungen', in Adolf M. Birke and Kurt Kluxen, eds., *England und Hannover* (Munich, 1986), pp. 145–75; Nicholas Harding, 'Hanoverian Rulership and Dynastic Union with Britain, 1700–60', in Rexheuser, ed., *Die Personalunionen von Sachsen-Polen 1697–1763 und Hannover-England 1714–1837*, pp. 389–414.

55 See Jürgen Habermas, *The Structural Transformation of the Public Sphere: An Inquiry into a Category of Bourgeois Society*, trans. Thomas Burger (Cambridge, MA, 1989); James Van Horn Melton, *The Rise of the Public in Enlightenment Europe* (Cambridge, 2001); T. C. W. Blanning, *The Culture of Power and the Power of Culture: Old Regime Europe 1660–1789* (Oxford, 2002).

ence and urbanity. At first glance, it might appear to have derived from a comparatively open legal environment; England's system of preliminary censorship lapsed in 1695, ten years before Hanover established an equivalent. But in any history of the dynastic union, this apparent difference recedes into the background. Dynastic union's connection to the British succession naturally attracted Jacobite commentary, which was liable to retroactive censorship. Much of this slipped by the authorities, but so did its Hanoverian equivalent. Unorthodox Hanoverian voices also published their views elsewhere in Germany, confident that their pamphlets would make their way back to Hanover. This was especially true of the period after 1789, in which the public sphere was putting down roots in Germany. Indeed, the Hanoverian debate on union came to dwarf its British analogue. This was partly due to mistrust of a foreign ruler, which likewise explains the prominence of Hanover in British discourse before 1760.

These differences notwithstanding, there were parallels between the countries. As has been seen, both were sensitive to domination and subjection – the hallmark of empire. This partially emerged from similar regional dynamics. Both the Hanoverian electorate and the British empire comprised several principalities, each with its own political assemblies and laws. Yet both experienced centripetal forces unifying these disparate possessions; the elector's inheritance of the principality of Celle (1705) antedated the Anglo-Scottish Act of Union by two years. In the electorate, this aggregated more influence to the principality of Calenberg and Göttingen, which contained the capital city of Hannover. George II endowed the principality with further cultural heft when he founded the university at Göttingen in the 1730s. Britain possessed a far more ancient and dominant center in London, whose population outgrew that of the electorate over the course of the eighteenth-century. With the lion's share of cultural production, both the British and Hanoverian metropolises would have dominated discussion of dynastic union in any case. They even absorbed immigrants such as John Toland, Edmund Burke, and Ludwig Timotheus Spittler, who wrote for metropolitan audiences. When peripheries did take an interest in the British-Hanoverian relationship, as did the North American colonies in the 1760s and 70s, they subordinated it to the theme of their own relations to the center. It was the latter in both Britain and Hanover which took an extraordinary interest in the connection, which potentially threatened the dominance of each in its respective country.

But for all the chronological and conceptual differences between British and Hanoverian commentary on union, the fact remains that both countries contained equivalent discourses of imperial dependency and supremacy. These interpretations do not suffice to explain the totality of the British-Hanoverian relationship, any more than personal union did. As did the latter, they more accurately illustrated particular episodes from its history. A familiarity with all contemporary perspectives on the British-Hanoverian relationship is necessary for present-day understanding of this ambiguous phenomenon, which tended towards intimacy and dissociation by turns. Of course, this experience was by no means singular in British imperial history. Hopefully the recognition of Hanover's place in British history will lead to a greater appreciation of Britain's European identity.

# 1

# *Prehistory*

When English and Hanoverian observers began to contemplate their prospective union, both did so with reference to their most recent respective imperial experiences. For England, this had been conquest and reconstruction at the hands of William III and the Dutch state. Although most Englishmen and women continued to support the Revolution settlement against the French-supported Stuarts, they were uneasily aware that it had been imposed by another foreign power. And they extended their ambivalence to the prospect of yet another union with a foreign country. For their part, Hanoverians viewed union with Britain through the prism of the Holy Roman Empire. They approved of the post-1648 Empire, and hoped union with Britain would establish a similar status quo on the European level. Imperial conceptions of the Anglo-Hanoverian union dominated from the beginning.

Britain's union with Hanover was made possible by the Glorious Revolution of 1688. Although historians have often emphasized the Revolution's British origins, it was primarily a Dutch conquest. Jonathan Israel has shown that the invasion served the interests of the Dutch state as well as those of William III, thereby foreclosing an entirely dynastic (and mostly domestic) account of the Glorious Revolution. The Dutch estates signed off on the expedition in order to bring England into their commercial war against France. The war bequeathed two peculiarly Dutch phenomena to England. The need to reassure a religiously diverse coalition led to England's first lasting religious toleration.[1] The war also consolidated the already perceptible Dutch influence over English public finance, where long-term debt came to supplement the excise tax.[2] Israel also dated the rise of the English parliament to its reaction against Dutch power, once the pacification of Ireland allowed William III to transfer his Dutch army to the continent in 1691.[3] This reaction peaked during the standing-army controversy of

---

1  Jonathan I. Israel, 'The Dutch Role in the Glorious Revolution', in Jonathan I. Israel, ed., *The Anglo-Dutch Moment: Essays on the Glorious Revolution and Its World Impact* (Cambridge, 1991), pp. 105–62.
2  Jonathan Scott, *England's Troubles: Seventeenth-Century English Political Instability in European Context* (Cambridge, 2000), esp. pp. 484–90.
3  Israel, 'The Dutch Role in the Glorious Revolution', pp. 159–60.

1697–9, when parliament frustrated the king's plan for a peacetime standing army and sent his Dutch bodyguard back to the United Provinces.[4] The Dutch union was an important interlude in the European history of British empire in its own right, but it also colored Britain's later imperial relationship with the continental electorate of Hanover. Union with Hanover followed from the Dutch invasion, as naturally as the Angevin empire issued from an earlier William's conquest.

In both these cases, the second union began more peacefully than its violent predecessor. When parliament had bestowed the crown on William and Mary, it had in some sense endorsed a fait accompli. When England returned to the question of a foreign succession after the 1700 death of Princess Anne's only son, the duke of Gloucester, her likeliest Protestant heir and his army were far away. This was Elector Georg Ludwig of Hanover, who was more likely to succeed than his aged mother, Electress Sophia. The elector's remove gave England more latitude to consider his succession than it had devoted to that of King William. James Vernon, the secretary of state, observed that 'the house of Hanover is much spoken of. The objection is, "What, must we have more foreigners?", which is not very obliging towards the king. But I hope people will at last resolve that it is better to have a prince from Germany than one from France.'[5]

The latter phrase was key. The Revolution and its consequent innovations had been tremendously controversial, but their repeal under a Stuart restoration would have heralded further instability. The easiest solution was therefore to reaffirm the precedents of 1689. Such a scenario called for the English parliament to reconcile the twin imperatives of heredity and Protestantism 'so as that', as Daniel Defoe was to put it, 'the *right of descent* and the *right of election* may go hand in hand, and kiss each other'.[6] But if parliament followed the example of 1689 with respect to the Protestant succession, it deviated from it by considering additional conditions no one had thought to apply to William and Mary. A month after Gloucester's death, a correspondent of Robert Harley, a leading member of parliament, wrote that 'some provisionary laws may be needful in case of a foreigner'.[7] Harley took this

[4] For the standing-army controversy, see Lois G. Schwoerer, 'The Literature of the Standing Army Controversy, 1697–1699', *The Huntington Library Quarterly* 28 (1965), pp. 187–212; Lois G. Schwoerer, *No Standing Armies!* (Baltimore, 1974), pp. 155–87.
[5] Vernon to Shrewsbury, 15 Aug. 1700, published in G. P. R. James, ed., *Letters Illustrative of the Reign of William III from 1696 to 1708 Addressed to the Duke of Shrewsbury by James Vernon, Esq., Secretary of State* (3 vols., London, 1841), iii, p. 129.
[6] [Daniel Defoe], *The Succession to the Crown of England Consider'd* (London, 1701), p. 21. For the attribution, see P. N. Furbank and W. R. Owens, *A Critical Bibliography of Daniel Defoe* (London, 1998), pp. 25–6.
[7] Guy to Harley, 31 Aug. 1700, published in Historical Manuscripts Commission (HMC), *The Manuscripts of His Grace the Duke of Portland Preserved at Welbeck Abbey* (10 vols., 1891–1931), iii, p. 625.

suggestion to heart. Presiding over the succession debate as speaker of the house, he observed that 'the haste the nation was in when the present government was settled had made us go too fast, and overlook many securities, which might have prevented much mischief, and . . . he hoped they would not now fall into the same error'.[8] The tory member of parliament Simon Harcourt added that it had previously limited certain aspects of Felipe II's prerogative when he married Mary I and assumed the dignity of king.[9] The commons determined that similar conditions should apply to an eventual Hanoverian successor.

If Harley was to be the legal architect of union, then his publicist John Toland laid its foundations in English political discourse.[10] Toland was an Irish expatriate with a talent for controversy, who had impressed Harley with his exertions against William III's peacetime standing army. Toland made the case for affixing conditions to the Hanoverian succession in *Limitations for the Next Foreign Successor, or New Saxon Race*,[11] which was 'timed . . . to coincide with the first vote of the commons upon the question of the Protestant succession on 3 March 1701'.[12] The *Limitations* did not deny the attractions of dynastic union with Hanover. Toland admitted that 'it might probably be for the honor of *England*, and perhaps her interest, to have her king an elector of the Empire because it would strengthen us by a considerable foreign alliance and probably assure us of the friendship of the Empire'.[13] But largely, the *Limitations* expressed fears of Hanoverian empire over England.

Toland grounded his apprehensions in mistrust of the Holy Roman Emperor, whose universal pretensions had contributed mightily to the defensive element of the English imperial ideal as expressed by parliament during the 1530s. Toland wrote that

8   Gilbert Burnet, *Bishop Burnet's History of His Own Time* (2 vols., London, 1724–34), ii, p. 270.

9   D. W. Hayton, ed., *The Parliamentary Diary of Sir Richard Cocks, 1698–1702* (Oxford, 1996), p. 71.

10  For Toland, see Justin Champion, *Republican Learning: John Toland and the Crisis of Christian Culture, 1696–1722* (Manchester, 2003).

11  The pamphlet's republican tone led at least one contemporary to identify it as Toland's work, writing 'the drift of it tends to a commonwealth, and the design of it seems wholly to aim at what [Toland] is so great a lover of: democracy and confusion'. Captain D---by, *Animadversions on the Succession to the Crown of England Consider'd* (London, 1701), p. 24. Subsequent scholars have tended to vindicate this opinion, even though Toland denied writing it: Giancarlo Carabelli, *Tolandiana* (Florence, 1975), p. 82; J. A. Downie, *Robert Harley and the Press* (Cambridge, 1979), p. 44. For Toland's claim that it was written by a Scottish gentleman, see T. Burnet to Sophia, 13/23 June 1701, London, published in Onno Klopp, ed., *Die Werke von Leibniz* (11 vols., Hannover, 1864–84), viii, p. 265.

12  Downie, *Robert Harley and the Press*, p. 44.

13  [John Toland], *Limitations for the Next Foreign Successor, or New Saxon Race* (London, 1701), p. 9.

we cannot be sure but an elector once king of *England* might have his ambition enlarged with his dominions. And since every elector has a right to put up to be chosen king of the *Romans*, it is not impossible but an elector of *Hanover* being at the same time king of *England* might make use of our power to set the imperial crown upon his own head and make it hereditary to his posterity, which would at once deprive us of our king and subject us to the Empire.[14]

The likelihood of a Hanoverian emperor was low (the house of Brunswick had last occupied the imperial throne in 1218, and the Habsburg dynasty had monopolized it since 1438), and that of converting the imperial monarchy from elective to hereditary status practically nonexistent. But Toland was not entirely dependent upon Reformation defenses of English sovereignty. He also referred to a medieval statute, 14 Edward III St. 3, which he inaccurately implied had prohibited dynastic union with France. But the illustration was nonetheless apt, for it had provided that the king's English subjects were not subject to him in his (putative) role as king of France.

Yet Hanover did not need its elector's elevation to Holy Roman Emperor to threaten dominance of England. The elector could do this by governing England as absolutely as Toland believed he did Hanover. One way to do this would be to extend Hanoverian institutions to England, virtually incorporating the kingdom into the electorate. A more subtle method would be to fashion English analogues to electoral institutions, thereby confining Hanoverian influence to the more indirect realm of example. These were the scenarios which would occupy Toland's *Limitations* and the subsequent literature on Hanoverian empire over England.

Toland's immediate fear was that any elector-king might cultivate what he considered to be England's constituency for absolute government, the Anglican clergy. Toland had notoriously assaulted the church hierarchy in *Christianity not Mysterious* (1696), and renewed the attack in the *Limitations*. He wrote that if

> a politic and ambitious *Lutheran* prince succeeds to our throne, and . . . he has a mind to make himself as arbitrary in *England* as most of the princes are in *Germany* . . . he may readily fall upon a method to effect it. He has no more to do but to fall in with our bigoted ceremonialists, as all our kings of the *Scots* race ever did; and provided he give them leave to persecute others, they will advance his prerogative as high as he pleases . . . The Lutherans . . . are rather for augmenting than diminishing ceremonies in worship.[15]

In describing Hanover, Toland adapted his Irish friend and patron Robert Molesworth's criticisms of Denmark. The link which allowed him to do so

---

14 [Toland], *Limitations*, p. 9.
15 [Toland], *Limitations*, pp. 7–8.

was both countries' common Lutheranism. In *An Account of Denmark* (1694), Molesworth had characterized the Lutheran religion as supporting absolute government alongside the army. The *Account of Denmark* was not without some basis in Danish self-description. Toland reported that a Danish tract of 1687, Hector Gottfried Masius' *Interesse principum circa religionem evangelicam*, argued that Lutheranism 'invests [princes] with more power than the principles of any other church'.[16] But Toland's reliance on the Danish model, however accurate in and of itself, revealed the level of English ignorance concerning Hanover.

Somewhat more distantly, Toland feared outright takeover by a Hanoverian institution – that of its standing army. Here, Toland returned to the republican suspicion of professional soldiers that he had already displayed in opposition to William III's peacetime standing army. Toland wrote that the Hanoverian successors

> will lie under a mighty temptation to enlarge their dominions beyond sea, in order to make the communication betwixt their old and new dominions more speedy and easy. This the family of *Hanover* may attempt by falling down upon the *Elbe* and the *Weser*, and swallowing up *Hamburg*, *Bremen*, *Emden*, etc. . . . [so] that if at any time we come to struggle with those princes for our privileges they will have an opportunity of landing men upon us from their foreign dominions, which may prove as fatal to our liberty, as the *German* invasion did formerly to our ancestors.[17]

Although Toland adverted to the ancient Saxon conquest of his subtitle, he must also have considered the more recent Dutch one. Indeed, many republicans considered William III might stage a sequel to effect his will in England. This view had already been expressed in a pamphlet of 1695 by Robert Ferguson the former Exclusionist.[18]

Although Toland devoted the majority of the *Limitations* to the argument that dynastic union imperiled English domestic liberty, he did consider that it might also endanger European freedoms in the process. The concept of absolute monarchy within a single state had an international analogue, which, like it, had acquired increasingly negative connotations over the centuries – that of universal monarchy.[19] Although contemporary theorists

16 John Toland, *Anglia Libera, or the Limitation and Succession of the Crown of England Explain'd and Asserted* (London, 1701), p. 183.
17 [Toland], *Limitations*, pp. 9–10.
18 [Robert Ferguson], *A Brief Account of Some of the Late Incroachments and Depredations of the Dutch upon the English* (n. p., 1695), p. 25.
19 See Franz Bosbach, *Monarchia universalis. Ein politischer Leitbegriff der frühen Neuzeit* (Göttingen, 1988). For a synthesis in English, see Franz Bosbach, 'The European Debate on Universal Monarchy', in David Armitage, ed., *Theories of Empire, 1450–1800* (Aldershot, 1998), pp. 81–98. For the concept's English history, see Steven Pincus, 'The

usually ascribed designs of a universal monarchy to France's Louis XIV, Toland apprehended that other European powers might perceive something similar in an eventual dynastic union between England and Hanover. He wrote that if a prospective elector-king annexed the Hanseatic cities in an effort to improve communications between the two dominions, 'it will occasion a jealousy in the *Dutch* and the Northern princes . . . [in which] case they will be sure to join with *Scotland* to keep the balance equal'.[20] Toland referred to a regional balance of power, corresponding to the European balance which supposedly preserved the political status quo from the threat of universal monarchy. Toland may have been attracted by the balance of power's resemblance to the Polybian or mixed constitution,[21] which had been a staple of English republicanism since its paradoxical introduction by Charles I in *His Majesty's Answer to the Nineteen Propositions of Parliament* (1642).[22] As Jonathan Swift wrote in 1701, 'there is a balance of power to be carefully held by every state within it self, as well as among several states with each other'.[23]

Toland thus concluded that dynastic union with Hanover would be detrimental to English and European freedom. But he considered that it might be rendered harmless in two ways. As the Hanoverian heirs' experience of absolute monarchy in Hanover might predispose them to rule England despotically, Toland suggested that they be brought to England to be reeducated in the principles of the English faith and constitution.[24] This view actually dovetailed with that of the king himself, who repeatedly suggested that Georg Ludwig's son and heir (the future George II) take up residence in England.[25] The king's own publicist Daniel Defoe echoed Toland,[26] and even reflected that

His present Majesty was the best acquainted with our *constitution, laws, temper,* and whatever was *needful* to qualify him *for the government of this nation,* of any

English Debate over Universal Monarchy', in John Robertson, ed., *A Union for Empire: Political Thought and the British Union of 1707* (Cambridge, 1995), pp. 37–62.

[20] [Toland], *Limitations*, p. 25.

[21] Herbert Butterfield, 'The Balance of Power', in Herbert Butterfield and Martin Wight, eds., *Diplomatic Investigations* (London, 1966), p. 141. See also Martin Wight's more detailed elaboration of this idea in 'The Balance of Power and International Order', in Alan James, ed., *The Bases of International Order* (London, 1973), pp. 96–8.

[22] See Corinne Comstock Weston, 'The Theory of Mixed Monarchy under Charles I and after', *The English Historical Review* 75 (1960), pp. 426–43.

[23] [Jonathan Swift], *A Discourse of the Contests and Dissensions in Athens and Rome* (London, 1701), p. 5.

[24] [Toland], *Limitations*, p. 8.

[25] See the Hanoverian envoy's dispatches to the elector, published in Georg Schnath, *Geschichte Hannovers im Zeitalter der neunten Kur und der englischen Sukzession 1674–1714* (4 vols., Hildesheim, 1938–82), iv, pp. 556, 562.

[26] [Defoe], *The Succession to the Crown of England*, pp. 22–4.

prince in the world that had lived all his time abroad, and yet I doubt not but His Majesty has experienced some *disadvantages* he receives as to *immediate management of affairs* for want of a more complete personal knowledge both of *things* and *men*.[27]

That no less a critic of English xenophobia than Defoe could express such reservations about foreign rulers testified to the ambiguous legacy of William's rule. The question of an invitation to one or more members of the Hanoverian dynasty remained a recurrent issue in English politics after William's death, but foundered upon Anne's passionate opposition.

Defoe's proposal demonstrated that any foreign successor would have been problematic, whether or not they ruled foreign dominions as well. Electress Sophia was an example of a foreigner whose succession would not immediately entail dynastic union. But Toland contemplated the prospect of dynastic union under her son with even greater apprehension, and he recommended that parliament rule out dynastic union with Hanover before the fact. He wrote that

> it ought to be well weighed whether it be the interest of England to have an elector of the Empire for their prince, and whether such of that family as happens to be our king should not be obliged for himself and the first of his male issue in all generations to renounce his dominions in *Germany*.[28]

Such conditions were unusual, but not entirely unheard of in Europe. In fact, recent history provided Toland with one such example. Spain had resolved its concurrent succession crisis by selecting the duke of Anjou to be its new king, overlooking his father and older brother and extracting a renunciation of his French rights so as to prevent an eventual dynastic union between the two countries.[29] It was a seductive proposal, given the distasteful alternatives of dynastic union with Hanover or a Stuart restoration. But such a provision would nevertheless have depended upon the electoral family's doubtful compliance, and had no precedent in British history.

In response to the *Limitations'* image of Hanoverian empire, other books hatched British imperial designs upon the electorate. The first of these was *Animadversions on the Succession to the Crown of England Consider'd*, whose anonymous author argued against the *Limitations*. He dismissed Toland's religious concerns out of hand, saying the English had nothing to fear from the Hanoverian family in terms of ceremonial innovations.[30] He furthermore

---

27 [Defoe], *The Succession to the Crown of England*, p. 24.
28 [Toland], *Limitations*, p. 9.
29 [Toland], *Limitations*, p. 8.
30 Captain D---by, *Animadversions*, p. 28.

reproved Toland for suggesting that the Hanoverian successors should renounce their rights in Germany, writing that 'it is unbecoming the spirit of an Englishman to repine at their sovereign's greatness, or murmur at the extent of his dominions'.[31] The *Animadversions'* monarchist tone distinguished it from the republican *Limitations*.

But while the *Animadversions* rejected Toland's religious and civic objections to union with Hanover, it spent more time introducing an economic rationale for it. It compared Hanover favorably with Scotland, where some considered the succession crisis an opportunity to terminate the union with England which they blamed for the recent failure of the Darien venture in Panama. The author of the *Animadversions* accepted the possibility of a Scottish defection from the union of crowns with equanimity, writing

> we have hitherto received so little advantage from our union with [Scotland], and such poor sums have flow'd into the English exchequer from the contributions in war or their revenues in peace, that we ought not to relinquish the prospect of benefit we shall have from a *Lüneburg* successor because of such an apprehension as the fear of so small a loss which carries the face of gain in it. Since the fat campaign country of *Hanover* as much excels the lean hungry mountains of *Scotland* as the garden of *Eden* does the northernmost parts of *Swedeland*.[32]

The *Animadversions* reinforced its impression of Hanoverian wealth by reminding its readers that Hanover would become even more consequential upon the elector's eventual inheritance of the principality of Celle from his uncle.[33] This fact notwithstanding, the pamphlet clearly exaggerated Hanover's economic attractions. Yet this mistake revealed an important attitude of some English thinkers: that dynastic unions ought to furnish larger countries with the opportunity to exploit the economies of smaller countries.

In June parliament finalized the Act of Settlement, which named Sophia and Georg Ludwig as the official successors. Parliament declined to enact Toland's suggestion that Georg Ludwig forfeit his electoral inheritance. But it did apply several other conditions to the Hanoverian succession. One of these required parliamentary approval for the monarch's travel outside the three kingdoms. This provision was probably partially inspired by, although stronger than, the injunction upon Mary I's removal from her dominions 'unless she pleas'd'.[34] But it was also clearly motivated by frustration with William's long absences abroad, which amounted to five of his reign's thirteen years.[35] Another proviso, which stipulated that England not be

[31] Captain D---by, *Animadversions*, p. 29.
[32] Captain D---by, *Animadversions*, p. 23.
[33] Captain D---by, *Animadversions*, p. 16.
[34] Toland, *Anglia Libera*, p. 136.
[35] Schwoerer, *No Standing Armies*, p. 156.

involved in wars on behalf of foreign dominions, may also have derived from the Marian conditions. Of course, it also articulated the perception of some that the Nine Years' War had suited Dutch rather than English interests. A third provision reserving public office for persons born in the three kingdoms more closely reprised a similar Marian condition than enacted Toland's weaker prescription of parliamentary consent for such appointments.[36] It also reflected resentment at William's having rewarded many of his Dutch intimates with English offices and titles. Lastly, the Act of Settlement required the king to communicate with the Church of England.

The Act of Settlement induced Toland to switch from a defensive to an expansionist posture. Toland's volte face on union corresponded to the changing political needs of his patron Harley, who needed to legitimize the agreement to the English public as well as to the Hanoverian court. Having disavowed any involvement with the *Limitations*,[37] Toland felt no obligation to maintain ideological consistency between the two works. He even scoffed at the possibility of a Hanoverian invasion, which he had mooted in the *Limitations*. Among the factors protecting British liberty from a Hanoverian king, Toland wrote in *Anglia Libera*, was 'the distance of his other dominions if he shou'd attempt anything against these kingdoms by their assistance: a thing in itself absolutely impossible, considering the several countries lying betwixt us, especially our good friends of *Holland*'.[38] In less than a year, Toland had moved from concern to complacency respecting the North Sea littoral between Hanover and Britain.

The retraction of his assertion that dynastic union would endanger the independent cities and principalities of the North Sea coast implied of itself that Toland no longer perceived a threat to the balance of power from the dynastic union, since the latter had followed from the former in the *Limitations*. Indeed, Toland now believed Anglo-Hanoverian dynastic union would positively support the European balance of power. At first glance, his argument might seem defensive rather than ambitious. But a concern for the balance of power was quite capable of instigating imperial undertakings, as the Dutch conquest of Britain had recently shown.[39] Toland furthermore believed that maintaining the balance of power fulfilled England's national mission and earned it immortal glory. 'Settling the succession in the house of Hanover', he wrote, 'is the most likely way in the world of restoring and preserving to *England* her ancient privileg'd greatness of holding the balance of *Europe*.'[40] The idea that England played a pivotal role in the European

---

36 [Toland], *Limitations*, p. 13.
37 T. Burnet to Sophia, 13/23 June 1701, London, in Klopp, ed., *Die Werke von Leibniz*, viii, p. 265.
38 Toland, *Anglia Libera*, p. 147.
39 Israel, 'The Dutch Role in the Glorious Revolution', p. 120.
40 Toland, *Anglia Libera*, p. 144.

balance had been introduced by Geffray Fenton in the dedication to Queen Elizabeth of his 1579 translation of Guicciardini,[41] who had earlier applied the balance of power idea to fifteenth-century Italy. Subsequent theorists explained England's special role in terms of its sea power.[42] England's ability and will to defend the European balance of power were two different things, as Toland and others argued in the cases of Charles II and James II.[43] But William III's war against France reassured them that England had once again assumed its privileged role maintaining the balance. Toland wrote in *Anglia Libera* that the king's

> finishing stroke in making us the arbiters of *Europe* as well as a particular balance against *France* was the present *Act of Succession*, whereby the crown of *England* descends to one of the powerfullest families in the *Empire* for their territory and more diffusive than all the rest in their kindred and alliances.[44]

Thus did Toland imply that England could preserve the sovereignty of other great powers by manipulating, and thereby violating, that of a smaller one.

The balance of power was the only theme from the *Limitations* which Toland turned to the dynastic union's advantage in *Anglia Libera*. But he turned to the related topic of the Protestant interest, which he had not developed in the earlier book. The idea of a Protestant foreign policy had grown up alongside that of a balance of power, until they overlapped for English observers concerned about international freedom.[45] 'Besides maintaining the *balance of Europe*', Toland wrote, 'it has been likewise another maxim of *England* since the Reformation *to keep it self the head of the Protestant religion all over the world*'.[46] Toland had good reason to fear for international Protestantism. In 1685, the same year in which Louis XIV had revoked the Edict of Nantes, Catholic dynasties had ascended to historically Protestant thrones in Britain and the Palatinate. And while the Catholic succession had proved to be temporary in Britain, the leading Protestant prince in Germany, the elector of Saxony, had converted to Catholicism in order to ascend the Polish throne in 1697. Toland was able to ascribe Hanover a certain sanctity within the English tradition of a Protestant foreign policy – Sophia's mother was Queen Elizabeth of Bohemia, the English princess whose misfortunes during the Thirty Years' War had rallied

[41] Martin Wight, 'The Balance of Power', in Butterfield and Wight, eds., *Diplomatic Investigations*, p. 164.

[42] Christoph Kampmann, 'Die englische Krone als "Arbiter of Christendom"? Die "Balance of Europe" in der politschen Diskussion der späten Stuart-Ära (1660–1714)', *Historisches Jahrbuch* 116 (1996), p. 332. See also p. 336.

[43] See, for example, Toland, *Anglia Libera*, pp. 141–2.

[44] Toland, *Anglia Libera*, p. 142.

[45] Andrew C. Thompson, *Britain, Hanover and the Protestant Interest, 1688–1756* (Woodbridge, 2006).

[46] Toland, *Anglia Libera*, p. 148.

the Protestant internationalists of her homeland.[47] He found it more difficult to elucidate a mechanism by which the dynastic union might strengthen international Protestantism. Toland exaggerated Hanover's familial ties to various Protestant potentates, adding that 'all the *Protestant* states are by this family as well as their principles united to us'.[48] In fact, the Hanoverian dynasty was relatively isolated from international Protestantism. While it did possess a close matrimonial alliance with the Protestant court of Prussia, its other close relations were mostly Catholic. This might have led *The Observator* to opine in 1703 that 'this Act of Settlement is the greatest tie upon the successors to the crown to keep themselves entirely in the *Protestant* interest'.[49] Britons did not know that Georg Ludwig was more reliably Protestant than his father, who had flirted with Catholicism for political gain.

Yet another costly war, the War of Spanish Succession, was to add a dimension to Toland's observations on the dynastic union's possible role in British foreign policy. When Toland returned to the issue of dynastic union in May 1714, he argued that 'whenever occasion shall raise up the seeds of war again in the Netherlands, which will but too often present, our native blood and treasure may in a great measure be spared by convenient succors and supplies drawn from Hanover'.[50] Toland hoped that it might use Hanover as its continental surrogate through the mechanism of dynastic union.

Nevertheless, Toland had already anticipated the peacetime economics of dynastic union when he wrote *Anglia Libera* in 1701. He adopted the argument of the *Animadversions* that dynastic union with Hanover would enrich England. 'Provinces and colonies', he wrote in *Anglia Libera*, 'are acknowledg'd to transmit all their riches to the seat of empire. But where several independent governments are united under one head the riches of the rest must flow of course into that country where the prince chooses or is oblig'd to keep his court, of which we need not go out of this island for examples.'[51] Toland's economic analysis flattened his constitutional distinction between empires and personal union, in that both directed wealth to the prince's residence. Toland's word 'oblig'd' reminded his readers that the Act of Settlement had reserved that honor to metropolitan Britain by subjecting royal travel abroad to parliamentary review. In 1714, Toland considered that 'it was for our own welfare and interest we enter'd into this settlement . . . on conditions more advantageous to ourselves than [Hanoverians]',[52] perhaps conscious that the supposedly despotic electoral constitution possessed no

---

47 Toland, *Anglia Libera*, p. 144.
48 Toland, *Anglia Libera*, p. 144.
49 *The Observator* no. 90 (27 Feb. – 3 Mar. 1703), p. 2.
50 [John Toland], *Characters of the Court of Hannover* (London, 1714), p. 8.
51 Toland, *Anglia Libera*, pp. 145–6.
52 [Toland], *Characters of the Court of Hannover*, p. 9.

equivalent to the Act of Settlement. Toland now portrayed the Act of Settlement as an instrument of influence.

In *Anglia Libera*, Toland did more than promote the Act of Settlement. The book also courted Electress Sophia, whom it described as 'one of the most learned, polite and accomplished ladies in the world'.[53] As part of his effort to woo the electoral court, Harley dispatched Toland with his book in the train of the earl of Macclesfield's extraordinary embassy conveying the Act of Settlement to Hanover. The visit confirmed Toland in the change of heart he had expressed in *Anglia Libera*, and he developed a lasting infatuation with the house of Hanover. Toland's *Account of the Courts of Prussia and Hanover*, published in 1705, accordingly extended Sophia's personal virtues to her entire family. 'The [Hanoverian] court,' it remarked, 'is extremely polite, and even in Germany it is accounted the best both for civility and decorum.'[54] Toland's emphasis upon politeness further marked a departure from his republican predictions about the relationship with Hanover. In the context of Hanover, Toland's evolution mirrored his old comrade the third earl of Shaftesbury's contemporaneous exchange of martial for sociable virtues.[55] It must be said that Shaftesbury's progression in this matter did not extend to Hanover, whose court (along, implicitly, with all others) he characterized in the manner of an old republican as 'despotic'.[56] He left the Hanoverian applications of politeness to his erstwhile protégé, Toland. Yet Toland's grasp of the concept's political potential was slight enough that he failed to ascribe to its Hanoverian variant any mechanism which might affect England in union.

Strangely, Toland was more original and provocative on the subject of the prospective dynastic union when he had comparatively little knowledge of the electorate (he admitted in *Anglia Libera* that he was 'yet a perfect stranger to that country'[57]) than he was after his visit. The publications on the subject which followed Toland's first visit in 1701 mostly repeated views he expressed in *Anglia Libera*. Electress Sophia wrote to Gottfried Wilhelm Leibniz as early as 1702, complaining that 'if there are not more novelties in the recent tomes of Toland than in the first ones, they are not worth the trouble of reading'.[58] It is true that Toland's post-1701 publications on the

---

53  Toland, *Anglia Libera*, pp. 72–3.
54  John Toland, *An Account of the Courts of Prussia and Hanover* (London, 1705), p. 53.
55  Lawrence Klein, 'The Third Earl of Shaftesbury and the Progress of Politeness', *Eighteenth-Century Studies* 18 (1984–5), p. 213. Lawrence E. Klein, 'Liberty, Manners, and Politeness in Early Eighteenth-Century England', *The Historical Journal* 32 (1989), pp. 586–7. Lawrence E. Klein, 'Shaftesbury, Politeness and the Politics of Religion', in Phillipson and Skinner, eds., *Political Discourse in Early Modern Britain*, p. 288; Lawrence E. Klein, *Shaftesbury and the Culture of Politeness* (Cambridge, 1994), p. 148.
56  Shaftesbury to Gwinn, 19 Apr. 1704, Rotterdam, published in Benjamin Rand, ed., *The Life, Unpublished Letters and Philosophical Regimen of Anthony, Earl of Shaftesbury* (London and New York, 1900), p. 323.
57  Toland, *Anglia Libera*, p. 72.
58  Sophia to Leibniz, 6 Sept. 1702, Herrenhausen, in Klopp, ed., *Die Werke von Leibniz*, viii, p. 359.

subject of dynastic union mostly recapitulated the argument of *Anglia Libera*. But if Toland found it difficult to be as original as he had been in 1701, then so did all subsequent publicists. For in the *Limitations* and in *Anglia Libera*, Toland had pioneered many major British arguments addressing the Hanoverian union. This was due in part to his patron Harley's shifting political needs, which required him to condemn and praise the prospective dynastic union in turn. But it was also due to Toland's omnivorous intellect, which made him equally comfortable writing about religion, politics, or economics.

The expansionist vision of union with Hanover propounded in *Anglia Libera* provoked the first British enunciation of the argument later identified with the legal doctrine of personal union. This was the *History of the Last Parliament*, which the tory physician James Drake published in early 1702. Like Toland, Drake approved of the Act of Settlement. But he was more concerned to ingratiate himself with Princess Anne, the heiress presumptive, than with the more distant Hanoverian successors. Drake even accused the whig party of conspiring to supplant Anne in the succession with Sophia in the event of the king's demise.[59] Drake's political objective required him to praise the Act of Settlement less for its guarantee of English influence over Hanover than for its prevention of Anglo-Hanoverian empire. So although Drake's *History* supported union with Hanover as much as Toland's *Anglia Libera*, its arguments drew more upon Toland's *Limitations*.

Drake echoed the *Limitations'* fear that the English succession might encourage the Hanoverian electors to seek the imperial German dignity, against whose universal claims the English had defined their sovereignty during the Reformation. Drake wrote

> suppose then that the accession of *Great Britain* and *Ireland* to his other dominions shou'd raise the ambition of our prince and prompt him to aspire (for example) in *Germany* to the *Empire*, and to employ our wealth and power to procure it or to make such other conquests and acquisitions upon his neighbors, and he shou'd succeed in his attempts. The consequence of this wou'd be that, when he had acquir'd to himself a larger . . . more absolute *empire* abroad than that of these kingdoms, he wou'd fix his residence there and leave us to be govern'd by a viceroy, and perhaps a foreign army to secure our obedience, and we be made the instruments of our own slavery or at least of depriving our selves of the benefit of our king's presence among us.[60]

Drake took up the *Limitations'* apprehension that a Hanoverian union might involve foreign military occupation, and expanded upon its suggestion that the Imperial dignity would require the king's absence from England. But he

---

[59] [James Drake], *The History of the Last Parliament* (London, 1702), p. ix.
[60] [Drake], *The History of the Last Parliament*, pp. 44–5.

took comfort in the fact that the Act of Settlement had limited royal travel abroad.

As had Toland in the *Limitations*, Drake feared that Hanover might exercise empire over England even if its German imperial ambitions stumbled. This would consist in the elector's establishment of absolute rule in England. 'Suppose then we shou'd at any time see upon our throne . . . a prince who shou'd have other hereditary dominions in which he was absolute', posited Drake. 'Would it not be natural for him to wish for the same power here?'[61] Drake's concurrence with Toland on this matter was not remarkable in itself, in that both merely articulated the widespread English belief that continental European princes ruled more or less absolutely. But interestingly, Drake also accepted the religious basis of Hanoverian despotism which Toland had proposed in the *Limitations*. Drake warned that

> the *Lutheran* churches approach somewhat too near the *Romish* superstition in some points of doctrine and ceremony to meet with a favorable reception here. Besides they are the growth of those countries only, where the several sovereigns are arbitrary and despotical, where the people know no happiness but what is . . . owing to the gracious disposition of their prince, who may tyrannize if he pleases.[62]

Drake appropriated the arguments of men his party considered the country's most notorious and unrepentant heretics, and domesticated them to the tory cause. Where Toland had feared that an elector-king might establish absolute government with the English clergy's collaboration, Drake worried that it might instead proceed at the behest of the Hanoverian clergy. Because of the correlation between Lutheranism and absolute government, he wrote,

> their clergy may by a people so jealous of their liberties as we are . . . be suspected of leaning too much towards the prerogative and indulging sovereign power too far. Nor is it unnatural to imagine that any sort of men who have known liberty only by theory and speculation shou'd have very narrow ideas of it, and probably disrelish the exercise of it, when they shall find it the only obstacle to their settlement here, the only bar to their grandeur and preferment. May we not likewise . . . suppose them to be as strongly persuaded of the truth of their own opinions, and the necessity of believing 'em to salvation, as zealous for the propagation of 'em, as other priests usually are? . . . Wou'd not these things . . . tempt any persons . . . to solicit the prince whose conscience shou'd be under their direction to employ his credit (if not his authority) in their favor to procure 'em such footing and establishment here as might give them hopes of advancing?[63]

---

61 [Drake], *The History of the Last Parliament*, p. 32.
62 [Drake], *The History of the Last Parliament*, p. 30.
63 [Drake], *The History of the Last Parliament*, pp. 30–2.

Drake eschewed Toland's account of religious tyranny, wherein Anglican bigots took Hanover for an example, and replaced it with one which extended Hanoverian doctrine and personnel to England. He thereby addressed the English clergy's anxiety about professional advancement, and established the durable fear that German divines might be preferred at its cost under a Hanoverian regime.[64] Nevertheless, Drake hoped that the chances of religious domination from Hanover were slight, once the Act of Settlement required successors to communicate with the Church of England.

Drake also feared the possibility that Hanover might impose absolute rule upon England indirectly, by example. He warned that the Hanoverian successors would be

> princes who have great dominions, alliances and expectations abroad where their power is more absolute and uncontrollable, which may invite 'em to take up their residence longer in those parts than may be consistent with the interest and good government of *England* . . . Not only vast treasures wou'd be constantly convey'd out of the nation, but our nobility and gentry wou'd be tempted from home and, by compliance with the fashions of the court which they wou'd follow for preferment and degrees, be tinctur'd with principles and habituated to customs different from those of their own country, which might in time endanger the overthrow of our constitution.[65]

The monarch's extended absence abroad would gradually drain the English gentry and nobility of the means, both material and moral, to resist his absolute governance of their country. The idea that wealth and martial virtue enabled resistance to a standing army had been a republican staple for years.[66] Drake hoped the Act of Settlement's restriction upon royal travel abroad would conserve both.

If impoverishment could cause Hanoverian empire over England, it would also result from English empire over Hanover. This was one area in which Drake did not draw upon Toland's *Limitations*, and was entirely original. Drake historicized the risk of English empire over Hanover, writing that

> though we have been so quiet and undisturb'd at home, we have not been so happy in the maintenance of our possessions abroad, to maintain which the sword was in a manner constantly drawn for near four hundred years 'til at last we . . . lost *Normandy, Aquitaine,* and *Guienne* to enemies . . . Nor are we perhaps to esteem ourselves the weaker for that loss. For though those provinces were rich and populous, yet were they no accession of strength to our crown,

---

[64] For later manifestations of this fear, see George Every, *The High Church Party* (London, 1956), pp. 114–15, 142, 144–5.

[65] [Drake], *The History of the Last Parliament*, pp. 47–8.

[66] For a concise statement of this position, see J. G. A. Pocock, 'Civic Humanism and Its Role in Anglo-American Thought', in J. G. A. Pocock, *Politics, Language and Time* (London, 1971), pp. 90–4.

but on the contrary a continual charge, a drain to our treasury, and a burying place to our bravest men . . . So hard it is for a prince or state to keep possession of a country never so little disjoin'd from the main dominions.[67]

Drake complained that Hanover threatened to reestablish the continental credentials of the British empire, which had been redefined as maritime since the loss of Calais.[68] He likely drew his inspiration from the more recent publicity campaign waged by the Jacobites against the Nine Years' War. A Jacobite pamphlet of 1694 claimed that England fought France in the interest of the United Provinces, and likened the latter to the Plantagenet possessions in France.[69] Yet Drake believed the Act of Settlement's limitation upon military assistance to Hanover foreclosed a recurrence of these historical phenomena.

Drake seemed to contradict his doubts about the strategic value of England's medieval possessions on the continent when addressing the issue of foreign office holders. He wrote that 'perhaps the swarms of locusts which those countries daily sent over hither was none of the least reasons why the *English* parted so tamely with so considerable a barrier to *England* as *Normandy* and *Aquitaine*'.[70] Along with war in Hanover's interest, Hanoverian office holders would also drain England of its wealth. Using a more recent historical illustration, Drake spoke of a Dutch individual who had been

encumber'd with vast salaries and perquisites and laden with private bounties and grants . . . yet thought not fit to trust this nation with the protection of that wealth . . . but converting into money her palaces, royalties, lands and tenements has convey'd into another land a greater estate than any of her ancient and genuine nobility enjoy at home.[71]

He doubtlessly referred to the king's good friend Hans Willem Bentinck, the earl of Portland. Drake apprehended similar usage under Hanoverian successors, of whom he wrote that

the community of speech, religion and customs, past confidence and familiarities, and other engagements of an elder date make conversation with his *foreign subjects* infinitely more easy and pleasing to a *new king* of *foreign birth* and *education* than with his *new ones*, whom 'tis a great while e're he knows and longer e're he readily understands.[72]

---

67 [Drake], *The History of the Last Parliament*, pp. 42–3.
68 See David Armitage, *The Ideological Origins of the British Empire* (Cambridge, 2000).
69 *Reply to the Answer Doctor Welwood Has Made to King James's Declaration* ([London, 1694]), pp. 8, 39.
70 [Drake], *The History of the Last Parliament*, p. 80.
71 [Drake], *The History of the Last Parliament*, pp. 61–2.
72 [Drake], *The History of the Last Parliament*, p. 83.

This was the first English articulation of the case for pro-Hanoverian favoritism by foreign-born kings. But Drake was also confident that this impulse
was restrained by the Act of Settlement's ban on office-holding by individuals born outside the three kingdoms.

Drake's introduction of the personal union thesis completed England's
debate about the Hanoverian relationship, in which it ranked alongside
those tending towards English or Hanoverian empire. Drake had been quite
skeptical about dynastic union with Hanover, believing that only the Act of
Settlement preserved English independence. If it experienced the slightest
violation, his logic might easily revert back to one of the two imperial interpretations. But for the moment, Drake's argument appears to have quieted
English apprehensions about union with Hanover.

Hanover was not faced by a comparable succession crisis, and could respond
to British events in a leisurely manner. Yet the electoral government saw to
it that Hanover's debate was comparatively restrained. Where England had
allowed its Licensing Act to lapse in 1695, Hanover was redoubling its
efforts at censorship.[73] Georg Ludwig even suppressed Friedrich August
Hackmann's German translation of Toland's *Anglia Libera* before the
sections relating to dynastic union could be published.[74] Censorship, and the
related underdevelopment of a Hanoverian press, restricted discussion of
union to the court. This dialogue differed from England's as much in terms of
opinion as in terms of structure. Where imperial considerations led
Englishmen and women to be ambivalent about union, they almost wholly
encouraged Hanoverians. This was because Hanoverians' experience of their
own multi-state system, the Holy Roman Empire, had been so positive since
the Peace of Westphalia. The Emperor no longer threatened to impose
universal monarchy, but had so far frustrated its latest claimant the king of
France. Moreover, Hanover had profited from its loyalty to the Emperor in
this endeavor, securing the ninth electorate in 1692. The prospect of
securing England's support for the territorial status quo in Europe was reason
enough for Hanoverians to support union with that country.

Georg Ludwig's misgivings about the English succession were real, for all
that recent historiography has tended to obscure them.[75] It is unclear how
much they initially involved fears about the effect of his absence on
Hanover, fears which later came to dominate all others after his eventual
succession. In a letter to his ambassador in London, Georg Ludwig worried
about 'whether our condition or conjunctures will allow us to absent our

---

73 See Schnath, *Geschichte Hannovers*, iii, p. 276.
74 Schnath, *Geschichte Hannovers*, iv, pp. 58–9.
75 Edward Gregg, *The Protestant Succession in International Politics, 1710–1716* (New
York, 1986).

[Hanoverian] lands'.[76] Georg Ludwig may have feared his absence would disrupt his ability to apply reason for the good of his subjects, the central ideological justification for his rule as elector. But the elector may have simply worried about his age upon the succession, a concern voiced frequently by his seventy-year old mother. Solicitude for Hanover does not seem to have featured overmuch in Georg Ludwig's initial reservations about the English succession.

These mostly concerned England's turbulent recent history, and the limitations upon monarchy which had emerged from it. Soon after the duke of Gloucester's death, Sophia wrote to the English diplomat George Stepney:

> it is to be feared that after my death, my sons will be considered foreigners. The eldest is a lot more accustomed to acting the sovereign than the poor prince of Wales, who is too young to profit from the example of the king of France, and who will be so visibly happy to have recovered what the king his father so thoughtlessly lost that one will be able to do with him what one would like.[77]

Sophia's comments reveal more about her son's attitude than about English prejudices, which they would have bolstered if publicized by Stepney. Georg Ludwig clearly worried about the condition of his prospective English empire, if empire is understood in its sense of a ruler's power over his subjects. He could not have known that English empire had early on been attributed not solely to the king, but to the king in parliament. But his reservations are nonetheless peculiar, considering Germany's extensive experience with dispersed sovereignty. Georg Ludwig not only owed fealty to the Holy Roman Emperor, but he had to submit taxation to the approval of his Hanoverian estates. But since the Peace of Westphalia (1648), practical power had been slipping from the Emperor and the provincial estates to the territorial princes. So it is unsurprising that Georg Ludwig mistrusted the English parliament, whose deliberations he termed 'a far too troublesome, uncertain affair'.[78] This skepticism increased after the Act of Settlement imposed even further limitations upon his prospective freedom of action as king of England. News of its provisions moved him to 'declare loudly that he does not want to be king of England', Sophia reported.[79] In many ways, the

---

[76] Georg Ludwig to Schütz, 4 Feb. 1701, Hannover, published in Schnath, *Geschichte Hannovers*, iv, p. 561.

[77] Sophia to Stepney, undated (c. 1700–1), Pyrmont, first published in Philip Yorke, 2nd earl of Hardwicke, ed., *Miscellaneous State Papers from 1501 to 1726* (2 vols., London, 1778), ii, p. 442. I do not agree that Sophia was being ironic, as argued in Waltraut Fricke, *Leibniz und die englische Sukzession des Hauses Hannover* (Hildesheim, 1957), p. 15.

[78] Georg Ludwig to Bothmer, 26 June 1702, quoted in Gert Brauer, *Die hannoversch-englischen Subsidienverträge 1702–1748* (Aalen, 1962), p. 18.

[79] Sophia to Christian Heinrich, undated, quoted in Schnath, *Geschichte Hannovers*, iv, p. 36.

prehistory of the Hanoverian succession in Britain is the story of how its English and electoral supporters wore down Georg Ludwig's resistance to it.

In correspondence or conversation with Hanoverians, Britons hastened to downplay the Act of Settlement's limitations. William III told the Hanoverian envoy in London that the Act of Settlement contained no new limitations on the royal prerogative, a point of view which Queen Anne put directly to the elector nine years later.[80] But other Britons undermined the royal opinion by hinting that the offending clauses might be undone. The earl of Marlborough suggested to Hans Caspar von Bothmer, the electoral representative at The Hague, that parliament might repeal some of the limitations after the eventual successor had won the nation's trust.[81] Marlborough's argument was not only prescient, as the partial repeal of 1716 confirmed, but also strongly inclined Hanoverian counsels to favor the succession.[82]

Georg Ludwig naturally put more credit in the opinion of his Hanoverian advisers, who strongly pushed the English succession. The Privy Council argued that the Act of Settlement was more obviously an insult to William III than to the elector and his family. It continued, writing that

> the most prominent cause of the dissatisfaction with the king of England is that he, from mere passion, raised the servants he brought from Holland to the most eminent and profitable charges in the kingdom, and not only made them equal, but even partly preferred them, to the old families, which the nation could not possibly approve. If the king had moderated himself in this, things would have gone a lot better. And if a future king abstains from this, he can also expect fewer inconveniences.[83]

In their advice to Georg Ludwig about how he might avoid the domestic unrest which had troubled William III, his electoral ministers prescribed personal union. They advised him to govern England more or less as if he did not already rule Hanover. But Georg Ludwig's Privy Council contradicted themselves when they admonished him to use the English succession to achieve Hanover's German objectives. They observed that 'through the elevated figure which the candidacy for the English crown would give Your Electoral Highness, you would be able to settle all the earlier the weighty matters of the electorate and the combination of principalities'.[84] The ministers felt the English succession would help Georg Ludwig attain universal

---

80 Schnath, *Geschichte Hannovers*, iv, pp. 33, 232.
81 Schnath, *Geschichte Hannovers*, iv, p. 34.
82 Gregg, *The Protestant Succession*, p. 16.
83 'Gutachten der Geheimen Räte für den Kurfürsten Georg Ludwig betr. die Ubernahme der englischen Thronfolge', 9 July 1701, published in Schnath, *Geschichte Hannovers*, iv, p. 574.
84 'Gutachten der Geheimen Räte', in Schnath, *Geschichte Hannovers*, iv, p. 575.

recognition of his pretension to electoral rank, as well as of his right to inherit the principality of Celle. Thus, the ministers also saw England as furthering Hanover's imperial expansion.

Georg Ludwig's ministers were ultimately less influential in this matter than a courtier whose intellectual fertility outweighed his personal distance from the elector. For Gottfried Wilhelm Leibniz, the English succession offered the prospect of patronage and prestige in a more cosmopolitan setting. He set out to convert Georg Ludwig to the English succession using an entirely imperial argument. Leibniz hoped to establish the elector's mastery over England's politics, which the latter might then use to manipulate that country in the interest of the European territorial status quo. For Leibniz and for many Hanoverians, empire implied conservation more than conquest.

Leibniz's thinking on the first front took shape in response to a letter from the Scottish philosophe, Thomas Burnet of Kemney. Burnet wrote to Leibniz on this occasion that the Act of Settlement burnished 'not only the prerogative's jewels but those of the people's liberty and privileges, which render the former more glorious and less burdensome' to the king as well as his subjects.[85] Like William III and Marlborough, Burnet aimed to reconcile the electoral court to the Act of Settlement. But Burnet's emollient language did not conceal his association of political liberty with the people and (by implication) the parliament. This sentiment provoked what one scholar has called Leibniz's 'most important purely political letter'.[86]

Leibniz's response was, in the strictest sense, a refutation of Burnet's letter along theoretical lines. Leibniz reproached his sense of political liberty as far too uncritical, explaining that 'true liberty . . . is one of the greatest jewels of human nature, but after reason; liberty, as I have told you on other occasions being only the power of following reason'.[87] Leibniz demoted liberty because, unlike reason, it was subject to corruption. He wrote, 'it is quite certain that liberty [which has] degenerated into license will disappear and will relapse into arbitrary power'.[88] If Burnet's definition of liberty was unsatisfactory, so was the assumption that it – or arbitrary power, for that matter – were specific to particular political institutions. Leibniz cautioned that 'arbitrary power is found not only in kings, but also in assemblies, when cabals and animosities prevail over reason'.[89] Yet Leibniz's objections extended beyond theory; like Burnet, he had practical political designs.

[85] T. Burnet to Leibniz, quoted in Gottfried Wilhelm Leibniz, 'Leibniz sur les formes de gouvernement', published in Klopp, ed., Die Werke von Leibniz, viii, p. 266.
[86] Gottfried Wilhelm Leibniz, Political Writings, trans. and ed. Patrick Riley (Cambridge, 1988), p. 23.
[87] Leibniz to T. Burnet, [1701], published in Leibniz, Political Writings, trans. and ed. Riley, p. 194.
[88] Leibniz to T. Burnet, [1701], in Leibniz, Political Writings, trans. and ed. Riley, p. 194.
[89] Leibniz to T. Burnet, [1701], in Leibniz, Political Writings, trans. and ed. Riley, p. 193.

When speaking of wicked assemblies, Leibniz clearly had the English parliament in mind. Indeed he cruelly caricatured that body's conduct during the standing-army controversy, in a passage which he prudently omitted from his final letter to Burnet:

> if, during a parliamentary debate, some extravagant people claimed that England could support itself against every foreign power without regular troops at home and without alliances abroad, provided it had a good fleet; if a naval officer observed that a fleet cannot be everywhere, and that this would put the security of the state at the mercy of the winds and waves, and that such a solitary fleet could not protect against the descent of a considerable force, as recent examples prove; and if this remonstrance was scorned by a cabal of malintentioned persons, I would say that this cabal exercises an arbitrary power in such an assembly brazenly rebelling against the empire of reason.[90]

Leibniz contrasted England's anarchic parliament with Sophia, who 'is entirely for reason'.[91] This implied firstly the current superiority of the electoral constitution as described by Sophia to Stepney. Leibniz even considered that 'the absolute power of kings is more tolerable than the license of individuals'.[92] He further implied that Hanover's moral superiority would become equality if reason established itself in English politics. This emphasis upon reason and natural law at the expense of institutional differences was immediately calculated to domesticate English politics for the reluctant elector. But it later encouraged many Hanoverians to compare the British and Hanoverian constitutions once the latter succeeded Queen Anne in 1714.[93]

Having established his patron's right to guide English politics, Leibniz had to put it to good use. He exhorted Georg Ludwig to use his eventual good fortune to secure England's defense of the European balance of power. Leibniz first linked the balance of power to the British succession in a memorial which emerged from a discussion with Sophia and Georg Wilhelm of Celle in early 1701.[94] The concept had taken on renewed relevance as Europe contemplated the prospect of a Bourbon secundogeniture in Spain. Yet Leibniz invested the British succession with even more importance for the balance of power, writing

---

90 Leibniz, 'Leibniz sur les formes de gouvernement', in Klopp, ed., *Die Werke von Leibniz*, viii, pp. 269–70.
91 Leibniz, 'Leibniz sur les formes de gouvernement', in Klopp, ed., *Die Werke von Leibniz*, viii, p. 267.
92 Quoted in Leibniz, *Political Writings*, trans. and ed. Riley, p. 24.
93 See Hermann Wellenreuther, 'Göttingen und England im achtzehnten Jahrhundert', *Göttinger Universitätsreden* 75 (1985), p. 52.
94 Fricke, *Leibniz und die englische Sukzession*, p. 22 (text and note).

the three kingdoms which make up Great Britain form a power which was once very formidable, and which has maintained a manner of balance in Christendom until now. So does not Europe's fate depend on the resolutions which are presently taken there? It is true that a king of England needs a lot of prudence and moderation to govern people so difficult and jealous of their liberty. But the glory of a prince is not to attach himself to his ease and pleasure, but to think that he is only great in order to procure the general good.[95]

Leibniz urged his patron to put aside his comfort in the interest of all Europeans. This was because Britain's maintenance of the balance of power was not automatic, but issued from its monarch's personal virtue. Leibniz's criticism of Charles II's and James II's 'intrigues with France'[96] reminded the electoral court of the Catholic pretender's indifference to the balance of power. The Hanoverian succession in Britain was the only chance to avert British recidivism in the matter of the balance of power. Leibniz later extended this analysis to the Protestant interest, which was held to defend religious liberty in much the same manner as the balance of power did civil liberty.[97]

As had Toland's, Leibniz's use of the balance of power had imperial resonance. But it differed from Toland's meaning, whereby England manipulated smaller countries to procure a balance of power and thereby derived glory. Leibniz ascribed more glory to Georg Ludwig's person than to Hanover itself, a recent creation with none of England's ancestral self-regard. But he did relate the balance of power to Germany's own medieval relic, the Holy Roman Empire, envisioning the two as concentric mechanisms for the preservation of peace. Admittedly, Karl Otmar von Aretin has distinguished between the two on mechanical grounds. The post-1648 Empire proved more respectful of smaller communities' rights and territories than the balance of power, though the latter system did not reveal its capacity for justifying the cupidity of Europe's great powers during Leibniz's lifetime.[98] Most importantly for Leibniz, the Empire and balance of power both aimed at peace. As Aretin

---

[95] Gottfried Wilhelm Leibniz, 'Considerations sur le droit de la maison de Bronsvic-L., à l'égard de la succession d'Angleterre', [1701], published in Klopp, ed., *Die Werke von Leibniz*, viii, p. 228.

[96] Leibniz, 'Considerations sur le droit de la maison de Bronsvic-L.', in Klopp, ed., *Die Werke von Leibniz*, viii, p. 229.

[97] 'The interest of the house of Brunswick in this point [the succession] is that of liberty and religion, and not only all of Protestant Europe, but even all of Europe which is interested in the public liberty, must be favorable to it. This shows that . . . its pretension [to the English throne] . . . conforms not only to law and interest, but to an indispensable duty.' Gottfried Wilhelm Leibniz, 'Considérations sur l'affaire de la succession d'Angleterre', [1701], published in Klopp, ed., *Die Werke von Leibniz*, viii, p. 254.

[98] Karl Otmar von Aretin, *Das Reich: Friedensgarantie und europäisches Gleichgewicht 1648–1806* (Stuttgart, 1986), esp. pp. 55–75.

himself conceded, 'the imperial system . . . and European balance were admittedly expressions of the desire for peace manifested in the Peace of Westphalia and of the intention to order the relationship of European states with one another in place of the old Christian formula for European peace'.[99]

Britain's separate peace with France, concluded at Utrecht in 1713, vindicated Leibniz's argument for the British succession based upon the balance of power. For the first time, Georg Ludwig's Hanoverian ministers justified the succession with the balance of power. Complaining of Georg Ludwig's refusal to fund a Dutch invasion of Britain in 1714, they admonished him that the succession concerned 'not only the interest, advantage, glory and reputation of Your Electoral Highness and your house, but the good of all Europe'.[100] And when Georg Ludwig appeared to retreat from a belated attempt to procure Anne's invitation for his son (the future George II), they again balked.[101] They stressed the importance of 'a crown whose possessor gives the balance in all Europe', and that

> the common good and the freedom of all Europe, as well as the salvation of Protestantism from its complete ruin, are interested that the pretender does not ascend to the British throne and that the same throne entails upon, and remains conserved in, Your Electoral Highness's noble house.[102]

Leibniz, assisted by events, had made the balance of power the single greatest 'legitimation' of dynastic union in Hanover.[103]

Both Hanover and England contemplated their prospective union in terms of recent imperial experience. The Dutch conquest made the English ambivalent about yet another foreign union, a sentiment which only diminished after the Act of Settlement appeared to preserve national independence or extend English empire to the electorate. Hanoverians' overwhelmingly more positive experience of the post-1648 Holy Roman Empire fostered more optimism for union with England, obscuring Georg Ludwig's personal misgivings about the Act's restrictions on his regal powers. The imperial tone for discussing the Anglo-Hanoverian union was established, although its context inevitably shifted in later years.

99   Aretin, *Das Reich*, p. 75.
100   Privy council to Georg Ludwig, 22 Feb. 1714, Hannover, published in Schnath, *Geschichte Hannovers*, iv, p. 730.
101   Schnath, *Geschichte Hannovers*, iv, p. 396.
102   'Gutachten der Geheimen Räte über die dringende Notwendigkeit, den Kurprinzen zur Rettung der Sukzession nach Engalnd zu schicken. Beschwörende Mahnung, sich der großen Stunde nicht zu verschließen', 5 June 1714, published in Schnath, *Geschichte Hannovers*, iv, pp. 745–6.
103   Hermann Wellenreuther, 'Die Bedeutung des Siebenjährigen Krieges für die englisch-hannoveranischen Beziehungen', in Adolf M. Birke and Kurt Kluxen, eds., *England und Hannover* (Munich, 1986), p. 157.

# 2

# Succession

If the Glorious Revolution had overshadowed the prehistory of dynastic union, then the Treaty of Utrecht haunted its early years. Concluded in 1713, a year before the Hanoverian succession, Britain's separate peace with Louis XIV represented a victory for the proponents of maritime policy. In advance of the treaty, the tory ministry of Robert Harley emphasized the imperial conflict at the expense of its European equivalent. And at Utrecht itself, Britain acquired Nova Scotia and the right to supply the Spanish empire with slaves. While the treaty also left Britain with European possessions in Minorca and Gibraltar, these were important naval bases which could be reconciled with maritime strategy. Nevertheless, they were leftovers of an earlier, more singularly European policy. The same was true of Hanover. At Utrecht, the British government procured French recognition of Hanover's electoral status and its ruling dynasty's right to rule in London. Here the Protestant succession trumped the government's maritime inclinations, leaving its winnings with a more European character than they would have had otherwise. Still, Utrecht offended Georg Ludwig. It abandoned the Holy Roman Empire, and its ruler's claims to the Spanish succession. And notwithstanding its language to the contrary, the treaty seemed to imperil the balance of power – which seemed to embody the Imperial ethic on a European scale. Rather than reinforcing Hanoverian ambivalence about the British succession, Utrecht bolstered arguments for it – particularly that which relied upon the balance of power. Hanoverians saw that Britain's supposed maintenance of the balance of power was not inevitable, but dependent upon the will of its ruler. They became increasingly resigned to the loss of their ruler.

Just as support for dynastic union derived from support for the Protestant succession, the opposition to both correlated highly. Thus it was that Jacobites were the foremost opponents of dynastic union during its early years. They feared Hanoverian ascendancy over Britain, but were initially uncertain about its character. Given the prominence of Anglican theologians in the ranks of British Jacobitism, it is unsurprising that scrutiny initially focused upon religion. Yet as in so many other instances, the Catholic pretender soon cut the ground out from under his nonjuring supporters.

The Kentish clergyman Theophilus Dorrington provoked the Jacobite examination of Britain's relationship with Hanover by republishing his English translation of Samuel von Pufendorf's *Jus feciale divinum sive de consensu et dissensu protestantium*. Dorrington clearly considered the *Jus feciale*, a plea for intra-Protestant doctrinal reconciliation, to speak to England's contentious religious divisions. Dorrington betrayed his political objectives in his various English translations of the work's title. He called his original 1703 edition *The Divine Feudal Law, or Covenants with Mankind Represented together with Means for the Uniting of Protestants. In which the principles of the Lutheran Church Are Stated and Defended*. As Pufendorf's original title said nothing explicit about Lutheranism, it may be that Dorrington hoped to vindicate the faith and homeland of Anne's consort, Prince George of Denmark, from Molesworth's libel. Dorrington again curried favor with his second edition in 1714, now entitled *A View of the Principles of the Lutheran Churches Showing How Far They Agree with the Church of England, Being a Seasonable Essay for the Uniting of Protestants upon the Happy Accession of His Majesty King George to the Throne of These Kingdoms*. The word 'seasonable' hinted at a sales strategy based upon the work's topicality. But Dorrington also courted George I by flattering what he supposed were the new monarch's intentions. Unfortunately, Dorrington did not explain what he meant by the word 'uniting'.[1]

Some Jacobites believed Dorrington aimed at institutional and doctrinal union with the Hanoverian church. This argument was advanced by another Kentish clergyman, the future nonjuror Thomas Brett, in his *Review of the Lutheran Principles*. The *Review* took the form of a letter to a friend who had supposedly represented Dorrington's viewpoint in more explicit terms. Brett's interlocutor intoned 'that His Majesty's subjects in the duchy of *Brunswick* were all *Lutherans*, and therefore, as we were now united under one king, it was very expedient that we should also be united in one religion'.[2] Whether religious union was desirable was one thing; whether it was possible was another. Brett's correspondent admitted that England and Scotland had retained their separate churches despite the unions of 1603 and 1707. But he

> conceiv'd we might much more easily unite with the *Lutherans* than with the *Scots*, or any other of the *reform'd* who were [geographically] nearer to us [than the Hanoverians] because the *Scots* and all those call'd the *reform'd* were profess'd *presbyterians* and declar'd enemies to episcopacy and liturgy, and would allow no ceremonies in religious worship. But the *Lutherans* were more ceremonious in their worship than the Church of *England*.[3]

---

[1]  For another Englishman's efforts to unite the Protestant churches, see Norman Sykes, *William Wake, Archbishop of Canterbury 1657–1737* (2 vols., Cambridge, 1957), ii, pp. 1–88.

[2]  Thomas Brett, *A Review of the Lutheran Principles* (London, 1714), p. 4.

[3]  Brett, *A Review of the Lutheran Principles*, p. 5.

Brett's correspondent further envisioned the manner of effecting such a union, saying that 'some few alterations in indifferent things might bring so great a number of His Majesty's subjects, as the Lutherans were, into our communion'.[4]

Brett, for his part, rejected religious union with Hanover. He wrote that the king

> was oblig'd by act of parliament to join in communion with the Church of England . . . since it was not thought reasonable to make any alterations in the doctrine or discipline of the establish'd church for the sake of His Majesty and his royal family, I could see no occasion there was for the making alterations for the sake of any of his subjects.[5]

Indeed, Brett suggested that the king's conformity to the Church of England might even set an example for religious union along exclusively English lines. He concluded his pamphlet with the wish that the Hanoverians 'will easily be persuaded to follow the great example of our gracious sovereign King *George* and most heartily embrace [our] communion'.[6] Here was a rare instance of religious expansionism directed at Hanover. But Brett was in fact skeptical that the Church of England could comprehend thousands of Hanoverian Lutherans. Whereas ceremonies had marked clerical influence in Toland, Brett dismissed them (and the apparent similarity of the Anglican and Lutheran liturgies) as unimportant.[7] He went on to examine differences with German Lutheranism in what he considered to be weightier matters: those of church government and doctrine.

Brett anathematized Lutheran doctrine by comparing it to that of Catholicism. He did this almost entirely on the basis of the Lutheran belief in the ubiquity of Christ's real body in the cosmos. Brett ridiculed this tenet on logical grounds,[8] but he also used it to introduce an attack on the related doctrine of consubstantiation. Brett scorned consubstantiation on its own merits,[9] but also compared it to the more familiar (at least to English ears) Catholic doctrine of transubstantiation. Brett enunciated this argument in some detail, writing:

---

4 Brett, A *Review of the Lutheran Principles*, p. 8.
5 Brett, A *Review of the Lutheran Principles*, pp. 7–8.
6 Brett, A *Review of the Lutheran Principles*, pp. 48–9.
7 Brett, A *Review of the Lutheran Principles*, p. 7.
8 "Tis the essence of a body to be circumscribed and bounded with certain limits, so that to talk of an infinite or omnipresent body is a contradiction.' Brett, A *Review of the Lutheran Principles*, p. 29.
9 Brett later wrote that Christ's apostles 'saw enough to tell them that it was not the *natural* body of their Lord that they ate [at the last supper] . . . for Christ's *natural human* body was there present'. [Brett], A *Letter to the Author of the History of the Lutheran Church*, pp. 33–4.

both [Catholics and Lutherans] agree that in the *Eucharist* we eat and drink the real, substantial body and blood of *Christ* . . . only the *papists* say we eat and drink them *in* the elements, which are substantially converted into them, and the *Lutherans* say we eat and drink them *with* the elements. But both maintain that we eat and drink the very body and blood of *Christ* . . . with our mouths, which is blasphemy. Whereas our church teacheth that *the body of* Christ *is given, taken, and eaten in the supper only after an heavenly and spiritual manner* . . . So that the *Lutherans* are in this case as far from the doctrine of our church as the *papists*. And when either *papists* or *Lutherans* are press'd with arguments drawn from the senses against their doctrine, they have recourse to God's omnipotence.

Now he that can believe what is contrary to the judgment of his sense and the nature of things, and supposes that God's omnipotence can reconcile contradictions, as . . . the *Lutherans* do in this case, may easily believe *transubstantiation*.[10]

This argument had first arisen during the Scottish parliament's 1703 debate about the Hanoverian succession, in one of the few instances in which a deputy addressed the future relationship with Hanover as well as the present one with England.[11] Although the speaker had admitted the anglophobic force of his argument, it was introduced to an English readership in the following year by Charles Leslie. An Irish-born nonjuror, Leslie adapted the protest of Scottish presbyterians to the uses of Anglican Jacobites.

Where Leslie likened Lutheran doctrine to that of Catholicism, he compared its church government to presbyterianism.[12] This argument was also taken up by Brett in 1714. He observed 'that the *Lutherans* have no *bishops* [and] that their *superintendents* . . . are only mere *presbyters* who have . . . a jurisdiction like that of our *archdeacons* . . . and consequently are as mere *presbyterians* as the *Calvinists* themselves'.[13] In a later text, Brett again implied the desirability of the Anglican hierarchy's extension to Hanover. But he doubted the Hanoverians would consent to the restoration of episcopacy,

for all those lands that in the times of popery did belong to that *order* are now dispersed among the *laity* . . . must be resumed [by bishops]. So that all the present proprietors, who are the chief leading men in those nations, must use

---

10 Brett, *A Review of the Lutheran Principles*, pp. 40–1.
11 [George Ridpath], *The Proceedings of the Parliament of Scotland Begun at Edinburgh, 6th May 1703*, (n. p., 1704), pp. 28–9. For the argument's later reiteration by Andrew Fletcher of Saltoun, see John Robertson, 'An Elusive Sovereignty: The Course of the Union Debate in Scotland 1698–1707', in John Robertson, ed., *A Union for Empire: Political Thought and the British Union of 1707* (Cambridge, 1995), p. 212.
12 [Charles Leslie], *The Wolf Stript of his Shepherd's Cloathing* (London, 1704), p. 44.
13 Brett, *A Review of the Lutheran Principles*, p. 17.

their utmost interest and endeavors to prevent their uniting with us upon those terms.[14]

But Brett feared that ecclesiastical union without the restoration of the Hanoverian episcopacy might in turn prove a pretext 'to take our bishops' lands and to overthrow the hierarchy amongst us'.[15] Brett feared Hanover's religious domination of England was more likely than vice versa.

Not surprisingly, Brett's *Review* attracted immediate censure. A *Second Review of the Lutheran Principles*, probably written by yet another Kentish clergyman, John Lewis, made the most robust rebuttal. Lewis considered that Brett had misconstrued the sense of the word 'union' in Pufendorf and Dorrington as requiring 'alterations' in either church. It insisted that such a union was unlikely,

> His *Majesty* knowing very well that all particular churches have a power to ordain their own rites and ceremonies and that 'tis the duty of every one to take them as they find them, the unity of Christians not lying in the *same circumstantials* of religion but in maintaining the *unity* of the *faith*.[16]

Lewis suggested that the latter sort of union might consist merely in the joint celebration of the eucharist. According to this interpretation, King George's adherence to the Church of England was exemplary not because it might encourage his Hanoverian subjects to convert, *pace* Brett, but because 'it was very agreeable to the principles of catholic unity to continue in the communion of the *Lutheran* churches while he was among *them*, and is so to conform to ours now he is *here*'.[17] This recollection of the Act of Settlement's requirement that foreign successors communicate with the Church of England seemed to oppose Brett's defensive stance against Hanoverian empire with Drake's vision of the personal union thesis.

The trouble with reducing religious union to communion was that Lutherans and Anglicans disagreed so obviously over this very sacrament. Lewis conceded that consubstantiation was erroneous.[18] But he noted that Lutherans had communicated with Anglican churches in the past, despite their variance of opinion on the matter.[19] He concluded that

---

14 [Thomas Brett], *A Letter to the Author of the History of the Lutheran Church from a Country School-Boy* (London, 1714), pp. 28–9. See also Brett, *A Review of the Lutheran Principles*, p. 15.

15 Brett, *A Review of the Lutheran Principles*, p. 15.

16 [John Lewis], *A Second Review of the Lutheran Principles, or an Answer to Dr. Brett's Late Insolent Libel against the Lutheran Churches, Showing That There Is No Essential Difference between Them and the Church of England* (London, 1714), pp. 43–4.

17 [Lewis], *A Second Review of the Lutheran Principles*, p. 30.

18 [Lewis], *A Second Review of the Lutheran Principles*, p. 29.

19 Quoted in [Lewis], *A Second Review of the Lutheran Principles*, pp. 20–2.

the *manner* in which the body of Christ is present in the sacrament is not made a *fundamental* point, either by the *Lutherans* or those who *differ* from them . . . how wide soever *consubstantiation* may be from the truth, it is only a speculative opinion, and has no ill influence upon practice. For the *Lutherans* do not idolatrously worship and give divine homage to the body of Christ, which they suppose to be present in the eucharist. Nor do they pretend to offer it again to almighty God as a *propitiatory sacrifice* for the sins of mankind.[20]

This was, of course, intended to absolve Lutherans of Brett's smear that their belief in consubstantiation qualified them as crypto-Catholics. Lewis had somewhat less difficulty in the matter of episcopacy, arguing that Brett's distinction was semantic rather than functional. 'Their *superintendents* are very like', he wrote, 'and have all that is of the essence of our *bishops*.'[21]

Yet by the time Lewis had attacked him, Brett had already shifted the basis of his argument against Lutheranism in a postscript to the second edition of the *Review*. Brett had hitherto stressed that salvation was at issue in the question of religious union.[22] But, in the second edition, he shifted the stakes from heavenly bliss to earthly freedom. Brett now based his argument upon the *Account of Denmark*, which he had not even mentioned in his previous treatments of Lutheranism. In particular, he quoted from those passages in which Molesworth had linked Lutheranism to absolute monarchy.[23] Brett's reliance upon the notoriously freethinking Molesworth, and his tacit adoption of the religious argument against union with Hanover from Toland's *Limitations*, were remarkable for an Anglican divine. But Brett was trying to reconcile his criticism of Lutheranism with the entirely secular case against Hanover presented by the pretender, whose manifesto of 29 August 1714 reached Britain during November.

James Stuart's first public response to the Hanoverian succession and the attendant dynastic union shocked its British readers, none more than the Jacobites themselves, by its whiggish content.[24] While criticizing the Revolution settlement as republican, the pretender displayed a sensitivity to professional soldiery that was itself indebted to classical republicanism. The

---

[20] [Lewis], *A Second Review of the Lutheran Principles*, pp. 34–5.

[21] [Lewis], *A Second Review of the Lutheran Principles*, p. 43. See also [Robert Watts], *Two Letters to the Right Honourable the Lord Viscount Townshend Shewing the Seditious Tendency of Several Late Pamphlets* (London, 1714), pp. 29–30; *British Advice to the Free-Holders of Great Britain* (London, 1715), p. 14.

[22] For example, he had written that consubstantiation 'destroyeth an article of our faith . . . which we are bound to believe under pain of *everlasting punishment*'. [Brett], *A Letter to the Author of the History of the Lutheran Church* , p. 31.

[23] Thomas Brett, *A Review of the Lutheran Principles . . . to Which Is Added a Postscript Containing Some Transient Remarks on a Late Virulent Pamphlet Entitled Two Letters to the Right Honourable the Lord Viscount Townshend, &c.* (London, 1714), pp. 42–3.

[24] 'Many, and in particular most of the *Jacobites*, were at first of opinion, that this piece was spurious, and a contrivance . . . But it was soon generally acknowledged that the said *declaration* was genuine.' *The Political State of Great Britain* 8 (1714), p. 470.

Stuart court had not experimented with republicanism since an abortive episode in April 1693.[25] But the British populace was unaware of the pretender's exposure to whiggish arguments by his court's Anglican chaplain, Charles Leslie. Leslie had first realized republicanism's anti-Hanoverian potential in 1705, when he was still in Britain. At that time, James Drake supported the tory leadership's invitation to Sophia to visit England on the republican grounds that it would inhibit political corruption and the influence of the army.[26] Leslie deconstructed Drake's argument, noting that a visit might instead necessitate a standing army to repulse attacks from both Scotland (which had not yet recognized the Hanoverian succession) and from the electorate itself. He particularly worried that a Hanoverian successor might emulate William III's introduction of Dutch guards into the realm, a symbol of conquest par excellence.[27] At first, republican misgivings about Hanover sufficed to dispute Drake's ideological consistency. But after his flight to the continent in 1711, Leslie retailed them to the pretender himself. He warned James Stuart that a 1709 act for naturalizing foreign Protestants might provide cover for a Hanoverian invasion,[28] a warning which the pretender soon repeated to his half-sister Queen Anne.[29] Republican argumentation against Hanover allowed the pretender to avoid potential religious pitfalls. He could hardly raise the question of George I's Lutheranism, knowing that he was vulnerable because of his own exotic Catholicism. Jacobites (including the Scottish member of parliament George Lockhart) knew that Catholics were as open to the charge of supporting absolute rule as Lutherans.[30] Furthermore, James Stuart's Catholicism made him less sympathetic towards polemic which elevated Anglican doctrine or church government above those of other denominations. Mindful of his party's religious divisions, the pretender hoped to maintain cohesion by hewing to secular language.

James Stuart's secular criticisms of the Hanoverian connection worked on two levels, addressing Britain and Europe in turn. He first labeled George I 'a foreigner, a powerful prince, and absolute in his own country, where he has never met with the least contradiction from his subjects. He is ignorant of our laws, manners, customs, and language, and supported by a good army of

---

[25] For this, see Paul Monod, 'Jacobitism and Country Principles in the Reign of William III', *The Historical Journal* 30 (1987), p. 299.

[26] *Mercurius Politicus* 1 nos. 33–5 (29 Sept. – 9 Oct. 1705).

[27] *The Rehearsal* 1 no. 69 (24–31 Oct. 1705), p. 2.

[28] [Charles Leslie], 'The Memorial of the Sieur Lamb', in James Macpherson, ed., *Original Papers Containing the Secret History of Great Britain from the Restoration to the Accession of the House of Hanover* (2 vols., London, 1775), ii, p. 217.

[29] James Francis Edward Stuart to Queen Anne, May 1711, published in Macpherson, *Original Papers*, ii, p. 224.

[30] See Anthony Aufrere, ed., *The Lockhart Papers, Containing Memoirs and Commentaries upon the Affairs of Scotland from 1702 to 1715 by George Lockhart, Esq., of Carnwath* (2 vols., London, 1817), i, pp. 474–5.

his own people'.[31] The manifesto's vagueness allowed for the most expansive interpretation: that the electoral army supported absolute rule in Hanover, and might eventually serve the same purpose in Britain. This was nothing less than the domestic fear expressed in Toland's *Limitations*, and the pretender followed up with an international corollary from the same work. He added that

> all Christian princes and potentates . . . will reflect upon . . . the formidable effects they are threaten'd with from such an united force as that of England and Hanover, and that they'll seriously consider whether the exorbitant power that now accrues to the house of Brunswick be consistent with the balance of power they have been fighting for all this last war.[32]

James Stuart thereby echoed Toland's charge from the *Limitations* that the union with Hanover threatened the balance of power, broadening Toland's original scope from northern Europe to the entire continent.

If the pretender echoed the fear of Hanoverian dominance first mooted in Toland's *Limitations*, then his opponents answered with the case for British superiority made in the same author's *Anglia Libera*. In *Remarks on the Pretender's Declaration*, Toland's friend and fellow freethinker Matthew Tindal dismissed the pretender's contention that union with Hanover damaged Europe's political equilibrium. Tindal wrote that the pretender's 'good friends the late blessed peacemakers have taken effectual care that *Britain*, though it were to be united with all her late allies as well as *Hanover*, should not be too powerful'.[33] On the contrary, he assured his readers that 'by the union of *England* and *Hanover*, they have got that balance of power all *Europe* has been so long fighting for'.[34] But where Tindal doubted the pretender's European argument, he conceded the related charge that George I ruled Hanover absolutely. 'It is so far true', Tindal admitted, 'the elector never met with the least contradiction from his subjects. But then 'tis as true he never required anything of them but what was for their good.'[35] But where this interpretation had led the pretender to envision Hanoverian empire over Britain, it enabled Tindal to argue just the opposite.

Tindal was confident that George I would govern Britain according to its own, rather than Hanoverian, practice. Misunderstanding the pretender's use of the word 'foreigners', which referred to the dynasty rather than its

---

31 James Francis Edward Stuart, *James R. James the Third, by the Grace of God King of Great Britain, France & Ireland, Defender of the Faith, &c.: To All Kings, Princes, & Potentates and Our Loving Subjects Greeting* (n. p., 1714), p. 1.

32 James Francis Edward Stuart, *James R. James the Third*, p. 2.

33 [Matthew Tindal], *Remarks on the Pretender's Declaration Dated at Plombieres, August 29th 1714 N. S.* (London, 1715), p. 9. For the attribution, see N. Tindal, *The Continuation of Mr. Rapin's History of England* (21 vols., London, 1763), xviii (vi), p. 333 (note).

34 [Tindal], *Remarks on the Pretender's Declaration*, p. 12.

35 [Tindal], *Remarks on the Pretender's Declaration*, p. 21.

retinue, Tindal emphasized that they, 'by the laws of which our king has shown himself a most religious observer, are excluded from all places of trust and profit'.[36] Tindal's juxtaposition of the Act of Settlement against Hanover's somewhat weaker constitutional protections highlighted a British opportunity to exploit the electorate. He wrote that

> wherever the seat of empire is, there the riches of the distant provinces must all center; and consequently all we shall suffer by a foreign prince coming among us is to have the riches of his other dominions by degrees brought in here, as well as to have their strength, as often as we have occasion, employ'd for our service.[37]

This was nothing less than a synthesis of the economic and strategic arguments for British empire over Hanover made by Toland in *Anglia Libera* and subsequent books. Tindal even collapsed Toland's original (but admittedly weak) distinction between territorial empires and dynastic unions. The economic case for empire over Hanover received a further fillip with the publication of an optimistic account of its resources in Guy Miège's *The Present State of His Majesty's Dominions in Germany*, although Miège evinced some uncertainty as to the nature of its relationship to Britain by paginating it separately from the new edition of his *Present State of Great Britain and Ireland*.[38]

By reviving the economic rationale for union with Hanover, Tindal opened up yet another secular theme for Jacobites. This was first introduced by Bishop Francis Atterbury of Rochester, in *English Advice to the Freeholders of England*. Atterbury addressed Drake's concern that union might siphon wealth from Britain to Hanover rather than vice versa. He reported evasion of the Act of Settlement's provision prohibiting the appointment of Hanoverians to British office, conjecturing that the Hanoverian diplomat 'Baron Bothmer is trusted with the privy purse, that the king may dispose his money here or send it to *Hanover* without the privity of the *English*'.[39] Atterbury suspected Hanoverian courtiers in Britain of forming an economic fifth column in Britain, where Toland and Tindal had believed they would import electoral wealth. Atterbury pointedly doubted the possibility of the latter scenario, noting that the British civil list of £700,000 was 'more by one full half than all *Brunswick, Lüneburg*, and *Hanover* put together can raise'.[40]

---

36 [Tindal], *Remarks on the Pretender's Declaration*, p. 21.

37 [Tindal], *Remarks on the Pretender's Declaration*, p. 28.

38 Guy Miège, *The Present State of His Majesty's Dominions in Germany* (London, 1715).

39 [Francis Atterbury], *English Advice to the Freeholders of England* (n.p. 1714), p. 25, depending upon the edition.

40 [Atterbury], *English Advice*, p. 22.

Atterbury originated the case for Hanover's original poverty, best implied later by the title of the Scots Jacobite ballad 'The Wee, Wee German Lairdie'.[41]

Charles Leslie reiterated Atterbury's fears for the Act of Settlement in a subsequent pamphlet, *The Church of England's Advice to Her Children*. Expanding Atterbury's economic argument, he wrote that George I

> was reported so vastly rich as to give everybody hopes of a mighty flux of *silver* and *gold* after his arrival. Whether he were rich before his coming to you is a doubtful question, but if he stays any time with you, it is not to be doubted but he and his people will be so.
>
> It was said that the treasure of *Hanover* was to pay the debts of the *English* nation. But all that you have seen of that was what entered the City of *London* with him (in a cart) under the appearances of *mops, brooms, buckets, tubs, earthen pans, and close stools*, which will not go a great way in paying the debts of the nation, if they should be ever so well sold.[42]

Leslie recalled the anxiety, first articulated by Toland and Drake, that the elector-king's elevation to Holy Roman Emperor might require his residence in Germany. He wrote that 'large sums may be drawn by it from the remoter dominions to center in the nation where the sovereign resides, that part of his dominions being his principal care as the mistress of all the rest'.[43]

The Jacobites located George I's complicity in wealth transfers to Hanover in a bias towards his native electorate. Drake had already prophesied this, and Jacobites had echoed him when the elector appeared to jeopardize his British inheritance by first withdrawing his troops from their British paymasters to protest Anne's peace negotiations at Utrecht and then demanding arrears in their pay.[44] Bishop Atterbury explained in *English Advice* that

> nothing is more natural than for the king's old subjects to have the advantage, in point of his affection, over his new. By speaking the same language, their conversation is most agreeable to him; and by having been partners with him in his pleasures, which open the heart, they may know . . . how to win upon his nature and to render themselves more acceptable than the *English*. There is

[41] The poem begins, 'Wha the deil hae we got for a king, but a wee, wee German lairdie!' *Jacobite Minstrelsy* (Glasgow, 1829), pp. 46–7.

[42] [Charles Leslie], *The Church of England's Advice to Her Children, and to All Kings, Princes, and Potentates* (London, 1721), p. 51. For Leslie's reference to the national debt, see [Tindal], *Remarks on the Pretender's Declaration*, p. 22.

[43] [Leslie], *The Church of England's Advice*, p. 48.

[44] Aufrere, ed., *The Lockhart Papers*, i, p. 469.

likewise on their side a natural inclination most people have for their country-men.[45]

Atterbury followed Drake in his sympathetic account of the Hanoverian successor's natural affinity for his homeland. But he ascribed no such honor-able motives to British whigs, who 'will desire an inlet may be made for foreigners into employments . . . to establish their present power'.[46] Thus did dynastic union exacerbate British political corruption.

Leslie agreed with Atterbury's interpretation of the royal motives for enriching Hanover at Britain's expense,[47] but added two others. Referring to his scenario of the imperial succession, he informed his readers that 'when you become a province of the Empire . . . you will be impoverish'd by all the means in your pretended king's power to continue your subjection to him'.[48] Leslie reminded his readers of Drake's linkage of wealth with the capacity to resist a standing army. He nonetheless recognized that fiscal-military oppres-sion might not secure Hanoverian empire over Britain, and wrote that

> in case a standing army should not answer all the ends proposed, . . . it may be expected that he should make use of your *blood* and *treasure* before his *harvest* be over, to enlarge his dominions in the *Empire* and to fill his *foreign* coffers, that if the princes abroad or the people at home should oblige him to retire he may have the larger country and the better purse to retire to.[49]

According to this perspective, George I feathered his electoral nest in advance of an inevitable Jacobite restoration.

Their republican themes required both Atterbury and Leslie to account for the elector-king's tendencies towards absolute government, which they both traced to the Hanoverian precedent. Atterbury cautioned that George I 'was uncontrollable at home, could command the lives, liberties, fortunes . . . and wills of his former subjects, and probably hath brought with him a desire to be not less absolute over us'.[50] He hinted further that Hanover's standing army might serve not only as model, but catalyst, for the establishment of absolute rule in Britain. Atterbury noted ominously that George I had recently expanded his electoral army,[51] although this was in preparation for war with Sweden rather than with Britain.[52] Leslie elaborated upon this suspicion, writing that '*Dutch* bottoms can bring in more *Prussians* and

---

[45] [Atterbury], *English Advice*, p. 24 or 25, depending upon the edition.
[46] [Atterbury], *English Advice*, p. 24.
[47] [Leslie], *The Church of England's Advice*, p. 52.
[48] [Leslie], *The Church of England's Advice*, p. 48.
[49] [Leslie], *The Church of England's Advice*, p. 47.
[50] [Atterbury], *English Advice*, p. 25 or 26, depending upon the edition.
[51] [Atterbury], *English Advice*, p. 19. See also p. 27.
[52] Hans-Joachim Finke, 'The "Hanoverian Junta" 1714–1719' (Ph. D. dissertation, University of Delaware, 1970), p. 132.

*Hanoverians* . . . The army being obtain'd, [George I] may . . . make himself as absolute in *England* as he was in *Hanover*.'[53] Leslie felt obliged to defend his master from the same charge of autocratic ambition, to which he was also vulnerable. He considered it absurd that

> he who never knew the least *restriction*, but always a power without any *limitation*, must be placed in the gap to keep out a power which it is only supposed might prove *absolute*, which is as if the taking one into your house with the *plague* upon him were the best remedy against that distemper.[54]

Finally, Leslie concluded his remarks by echoing the pretender's fear that dynastic union threatened European as well as domestic liberties by upsetting the balance of power.[55]

Atterbury and Leslie seconded and greatly elaborated James Stuart's secular case against union with Hanover. While it is true that Atterbury rehearsed Brett's objections to George I's religion,[56] these were curiously muted considering they appeared in the work of a theological controversialist. The equally pious Charles Leslie downplayed them further in *The Church of England's Advice*, merely terming George I an 'occasional conformist'.[57] In favoring secular argument, they pointed the way forward for subsequent Jacobite comment on Hanover's putative empire over Britain.

While it is true that imperial interpretations dominated early commentary on the British-Hanoverian relationship, they prompted a reaction which more closely resembled the personal union thesis. This began in Britain, where at least one pro-government publicist dissented from Tindal's imperial designs upon Hanover. By denying that the elector ruled absolutely and upholding the privileges of the Hanoverian estates, this anonymous author implicitly emphasized the autonomy of Hanoverian institutions from Britain. Leibniz subsequently adopted this argument and introduced it in the electorate, revolutionizing Hanover's political self-image.

The anonymously authored *British Advice to the Free-Holders of England* refuted Atterbury's earlier *English Advice*, but also implicitly differentiated itself from Tindal's response to the pretender. It did concur with Tindal in attacking Atterbury's economic argument, writing that 'His Majesty is so far from sending any money from *England* to *Hanover*, that everyone about him knows he has sent for money from *Hanover* to subsist the *Germans* who had the honor to attend him hither.'[58] Pro-union publicists still agreed that

---

53  [Leslie], *The Church of England's Advice*, p. 44.
54  [Leslie], *The Church of England's Advice*, p. 41.
55  [Leslie], *The Church of England's Advice*, p. 46.
56  [Atterbury], *English Advice*, p. 20.
57  [Leslie], *The Church of England's Advice*, p. 40.
58  *British Advice to the Free-Holders of Great Britain* (London, 1715), p. 17.

union enriched, rather than impoverished, Britain. But in assaulting Atterbury's accusations respecting George I's supposedly absolute rule in Hanover, *British Advice* distanced itself from Tindal's more imperial view. The pamphlet argued that George I would respect parliamentary prerogatives because of his experience with similar institutions in Hanover. *British Advice* observed of Hanoverians that their elector 'was not guilty of the least act of violence or injustice to any of them, that he never rais'd any taxes upon them, without the consent of the states of the country'.[59] *British Advice* was the first work to highlight the Hanoverian estates' consultative role in state finance. While it remained eccentric within British political culture, it was to have remarkable influence in Hanover.

*British Advice* greatly influenced Leibniz's own response to Atterbury, which he entitled *Anti-Jacobite*.[60] Leibniz did not footnote *British Advice*, but the court library he supervised obtained a copy as well as its French translation.[61] But there were original segments of Leibniz's book, particularly that in which he expanded *British Advice's* refutation of Atterbury's religious arguments. The Hanoverian court had sought to compare Lutheranism with Anglicanism ever since Sophia had crudely conflated the two in a letter to Gilbert Burnet of 1689.[62] And Leibniz's part in this effort befitted that of a philosopher who had labored his entire life to reunify western Christendom.[63] Yet theological views of the British-Hanoverian relationship were waning in Hanover as well as Britain.[64] *Anti-Jacobite's* greatest contribution was its transmission of *British Advice's* novel interpretation of Hanoverian civil liberty to the electorate itself. Leibniz simply repeated that 'the king has never taxed his subjects without the consent of the country's estates, [and] he has never used despotic power', which would have been against his oath of investiture.[65] It was true that George I had afforded his Hanoverian estates

---

59 *British Advice*, p. 20.

60 Leibniz wrote in a letter of 4 July 1715, 'I am stunned that the *Anti-Jacobite*, which was not published at Hannover, has been attributed to me.' Emile Ravier, *Bibliographie des œuvres de Leibniz* (Paris, 1937), p. 37 (note). He thus distanced himself from the *Anti-Jacobite*, without actually denying that he wrote it. Leibniz further misled his correspondent, for the book was published in Hannover after all. *Nouvelles Litteraires* 2 (1715), p. 36; *Neue Zeitungen von Gelehrten Sachen* (Leipzig, 1715), p. 497.

61 The French translation was called *Remarques sur le libelle intitulé English Advice to the Freeholders* (The Hague, 1715). Both editions are still to be found in the former electoral library, which has recently taken Leibniz's name.

62 Sophia to G. Burnet, [1689], published in Onno Klopp, ed., *Die Werke von Leibniz* (11 vols., Hannover, 1864–84), vii, p. 76.

63 See Paul Eisenkopf, *Leibniz und die Einigung der Christenheit* (Paderborn, 1975); Hans Friedrich Werling, *Die weltanschaulichen Grundlagen der Reunionsbemühungen von Leibniz im Briefwechsel mit Bossuet und Pellisson* (Frankfurt, 1977).

64 For the persistence of the Protestant interest, see Andrew C. Thompson, *Britain, Hanover and the Protestant Interest, 1688–1756* (Woodbridge, 2006).

65 [Gottfried Wilhelm Leibniz], *Anti-Jacobite, ou faussetés de l'avis aux proprietaires anglois* ([Hannover], 1715), p. 66.

markedly more respect than his electoral predecessors had.[66] Although Leibniz had made a career of ascribing his electoral patrons an expansive degree of latitude, he had always acknowledged external brakes upon their power – such as the Holy Roman Empire and its constitution. He was less comfortable highlighting the Hanoverian estates' internal limitations upon the elector's power, which probably accounted for his reluctance to elaborate upon *British Advice*. Yet even this brief reference to the estates, which had slumbered for decades, revived interest in them.

Leibniz's timing helped to resuscitate public interest in the estates. Where the elector had long overshadowed them, he was now absent in Britain. Hanoverians, particularly younger ones, rediscovered political institutions closer to home. David Georg Strube, the son of a Celle judicial official, incorporated them into his Leiden university dissertation several years later. Strube directly quoted the short passage from the *Anti-Jacobite*, and added that

> the most powerful king of Great Britain shows himself to be no less fair and liberal [than the Emperor in Austria] towards the estates of his German dominions. For he is so far from using that power by which he might suppress them that we must rather acknowledge that His sacred Majesty the king is more solicitous to conserve their rights than he is to violate them.[67]

Strube's confidence in the Emperor's conduct towards his Austrian estates was peculiar; it is possible that he assumed they experienced the same lenience as the Imperial estates in Regensburg. Strube was equally expansive when discussing the Hanoverian estates, preferring the elastic expression 'rights' to Leibniz's more cramped talk of the estates' consent to taxation.

Already more generous than Leibniz's account, Strube's rendition of the estates' rights was further embellished by Helmstedt professor Gottlieb Samuel Treuer. Treuer affirmed that

> the serene house of Brunswick-Lüneburg, which has the glory just as well as the archducal Austrian house that it has never sired tyrants, has at all times left the estates their rights uninjured. That is why the author of the *Anti-Jacobite* against the tories showed that His Royal Majesty of England puts up with the traditional rights and customs of his provincial estates even in his German lands, nor has he ever allowed himself to be seen to discard these in the least. The estates and their recesses are known only too well in these lands, and how graciously the prince has left everything at the old tradition.[68]

66 Georg Schnath, *Geschichte Hannovers im Zeitalter der neunten Kur und der englischen Sukzession 1674–1714* (4 vols., Hildesheim, 1978), iii, pp. 29–30.
67 David Georg Strube, *De origine nobilitatis germanicæ et præcipuis quibusdam ejus juribus* (Leiden, 1718), p. 66.
68 Wilhelm Freiherr von Schröder, *Disquisitio politica vom absoluten Fürsten-Recht*, ed. Gottlieb Samuel Treuer (Leipzig and Wolfenbüttel, 1719), pp. 94–5.

Treuer stuck with Strube's broad formulation of 'rights', and further indicated that these might be discerned from princes' historical concessions to estates. Strube and Treuer acknowledged their debt to *Anti-Jacobite*, but expanded its terse defense of dynastic union into a new understanding of the Hanoverian constitution in the matter of a few years. They went on to promote what became this point of view from increasingly exalted positions; Treuer was appointed the first lecturer in Hanoverian law at the new university of Göttingen, while Strube became the electorate's highest-ranking legal officer. The estates' rehabilitation had thus acquired substantial momentum before Montesquieu's *De l'esprit des loix* further popularized 'intermediate bodies'.

Whereas *Anti-Jacobite*'s young acolytes moved away from Leibniz's use of natural law,[69] their focus upon institutional liberties initially strengthened its argument for the similarity of British and Hanoverian government. Treuer quoted Sir William Temple's *Observations upon the United Provinces of the Netherlands* to demonstrate the common Germanic pedigree of almost all European constitutions.[70] One publicist even argued that the Hanoverian Succession renewed the British civil liberties established by the (first) Saxon invasion. He wrote of Britain that

> Es läßt sich seine Macht durch Sachsens Ruh verstärcken/
> So bleibt das Land so wol als die Gewissen frey.
> Es hat sich England sonst mit Sachsen schon verbunden/
> Nun hat es wiederum daselbst sein Heyl gefunden.[71]

> It strengthens its power with Saxony's peace; so the land as well as consciences remain free. England has already bound itself to Saxony once; now it has once again found its salvation there.

The passage amply illustrates the self-congratulatory mood in which Hanoverians contemplated Britain's successes in the period directly following 1714.

But while the revival of interest in institutional liberties initially reinforced Hanoverians' sense of constitutional affinity with Britain, it simultaneously encouraged them in a distinctiveness which had been lacking in a discourse based entirely on natural law and princely rule. The estates were potential mascots for Hanoverians who might use personal union to preserve Hanoverian sovereignty from perceived British incursions. Thus *British Advice* had greater success propagating its anti-imperial view of dynastic union in Hanover than in Britain. This revival of interest in the Hanoverian

---

69 See Schröder, *Disquisitio politica vom absoluten Fürsten-Recht*, ed. Treuer, p. 223.

70 Schröder, *Disquisitio politica vom absoluten Fürsten-Recht*, ed. Treuer, pp. 45–6.

71 Johan Conrad Stephan Hölling, *Ihrer Königlichen Majestät von Groß-Britannien Georg dem Ersten* (Hannover, 1714).

estates is a significant exception to Wellenreuther's rule that 'neither English influences on [Hanoverian] political thought nor absorption from England in the areas of education, culture, agriculture or manufactures can be proven'.[72] And it proceeded not from the anglophilia which sometimes seized eighteenth-century continental societies, but from the British relationship itself.

Back in Britain, Jacobites continued to push their argument against Hanoverian empire. Part of their early confusion about whether to pursue religious or secular themes had resulted from George I's initial failure to pursue an obviously imperial policy. Their ultimate adoption of a secular viewpoint owed more to the rhetorical needs of the Stuart cause. George I's actions soon seemed to justify this decision. His government's religious policy greatly upset nonjurors, but did not appear to aim at a merger with the Hanoverian church. But Jacobites detected Hanoverian machinations behind two secular phenomena, the Northern War and the South Sea Bubble. Their pro-government opponents tended to take a British imperial viewpoint during the early years of the former, but later gravitated towards personal union as ministers sought to exclude Hanoverian influence over British affairs.

During 1715, Britain became increasingly involved in the Northern War which had ranged a number of Baltic nations against Karl XII of Sweden since the last century. George I dispatched a naval task force under Sir John Norris to the Baltic, ostensibly to protect British commerce from Swedish privateering. This action was unremarkable in one sense, for it followed precedents from the reign of Queen Anne.[73] But it also followed Hanover's treaty with Denmark of 2 May 1715, by which the latter 'sold' the German duchies of Bremen and Verden to the electorate in exchange for a declaration of war on Sweden. These duchies were not Denmark's to sell, strictly speaking. Firstly, they had been awarded to the Swedish crown by the Treaty of Westphalia in 1648. Secondly, Denmark was not even in possession of Verden, which Hanover had occupied since 1712.[74] But the treaty did ultimately deliver the hitherto Danish-occupied duchy of Bremen to Hanover on 14 October 1715, after Norris had been ordered to leave eight of his ships in Denmark's command.[75] This appeared to be British expense on Hanover's account.

---

[72] Hermann Wellenreuther, 'Von der Interessenharmonie zur Dissoziation. Kurhannover und England in der Zeit der Personalunion', *Niedersächsisches Jahrbuch für Landesgeschichte* 67 (1995), p. 35.

[73] John J. Murray, *George I, the Baltic, and the Whig Split of 1717* (Chicago, 1969), pp. 85–6.

[74] Walther Mediger, 'Die Gewinnung Bremens und Verdens durch Hannover im Nordischen Kriege', *Niedersächsisches Jahrbuch für Landesgeschichte* 43 (1971), p. 40; Schnath, *Geschichte Hannovers*, iii, p. 668.

[75] Murray, *George I, the Baltic, and the Whig Split of 1717*, p. 187.

The duchy of Bremen had long featured in the diplomacy of the exiled Stuart court,[76] but the province did not appear in its publicity until the Danish handover. James Stuart preceded his embarkation for Scotland, where an insurrection had risen in his behalf, with another declaration of 25 October 1715. 'By taking possession of the duchy of Bremen in violation of the public faith', the pretender warned his would-be subjects, 'a door is opened by the usurper to let in an inundation of foreigners from abroad and reduce these nations to the state of a province to one of the most inconsiderable provinces of the Empire.'[77] The pretender's manifesto was largely the project of his secretary of state, Lord Bolingbroke, who composed, printed, and distributed it.[78] Bolingbroke had abandoned his early enthusiasm for the Hanoverian Succession,[79] especially in the wake of Hanoverian opposition to the peace policy he implemented as Queen Anne's secretary of state. Thereafter he contemplated tightening the Act of Settlement in certain signal respects.[80] But it was only proscription and prosecution under George I which drove him to France, and the pretender's service. James Stuart revised some of Bolingbroke's language respecting the Churches of England and Ireland,[81] provoking the first in a series of rows which culminated in his dismissal of the latter. But he did not alter Bolingbroke's original language on Hanover.

Bolingbroke's anti-Hanoverian rhetoric was firmly in the 'republican' tradition of earlier Jacobite pieces. Yet Bolingbroke was not entirely without influence upon the content of Stuart publicity; the course of events allowed him to add a Baltic dimension to it. Most conspicuously, he revived the invasion theory which had dogged the dynastic union since 1701. Hanover had possessed a viable seaport since Georg Ludwig had inherited Harburg in the principality of Celle from his uncle in 1705. But the duchy of Bremen included a relatively capacious North Sea coastline stretching from the Elbe estuary to that of the Weser, a more strategic maritime position than the electorate had ever commanded before. 1715's diplomacy appeared to fulfill Toland's prediction from the *Limitations* that Hanover would seek portions of the North Sea littoral in order to facilitate communication with, and perhaps

---

[76] For diplomacy, see 'A Memorial Shewing That It Is the Interest of the King of Sweden to Hinder the Hannoverian Succession', carried to Versailles 22 Sept. 1706, in Macpherson, *Original Papers*, ii, p. 23. The year 1706 was probably a misprint, because the memorial mentions the 1708 death of Prince George of Denmark.

[77] James Francis Edward Stuart, *His Majesty's Most Gracious Declaration* (n. p., 1715).

[78] See Philip Henry Stanhope, Viscount Mahon, *History of England from the Peace of Utrecht* (7 vols., London, 1836), i, appendix, pp. xxvii–xxxi, passim; Historical Manuscripts Commission, (HMC), *Calendar of the Stuart Papers*, i, pp. 432–51, passim.

[79] St. John to Trumbull, 13 Aug. 1701, Lidiard, published in HMC, *Report on the Manuscripts of the Marquess of Downshire* (6 vols., London, 1924), i, p. 805.

[80] Edward Gregg, *The Protestant Succession in International Politics, 1710–1716* (New York, 1986), pp. 201–2.

[81] See Bolingbroke to James Francis Edward Stuart, 2 Nov. 1715, Paris, in Mahon, *History of England from the Peace of Utrecht*, i, appendix, p. xxx.

even coercion of, Britain. Bolingbroke's treatment of the supposedly-violated 'public faith' was more oblique. He could have meant George I's treaty commitments to Sweden, either as elector or as king. But he more probably considered the Act of Settlement's war clause, which the pretender could not overtly support.

The accusation that George I's Baltic policy had subverted the Act of Settlement's war clause was refuted by the whig journalist Sir Richard Steele. 'Our sovereign', Steele wrote, 'has obtained (since his accession) from his own coffers, not by the expense of our blood or that of the subjects of any other his nations, new duchies, new territories.'[82] While Steele addressed Bolingbroke's implication that Hanover would dominate Britain by draining it of money and men, he left the more explicit invasion thesis to his former associate Joseph Addison. The latter attacked the Stuart proclamation, asking the pretender

> do you then really believe the mob-story, that King *George* designs to make a bridge of boats from *Hanover* to *Wapping*? We . . . don't find that *William* the Conqueror ever thought of making *England* a province to his native duchy of *Normandy*, notwithstanding it lay so much more convenient for that purpose. Nor that King *James* the first had ever any thoughts of reducing this nation to the state of a province to his ancient kingdom of *Scotland*, though it lies upon the same continent . . . we are no more afraid of being a province to *Hanover*, than the *Hanoverians* are apprehensive of being a province to *Bremen*.[83]

Just as the pretender's manifesto had recalled the invasion thesis of Toland's *Limitations*, Addison's answer echoed the same author's subsequent renunciation of it.

Addison also highlighted the absurdity of the pretender's invasion scenario, juxtaposed as it was with a description of Hanover as 'inconsiderable'. But both he and Steele hastened to dispel the image of Hanover as weak. Steele disputed Jacobite disdain for Hanover in a manner which marked an important moment for pro-union publicity. He considered that George I as elector 'is at once, to this nation, a good and gracious prince, and a rich and powerful ally'.[84] Steele was the first publicist to term Hanover an 'ally', implying the electorate's diplomatic equality with Britain, and the consequent existence of a personal union between the two countries. Yet the designation of 'allies' may not have been the most felicitous term with which to argue for personal union, in the absence of a treaty. Steele exerted little

---

[82] Sir Richard Steele, *The British Subject's Answer to the Pretender's Declaration* (1716), in Rae Blanchard, ed., *Tracts and Pamphlets by Richard Steele* (Baltimore, 1944), p. 399.
[83] *The Freeholder* no. 9 (20 Jan. 1716), in Joseph Addison, *The Freeholder*, ed. James Leheny (Oxford, 1979), pp. 79–80.
[84] *Town-Talk* no. 5 (13 Jan. 1716), in Blanchard, ed., *Tracts and Pamphlets by Richard Steele*, p. 383.

influence on British readers, who continued to construe their relationship to Hanover using imperial models.

One of those was probably Joseph Addison. Addison also denied Hanover's insignificance, holding that George I's 'court at *Hanover* was always allow'd to be one of the politest in *Europe*'.[85] Addison thereby corroborated Toland but ascribed politeness no more agency within dynastic union than had his predecessor. Addison's major argument for union was that 'the duchy of *Bremen* . . . [has] considerably strengthened [George I's] interests in the Empire, and given a great additional weight to the Protestant cause'.[86] He thereby not only contested the pretender's insult to Hanover but also hinted at one of Toland's original arguments for union, whereby Britain would manipulate Hanover as part of its leadership of the Protestant interest in Europe.

This argument was refuted by the Swedish ambassador, Count Gyllenborg. He anonymously circulated a pamphlet, *An English Merchant's Remarks*, which purportedly proved a memorial of the British ambassador in Stockholm detailing British losses to Swedish piracy to be a Jacobite forgery. In actuality, the *Remarks* articulated the position of the Jacobites, with whom Gyllenborg was negotiating. Gyllenborg uncoupled dynastic union from the Protestant interest in Europe, to which it had been joined by thinkers from Toland to Addison, saying that the George I's foreign policy would 'destroy' the 'friendship so necessary between the *Protestant* princes'.[87] This was particularly effective, as Sweden's heroic accomplishments during the Thirty Years' War made it Britain's chief rival for the symbolic leadership of European Protantism. But the crux of Gyllenborg's argument was that George I had made 'a breach in the Act of Succession (the very Act that happily set the crown on his head) as to increase his dominions in *Germany* at the expense of the *British* blood and treasure'.[88] The Swede thereby recapitulated the Jacobite argument against Hanoverian empire.

Molesworth responded to Gyllenborg in *Observations upon a Pamphlet Called An English Merchant's Remarks*. Molesworth defended the Hanoverian purchase of Bremen and Verden from his old bête noire, Denmark. If Denmark had retained possession of the duchies, he noted, it

wou'd have entirely pent up the electorate of *Hanover*. For the country of *Bremen* extending from the *Elbe* to the *Weser*, and His *Danish* Majesty having the town of *Glückstadt* on the other side of the first of these rivers, and the county of *Oldenburg* on the other side of the second, all this tract of territory wou'd have

---

85 *The Freeholder* no. 7 (26 Dec. 1715), in Addison, *The Freeholder*, ed. Leheny, p. 66.
86 *The Freeholder* no. 2 (26 Dec. 1715), in Addison, *The Freeholder*, ed. Leheny, p. 46.
87 [Karl, Count Gyllenborg], *An English Merchant's Remarks upon a Scandalous Jacobite Paper, Publish'd the 19th of July Last in the Post-Boy under the Name of a Memorial Presented to the Chancery of Sweden by the Resident of Great Britain*, in *The Political State of Great Britain* 12 (1716), p. 319.
88 [Gyllenborg], *An English Merchant's Remarks upon a Scandalous Jacobite Paper*, p. 319.

become contiguous had he kept the duchy of *Bremen*. By which means *Denmark* might in time have come to be mistress of all the commerce of the *Elbe* and *Weser*, and by consequence of that of all *Germany* . . . In these circumstances His Majesty acquired that country of the king of *Denmark* for a very considerable sum, and by so doing provided for the safety of His own electorate and of His neighborhood.[89]

Molesworth presented a judicious account of the rationale underlying the electoral acquisition of Bremen and Verden. But he neglected to explain how that purchase corresponded to British interests.

This had already been done in private by the secretary of state for the southern department, James Stanhope. In response to a hint from his colleage of the north, Lord Townshend, that George I sacrifice the duchies in view of his worsening relations with Russia,[90] Stanhope wrote that

Cromwell, who understood very well the interest of England with respect to foreign powers, fitted out more than one fleet to the Baltic with no other view than to secure that . . . a freedom of trade to the Baltic should be preserved to all nations. He frequently offered considerable sums of money to the king of Sweden for Bremen.[91]

Stanhope defined Britain's interest in Hanover as economic, in the tradition of Toland and Tindal. But where the latter had described the electorate as an unwitting contributor of wealth to the residence of its absent elector, Stanhope conceived of it as a geostrategic sentinel astride crucial British shipping lanes. This controverted Drake's claim that Hanover would dilute the British empire's maritime identity, showing that it was fully consistent with the latter. Stanhope even replaced Drake's historical allusion to the allegedly continental empire of medieval England in France with Cromwell's more obviously maritime and commercial policy. No figure was better suited to establish Hanover's utility to British rather than dynastic interest. This case was persuasive enough to convince Townshend, who later repeated it to the Dutch official Simon van Slingelandt even though his differences with Stanhope over Northern policy had resulted in his demotion to lord lieutenant of Ireland.[92]

Stanhope's argument finally reached the public after the king requested Baltic funds from the parliament in early April 1717. An anonymously

---

[89] [Robert Molesworth], *Observations upon a Pamphlet Called An English Merchant's Remarks* (London, 1717), p. 59.

[90] Townshend to J. Stanhope, 23 Sept./4 Oct. 1716, published in William Coxe, *Memoirs of the Life and Administration of Sir Robert Walpole* (3 vols., London, 1798), ii, p. 86.

[91] J. Stanhope to Townshend, 16 Oct. 1716, Göhrde, in Coxe, *Memoirs of the Life and Administration of Sir Robert Walpole*, ii, p. 109.

[92] See Coxe, *Memoirs of the Life and Administration of Sir Robert Walpole*, i, p. 87.

published pamphlet, *Some Considerations upon His Majesty's Message and the Dutchies of Bremen and Verden*, repeated Molesworth's assertion that the Hanoverian purchase had spared the north German waterways from a Danish chokehold. But the *Considerations* examined Bremen and Verden in terms of British rather than Hanoverian interest. Considering the volume of British trade on the Elbe and Weser, its author reflected that

> 'tis not possible a greater advantage could happen to us than that our king should hold the keys of both those rivers, which *next to the* Thames *and the* Severn *are of the greatest consequence to* Britain *of any two rivers in the known world, and through whose streams so great a part of our riches flows continually home to us* . . . the same gracious prince will without doubt endeavor to secure us such a freedom of navigation in those parts as is absolutely necessary to the very being of *Britain.*[93]

*Some Considerations* elaborated and publicized Stanhope's previously private argument that Hanoverian territorial expansion was in Britain's economic interest. Indeed Stanhope repeated his argument to the house of commons,[94] and even likened Hanover to a British province in conversation with an Austrian diplomat.[95]

However ingenious *Some Considerations* was, it could not palliate disgruntled whigs. The motion for supply was plagued by whig abstentions, and passed by only four votes in the commons. Friedrich Wilhelm von der Schulenburg, the brother of George I's mistress, reported to a Hanoverian correspondent that

> the debaters attacked the German ministers on the pretext that this supply would prosecute the war . . . against Sweden in order to keep Bremen and Verden, which were of no importance to Great Britain. The prince [of Wales] himself is said to have claimed that it would be used for the conservation of this acquisition, for which he cared little, in order to make himself agreeable to the nation.[96]

Schulenburg blamed the difficulty on the prince, who distanced himself from his Hanoverian homeland as part of his opposition to his father. But it was also due to disaffection within Townshend's political clientele. The king dismissed his lord lieutenant, who was voluntarily accompanied into opposition by his able brother-in-law Robert Walpole. The whig party's feud

---

[93] *Some Considerations upon His Majesty's Message and the Dutchies of Bremen and Verslen* (n. p., 1717), pp. 10–1.

[94] See the speech of 12 Apr. 1717 reprinted in William Cobbett, ed., *The Parliamentary History of England* (36 vols., London, 1806–20), vii, col. 444.

[95] Derek McKay, 'The Struggle for Control of George I's Northern Policy', *The Journal of Modern History* 45 (1973), p. 372.

[96] Schulenburg to Görtz, 20 Apr. 1717, London, Hessisches Staatsarchiv Darmstadt (HStAD), F 23 A Nr. 153/6, f. 31.

presented the Jacobites with an unprecedented opportunity to convert the dissenters to their position on dynastic union, if not their position on the succession.

Jacobites hoped to capitalize upon whig dissension by publishing a letter *To Robert Walpole, Esq.*. To attract Walpole's following, its anonymous author pretended to have once supported whig imperial designs upon Hanover. He wrote that George I's 'foreign dominions, we expected, should [secure] to us riches and power, strength to the *Protestant* interests, [and] more allies'.[97] Instead, he echoed Gyllenborg in pronouncing 'the Protestant interest extremely injur'd' by Britain's anti-Swedish policy.[98] And where

we expected a treasure from *Hanover* that would largely reduce the debts of the nation . . . the king has lent vast sums of *English* money thither, and it's to be fear'd the foreign dominions will load the nation with debts that will complete its destruction. Besides, the *Turks* [George I's two manservants] and others that came over with the king have sent large sums to the other side, which makes 'em a design upon the nation that will sue out its *cash*, make *Hanover* the greatest treasury in *Europe* and *England* only a feeding pond to it, which will make *Hanover* principal and *England* a province to it.[99]

The author echoed Leslie's caricature of the economic case for empire over Hanover and used Atterbury's argument for the reverse, in which George I's Hanoverian retainers supposedly shipped British wealth back to their homeland.

The anonymous author also discredited the personal union thesis by casting doubt on the Act of Settlement's efficacy. He wrote that

the Act of Limitation was thought the best fence that ever was made for our liberties, and without [it] we should not have thought ourselves safe in electing a stranger for our king. But that was broken through in the purchase of the principalities of *Bremen* and *Verden* for enlarging the electorate of *Hanover*, for it was made with English money, blood and shipping without leave from, or once putting the question to, parliament.[100]

The author considered that 'the king would endeavor to make his will the law of our lives and fortunes as it was those he rul'd before we constituted him our ruler'.[101] If George I extended the Hanoverian political model to Britain, he also sought the same hegemony within Germany by upsetting the Holy Roman Empire's internal balance of power.[102] The latter charge was one more variation on the theme of dynastic union's threat to various

---

97  'William Thomas', *To Robert Walpole, Esq.* (n. p., [1717]), p. 1.
98  'Thomas', *To Robert Walpole, Esq.*, p. 6.
99  'Thomas', *To Robert Walpole, Esq.*, p. 3.
100  'Thomas', *To Robert Walpole, Esq.*, p. 2.
101  'Thomas', *To Robert Walpole, Esq.*, p. 1.
102  'Thomas', *To Robert Walpole, Esq.*, p. 6.

balances of power, from that of the North (found in Toland's *Limitations*) to that of all Europe (as expressed by the pretender and Charles Leslie).

The anonymous Jacobite author recommended two courses of action to Walpole and the dissident whigs. He wrote,

> if a war be enter'd into in defense of the foreign dominions, there are but two expedients left to prevent the utter ruin of this unfortunate nation. One is by calling in our exil'd king, which will put an end to it. And the other, by obliging the foreign dominions to defray the whole expense of the wars that *England* may enter into their defense.[103]

Yet the author made his preference for the former choice clear, saying

> nothing now can serve us but the king's restoration, for if the foreign dominions were sold outright, their whole worth will not maintain a war to years if a war to come should prove as expensive as the war past, besides the recompense we ought to think of for the loss of blood and interruption of our trade.[104]

Although *To Robert Walpole, Esq.* had already envisioned future Hanoverian wealth, founded upon the economic exploitation of Britain, he doubted that this had already redressed the electoral poverty first revealed by Atterbury and Leslie.

The Northern War was not the Jacobites' only dispute with Hanover, as was demonstrated by a renewed debate over the size of Britain's standing army. The anonymously-authored *Necessity of a Plot* asked in 1717,

> is it not likewise a great honor to us that a standing army will very near reduce us to the state of our fellow-subjects in Hanover? Where we hear of no complaints against the government? Where the army is part of the constitution, and the people all hope to have their share therein? Where the men go to war according as they are hired out, and the women manure the ground and bring in the harvest?[105]

*The Necessity of a Plot* further observed that Prince Frederick remained in Hanover to learn from his grandfather's example. But the above-quoted passage was the most influential part of its argument. The Jacobite member of parliament William Shippen was committed to the tower for making the same case in the commons.[106] Publicists from Toland to Leslie had represented the electoral army as a direct threat to British liberty. For Shippen and the author of *The Necessity of a Plot*, the Hanoverian military was more of a blueprint for despotism raised with British resources.

---

103 'Thomas', *To Robert Walpole, Esq.*, p. 7.
104 'Thomas', *To Robert Walpole, Esq.*, p. 7.
105 *The Necessity of a Plot, or Reasons for a Standing Army* (n. p., c. 1717), p. 11.
106 See Cobbett, ed., *The Parliamentary History of England*, vii, col. 508.

Yet responses invariably justified Britain's standing army with reference to the Northern War. Defending the army, *The Critick* wrote of Karl XII that

> it may indeed be objected that he is not at war with the king of *Great Britain* so properly as the elector of *Brunswick*. But the distinction is only in words . . . 'Twas upon this presumption the states of *Saxony* formerly rely'd when the same lawful prince wag'd war against the king of *Poland*. And what was the event? He came down upon them and ravag'd their country at pleasure.[107]

If it differed from Jacobites' opinion about the army, *The Critick* nevertheless implicitly confirmed their position on Hanoverian empire by its comparison of Britain to Saxony. Later Jacobites preferred to liken Britain to Poland, a constitutional monarchy whose monarch (Augustus II) had usurped another (Stanislas Leszczynski) and spent substantial time in his German electorate.[108] But *The Critick's* main point was that neither Saxony's nor Poland's opinion on the nature of their relationship had mattered as much as that of Sweden. It argued that a personal union was only as good as the respect it received from one of the components' enemies.

Despite *The Critick's* caveat, non-Jacobite opinion was converging upon the personal union thesis. Responding to *To Robert Walpole, Esq.*, the anonymously published *Vindication of the Honour and Justice of His Majesty's Government* declared that '*Hanover* could no more be expected to lessen our national debts, though wealthy of itself, than it is possible for any *English* money to be applied to any foreign service.'[109] This was a denial of the Jacobite diagnosis of Hanoverian empire over Britain, but it also abjured the reverse scenario which *To Robert Walpole, Esq.* had crudely caricatured. This left the *Vindication* positing the existence of a personal union.

The non-Jacobite trend towards personal union was exemplified by Earl Stanhope, hitherto the foremost exponent of British empire over Hanover. Far from being passive vessels of British influence, the Hanoverian ministry actively intervened in British politics. Stanhope had no cause to publicize this fact while he still availed himself of Hanoverian influence against Townshend and Walpole. But now that they were gone, the Hanoverian ministers replaced them as the single greatest threat to Stanhope's foreign policy. Stanhope recanted his earlier arguments in 1718 by declaring that Bremen and Verden were 'of no use' to Britain,[110] while his fellow turncoat Molesworth even suggested their return to Sweden in order to procure peace

---

[107] Quoted in *The Political State of Great Britain* 15 (1718), p. 457.

[108] See for example *Seasonable Advice, with the Characters of the Late King Stanislaus, Augustus King of Poland, His Son the Prince. To Which Is Added Some Thoughts Concerning the Said King Augustus's Going So Often out of His Kingdoms to Visit His German Dominions* (London, 1725).

[109] *A Vindication of the Honour and Justice of His Majesty's Government* (London, 1717), p. 18.

[110] Quoted by McKay, 'The Struggle for Control of George I's Northern Policy', p. 374.

with Russia in 1721.[111] Stanhope's defensive maneuvering against Hanoverian interference, which finally obtained royal favor in 1719, left little energy for the extension of British influence to the electorate. Playing the elector's secretary Jean de Robethon against his chief minister, Andreas Gottlieb von Bernstorff, Stanhope wrote the duke of Newcastle that 'whilst we are excluding the Germans avowedly from meddling in English business we cannot openly support him'.[112] Stanhope had come to support the appearance (if not the spirit) of personal union.

The Northern War had vindicated fears of Hanoverian empire over Britain, and would remain a powerful illustration of it for future generations. But its immediate relevance to British politics receded after Sweden officially recognized Hanoverian possession of Bremen and Verden in 1719. And although the Northern War had not been the sole reason for their opposition, its end eased the return of Townshend and Walpole to government as well as the prince of Wales' reconciliation with his father. But the South Sea Bubble renewed Jacobite hopes and efforts, because a royal visit to Hanover had appeared to play a role in the financial panic. The Huguenot chronicler and government loyalist Abel Boyer reported in June 1720 that the king's departure deflated the price of South Sea Company stock. He wrote that 'many persons who were to follow the king to *Hanover* . . . were . . . desirous to turn their stock into money, so that for some days the number of *sellers* exceeded that of *buyers*'.[113] This event took on more significance after the price irrevocably crashed later in the summer. A 1722 pamphlet retrospectively added that the king's presence in Hanover had only compounded the crisis, for George I 'could not easily quit his *German* dominions to come to our assistance, and a parliament could not well be call'd at this extraordinary juncture without his royal presence'.[114]

Where the Northern War had focused Jacobite attention on supposed violations of the Act of Settlement's war clause, the South Sea bubble shifted it to parliament's 1716 forfeiture of its right under the same Act to review royal travel to the European continent. Parliament's justification for the repeal – that George I's 'numerous progeny . . . and in particular . . . a prince endowed with all virtues and qualifications requisite to render posterity flourishing and happy' obviated any danger to the succession[115] – was disingenuous. The limitation upon royal travel abroad had not been intended to safeguard a tenuous succession in the house of Hanover, as the

---

111 Cobbett, ed., *The Parliamentary History of England*, vii, col. 846.
112 Stanhope to Newcastle, 24 Oct. 1719 O. S., Hanover, British Library (BL), Add. MS 32686, f. 156.
113 *The Political State of Great Britain* 19 (1720), p. 656.
114 *A Compleat History of the Late Septennial Parliament* (London, 1722), p. 40. See also *The Freeholder's Journal* 1 no. 7 (14 Mar. 1721 O. S.), p. 38.
115 See 1 George I st. 2 c. 51 in Owen Ruffhead, ed., *Statutes at Large from Magna Charta to the End of the Last Parliament, 1761* (8 vols., London, 1768–70), v, p. 87.

selfsame prince (the future George II) was already alive and practically an adult in 1701. It was instead designed to prevent the court from spending British specie abroad, a fear borne out by Uta Richter-Uhlig's finding that Britain actually did cover the costs of George II's visits to his electorate during the 1730s.[116]

Parliament's repeal of the limitation upon royal travel to the continent reinforced the Jacobites' belief in the Act of Settlement's essential toothlessness. They now furnished a colorful history of royal travel to Hanover, in preparation for the 1722 parliamentary elections. Charles Hornby detailed repeal's consequences in his sequel to Atterbury's *English Advice*. He wrote that George I's

> old counselors at *Hanover* may turn his heart more and more against his new subjects. New leagues may be entered into to our prejudice, either for transporting *foreign forces* hither or involving us in *foreign wars* against our interest. And . . . here is such a constant drain upon us of our *current specie* that in a few years we may have none.[117]

This was a précis of the Jacobite argument against Hanoverian empire, viewed through the lens of royal visits to the electorate.

Of Hornby's litany, the most sensitive component in 1722 was that relating to economics. Hornby related that in George I's first return to Hanover as king,

> all the money, plate and jewels which had been got for *titles*, *garters*, *places* and *grants* were packed up and carried off. Some *great ladies* [George I's two female intimates] who came here with wooden shoes went away with chests full of gold and silver. All their utensils for the chamber, table, nay the kitchens were massy plate, and particular directions given the gold and silver smiths to make everything as thick and heavy as possible; and . . . there was a particular order that no custom-house officers or proper searchers should go on board such ships as were loaded with the pillage of the three kingdoms.[118]

Hornby's scurrilous accusations illuminate Jacobite strategy more than they do actual fact. The vast majority of his contemporaries measured national wealth in terms of circulating coin, and consequently discouraged the stockpiling of bullion, especially of jewelry or plate, by private individuals.[119] So

---

116 Uta Richter-Uhlig, *Hof und Politik unter den Bedingungen der Personalunion zwischen Hannover und England* (Hannover, 1992), pp. 59–62.
117 [Charles Hornby], *The Second and Last English Advice to the Freeholders of England* (London, 1722), p. 26.
118 [Charles Hornby], *The Second and Last English Advice*, p. 27.
119 Eli Heckscher, *Mercantilism*, trans. Mendel Shapiro (2 vols., London, 1934), ii, pp. 212–15.

Hornby's Hanoverians sinned twice against the British economy: first by transporting bullion out of Britain, and secondly by hoarding it in the form of plate. These were moreover the very courtiers whom pro-union publicists since Toland had believed would contribute to British wealth by their presence in London.

Hornby referred to the South Sea Bubble as 'the second plunder of the nation'.[120] He gave an account of how royal travel provoked the South Sea Bubble, writing that

> when the king himself sold out a vast deal of South Sea stock and subscriptions at 800 and 900 percent . . . we all knew . . . the greater part of those sums was paid to the king, the Duchess of *Kendal*, Madame *Kielmansegg* . . . and the rest of the Hanoverian favorites, and it was all likewise spirited away to *Hanover*.[121]

Ragnhild Hatton has shown that Hanoverian courtiers' fortunes varied as much as those of other investors.[122] But Hornby's argument was firmly in the Jacobite tradition of blaming the king and his retainers for exporting British wealth to the electorate. Hornby added that George I exacerbated the crisis by hesitating to return to Britain. 'His Majesty', he continued, 'was engaged in building a magnificent palace at *Herrenhausen* . . . and either was kept ignorant of our situation or did not think fit to come until the time he first prefixed to move.'[123] But where Hornby believed the king and his courtiers absent-mindedly provoked the South Sea Bubble, Matthias Earbery believed it to have been intentional. In the sarcastically titled *Historical Account of the Advantages That Have Accrued to England by the Succession in the Illustrious House of Hanover*, he called the Bubble a plot to finance various Hanoverian objectives including the purchase of Mecklenburg.[124]

Jacobites had to account for George I's supposed bias towards the electorate. Hornby's ambivalence on this matter mirrored that of his movement. Feeling generous at one point, he wrote that

> the *German* ministry are without doubt the more excusable since they have acted for the interest of their country, but the *English* to the prejudice and ruin of theirs. And His Majesty in his whole transaction hath acted a natural part for though he be king of *England*, *Hanover* is the place of his birth and education.[125]

---

120 [Hornby], *The Second and Last English Advice*, p. 27.
121 [Hornby], *The Second and Last English Advice*, p. 27.
122 Ragnhild Hatton, *George I: Elector and King* (Cambridge, MA, 1978), pp. 151–3; pp. 251–4.
123 [Hornby], *The Second and Last English Advice*, p. 37.
124 [Matthias Earbery], *An Historical Account of the Advantages That Have Accrued to England by the Succession in the Illustrious House of Hanover* (London, 1722), pp. 14–16, 43.
125 [Hornby], *The Second and Last English Advice*, p. 30.

It was by now traditional to follow Drake and Atterbury in complimenting George I on his Hanoverian patriotism, in turn indicting Britain's lack of corresponding virtue.

But Hornby also contradicted himself by insinuating that the king preferred residence amongst Hanoverians 'from the absolute state of servitude which they are in towards him, contracting a full dislike against all others of his subjects who should refuse to be as abject slaves as they'.[126] And Earbery implied that economic exploitation such as the South Sea Bubble was aimed at reducing Britons to the same condition.[127] He advanced the notion, hinted at in Drake's *History*, that a king-elector might plunder British resources, not only to enrich his electoral possessions but to consolidate his rule in Britain. This was in turn merely part of a larger plan, which he imagined the Dutch Pensionary Heinsius suggested to George I on his way to Britain in 1714. Heinsius supposedly informed the elector-king that

> by strengthening the *Dutch* with the *English* trade, he only secured himself the more in the possession of his crown, . . . which would so far enable him to advance his interests in *Germany* that one day it might happen *that a prince of his house might sit at the head of the Empire.*[128]

This was a pure relic of the days in which dynastic union was first envisioned, when memories of the Dutch invasion were fresh and when publicists breathlessly reported Hanoverian designs upon the imperial diadem. Earbery even invented a story that George I sought to procure his grandson Frederick's election as king of the Romans.[129]

Jacobite publicity inevitably sensitized government officials to the unpopularity of George I's absences. Ministers routinely used discontent to mask their own reasons for opposing the visits, such as their fear that Hanoverian ministers would reestablish primacy in the king's councils. In a confidential memorandum to George I, Townshend employed a powerful analogy from another of Britain's imperial relationships:

> should Your Majesty . . . think it proper and advisable immediately after the ending of this short [parliamentary] session again to visit your foreign dominions, you would thereby give an opportunity to the disaffected to insinuate that the same inclinations which call Your Majesty abroad this summer . . . will always produce the same effect, and Britain thereby be seduced to the same state with Ireland, where the lord lieutenant never appears but when the parliament is called to give money, and never enjoy the blessing of Your Majesty's presence any longer than while this service lasts.[130]

126 [Hornby], *The Second and Last English Advice*, p. 26.
127 [Earbery], *An Historical Account*, pp. 39–40.
128 [Earbery], *An Historical Account*, p. 12.
129 [Earbery], *An Historical Account*, p. 39.
130 Townshend to George I, early 1724, published in Coxe, *Memoirs of the Life and Administration of Sir Robert Walpole*, ii, pp. 298–9.

Townshend envisioned Hanoverian empire over Britain more vividly than any Jacobite ever had, at a time when government opinion was tending towards the personal union thesis.

Of course, George I's absence did not trouble Jacobites provided it remain permanent. In a manifesto of 10 September 1722, composed by Lord Lansdowne,[131] James Stuart exhorted George I to quit Britain permanently for Hanover, 'where an uncontested right will free him from the crime and reproach of tyranny and usurpation'. He contrasted George's 'calm, undis-turbed reign over a willing and obedient people' in Germany with his 'rest-less possession in a strange land where authority, forcing the inclinations of the people, can only be supported by blood and violence'.[132] The pretender managed to reconcile republicanism with the Jacobite doctrine of indefea-sible hereditary right, by presuming that the latter was the decided convic-tion of the British people. The declaration of 1722 inverted the 1714 formula: now George I tyrannically ruled Britain instead of Hanover. But the pretender was otherwise consistent in his secular definition of civil liberty.

The pretender was answered by Bishop Benjamin Hoadly of Hereford. Hoadly followed Tindal in agreeing with the pretender's characterization of Hanoverian politics. The bishop wrote of George I that

> neither his *uncontested right*, nor the unbounded extent of his *authority* over his *subjects* in his *native dominions*, ever created an inclination in his breast towards a single *act* of *tyranny*; and where his *will* alone has been always his *law*, there the *law* of justice and equity alone has been always his *will*.[133]

But where Tindal had believed George I's control over Hanover would facili-tate British empire over that electorate, Hoadly was content to demonstrate that the elector-king would rule Britain differently. 'In our *country*, in which written laws are the *rule* of *power*', Hoadly considered, George I 'has conducted himself in every step of his *administration* by the direction of those laws with as much ease and address as if he had been used, throughout his whole life, to none but a *limited* government'.[134] This was, of course, part of the case for empire over Hanover. But the failure to mention Hanover's lack of an equivalent to the Act of Settlement, and the opportunities it afforded for British empire, skewed Hoadly's argument towards personal union.

The period of Jacobite dominance in British discussion of the Hanoverian

---

[131] For the attribution, see Paul Chapman, 'Jacobite Political Argument in England, 1714–1766' (Ph. D. dissertation, Cambridge, 1983), pp. 120–1.

[132] James Francis Edward Stuart, *Declaration of James the Third, King of England, Scotland, and Ireland, &c. To All His Subjects of the Three Nations and to All Foreign Princes and States to Serve as a Foundation for a Lasting Peace in Europe* (n. p., 1722), p. 2.

[133] *The London Journal* no. 75 (1 Dec. 1722), p. 1. For the attribution, see John Hoadly, ed., *The Works of Benjamin Hoadly, D. D.* (3 vols., London, 1773), i, p. xxi.

[134] *The London Journal* no. 75 (1 Dec. 1722), p. 1.

relationship came during the early 1720s, when the revelation of Atterbury's plot and consequent governmental repression dampened Jacobite publicity. But the Jacobites left a potent legacy to critics of dynastic union, one which fastened earlier theories of Hanoverian empire over Britain to the circumstances of the Northern War and South Sea Bubble. They had also helped to push their adversaries from support for British empire over Hanover to advocacy of personal union. This would attain further sophistication under pressure from the Jacobites' whig heirs during the administration of Sir Robert Walpole.

If Britons struggled to understand George I's visits to Hanover, then Hanoverians grappled doubly as hard with his prolonged absence from the electorate. Even if this nurtured renewed interest in the estates, Hanoverians had to account for the sudden disappearance of the figure which had until recently consumed all the country's political oxygen. Most of them belatedly accepted the argument which had prompted the electoral court to pursue the British succession, whereby they hoped Britain would manipulate the balance of power in such a ways as to afford Europe the kind of territorial security Germans found in the Holy Roman Empire. Yet that selfsame court believed the succession had already achieved this, and began to worry that the elector's absence threatened Hanover with British domination. This latter viewpoint motivated George I's serial attempts to provide for Hanover's eventual separation from Britain in his will.

Perhaps the first anticipation of how the electoral absence would affect Hanover had come in Lüneburg in 1706. Georg Ludwig traveled to the city to receive its homage, after inheriting the principality of Celle from his uncle. Comparing the elector to a full moon, one poet predicted that his princely government would persevere even if the British succession eventually necessitated his absence. He wrote,

> Ob Du auch künfftig sollst/wanns das Verhängnis schickt/
> Ein ander grosses Reich mit Deinen Strahlen zieren/
> Daß uns Dein Gnaden-Aug' von weiten nur erblick't/
> So wird Dein Scepter uns doch fort und fort regieren/
> Dein hocherhabner Schein erqvicket unser Land/
> Ob deiner Strahlen-Pracht gleich andern auch bekandt.[135]

If you should hereafter – when fate ordains it – adorn another great land with your beams, if your merciful eye only sees us from afar, your scepter will still rule on and on. Your sublime shine refreshes our land, even if the splendor of your beams is known to others.

---

135  J. J. Wolff, *Als der durchlauchtigste großmächtigste Fürst und Herr, Herr Georg Ludwig . . . die Erb-Huldigung in seiner erb-unterthänigen Stadt Lüneburg anzunehmen, seinen hoch-fürstlichen Einzug . . . hielt* (Lüneburg, 1706).

Celestial bodies were favorite metaphors for the elector, in that they combined the life-giving power known to the ancients with the rationality Newton's contemporaries liked to ascribe them. But if its astronomical motif was familiar, the poem's practical argument was innovative. It established that electoral bienfaisance was not necessarily diluted by distance or by large numbers of fellow-subjects.

Electoral apologists hit upon this argument in greater numbers, once George I's absence in London required it. One poet recapitulated this argument directly after the 1714 succession, replacing the full moon with the sun.

> Ob manche lieber schon mit Thränen sich benetzten/
>    Weil unser Vatter jetz sein eigen Land verläst.
> Doch kan die Sonne auch von ferne uns bescheinen.
>    Dem eig'nen geht ja vor das allgemeine Best.[136]

> If some would rather sprinkle themselves with tears because our father leaves his own land now, the sun can also illuminate us from afar. The general good comes before one's own.

Hanoverian dissatisfaction with the dynastic union (in the form of tears) was therefore noted from its very beginning. But the poet disarmed it with the familiar sun imagery. The sun obviously disregarded political and geographical boundaries. It was fortunate for those who argued on behalf of continuity that the best-known metaphor for electoral rule translated into the post-1714 circumstances.

'The general good' to which the above-quoted poet referred was the European balance of power, which justified dynastic union to the public as much as it had to the court. One Hanoverian poet sang to George I after he became king,

> Der beste Theil der Welt muß Seine Macht verehren/
>    Weil Er in selbigem das beste Land besitzt/
> Wil denn der Stoltzen Arm der schwächern Land verheeren/
>    So weiß man/wie es Gott durch England offt beschützt.
> Der Englische Monarch hält längst Europens Wage/
> Daß der gedruckten Macht nicht gäntzlich niederschlage.

> Zwar kan Hanover sich der Zähren nicht erwehren
>    Weil Deine Abfahrt folgt/doch dieser Thränen-Fluß

---

[136] Johann Arnold Noltenius, *Dem allerdurchlauchtigsten, großmächtigsten Fürsten und Herrn, Herrn Georg Ludewig . . . als Derselbe am 12. Augusti MDCCXIV in London, zum König, unter frölichem Zujauchzen des Volcks, war proclamiret worden* (Hannover, 1714).

Muß/weil er Wünsche führt/Dein grosses Glück vermehren/
Dein Glück ist unser Schutz und der des Glücks Genuß.[137]

The best part of the world must honor his power, because he possesses the best land in the same. If the arm of the proud wants to ravage the land of the weak, one knows how God often protects it with England. The English monarch has long held Europe's scale so that power does not entirely crush the oppressed. Admittedly, Hanover cannot refrain from tears because your departure follows. But this river of tears must increase your happiness, because it brings wishes. Your good fortune is our protection and the enjoyment of the good fortune.

The poem made Hanoverians' interest in dynastic union clear: they were among the weak who would be protected by Britain's maintenance of the European balance of power. Britain's role behind the balance of power interested Hanoverians far more than its support for the acquisition of Bremen and Verden, which scarcely elicited comment in the electorate. A 1718 flood in the duchy of Bremen even led Schulenburg to complain that 'this acquisition will not return interest proportional to its price, still less to the trouble we have had keeping it'.[138]

Dynastic union would have been unnecessary if Britain's defense of the balance of power was consistent. But the tory peace with France had reminded Hanoverians of Britain's inconstancy in this respect, and fortified the arguments for union. Leibniz argued in the *Anti-Jacobite* that 'His Majesty has tried to return things in the [English] nation . . . to the condition which they were in before the last ministry, a condition which was applauded by all well-intentioned and well-informed people – even by all Europe, England's friend – and especially by those who love the Protestant religion and reasonable liberty.'[139] The tory ministry of 1710–14 played the role the later Stuarts had occupied in Leibniz's 1701 memoranda, proving that Britain's defense of the balance of power hinged upon its leaders' resolve. By this perspective, dynastic union amounted to a takeover of British foreign policy.

As he had in his 1701 memoranda, Leibniz associated British disregard for the balance of power with political corruption. But where he had then implied that French monies had sapped the later Stuarts' will to resist Louis XIV, he now argued that the tory ministry of 1710–14 had bought voters' acquiescence in its peace. Refuting Atterbury's charge that George I's government was corrupting the 1715 parliamentary election, Leibniz retorted that 'the king's intention is to leave it entirely up to the cities, boroughs, and shires. And if there have been some who tried to persuade him

---

137 Hölling, *Ihrer Königlichen Majestät von Groß-Britannien Georg dem Ersten*.
138 Schulenburg to Görtz, 18 Jan. 1718, London, HStAD, F 23 A Nr. 153/6, f. 159.
139 [Leibniz], *Anti-Jacobite*, p. 6.

to imitate the last ministry's cabals and use money, His Majesty responded generously that he did not want to corrupt his subjects.'[140] Leibniz contrasted the elector's supposed integrity as king with the unsavory political practices of British elites. *Anti-Jacobite* established the Hanoverian public's association of Britain with political corruption.

In arguing that George I was simply returning Britain to its pre-1710 policy, Leibniz again demonstrated his faith in natural law. As he had earlier to Burnet, he implied that Britain and Hanover were ruled similarly before 1710 according to the dictates of reason. But the rupture of 1710–14 allowed lesser Hanoverian publicists to ignore this in their attempt to credit George I with all rationality in British governance. Indeed, the deference shown to Britain in international policy yielded to a sense of equality in the field of domestic government, where Hanoverians added a self-congratulatory element to the anglophilia common in many eighteenth-century conti-nental states.[141] One poet praised George I, writing that England 'makes itself the wonder of this age through you'.[142] In a country where the personal rule of the elector was so important and its principles universal, Hanoverians could not imagine that Britain was governed differently. The logical conclu-sion was that Britain's greatness was but an amplification of previous Hanoverian achievements. The chronological progression is evident in a passage which followed the preceding quotation.

> Hier zeig ich nicht wie Du im Lüneburger Land
> Dich Wunderns-werth gemacht/es ist vorhin bekandt.
> Den Britten hatte ja Dein Glantz noch nicht geschienen/[143]

> I will not show here how you made yourself wondrous here in Lüneburg.
> Your luster had not yet shone upon the Britons.

Britain could only be allowed to be exemplary if it was first acknowledged that it owed its successes to Hanoverian principles. August Wilhelm von Schwicheldt toed this line, writing

> Daß Groß-Britannien in grösten Glücke lebet,
>   Seit dem das gantze Reich Georgens Scepter küßt.
> Das Plato Republic ist nur im Kopff errichtet,
>   Wie scheinbar auch ihr Grund auf dem Papiere läßt;
> Was von Utopien der kluge Morus dichtet,

---

[140] [Leibniz], *Anti-Jacobite*, p. 6.

[141] For this, see Michael Maurer, *Aufklärung und Anglophilie in Deutschland* (Göttingen, 1987).

[142] Christian August Zindel, *Als der allerdurchlauchtigste großmächtigste Fürst und Herr, Herr Georg . . . bey königl. hohen Vergnügen bißher gelebet* (n. p., 1719).

[143] Zindel, *Als der allerdurchlauchtigste großmächtigste Fürst und Herr, Herr Georg . . . bey königl. hohen Vergnügen bißher gelebet.*

Hält nur in dem Gehirn und nicht im Wesen fest.
Der Sevaramben Land ist treflich schön beschrieben,
    Nur Schade! daß kein Mensch den Regeln folgen kan,
Drum mögen andere die klugen Fabeln lieben:
    Wir sehen Albion als bestes Muster an.[144]

Great Britain lives in the greatest happiness, since the whole empire kissed George's scepter. Plato's republic was erected only in the head, no matter how plausible it appears on paper; the ingenious More's rhapsodies about Utopia hold true only in the brain and not in reality. The land of the Sevarambs is described admirably well; too bad that no one can follow its rules. Others may love clever fables; we see Albion as the best model.

The implication was, of course, that the Hanoverian constitution also exceeded Plato's republic and More's utopia in didactic effectiveness. Such commentary added a domestic Hanoverian aspect to the hitherto solely German imperialism directed at Britain.

One British characteristic which consistently struck foreign observers was its wealth. One Hanoverian poet asked on the occasion of George I's death in 1727

Wo ist so vieles Gold und Silber noch zu finden
Als dieses mächt'ge Reich in seinem Busen hägt?
Das zur Bewunderung die gantze Welt bewegt.

Where is as much gold and silver to be found as this powerful empire, which moves the whole world to admiration, contains in its bosom?

He quickly answered his own question:

Doch was Jerusalem hat vormals aufgewiesen,
Und was an Londen auch noch heute wird gepriesen,
Das zeigt Hannover uns in gleichem Wehrt und Grad:
Was herrlich, lieb und wehrt; was eine Zierde hat;
Was hoch zu achten ist, das alles ist vorhanden
In unsers Königs- Chur- und seinen Erbe-Landen,
Wer zählet Dessen Schatz an Gold und Silber aus?[145]

What Jerusalem once exhibited, and what is now prized in London, Hanover shows us in equal worth and degree. What is splendid, dear, and

---

[144] August Wilhelm von Schwicheldt, *Aller-unterthänigste Lob- und Ehren-Rede* (Wolfenbüttel, 1726), p. C1.
[145] *Betrachtungen einiger Umstände bey dem Tod des grossen Frieden-Stifters der europäischen Welt, des weyland allerdurchlauchtigsten und großmächtigsten Fürsten und Herrn, Herrn Georg des ersten* (n. p., 1727).

valuable, what is ornamental, what is highly esteemed is all there in our king's electoral and hereditary land. Who can count its treasures of gold and silver?

Importantly, Hanoverians believed their own plenty (such as it was) had originated not in economic exploitation of Britain but in an economic management which predated the British succession. The same poet accordingly thanked the elector-king,

> Was uns so offt ergötzt, und wir bisher genossen,
> Das ist von Deiner Krafft, o König! ausgeflossen,[146]

> What has so often amused us and what we have enjoyed, has flowed out from your strength o king!

Because it was believed that a country's wealth resulted from princely initiatives, it stood to reason that the Hanoverian economy was in the same flower as the British economy. Empire derived from British emulation rather than Hanoverian exploitation.

For all that Hanover's princely constitution inspired sympathy for Britain, however self-referential, it also begat a jealousy focused upon George I's long absences there. One Hanoverian poet addressing the theme of his absence commented that 'Germany and England begin a competition' over him.[147] Another writer, the Helmstedt professor Rudolph Friedrich Telgmann, went so far as to declare that Hanover was more deserving of the elector-king's presence than Britain, and wrote as if speaking to George I

> Wir haben größer Recht, Georg, Dich zu behalten/
> DIR hat uns eigentlich der Himmel anvertraut.

> We have more right to keep you, George; Heaven actually entrusted us to you.

Telgmann not only belittled George's parliamentary right in Britain, but argued further that the British had not earned his presence among them. Referring to the Jacobite '15, he asked the elector-king 'did you ever experience treachery with us?' The couplet immediately following the one quoted above made Telgmann's practical argument:

> DU kanst Dein Königreich dennoch sehr wol verwalten/
> Wenn es DICH gleich nicht selbst genug die Klugheit schaut.[148]

---

146 *Betrachtungen einiger Umstände.*
147 Heinrich Christoph Leopold Kirchmann, *Alleruntertänigste Zeilen auf die Abreise Sr. Königl. Maj. von Groß-Britannien* (Hannover, 1725).
148 Rudolph Friedrich Telgmann, *Das warhafftig klagende Zion über der abermahligen Abreise seines Königs* (Helmstedt, 1723).

You can still govern your kingdom very well even if it does not see your person, so long as it sees your reason.

Telgmann came dangerously close to *lèse majesté* in suggesting that George I rule Great Britain from Hanover rather than vice versa, but he was merely the most daring of the poets who vied to display their jealousy of Britain.

Solar imagery had been deployed to disarm such railing at the electoral absences. But it was just as capable of expressing dissatisfaction with them. George's peregrinations were easily compared to the sun's diurnal cycle. Hanoverians particularly favored nocturnal imagery in their desire to render the most melodramatic depiction possible of his absence. One poet welcomed George I's first return to Hanover in 1716 (parliament having forfeited its oversight of such visits under the Act of Settlement), writing

> Dein Abschied ließ uns zwar noch Sternen-Feur zurükke/
>   Des Mondes Wechsel-Schein trat öffters bey uns ein.
> Allein es blieb doch Nacht/die schönen Sonnen-Blikke
>   Die musten noch zur Zeit von uns entfernet seyn.
> Die Nacht/die lange Nacht/mit ihrem Kummer-Schatten
>   Hat unsern Geist gekränkt/auch endlich fast entseelt.[149]

> Your departure left behind starlight for us, and the moon's oscillating shine graced us often. But it remained night; the sun's beautiful beams had to be removed for us for a time. The night, the long night, with its worrisome shadows has hurt, and almost killed, our spirit.

Given that solar imagery usually referred to electoral initiatives, it appears that some Hanoverians feared that his absences in Britain interfered with this bienfaisance.

As it happened, George I further worried that his successors' absences in Britain might eventually corrupt Hanoverian sovereignty. George I's attempt to exclude females from the British succession may appear an imperial imposition of German practice, except that it aimed at a separation of the British and Hanoverian successions after the deaths of his son the prince of Wales and his grandson Prince Frederick. George I outlined his reasons in a will of 14/25 January 1716, saying that

> as long as our male line *ruled* in Great Britain, our electoral and other German lands would be thought to be a perpetual annexation and *dependency* of the British crown. This would not only be very disadvantageous to the well-being

---

[149] Henrich Friderich Engelhart, *Wie der aller-durchlauchtigste und groß-mächtigste Fürst und Herr, Herr Georg . . . sein Erb-Länder nach zwey-jähriger Abwesenheit durch seine hohe Gegenwart als eine wohlthätige Sonne zu grossen Vergnügen derer Unterthanen wiederum bestrahlete* (Stade, 1716).

of those lands in many ways, but could occasion all sorts of inconveniences for our descendents in their quality as elector. There is no other means to prevent this than a separation of the royal and electoral governments within our house.[150]

Far from believing in Hanover's empire over Great Britain, George I feared Great Britain would come to exercise empire over the electorate. It is probable that the elector-king's post-1714 exposure to similar ideas in Britain heightened the ambivalence towards union which he had harbored since 1700.

To prevent this from happening during the lifetimes of his son and grandson, George I attempted to provide for something like personal union. He required that his son and grandson '*permanently* maintain a court and government in our German lands, not only *so that* money stays and circulates within the country to promote the consumption and sustenance of the same, but so that there is a better opportunity to raise good and capable people who can profitably serve the fatherland'.[151] The retention of a court during periods of electoral absence was particularly striking, as George was an otherwise austere ruler who had slashed court expenditure when he became elector in 1698.[152] The provision, which attempted to forestall any drain of wealth resulting from the electoral absence, was curiously similar to the Act of Settlement's limitation (soon to be repealed) upon royal travel to the European continent.

If George I worried about electoral government under his son and grandson, he was even more troubled by the prospect of an eventual British-born successor who would possess no first-hand knowledge of Hanover. In a letter to his electoral representative in Vienna, he wrote that Hanover's well-being would suffer under rulers 'who have never lived in the Empire, who no longer know or respect the state, condition, or constitution of their and our Imperial lands'.[153] To counteract this possibility, he limited service in the electoral government to Germans in another parallel to the Act of Settlement.[154]

George I's misgivings about dynastic union sharpened as his Hanoverian ministers lost most of their influence over British affairs in 1719. He then asked his British ministers if an act of parliament might further solemnize his

150 Published in Richard Drögereit, 'Das Testament König Georgs I. und die Frage der Personalunion zwischen England und Hannover', *Niedersächsisches Jahrbuch für Landesgeschichte* 14 (1937), p. 181.

151 Drögereit, 'Das Testament König Georgs I.', pp. 184–5.

152 See Annette von Stieglitz, 'Hof ohne Fürsten: Residenzleben in Hannover unter Georg I. und Georg II.', in Rex Rexheuser, ed., *Die Personalunionen von Sachsen-Polen 1697–1763 und Hannover-England 1714–1837: Ein Vergleich* (Wiesbaden, 2005), pp. 369–88.

153 Drögereit, 'Das Testament König Georgs I.', p. 101.

154 Drögereit, 'Das Testament König Georgs I.', p. 185.

will's provisions. Doubting that Britain's parliament could legislate for Hanover, they replied equivocally.[155] Pressed for a further opinion, the ministers responded in language calculated to frighten the king. They reminded the king that

> if the parliament here once meddle in making any one law touching the estates in Germany, possibly following parliaments may thence take a handle to extend their power and try to offer other laws relating to those estates in matters within His Majesty's power which may one time or other make His Majesty or his successors uneasy.

Adducing an example of such unwelcome legislation, the ministers warned that an eventual successor might 'propose to his parliament to make the keeping those [Hanoverian] estates subservient to the trade and other advantages of this country . . . making those countries in effect provinces of England, which we presume His Majesty would carefully guard against'.[156] Parliamentary support for George I's will could actually magnify, rather than diminish, British influence over Hanover. But the British government declined to extend parliamentary sovereignty to the electorate, as it did for Ireland in the Declaratory Act the following year.

Discouraged from seeking British intervention, George nonetheless persisted in his electoral initiative. Moreover, the Hanoverian ministers' declining fortunes seem to have only increased their support for the will. In a series of 1721 memoranda which unfortunately perished during the 1943 bombing of Hannover, Bernstorff supported the king's will with reference to natural law. The first was sensitive to the charge of Hanoverian empire over Britain which had frequently been leveled at Bernstorff, noting that the proposed exclusion of female successors would lessen the likelihood of foreign rulers.[157] But Bernstorff worried more that future generations of British-born electors unfamiliar with Hanover's laws, constitution, and people would reduce Hanover to the status of Ireland, Britain's overseas colonies, or even Scotland.[158] A second memorandum hinted at British arguments for Hanoverian empire by saying that dissolution would stop flows of wealth to the electorate. But such flows existed for Bernstorff in the context of British empire over Hanover, for he again likened Hanover to Scotland.[159] Bernstorff's permanent departure from Britain in 1720 underscored his growing frustration with dynastic union. Bernstorff was not the only Hanoverian minister to compare Hanover's relationship to London with

---

155  BL, Stowe MS 249.
156  Niedersächsisches Hauptstaatsarchiv (NHStA), Hann. 92 Nr. 70, f. 118.
157  Drögereit, 'Das Testament König Georgs I.', p. 127.
158  Drögereit, 'Das Testament König Georgs I.', pp. 125–6.
159  Drögereit, 'Das Testament König Georgs I.', p. 130.

that of Britain's peripheral kingdoms. Bothmer wrote him from London in 1724 that 'Hanover will soon be a province of Great Britain much as Ireland is now.'[160]

George I also consulted the prince of Wales about his scheme after Princess Caroline gave birth to a second son, Prince William, in 1721.[161] Sir Robert Walpole informed Lord Chancellor King during the summer of 1725 that

> the prince and his wife were for excluding Prince Frederick from the throne of England, but that after the king and prince he should be elector of Hanover and Prince William king of Great Britain. But that the king said it was unjust to do it without Prince Frederick's consent, who was now of age to judge for himself.[162]

The prince lost interest in any settlement which preserved his son's British rights, and he later suppressed his father's will upon his succession as George II. But the idea of dividing Britain and Hanover between his two sons was to recur.

George I's will expressed the first Hanoverian misgivings about British empire. His solution to the problem was a personal union followed by outright dissolution of dynastic union. Interestingly, George I did not question what effect the latter might have upon the European balance of power. This, after all, had been Hanover's primary motive in seeking the British succession, its imperial scheme to establish the Holy Roman Empire on a European scale. It underlay Hanoverian imperial designs upon Britain which still predominated in the electoral populace, if tempered somewhat by worry at the elector's long absences.

The Treaty of Utrecht left the British empire with a greater commitment to the continent than is often realized. But there was some uncertainty about the location of empire's seat. Both Jacobite and Hanoverian publicity posited Hanoverian empire extending to Britain. Fewer people believed in Britain's empire over Hanover; its British constituency disappeared during the British government's struggle with Hanover's ministry. Meanwhile, the idea of personal union took off in both countries. This happened first in Hanover (although inspired by a singular British theorist), but later converted many former British adherents of empire over the electorate. These latter were to be the dominant voice in British discussion of union during the 1730s.

---

160 Quoted and translated by Hatton, *George I*, p. 168.
161 Hatton, *George I*, p. 168.
162 Peter King, 'Notes of Domestic and Foreign Affairs during the Last Years of the Reign of George I and the Early Part of the Reign of George II', published as an appendix in Peter, 7th Baron King, *The Life of John Locke, with Extracts from His Correspondence, Journals, and Common-Place Books* (2 vols., London, 1830), ii, p. 16.

# 3

# *Walpole*

Robert Walpole's imperial policy merited Edmund Burke's later caricature of 'salutary neglect', except perhaps when it came to patronage.[1] To the extent that he busied himself with foreign affairs, it was European diplomacy which attracted his attention. Walpole especially favored the language of international affairs (as opposed to empire) when considering Hanover's relationship to Britain. Walpole and his circle were the first to elaborate the personal union thesis first introduced by James Drake. But where the theory of England's and Hanover's countervailing sovereignties had allowed Drake and his heirs to separate the two countries legally and institutionally, it functioned to unite the two morally under Walpole. Indeed, Walpole's reputation for hostility to Hanover is greatly exaggerated.[2] He became more sympathetic to the electorate once the foreign policy initiative shifted from Hanover to Britain in the years surrounding 1720. Personal union went from shielding Britain against Hanoverian influence to protecting the electorate from British enemies. Britain's leaders never admitted a legal responsibility, but felt morally obliged, to insulate Hanover from their adversaries' allegedly incorrect interpretation of the two countries' relationship. Walpole's problem was that while he took Hanover's initial independence for granted, his assistance to the electorate could inculcate dependence on Britain. Indeed, some of his publicists revived previous generations' arguments for empire over Hanover. These horrified some opponents, who feared that continental obligations might ensue. Finally, other anti-Hanoverians remained loyal to the older diagnosis of Hanoverian empire over Britain. These were Britain's perspectives upon Hanover until the latter concluded a separate neutrality in 1741 to avoid French invasion. The neutrality ended discussions of empire over Hanover, by illustrating the electorate's independence from Britain. But while the separate peace vindicated Walpole's personal union thesis, it also made both unpopular leading up to the government's collapse in early 1742.

---

1 James A. Henretta, *"Salutary Neglect"*: *Colonial Administration under the Duke of Newcastle* (Princeton, 1972).
2 Nick Harding, 'Sir Robert Walpole and Hanover', *Historical Research* 76 (2003), pp. 164–88. For a summary of the traditional view, see Jeremy Black, *The Continental Commitment: Britain, Hanover, and Interventionism 1714–1793* (London, 2005), p. 39.

*

It has been seen that Hanoverian influence between 1714 and 1719 pushed most non-Jacobites into support for personal union. But this position was poorly defined, more often implied than explained. This changed with circumstances during the 1720s. Having used Britain's navy to secure Bremen and Verden for Hanover, George I began to privilege the interests of his kingdom even when this policy might endanger the electorate.[3] British opposition to Karl VI's trading company at Ostend led the Emperor to seek special privileges within the Spanish empire, which Felipe V's minister Ripperda conceded in the Treaty of Vienna (1725). When Britain and France opposed the Austro-Spanish alliance with a countervailing one concluded at Hanover, the flamboyant Ripperda responded by threatening an Austrian invasion of the electorate.[4] Where Hanoverian policy had once endangered Britain, British policy now imperiled Hanover. Hanoverian ministers accordingly opposed Britain's anti-Austrian policy,[5] but to no avail. To maintain their policy, Walpole and his ministers needed to assure the king that they would try to protect Hanover from its potential consequences. He pushed the house of commons to guarantee Hanover, arguing that British opposition to the Ostend company had exposed it to Austrian attack.[6] The idea that Hanover should not suffer because of British policy complemented the reverse proposition, which Walpole had already formulated during the Northern War, and completed a moral theory of personal union.

Naturally, the opposition sympathized more with Austria's imperial interpretation of the British-Hanoverian connection. William Shippen disputed the personal union theory, arguing that the parliamentary guarantee 'would engage the British nation in a war for the defense of His Majesty's dominions in Germany contrary to an express provision . . . in the Act [of Settlement]'.[7] Henry Pelham, the war secretary, corrected Shippen, reminding him that assistance to Hanover was permissible under the Act of Settlement if ratified by parliament.[8] Yet it was still possible to agree with Shippen on the fact of Hanoverian empire over Britain. The opposition whig William Pulteney traced the Austro-British tensions which threatened the electorate to 'the

---

3   Ragnhild Hatton, *George I: Elector and King* (Cambridge, MA, 1978), pp. 242–6.
4   W. Stanhope to Townshend, 27 Dec. 1725, Madrid, published in William Coxe, *Memoirs of the Life and Administration of Sir Robert Walpole, Earl of Orford* (3 vols., London, 1798), ii, p. 575.
5   See the letters published in Coxe, *Memoirs of the Life and Administration of Sir Robert Walpole*, ii, pp. 498–512.
6   See G. C. Gibbs, 'Britain and the Alliance of Hanover, April 1725 – February 1726', *The English Historical Review* 73 (1958), p. 428.
7   William Cobbett, ed., *The Parliamentary History of England* (36 vols., London, 1806–20), viii, col. 506.
8   Cobbett, ed., *The Parliamentary History of England*, viii, col. 506.

imperial court's backwardness in granting the investiture for Bremen and Verden'.[9] While it was true that Karl VI had yet to recognize Hanoverian rule in Bremen and Verden, Ragnhild Hatton has shown that the investitures were a relatively low priority for George I.[10] It was nevertheless plausible enough to keep the diagnosis of Hanoverian empire alive. Pulteney had been the whig most receptive to the Jacobite theory of Hanoverian empire during the Northern War,[11] and revived it now.

But opposition qualms had little effect on the house of commons during the height of Walpole's power. Parliament dutifully resolved that

> justice, gratitude, and honor . . . make it our indispensable duty to assure Your Majesty upon this occasion that if Your Majesty shall be at any time insulted or attacked by any prince or state whatsoever in any part of Your Majesty's dominions or territories not belonging to the crown of Great Britain in resentment of such measures as Your Majesty has taken for preserving and maintaining the trade and safety of this kingdom and of Your Majesty's having entered into the said defensive alliance [of Hannover] for that purpose, we are fully determined in vindication of Your Majesty's honor to exert ourselves to the utmost in defending and protecting such dominions from any such insults and attacks.[12]

Parliament's guarantee had practical consequences, most famously the subsequent employment of Hessian mercenaries to protect Hanover.[13] But it was also intellectually crucial. Promoters of personal union now found that justice and gratitude outweighed interest as foundational principles of their cause. Hanoverian sovereignty required British retaliation should Austria refuse to recognize the two countries' independence from one another.

The guarantee of Hanover targeted many audiences, including the public, members of parliament, and the king himself. The royal attitude towards Hanover might have changed in 1727, when George II succeeded his father. He spoke better English than George I, and his British mistress (Henrietta Howard) contrasted favorably with the late king's German intimacies. George II had moreover, as prince of Wales, actively defined himself against Hanover as part of his political opposition to George I. Upon leaving Hanover in 1714, he had declared that 'he had not one drop of blood in his

---

9  Cobbett, ed., *The Parliamentary History of England*, viii, col. 507.
10  Hatton, *George I*, p. 243. Jeremy Black still blamed Hanover's problems on the investitures in *British Foreign Policy in the Age of Walpole* (Edinburgh, 1985), p. 33. But the investitures would scarcely have excited Ripperda, who undoubtedly targeted Britain through the electorate.
11  See Hatton, *George I*, pp. 202–3.
12  Cobbett, ed., *The Parliamentary History of England*, viii, cols. 512–13.
13  See Jeremy Black, 'Parliament and Foreign Policy in the Age of Walpole: The Case of the Hessians', in Jeremy Black, ed., *Knights Errant and True Englishmen: British Foreign Policy, 1660–1800* (Edinburgh, 1989), pp. 41–54.

veins but what was *English* and at the service of his [father's] new subjects'.[14] Over two years later, the future George II had disparaged Bremen and Verden. The new king's anti-Hanoverian track record might have revived British hopes of empire over Hanover. But the pro-government constituency which would have sustained these hopes had already hitched its wagon to personal union. So did figures who had feared Hanoverian empire over Britain, if only temporarily. Pulteney's new journal, *The Craftsman*, now declared that 'the popular topics of a *new family* and a *foreign reign* are in a great measure remov'd, our present most gracious sovereign . . . having constantly resided amongst us for above these *thirteen years* and made our *language* and *constitution* familiar to him, which is more than can be said of the pretender'.[15] Even William Shippen, the Jacobite member of parliament, argued against George II's proposed civil list with the expectation that 'many particular expenses in the late reign, especially those for frequent journeys to Hanover, will be discontinued and entirely cease'.[16]

What ended this brief truce on the subject of Hanover was George II's resumption, in 1729, of his father's hugely controversial visits to Hanover. For Lord Hervey, the memoirist, the king's first visit to Hanover as elector was doubly significant. Firstly, it showed that George II's 'thoughts, whatever they might have been, were no longer turned either with contempt or dislike to his electoral dominions'.[17] Secondly, wrote Hervey, 'whilst the king was at Hanover he had several little German disputes with his brother of Prussia, the particulars of which [were] about a few cart-loads of hay, a mill, and some soldiers improperly enlisted by the king of Prussia in the Hanoverian state'.[18] For all its apparent absurdity, the Prusso-Hanoverian dispute might easily have escalated into a full-fledged war involving Britain. Unbeknownst to the public, George II prepared to have thousands of British regulars transported to Germany.[19] Harder to conceal were his appeals for assistance from British stipendiaries such as Hesse-Cassel. Hanoverian interests again drove British policy, as they had during the Northern War. Walpole's challenge was to serve George II without appearing to back away from his historical opposition to Hanoverian ascendancy within dynastic union.

Pulteney prepared to attack Hanover as he had not done since 1726. Then, he had revived the Jacobite critique of Hanoverian empire which

---

[14] Karl Ludwig, Freiherr von Pöllnitz, *The Memoirs of Charles Lewis, Baron de Pollnitz*, trans. Stephen Whatley (5 vols., London, 1745), iv, p. 233.

[15] *The Country Journal, or the Craftsman* no. 70 (4 Nov. 1727), pp. 1–2.

[16] Cobbett, ed., *The Parliamentary History of England*, viii, col. 601.

[17] John Hervey, 2nd Baron Hervey of Ickworth, *Some Materials towards Memoirs of the Reign of King George II*, ed. Romney Sedgwick (3 vols., London, 1931), ii, p. 485.

[18] Hervey, *Some Materials towards Memoirs of the Reign of King George II*, ed. Sedgwick, i, p. 102.

[19] Jeremy Black, *The Collapse of the Anglo-French Alliance 1727–1731* (Gloucester, 1987), p. 140.

dated from the Northern War. Now that the years had proved Hanover's vulnerability, he shifted to a no less critical interpretation of British empire over the electorate. This had first been anticipated by Drake in his 1702 *History*, but remained implicit in Pulteney's 1729 remarks to Hervey. Pulteney, warned that members of parliament might 'declare the Act of Settlement broken by the continuation of the Hessian troops in the English pay for the defense of Hanover'.[20] As Pelham had earlier done in response to Shippen, Hervey reminded Pulteney that assistance to Hanover was legal when approved by parliament.[21] But Pulteney was perhaps closer to one of the Act of Settlement's original rationales, the prevention of money from leaving Britain for Hanoverian purposes, when he condemned the 'vast and unnecessary and ridiculous expense of the Hessians'.[22] Pulteney even threatened that some members might suggest replacing George II as king with his eight-year-old son the duke of Cumberland,[23] the first time a whig had contemplated dissolving dynastic union since Toland's *Limitations*.

Walpole took this opportunity to amplify the rhetoric he had employed in 1726. He addressed the Prussian crisis in a pamphlet of January 1730, *Observations upon the Treaty between the Crowns of Great Britain, France, and Spain*. He was in the habit of commissioning a pro-government treatise on foreign affairs before each parliamentary session, but this year personally composed it in self-congratulation for having excluded Townshend (his former brother-in-law and current ministerial rival) from the negotiations which culminated in the Treaty of Seville with Spain. Walpole's scarcely concealed authorship garnered the pamphlet the highest profile possible. Although Walpole admitted that the Prussian crisis 'was so happily dissipated' by the time he wrote,[24] he happily returned to the subject in the *Observations*. He claimed that the Prusso-Hanoverian feud had evolved from Britain's continuing dispute with Austria, which had moreover worsened because of the Treaty of Seville. Walpole rightly observed that

> His Majesty's preferring an alliance with *Spain* is a strong proof that the interests of *Great Britain* have the chief place in his thoughts. His Majesty might certainly have promised himself not only security, but even great advantages, to his *German* territories from a reconciliation with the Emperor. And on the contrary, he may now perhaps meet with marks of resentment in those

---

[20] Hervey, *Some Materials towards Memoirs of the Reign of King George II*, ed. Sedgwick, i, p. 106.

[21] Hervey, *Some Materials towards Memoirs of the Reign of King George II*, ed. Sedgwick, i, p. 106.

[22] Hervey, *Some Materials towards Memoirs of the Reign of King George II*, ed. Sedgwick, i, p. 107.

[23] Hervey, *Some Materials towards Memoirs of the Reign of King George II*, ed. Sedgwick, i, p. 106.

[24] [Sir Robert Walpole], *Observations upon the Treaty between the Crowns of Great Britain, France, and Spain* (London, 1729), p. 26.

quarters. *Seckendorff*, the imperial minister at *Berlin*, will without doubt be again called upon to exert the credit which he pretends to have gain'd with His *Prussian* Majesty to induce him to quarrel once more with those to whom he ought by all the ties of blood, interest, and religion to be most closely united.[25]

Walpole's conflation of the Prussian case with its Austrian precedent functioned to deny claims of Hanoverian empire over Britain, and to renew the relevance of his 1726 arguments for personal union.

Personal union was not the only justification for assistance to Hanover. Walpole further argued that Hanover's Protestantism alone qualified it for British succor, writing

> I cannot see how it can be the duty of an *Englishman* to encourage foreign powers to invade the king's *German* dominions, and to excite the neighboring princes to oppress a people merely because they acknowledge the same sovereign that we do. That country, barren and despicable as it has been represented, has surely the common claim of all Protestant nations to our favor and good wishes, if not to our protection. The last as well as the present parliament have declared themselves to be in this way of thinking, and we need not surely repine at their quiet, nor are we under any temptation to disturb it. I hope therefore that the malicious desire which these false patriots have shown to distress the king's affairs *there* will have no other effect than to open the eyes of those who have been deceived by their specious pretenses of loyalty and affection for His Majesty. And it may reasonably be expected that the complaisant person who once condescended to make a private submission in the last reign for some free expressions that fell from him in public upon a subject not very unlike that which I have been now treating of will think this a proper occasion for showing once more his great address in making recantations.[26]

Walpole probably calculated that his prominent defense of Hanover would ease Townshend's inevitable departure from government, as the latter had been catering more enthusiastically to the king's favorite electorate;[27] but this passage targeted another rival. Pulteney was the 'complaisant person' who had had to apologize to George I in 1717 for his anti-Hanoverian remarks as part of Walpole's opposition. Walpole also associated Pulteney with the conviction that the electorate was 'barren and despicable', a paraphrase of the old Jacobite argument against Hanover. His object was not

---

[25] [R. Walpole], *Observations upon the Treaty*, pp. 23–4.

[26] [R. Walpole], *Observations upon the Treaty*, pp. 26–7 or pp. 27–8, depending upon the edition.

[27] The king still worried, declaring that 'his dependence for Hanover must now be upon' Townshend's successor. Newcastle to Harrington, 23 Apr./4 May 1730, London, published in William Coxe, *Memoirs of the Life and Administration of Sir Robert Walpole* (3 vols., London, 1798), ii, p. 689.

only to call Pulteney a Jacobite, but also to goad him and his followers into further attacks upon Hanover. Walpole obviously believed that Hanover's utility to his familiar strategy of smoking out Jacobitism[28] outweighed whatever disadvantages it possessed.

Walpole's attack obviously frightened Pulteney, who authored a meek rebuttal entitled A Short View of the State of Affairs. Even a bolder pamphlet, The Observations on the Treaty of Seville Examined, felt obliged to deny Walpole's aspersions. Its anonymous author considered that 'the people of Hanover are our friends, they are Protestants, they are subjects of the same prince. In all these respects, far from having that ignoble and wicked sentiment of repining at their quiet, we ought to wish for their prosperity.'[29]

But The Observations on the Treaty of Seville Examined did not spare Walpole's argument. It held that the Hanover's present crisis with Prussia did not derive from Austria's 'hatred to the Hannover treaty',[30] which had prompted the parliamentary guarantee of 1726, but from 'a few cartloads of hay [and] some irregular practices in listing or detaining a few sorry peasants'.[31] This allusion to electoral influence over British policy, taken alone, might have hinted at Hanoverian empire were it not for additional argument. The pamphlet concluded that

> there never can happen any disturbance in Lower Saxony by which we must not be alarm'd, nor any war there, wherein we must not be engag'd . . . If that ever comes to be our case, what advantage [can] we . . . reap from the situation of our country as an island or from the present happy establishment of our government? . . . Every man who labors . . . to introduce the notion that we are under other obligations of protecting His Majesty's German dominions than we are under of protecting any other state (I mean obligations of general interest and particular compact) [is] a man who betrays one of the most essential rights of the British nation . . . which we hold by the same tenure as His Majesty holds his crown.[32]

This elaborated the critique of British empire over Hanover which had remained implicit in Pulteney's earlier remarks to Hervey. It recalled the maritime bias against continental dependencies first applied to Hanover by

---

28 For this, see G. V. Bennett, 'Jacobitism and the Rise of Walpole', in Neil McKendrick, ed., Historical Perspectives (London, 1974), pp. 70–92; Paul S. Fritz, The English Ministers and Jacobitism between the Rebellions of 1715 and 1745 (Toronto, 1975).
29 The Observations on the Treaty of Seville Examined (London, 1730), p. 8 or p. 9, depending upon the edition.
30 The Observations on the Treaty of Seville Examined, p. 9 or p. 10, depending upon the edition.
31 The Observations on the Treaty of Seville Examined, p. 8 or p. 9, depending upon the edition.
32 The Observations on the Treaty of Seville Examined, pp. 9–10 or p. 10, depending upon the edition.

James Drake in his *History* of 1702. Drake's critique of British empire over Hanover had more life from now on.

The injunction that Britain restrain its foreign obligations to those of 'general interest and particular compact' had a remarkable effect upon supporters of assistance to Hanover. It was an unfair criticism of Walpole's *Observations*, in that he had justified assistance to Hanover in terms of Protestant solidarity. The government made rather less of this when the commons debated the Hessian subsidy, leaving the theme to sympathetic backbenchers. Sir Archer Croft even contradicted the government's emphasis on treaty, declaring he 'would be for maintaining the Hessians though the defense of Hanover should be alone the reason . . . And besides . . . it is a Protestant state . . . we see the Protestants abroad in all places oppressed, and . . . he wished there were more states of our religion under His Majesty than he is already possessed of'.[33] Protestantism could not neutralize the prejudice against continental dependencies, and at least one government loyalist opposed Croft with reference to 'particular compact'.[34]

This had been the line already taken by ministers themselves. Defending a renewal of the Hessian subsidy before the commons, Henry Pelham termed it

> a necessary measure to be prepared against any attempt [Austria] should . . . make not merely against His Majesty's electorate dominions but against any of the powers engaged in the alliance with us to maintain the Treaty of Seville.
>
> So little do all our allies look on this to be an electorate quarrel that as soon as the king of Prussia, influenced entirely by the Vienna councils, threatened to invade Hanover, France, Holland, Denmark, and Sweden declared to that prince that they looked on such an attempt as a cause wherein they were all concerned, not as a design to right himself in such trivial matters as listing a dozen soldiers or carrying away a load of hay, but that his purpose was under that pretence to disturb the tranquility of Europe and particularly to fall upon Holland.[35]

This argument was repeated to the commons the next day by Walpole's own brother Horatio. As had Pelham, Horatio Walpole echoed his brother's argument that Austria had incited Prussia's quarrel with Hanover.[36] But they betrayed misgivings by insisting that the Dutch, rather than Hanover, had necessitated the Hessian subsidies. While the emphasis upon international law was a response to the insistence upon 'particular compact' found in *The Observations on the Treaty of Seville Examined*, government supporters did not

---

[33] Historical Manuscripts Commission (HMC), *Diary of Viscount Percival, afterwards First Earl of Egmont* (3 vols., London, 1920–3), i, p. 30.

[34] HMC, *Diary of Viscount Percival*, i, p. 30.

[35] HMC, *Diary of Viscount Percival*, i, p. 26.

[36] A. N. Newman, ed., *The Parliamentary Diary of Sir Edward Knatchbull 1722–1730* (London, 1963), p. 104.

address the full implications of that pamphlet's insistence upon 'particular compact'. Horatio Walpole and Pelham dodged the opportunity to define Britain's relationship with Hanover, by changing the subject to that of the Dutch alliance. But their interest in international law indicated the government's further movement in the direction of personal union.

Although personal union was less controversial than British empire over Hanover, opposition figures attacked it nonetheless. Discounting Pelham's Dutch fears, Pulteney's cousin Daniel complained that

> we are to keep up [the Hessians] on account of the Hanoverian dominions, and this I think not proper for us to engage in, their interest and views [being] different. They have none of our countrymen in their councils, they have none of theirs in ours, and [it is] very hard that we shall be involved by the resolutions and treaties made by Hanoverian ministers who are by no means answerable for their conduct to us and the parliament.[37]

But he stopped short of a solution. In contrast, several opposition whigs wished it had never existed. The most important of these was John Barnard, a member of parliament for London, who criticized the Act of Settlement for failing to require the Hanoverian successors to renounce their German inheritance as Felipe V of Spain had done with his French rights.[38] John Toland had argued similarly before the Act's adoption in 1701,[39] but no other whig had repeated the view until Barnard. Barnard was even more original on a related point. Where Daniel Pulteney had accepted the government's contention that Britain and Hanover were in personal union, Barnard censured what he considered to be British empire over Hanover. Affecting sympathy for the electorate, he observed that the latter 'may be attacked only to destroy England and so suffer on that account which [it] otherwise would [not] have'.[40] This point of view was to become wildly popular among opposition politicians of the 1750s. But it did not take off in 1730, probably because it directly contradicted Barnard's opinion that Hanover had brought trouble upon itself.[41]

If Hanover's critics were divided, then so were its supporters. Just as Pelham and Horatio Walpole were denying the Hanoverian rationale for hiring Hessian mercenaries, an anonymously authored pamphlet conceded it. *The Treaty of Seville and the Measures That Have Been Taken for the Four Last Years Impartially Considered* asserted that the Hanoverians

---

37 Newman, ed., *The Parliamentary Diary of Sir Edward Knatchbull*, p. 148.
38 Newman, ed., *The Parliamentary Diary of Sir Edward Knatchbull*, p. 150.
39 [Toland], *Limitations for the Next Foreign Successor*, pp. 8–9.
40 Newman, ed., *The Parliamentary Diary of Sir Edward Knatchbull*, p. 150.
41 HMC, *Diary of Viscount Percival*, i, p. 28.

suffer upon a quarrel purely *English* – entirely so with respect to *Hanover*, which has no interest in our disputes with the *Emperor* or *Spain* . . . If they feel the miseries of a war, it is for no other reason but because they have the same prince for the governor with us – the king of *England* is *their* elector. What then can be more just than that *England* should join in their defense? 'Tis so manifest a piece of justice this, that nobody can pretend to be against it.[42]

But if the pamphlet's revival of the justice-based language introduced in the parliamentary resolutions of 1726 deviated from the government's more recent disavowal of Hanover's role behind the Hessian subsidy, it concurred with Walpole's evolving case for a personal union with that electorate. The injustice of Austria's threats to Hanover proceeded from the electorate's legal independence from Britain.

*The Treaty of Seville and the Measures That Have Been Taken for the Four Last Years Impartially Considered* was not only an important clarification of the pro-Hanoverian position; it forced an equally important response from *The Craftsman*. Pulteney's journal prudently avoided intemperate attacks upon personal union by agreeing with justice-based arguments for assistance to the electorate, averring that

> whenever it shall appear that His Majesty's *foreign dominions* are involv'd in any difficulties on account of *England*, we ought to *assist* and *support* them. On the contrary . . . any man who endeavors to make *England* a province to *those dominions* or to involve her in a war upon account of quarrels *entirely foreign to England* is an enemy to his *king* and a traitor to his *country*.[43]

Given its judgment that Hanover had endangered itself by its quarrel with Prussia, *The Craftsman* essentially forwarded a diagnosis of Hanoverian empire over Britain. This argument had been scarce since 1726, and diversified opposition rhetoric.

If opposition argumentation was becoming more heterogeneous, then that of the court was consolidating. In 1730 *The Treaty of Seville and the Measures That Have Been Taken for the Four Last Years Impartially Considered* had exonerated the Hanoverian calculations behind Hessian subsidies using arguments from justice, while government luminaries had instead ascribed the latter to Britain's Dutch alliance. These positions merged in the annual pamphlet which Walpole commissioned to open the parliamentary session of 1731. *Considerations on the Present State of Affairs in Europe* was written by veteran diplomat Stephen Poyntz in conjunction with Walpole's own brother Horatio, one of the foremost exponents of the Dutch interpretation

---

[42] *The Treaty of Seville and the Measures That Have Been Taken for the Four Last Years Impartially Considered in a Letter to a Friend* (London, 1730), pp. 28–9.
[43] *The Country Journal, or the Craftsman* no. 190 (21 Feb. 1730), p. 2.

during 1730.[44] International developments facilitated Horatio Walpole's self-reversal. The end of Hanover's Prussian crisis made it easier to blame its vulnerability on Britain's continuing froideur with Austria. He also wrote that 'as His Majesty might expect the like insults upon his *Hanover* dominions, out of resentment for the measures taken by him to make good his engagements as king of *England*, it would be unjust to leave him exposed as elector purely on that account'.[45] Here again was the justice-based case for assistance to Hanover. Anticipating the argument that Austria threatened Hanover out of a dispute more electoral than British, Horatio Walpole claimed that 'not one word had passed for some years before the conclusion of *Vienna* about [the imperial investitures for] *Bremen* and *Verden*'.[46] This provoked William Pulteney to declare before the commons that 'Bremen and Verden had been the foundations of . . . bad treaties . . . and were the real source of all the present disputes in Europe',[47] virtually repeating his remarks of 1726. This probably gratified the younger Walpole, who followed his brother's lead in associating criticism of the electorate with opposition to the Hanoverian succession in Britain.[48]

But while Horatio Walpole abandoned his reliance upon the Dutch alliance, he employed the language of international law which had underpinned it to bolster the justice-based case for assistance to Hanover. His system elevated Hanover from its previous subordination to Britain's foreign allies, now considering 'the electorate of *Hanover* as an ally of *Great Britain*'.[49] Horatio Walpole thereby revived Sir Richard Steele's 1716 conception of Hanover as 'a rich and powerful ally'. While the Treaty of Hanover obliged its signatories to defend the electorate as one of George I's dominions, neither he nor his son had ever explicitly acceded to it as elector. This hardly made Hanover a British ally in the conventional sense. Horatio Walpole recognized this weakness in his argument, for he continued that

> it is true indeed there is no formal alliance between *Great Britain* and *Hanover* for, the quality of king and elector residing in the same person, His Majesty could not contract with himself. But the union betwixt the two governments and the obligations of mutual defense and guarantee are as strongly and necessarily implied as the most formal treaties and conventions could possibly make them.[50]

---

[44] For the attribution, see HMC, *Diary of Viscount Percival*, i, p. 125.

[45] [Horatio Walpole and Stephen Poyntz], *Considerations on the Present State of Affairs in Europe* (London, 1730), p. 43.

[46] [Horatio Walpole and Poyntz], *Considerations on the Present State of Affairs*, p. 47.

[47] T. Pelham to Waldegrave, 22 Jan. 1731, London, published in Coxe, *Memoirs of the Life and Administration of Sir Robert Walpole*, iii, pp. 79–80.

[48] [Horatio Walpole and Poyntz], *Considerations on the Present State of Affairs*, p. 53.

[49] [Horatio Walpole and Poyntz], *Considerations on the Present State of Affairs*, p. 49.

[50] [Horatio Walpole and Poyntz], *Considerations on the Present State of Affairs*, p. 50.

Yet despite its self-confessed flaws, Horatio Walpole's argument enriched the conception of the British-Hanoverian relationship as personal union by its addition of international law.

The case for a quasi-alliance with Hanover inevitably provoked a response from the opposition press. The anonymously authored *Case of the Hessian Forces* sought to change the subject from justice to interest by agreeing, for argument's sake, with the younger Walpole's contention that the two countries were allies. 'Even supposing this to be the case', it asked, are the Hanoverian dominions 'not a weight upon the strength of *England*? Are they not a constant pledge, as it were, in the *Emperor*'s hands?'[51] Such language betrayed that the anonymous author considered Hanover to be more like an imperial dependency of Britain than an ally. He deliberately misconstrued Horatio Walpole's language to make it appear as if the minister's brother had as much as conceded this opinion. Noting that the younger Walpole had spoken of a 'union betwixt the two governments', its author inquired 'What UNION *of the two governments* can the *author* possibly mean? Though we have the happiness of living under the *same prince* . . . we do not live under the *same form of government*. Ours is *limited*, theirs is *absolute*, and whilst this difference subsists there can be no union between them.'[52] The word 'union' in Horatio Walpole's argument had undoubtedly referred to an alliance rather than political integration. But *The Case of the Hessian Forces* cleverly exploited the ambiguity of Horatio Walpole's words to attack continental dependencies.

These were inflammatory arguments. Yet again, the mainstream organs of opposition whig publicity stopped short of abjuring personal union. *The Case of the Hessian Forces* would have been satisfied with a change in behavior, trusting 'in His Majesty's wisdom that he will . . . consider himself in a *double capacity* as king of *Great Britain* and elector of *Hanover*'.[53] Not so opposition whig parliamentarians, whose animus against union with Hanover only increased during the annual debate on the Hessians. A member for Liverpool, Sir Thomas Aston, 'wished the king would part with Hanover to his second son', the duke of Cumberland, and was seconded by Barnard of London.[54] This was, of course, the reverse of the plan first mooted in private by Pulteney over a year before. It indicated that opposition whiggery's exceptions to Hanover had moved from the previous year's nostalgia to a programme increasingly more distinct, and thereby more dangerous to Walpole, from Jacobitism.

Aston and Barnard were opposed with the argument that Hanover was a

---

51 *The Case of the Hessian Forces in the Pay of Great Britain Impartially and Freely Examin'd* (London, 1731), p. 35.
52 *The Case of the Hessian Forces*, p. 35.
53 *The Case of the Hessian Forces*, p. 36.
54 HMC, *Diary of Viscount Percival*, i, p. 126.

'Protestant ally'.[55] Although the definition of ally had come under much scrutiny since the publication of *The Observations on the Treaty of Seville Examined*, the importance of Protestantism had been relatively neglected despite its appearance in the pamphlet of Walpole's which it had answered. This defect was remedied by an anonymously published pamphlet entitled *Some Observations on the Present State of Affairs*. It still maintained the Dutch conceit, but also admitted the Hessians' usefulness to Hanover. The author recalled that James I was rightly

> blam'd for not protecting a people of the reform'd religion and abandoning a nation which might have been useful in the Empire to the Protestant interest. If these arguments were of force against the conduct of King *James*, they must be of equal force to justify the conduct of the parliament now, the people of *Hanover* being a parallel case or rather still more deserving our protection as the difficulties they labor under proceed from our quarrels not their own.[56]

James I's failure to assist his son-in-law, the elector Palatine, during the Thirty Years' War remained a powerful totem for Protestant interventionists. Its recollection here revived the religious element of pro-Hanoverian literature, as well as recapitulating the justice-based argument for assistance to the electorate.

This argument for assistance to Hanover – the elements drawing upon the Palatine precedent and upon justice, in particular – was taken up by Sir Robert Walpole's favorite publicist, William Arnall.[57] To these Arnall appended the idea of personal union advanced by Horatio Walpole's *Considerations*, which he quoted at length. To this, he added,

> His Majesty's *German dominions* are no parcel of the *British* crown, nor are they to be swayed by the laws or councils of *Great Britain*. So far they are not entitled to protection as people who are subjects or as countries which are appendages to the crown. But then as a country in friendship with us, nay more as a *Protestant* state, . . . the king's dominions abroad are to be treated as in alliance with us, an alliance which gives some weight and authority *to us* in particular with important advantages to *Europe* in general, nor less deserve support and assistance *from us* as those are the mutual terms of every league and confederacy.[58]

Arnall further strengthened the idea of personal union by comparing Britain's relationship with Hanover to that between Hesse-Cassel and Sweden.[59]

---

[55] HMC, *Diary of Viscount Percival*, i, p. 126.
[56] *Some Observations on the Present State of Affairs in a Letter to a Member of the House of Commons by a Member of Parliament* (London, 1731), pp. 30–1.
[57] *The Free Briton* no. 65 (25 Feb. 1731), p. 2.
[58] *The Free Briton* no. 65 (25 Feb. 1731), p. 1.
[59] *The Free Briton* no. 65 (25 Feb. 1731), p. 2.

Sweden was another constitutional monarchy which had been joined to a German principality, upon the Swedish king's inheritance of Hesse from his father the previous year. Although it was too early to tell, Fredrik I looked as if he was governing his two countries as though they were entirely independent of one another.

Yet Sweden had no guarantee of independence analogous to Britain's Act of Settlement, which always featured highly in any assertion of personal union. Indeed, Arnall himself downplayed the Act's significance in British history. He conceded that it was directed at 'natural infirmities of temper' and 'wrong bias of mind' in future elector-kings, while shrewdly excluding George I and George II from such suspicion. But Arnall largely dismissed fears relating to Hanover, contending that drafters of the Act of Settlement 'did not at any time look upon these dominions as likely to injure the interests of *Great Britain*. Had this been their apprehension, they would have made it a condition that the *successor* should upon his accession renounce his title of his *electoral* countries. But they did not propose it.'[60] Arnall conveniently overlooked the debates over the Act of Settlement, particularly Toland's demand (made in the *Limitations*) that the Hanoverian successors disown their electoral pretences before ascending the English throne. This cavalier attitude towards the Act of Settlement seemed to bespeak something other than entire adherence to personal union.

Alongside personal union, Arnall also supported a relationship with Hanover that was much more imperial. He supposed that the drafters of the Act of Settlement expected eventual elector-kings

> would rather make the interests of the *lesser* country subservient to the *greater* than the *greater* to *the less*, and that there was no more probability *Hanover* would outweigh *Great Britain* in the royal mind than appeared to the people in Queen ELIZABETH's days that *England* would become a province to *Scotland*, though the *last* supposition was much more plausible than the first could be.[61]

Arnall betrayed an attraction to British empire over Hanover. Although his support for assistance to Hanover was clear, the two models associated with Sweden/Hesse (personal union) and England/Scotland (something more imperial) conflicted with each other.

Arnall's diatribe helped to provoke what had long been a Walpolean objective: a response by Bolingbroke. Bolingbroke had refrained from overt contemporary commentary while serializing his *Remarks on the History of England* in *The Craftsman*. But he finally took that bait when his narrative reached the episode of the Palatinate, asking,

---

60 *The Free Briton* no. 65 (25 Feb. 1731), p. 1.
61 *The Free Briton* no. 65 (25 Feb. 1731), p. 1.

how monstrous is the absurdity and impudence of *those* who have asserted that the case of the people of the *Palatinate*, invaded by a powerful enemy who pretended to nothing less than the conquest of them, is parallel to that of the people of *Hanover*, invaded by nobody and over whom no foreign power pretends any dominion? [62]

The pretender's former secretary of state gave Walpole and his publicists their opportunity to associate suspicion of Hanover with Jacobitism.

James Pitt, a dissenting schoolmaster from Norwich and friend of Toland's,[63] attacked Bolingbroke's comments in *The London Journal*. Not as close to the prime minster as Arnall, Pitt was nonetheless Walpole's man. Yet he downplayed the issue of personal union, preferring to speak in terms of British empire over Hanover. Pitt's empire was distinctive, relying more upon duty than advantage:

we had no other way to save ourselves from *certain ruin* [than] by choosing the *elector of Hanover* king. But it is ridiculous to suppose that the royal family *will part with that electorate*, especially made so advantageous by the additions of *Bremen* and *Verden* . . . It will be eternally our interest to *support the Protestant cause* as that case is the *cause of liberty*, so that if we had no *Hanover* dominions it might be the duty of *England on certain occasions* to keep troops in pay and princes too . . . *Whenever those occasions rise*, the *Hanover* dominions may be of the greatest service in the world to us, as they would engage us *to do that more warmly from necessity* which we should perhaps *do more cooly from reason*.[64]

Where Toland's *Anglia Libera* had imagined that dynastic union would secure the (implicitly unreliable) Protestant German principalities to the Protestant interest, the wayward country for Pitt was Britain.

The opposition countered that, far from extending British empire to Hanover, a policy of assisting that electorate made it master over Britain. *The Craftsman* charged that Pitt had 'not scrupled to assert the necessity of making Great Britain in some sort a province to foreign dominions'.[65] Although unaccompanied by analysis, this was the very same charge of British subjection to Hanover *The Craftsman* had made the previous year.

The virtue of *The Craftsman's* language was to force Pitt to make his more precise. Far from calling Great Britain a province of Hanover, Pitt claimed to have made '*Hanover* a province to *Great Britain*, for that country which is *defended or supported* by us may in some sort be said to be a *province* to us, but

---

[62] *The Country Journal, or the Craftsman* no. 253 (8 May 1731), p. 2.
[63] Simon Targett, 'Government and Ideology during the Age of the Whig Supremacy: The Political Argument of Sir Robert Walpole's Newspaper Propagandists', *The Historical Journal* 37 (1994), p. 316.
[64] *The London Journal* no. 616 (15 May 1731), p. 1.
[65] *The Country Journal, or the Craftsman* no. 258 (12 June 1731), p. 1.

that which *defends or supports* can IN NO SORT be said to be a province'.[66] Pitt clarified his earlier vision of British empire over Hanover, an empire of obligation more than profit.

Undeterred, *The Craftsman* intensified its condemnations of British submission to Hanover. It considered that

> if we lie under a *necessity . . . of paying armies and subsidies abroad* for the support of *foreign dominions*, we may find ourselves . . . even in a worse condition than that of a *province*, since though a *province* is obliged to follow the interest and policy of the *mistress country* she is likewise entitled to her protection. Whereas if we are obliged, at all times, to support *foreign dominions* whose interests are not immediately and necessarily united with ours and whose policy cannot be supposed to be directed by ours, we should really act the part of a *province* to those countries and it would be ludicrous to suppose that they could give us any protection in return.[67]

To Pitt's contention that the condition of being a province lay in duty, *The Craftsman* insisted upon an argument from advantage.

Diplomacy's ebb reduced the attention paid to dynastic union's role in British wars. But the 1731 publication of Voltaire's *Histoire de Charles XII* reanimated discussion of the dynastic union's role during the Northern War. English translators prudently excised Voltaire's tart speculation that George I 'seemed to have no right' to Bremen and Verden,[68] but could not avert the issue's revival. It prompted the eccentric demand by one tory member of parliament, Thomas Palmer, that the two duchies be placed under British sovereignty in the manner of England's medieval possessions in France. But it also induced several opposition whigs to call for union's dissolution,[69] and *The Craftsman* to imply that George I had violated the Act of Settlement in the matter.[70]

*The Craftsman's* review of Voltaire's biography prompted the last of James Pitt's responses. Most of it repeated his Protestant logic for British empire over Hanover. But replying to *The Craftsman's* extreme understanding of the Act of Settlement, Pitt added that

---

66 *The London Journal* no. 623 (3 July 1731), p. 2.

67 *The Country Journal, or the Craftsman* no. 264 (24 July 1731), p. 2.

68 Contrast Voltaire's 'George était entré dans la querelle . . . pour garder Brême et Verden, auxquels il semblait n'avoir d'autre droit que de les avoir achetés à vil prix du roi de Danemark, à qui ils n'appartenaient pas' (Voltaire, *Histoire de Charles XII* (Paris, 1968), p. 223) with his English translator's '[George came] to the business . . . with intent to hold *Bremen* and *Verden*, which he bought for a trifle of the King of *Denmark*' (Voltaire, *The History of Charles XII, King of Sweden* (London, 1732), p. 147).

69 HMC, *Diary of Viscount Percival*, i, p. 253.

70 *The Country Journal, or the Craftsman* no. 302 (15 Apr. 1732), p. 1.

though the king of *Great Britain* and the elector of *Hanover* are *two distinct powers*, yet those powers are lodged in *one person* . . . 'Tis impossible in the nature of things that the *king* should act *absolutely distinct* from the *elector*, or the *elector* from the *king*, or ever consider himself in any other light than as *king* and *elector*. The *king* will *naturally and necessarily* have regard to the *elector* and the *elector* to the *king*.[71]

This highlighted the government's personal union. Pitt held that Britain and Hanover were legally distinct from one another, but that there were circumstances in which both might treat each other as more than allies. One such eventuality was when the enemy of one failed to recognize their mutual independence.

But by the time of Pitt's journalistic volley with *The Craftsman*, this situation had altered. In exchange for Britain's ratification of its Pragmatic Sanction, Austria agreed in March 1731 to disband the Ostend Company. By burying its quarrel with Austria, Britain simultaneously relieved Hanover of its invasion fears. But Walpole also considered the Austrian treaty to have discharged Britain's obligations to Hanover, leaving the electorate to resolve the issue of investitures on its own a month later. Improving relations with Austria, and Walpole's miscalculated increase in the excise tax, temporarily removed Hanover from public consideration.

The War of Polish Succession brought Hanover back to the public's attention, but under circumstances which would diminish the electorate's popularity in Britain. This was because Britain remained neutral while Hanover furnished the Holy Roman Empire with troops for its war against France.[72] Hanover once again threatened to involve Britain in war, as it had during the Northern War. The government once again invoked personal union, but this time to distance Britain from Hanoverian policy. When tories in 1734 objected to a parliamentary guarantee of George II's 'rights and possessions . . . as might preserve the respect due to the crown of Great Britain'[73] on the ground that such terms were vague enough to include Hanover, Pelham assured them that 'His Majesty's German dominions . . . in no way belong to the crown of Great Britain'.[74] And when an anonymously authored pamphlet defended the government's foreign policy, it favored

---

[71] *The London Journal* no. 671 (6 May 1732), p. 1.
[72] Jeremy Black, 'British Neutrality in the War of the Polish Succession', *The International History Review* 8 (1986), pp. 345–66.
[73] Cobbett, ed., *The Parliamentary History of England*, ix, col. 188.
[74] Cobbett, ed., *The Parliamentary History of England*, ix, col. 191.

Horatio Walpole's personal union thesis over the more expansionist arguments of James Pitt.[75]

It was George II's 1735 visit to Hanover that further raised the electorate's public profile. This was because the king fell in love with Amelia Sophia von Walmoden, prompting him to make an unprecedentedly rapid return to Hanover in 1736. The trip's immoral objective only heightened British anxiety about wealth transfers to the electorate. Hervey reported that some malcontents wondered if 'parliament had given [George II] a greater civil list than any of his predecessors only to defray the extraordinary expenses of his traveling charges, to support his Hanover bawdy-houses in magnificence, and enrich his German pimps and whores'.[76]

George II's honeymoon with the British public, long in decline, was finally over. Hervey considered that the king's visits to Hanover 'convinced the distant part of the nation of what those who had the honor to be more near him had discovered long ago, which was his preferring his German to his English subjects at least as much as his father had done'.[77] But they also offended his British court to a greater extent than before. In his growing enthusiasm for Hanover, George II reflected rashly upon the freedoms Britons considered distinguished them from the electorate. The king complained to Hervey, for instance, that

> he was forced to distribute his favors here very differently from the manner in which he bestowed them at Hanover; that there he rewarded people for doing their duty and serving him well, but that here he was obliged to enrich people for being rascals and buy them not to cut his throat.[78]

On another occasion the king wished 'the devil may take all your bishops, and the devil take your minister, and the devil take the parliament, and the devil take the whole island, provided I can get out of it and go to Hanover'.[79] George II's remarks fed suspicions that he might act against British liberties. Queen Caroline's attempt to neutralize the king's comments by praising the British constitution over that of Hanover fell further flat; her assertion that Britain's liberties were its only asset was

---

75 *A Series of Wisdom and Policy Manifested in a Review of Our Foreign Negotiations and Transactions for Several Years Past, Being a Complete Answer to Politicks on Both Sides &c. in a Letter to a Member of the Present Parliament* (London, 1735), pp. 34–7.
76 Hervey, *Some Materials towards Memoirs of the Reign of King George II*, ed. Sedgwick, ii, p. 610.
77 Hervey, *Some Materials towards Memoirs of the Reign of King George II*, ed. Sedgwick, ii, p. 646.
78 Hervey, *Some Materials towards Memoirs of the Reign of King George II*, ed. Sedgwick, ii, p. 486.
79 Hervey, *Some Materials towards Memoirs of the Reign of King George II*, ed. Sedgwick, ii, p. 539.

unflattering, and her concession of the electorate's relative illiberality, reinforced fears it might contaminate British political culture.[80] The dowager duchess of Marlborough provocatively echoed Lockhart's unflattering comparison of Hanoverian with Stuart tyranny, asking 'which was the easiest servitude, under France or Germany?'[81]

Dynastic union's unpopularity encouraged the prince of Wales to use it in his opposition to George II, just as the latter had done as heir apparent. Frederick's political associates celebrated the birth of his daughter in 1737, knowing that Britain's and Hanover's different laws respecting the accession of female heirs would sunder the dynastic union. This prospect faded the following year, with the birth of a boy (the future George III) to Princess Augusta. But rumors nonetheless abounded that Frederick planned to renounce his electoral rights in favor of Cumberland, just as Aston had suggested, in return for an extra £50,000 a year.[82]

Although Caroline claimed that the king had already considered precisely the same step 'to mortify' Frederick and 'provide' for Cumberland,[83] she now opposed the plan as coming from the former. Caroline doubted her son's sincerity in any case for 'she was sure the prince looked upon Hanover as a retreat in case the Jacobites in England ever got the better', and even claimed he had considered fleeing hither during the worst of the Excise Crisis in 1733.[84] Thus did the queen confirm Leslie's caricature of Hanover as the royal family's insurance against a Jacobite restoration, although not his corollary that this role encouraged them to aggrandize and enrich the electorate at British expense.

Yet Walpole feared that this would be precisely the outcome of any decision to dissolve union upon George II's death. He told Hervey that

> should this be done, it will ever after be such a series of rapaciousness to hoard at Hanover for the duke's grandeur and profit and the queen's security and retreat. And Hanover in all foreign negotiations would so cross on all our measures, that it is impossible to foresee half the difficulties it would bring upon us. Not but that I own, at the same time, it would in futurity be

[80] Hervey, *Some Materials towards Memoirs of the Reign of King George II*, ed. Sedgwick, ii, pp. 487–8.

[81] Quoted in Frances Harris, *A Passion for Government: The Life of Sarah, Duchess of Marlborough* (Oxford, 1991), p. 317.

[82] Hervey, *Some Materials towards Memoirs of the Reign of King George II*, ed. Sedgwick, iii, p. 795.

[83] Hervey, *Some Materials towards Memoirs of the Reign of King George II*, ed. Sedgwick, iii, p. 795.

[84] Hervey, *Some Materials towards Memoirs of the Reign of King George II*, ed. Sedgwick, iii, p. 796.

the greatest real benefit the sagacity of all mankind combined could procure for this country.[85]

Walpole revealed a frustration with union – and perhaps even a sentimental opposition to it – when it no longer suited his purposes. Hervey did him one better, even rebutting Walpole's misgivings about dissolution:

> as to Hanover crossing on all your foreign negotiations and your finding it mixed – and troublesomely mixed – in every consideration, is it not so now? Has it not been so ever since the Hanover family came here? And will it not continue so as long as the union of the dominions continue? And as to the queen's hoarding there for herself, believe me Sir, she will never go there. Though she would look on her English son as the devil and her Hanover heir as an angel, she will stay in this paradise with her devil sooner than go to that hell with her angel. She has too much pleasure in grandeur to exchange that she has been accustomed to in this country for the mean indigent scenes she knows she would be reduced to there.[86]

While Townshend had criticized Hanover before his first resignation in 1717, a minister had not attacked union with the electorate before Hervey did in the mid-1730s.

The 1739 war with Spain did little to dislodge the preeminence of George II's trips to Hanover in British discourse respecting dynastic union. His voyage of 1740 provoked more consternation; even the cabinet tried to dissuade him from going. The earl of Egmont reported that a soldier 'said there was no occasion to fight against Spain, but we should go to war with Hanover'.[87] One pro-union pamphlet claimed that Friedrich Wilhelm I's mortal illness had inspired the trip, and hoped that hoped that 'through His M-----y's presence at *Hanover* . . . the strict amity . . . so highly necessary for strengthening of the Protestant interest might be restor'd between the courts of *Great Britain* and *Prussia*'.[88] This recalled an earlier argument by the Scottish whig, Thomas Gordon of Kirkcudbright, that royal visits to Hanover assisted British diplomacy.[89] By this logic, George II's geographical proximity to the Prussian successor would reconcile their estranged royal houses.

---

85 Hervey, *Some Materials towards Memoirs of the Reign of King George II*, ed. Sedgwick, iii, p. 800.
86 Hervey, *Some Materials towards Memoirs of the Reign of King George II*, ed. Sedgwick, iii, pp. 800–1.
87 HMC, *Diary of Viscount Percival*, iii, p. 133.
88 *The Consequences of His Majesty's Journey to Hanover at This Critical Juncture Considered in a Letter from a Member of Parliament in Town to a Noble Duke in the Country* (London, 1740), p. 6.
89 [Thomas Gordon], *A Supplement to Three Political Letters to a Noble Lord Concerning Liberty and the Constitution, with a Political Dissertation on the Act of Settlement* (London, 1721), p. 20.

*

As is now known, George II's presence in Germany failed to prevent Friedrich II's seizure of the Austrian provinces in Silesia in 1740. French opportunism stiffened Britain's resolve to observe the Pragmatic Sanction, which obliged it to uphold Maria Theresia's title to the Austrian hereditary dominions. On 8 April 1741 George II asked parliament to finance 12,000 Danish and Hessian troops, as well as a direct subsidy of £300,000 to Austria. In doing so, the government realized it was once again potentially endangering Hanover – not least by angering Prussia, whose ministers had just recently informed British officials that the electorate 'would only be a breakfast' for their army.[90] It was true that Hanover risked itself by supporting the Imperial candidacy of Maria Theresia's husband, the grand duke of Tuscany.[91] But British subsidies had added material to moral support, compounding the electorate's vulnerability.

Walpole opted for the formulas of the past in moving to secure Hanover. Although he was never again as forward in support of the electorate as he had been in 1730–31, he once again associated its cause with his own. His son-in-law the earl of Cholmondeley proposed the renewal of the 1726 guarantee in the house of lords. The resolution's language almost perfectly followed that used fifteen years earlier, as did that of the house of commons, extending protection to 'any part of His Majesty's territories or dominions, though not belonging to Great Britain' which might be attacked 'in resentment of the just measures which His Majesty has so wisely taken'.[92] And once again, the resolution was supported by appeals to justice. Hervey's old intimate, Stephen Fox, argued in the commons that since the Hanoverians

> suffer for the cause which we are engaged to support and suffer only by our measures, we are at least as allies obliged by the laws of equity and the general compacts of mankind to arm in their defense. And what may be claimed by the common right of allies, we shall surely not deny them only because they are more closely united to us because they own the same monarch with ourselves.[93]

So Fox revived Horatio Walpole's case that Hanover was an ally. But as the younger Walpole had admitted, no treaties existed to prove it. The earl of

---

[90] Quoted in Jeremy Black, 'Foreign Policy in the Age of Walpole', in Jeremy Black, ed., *Britain in the Age of Walpole* (New York, 1984), p. 155.

[91] Black, *The Continental Commitment*, p. 37.

[92] Cobbett, ed., *The Parliamentary History of England*, xii, col. 158.

[93] Cobbett, ed., *The Parliamentary History*, xii, col. 159.

Hardwicke, lord chancellor, explained that this was because 'the parliament hath restrained the king from making an alliance with the elector of Hanover as he can with any other prince'.[94] Believing this to be the upshot of the Act of Settlement's war clause, Hardwicke justified parliament's unilateral assurance to Hanover. But his argument further undercut the government's case for personal union.

Opposition whigs were just as divided. The earl of Chesterfield accepted that Britain was in personal union with Hanover, but used personal union to distinguish rather than bind the two. He argued that 'there is no more need of mentioning Hanover than any other ally . . . the Hanoverians are not ourselves, but our allies'.[95] Other opposition figures believed the relationship was not close enough to personal union. Lord Gage thought 'it necessary to declare that Hanover is always to be considered as a sovereignty separate from that of Great Britain'.[96] His subsequent echo of William Pulteney's description of Hanover as 'dominions from which we never expected nor received any benefit'[97] implied a critique of misguided British imperialism in Hanover. It was of course untrue that Britons had never expected any benefit from Hanover, but Pulteney's speech can be seen as an expression of whig disappointment on that count.

Parliament renewed its guarantee of Hanover just in time for elections that spring. The opposition press leapt upon it, most flamboyantly with an anonymously authored pamphlet entitled *The Plain Truth*. *The Plain Truth* was probably written by the opposition whig James Ralph,[98] an American friend of Benjamin Franklin and Henry Fielding. Ralph adopted the line that Hanover had assumed imperial influence over Britain. Complaining that royal travel to Hanover was enriching the electorate at Britain's expense, Ralph wrote

> as for [Hanover] being a rich country, I don't believe it, though I do believe it is a great deal richer now than it was some years ago . . . One would think indeed it should be a finer one than *Engl--d*, by somebody's leaving *Eng--d* so often to go to it. But for all that, I am assur'd it is a very bad one, and I see but . . . one person in the world who has ever been there that desires to go there again.[99]

94 Cobbett, ed., *The Parliamentary History*, xii, col. 152 (note).
95 Cobbett, ed., *The Parliamentary History*, xii, cols. 151–2 (note).
96 Cobbett, ed., *The Parliamentary History*, xii, col. 167.
97 Cobbett, ed., *The Parliamentary History*, xii, col. 162.
98 William B. Coley, 'The "Remarkable Queries" in *The Champion*', *Philological Quarterly* 41 (1962), p. 436.
99 [James Ralph], *The Plain Truth: A Dialogue between Sir Courtly Jobber, Candidate for the Borough of Guzzledown, and Tom Telltruth, School-Master and Freeman in the Said Borough* (London, 1741), p. 20.

Ralph drew heavily on Jacobite caricature of royal travel to an inconsider-able electorate, which was again an issue. George II had visited Hanover in 1740, despite the war with Spain, and was preparing to visit again in the summer of 1741.

Ralph also feared that Britain's export of specie to Hanover was not merely inadvertent, as in the case of royal travel there. He implied that George II actually orchestrated it in the form of British assistance to Maria Theresia, which might be used to purchase his vote for her husband in the upcoming imperial election. Ralph wrote that 'I would not give this same queen a sh-----g for her s-re of it. It's all devoted to el-----s and el--------s. There's an ele----n indeed in another country this year, and el----rs are always paid their travelling charges'.[100] In so arguing Ralph followed Atterbury and George Lyttelton[101] in linking dynastic union with political corruption (albeit German) revealing a republican sensibility. He also wrote essays for his newspaper, *The Champion*, under the historically resonant name of 'Lilbourne'. This association had also influenced the pamphlet's title: *Plain Truth, without Fear or Flattery* was a 1647 work often attributed to John Lilburne the leveller.[102]

Ralph's republican perspective also revealed itself in a concern for a balanced constitution. He wrote,

> don't talk to me of preserving the balance of power in *Europe* when the bal-ance of our c-nst------n at home is destroy'd, and all the weight thrown into the c---n scale. Besides I don't see that anything has been done to preserve the balance of power in *Europe*, but I see a great deal that has been done to destroy it. We pull'd down the Emperor's power so low that we can't set it up again, and we set up the power of *France* so high that we can't pull it down again, and all this for the sake of *Han---r* too.[103]

This also revived a dormant Jacobite case against union, which had last been raised by the pretender and Charles Leslie in 1714–15: that dynastic union upset the European balance of power. But the argument's details had changed. Where the Jacobites, and Toland's *Limitations* before them, had worried that dynastic union would upset the balance of power in and of itself, Ralph claimed that it had merely interfered with Britain's disinterested defense of it during the period during the late 1720s and early 1730s.

Finally, Ralph refined the opposition's historical sensibility respecting union. He opposed parliament's recent guarantee of Hanover because it was 'declared to be for *Han--er*, as every step we have taken in foreign affairs

---

100 [Ralph], *The Plain Truth*, pp. 21–2.
101 See [George Lyttelton], *Letters from a Persian in England to His Friend at Ispahan* (London, 1735), p. 167.
102 Coley, 'The "Remarkable Queries" in the *Champion*', pp. 435–6.
103 [Ralph], *The Plain Truth*, p. 19.

have in truth been'. This was the most categorical statement yet that Hanover's interest trumped that of Britain. This attitude had informed Earbery's *Historical Account* (1722), but had not been explicitly stated before Ralph.

*The Plain Truth* was a programmatic as well as ideological innovation. Previously, opposition whigs had restricted their calls for union's dissolution to the house of commons. Ralph wrote that 'Han---r has cost us five and twenty millions. And I don't believe the fee-simple on't, if sold (as I heartily wish it were), is worth one quarter of that money.'[104] What appeared to be just a reiteration of an old slight against dynastic union (found first in *To Robert Walpole, Esq.*) actually contained the first printed demand for its dissolution by an opposition whig.

Ralph's pamphlet represented an unfortunate rhetorical development for dynastic union, but it was followed by equally disastrous diplomatic events. After concluding an alliance with Prussia, Louis XV deployed an army of 40,000 under the marquis de Maillebois in Westphalia. France endangered Hanover more than Austria ever had during the period 1725–31; in so doing it also threatened George II himself, who was visiting his electorate. The earl of Harrington, the British minister accompanying him, asked his colleagues for military assistance, indicating that the electorate might conclude a separate neutrality with France and/or Prussia in its absence. Although the British government offered to supplement the 12,000 foreign mercenaries with 12,000 British regulars, George II deemed this to be inadequate and sought neutrality anyway. Although open to a British quid pro quo in the form of peace with France's ally Spain, he eventually secured neutrality by voting for its client Karl Albrecht of Bavaria in the Imperial election.[105] In retrospect, George II observed that he had 'entirely detached English from German affairs'.[106]

Such a course of action was entirely compatible with the theory of personal union articulated for years by Walpole's government. But the latter nonetheless suffered greatly from it, because many of its publicists had argued for British empire over Hanover as well as personal union. This position had been sustainable as long as Britain took the initiative, and appeared to endanger Hanover in the process. Having extricated itself from danger by deserting the cause of Britain's ally Austria, Hanover became a great deal less sympathetic. France's apparent endorsement of personal union further poisoned that theory for British imperialists, as Austria's rejection of it had made it more appealing between 1726 and 1731. From now on, supporters of the government had to take one or the other position.

---

104 [Ralph], *The Plain Truth*, p. 19.
105 For a précis of the diplomacy leading to neutrality, see Uriel Dann, *Hanover and Great Britain 1740–1760: Diplomacy and Survival* (Leicester, 1991), pp. 34–9.
106 George II to Hardenberg, 4/15 Feb. 1742, quoted in Gert Brauer, *Die hannoverschenglischen Subsidienverträge 1702–1748* (Aalen, 1962), p. 120.

The British government's quandary was epitomized by Pelham's brother the duke of Newcastle. The secretary of state for the southern department had long been suspicious of Hanover.[107] Nevertheless he appeared to acquiesce in both personal union and neutrality when corresponding with Harrington in 1741. When the latter first broached the subject in the summer, Newcastle responded that 'we cannot presume to interfere in any other measures that His Majesty, as elector, may think proper to take for the security of his electoral dominions'.[108] And when the neutrality appeared imminent, Newcastle instructed Harrington to distance Britain from the neutrality in a manner consistent with personal union.[109] But he displayed rather less regard for it in private correspondence. He wrote to Hardwicke that 'the parliament had assured the king of the assistance of this country for his electorate if he exposed it on their account, but that . . . he had given up the interest of this country in order to secure the electorate'.[110] The interest he referred to was the support of Austria. Hanover had been pried from the pro-Austrian coalition, as had the Danish and Hessian mercenaries in British pay which now lingered in northern Germany to protect the electorate. For Newcastle, this inaction belied claims that Hanover was menaced on account of Britain's support for Austria.[111] Newcastle portrayed a form of British empire over Hanover which conferred responsibility without benefit. Both he and his brother Henry attributed the imbalance to the royal family's 'partiality to Hanover'.[112]

The Hanoverian neutrality horrified the Pelhams' political opponents, but for the opposite reason. Bolingbroke would also have accepted Hanoverian submission to British dominance, writing George Lyttelton to 'let Britain protect Hanover and the whole Protestant interest in Germany'.[113] But Bolingbroke believed the situation was just the reverse, that Hanover sought dominion over Britain. The idea 'that the foreign

---

107 See Newcastle's letter of 24 Nov. 1719, London, British Library (BL), Add. MS 32686, f. 88; Newcastle to W. Stanhope, 12/23 June 1729, London, published in Coxe, *Memoirs of the Life and Administration of Sir Robert Walpole*, ii, p. 644.

108 Newcastle to Harrington, 31 July 1741, London, The National Archives (NA), SP 43/30, f. 112.

109 Newcastle to Harrington, 25 Sept. 1741, London, BL, Add. MS 32698, f. 62.

110 Newcastle to Hardwicke, 18 Sept. 1741, Claremont, BL, Add. MS 32698, f. 52.

111 Newcastle to Hardwicke, 9 Sept. 1741, Claremont, published in Philip C. Yorke, *The Life and Correspondence of Philip Yorke, Earl of Hardwicke, Lord High Chancellor of Great Britain* (3 vols., Cambridge, 1913), i, p. 269; For Horatio Walpole's contrary view, see William Coxe, *Memoirs of Horatio, Lord Walpole* (London, 1802), p. 236.

112 Newcastle to Pelham, 2 Oct. 1741, Claremont, published in William Coxe, *Memoirs of the Administration of the Right Honourable Henry Pelham* (2 vols., London, 1829), i, p. 21; Pelham to Newcastle, 8 Oct. 1741, published in Coxe, *Memoirs of the Administration of the Right Honourable Henry Pelham*, i, p. 24.

113 Bolingbroke to Lyttelton, 4 Nov. 1741, published in Robert Phillimore, ed., *Memoirs and Correspondence of George, Lord Lyttelton from 1734 to 1773* (2 vols., London, 1845), i, p. 197.

interests of Britain must be conducted in a certain subordination to those of Hanover', he wrote, 'has corrupted our politics from the time that Bremen and Verden were acquired in direct violation of the guarantee of the crown of Britain. And this violation was maintained and established by powerful squadrons that were sent into the Baltic and that cost the nation more than £1,200,000.'[114] Bolingbroke had been the first Briton (in his capacity as James Stuart's ghost writer) to raise the alarm about Bremen and Verden, but his assumption of the electorate's pervasive influence owed something to *The Plain Truth*.

Ralph returned to this theme himself in *The Groans of Germany*, where he wrote that 'the aggrandizement and preservation of the *electorate* was the principal spring of the conduct of the court of *London*' in appeasing France since 1714.[115] This led him to reiterate his allegation that Hanover had distracted Britain from its defense of the European balance of power. He asked,

> who could ever suppose that *German* Protestant princes would confederate with *France* in dissolving the natural band of friendship that had subsisted between those whose union was necessary for keeping that ambitious crown within bounds? The reasons for the *Act of Settlement* in *England* were founded chiefly on a presumption that the *equilibrium* between the houses of Austria and Bourbon was not to be preserved without calling the electoral family of H------ to the *British* crown. This was also the motive for investing the house of H-----r with the electoral dignity. Let those who dare dispute these points . . . show better reasons for advancing to so stupendous a height a family far inferior in power and alliance to several other Protestant princes in *Germany*.[116]

Ralph followed Toland in tracing dynastic union to the balance of power, which Hanover now betrayed.

Ralph also broadened his critique of dynastic union, grounding it in Britain's particular interest as well as the general interest of Europe. Unknowingly echoing Newcastle,[117] Ralph feared that George II had secretly compromised Britain's war with Spain to obtain neutrality for Hanover. Suddenly, Britain's anemic performance in the Spanish war became understandable. Ralph wrote that

> the march of *French* troops towards H------ was as much, or more, in favor of *Spain* as on any other consideration. And since *France* is not as yet a match for

---

114 Bolingbroke to Lyttelton, 4 Nov. 1741, published in Phillimore, ed., *Memoirs and Correspondence of George, Lord Lyttelton*, i, p. 196.
115 [James Ralph], *The Groans of Germany* (London, 1741), p. 28. For the attribution, see John Burke Shipley, 'James Ralph: Pretender to Genius' (Ph.D. disseration, Columbia, 1963), pp. 351–2; 691.
116 [Ralph], *The Groans of Germany*, pp. 23–4.
117 Newcastle to Hardwicke, 9 Sept. 1741, Claremont, published in Yorke, *The Life and Correspondence of Philip Yorke, Earl of Hardwicke*, i, p. 269.

*Great Britain* at sea, I don't know whether the route to *H------* may not be the surest and shortest road to a peace for Spain. The farthest way about is often the nearest way home. And though the distance between *Madrid* or *Paris* and *London* is not so far as to *H----nh----n*, yet as the latter is not situated on an island [it] consequently can more easily be come at.[118]

Ralph's Spanish conjecture was incorrect, for it had been George II's electoral vote which sealed the neutrality. But it revived the maritime critique of empire over Hanover.

Because opposition figures could not know the neutrality's provisions, they continued to suspect it contained constraints upon the Spanish war. Conspiracy theories abounded when Spanish troop convoys evaded a British Mediterranean squadron to attack Habsburg possessions in Italy. John, Lord Carteret alleged in the lords that 'the invasion of Italy is permitted to preserve Hanover from the like calamity',[119] implying the existence of a British quid pro quo within the electoral neutrality. With more justice, he also inquired why Britain's foreign mercenaries had 'never marched beyond the territory of Hanover, nor left that blissful country for a single day'.[120]

Carteret was answered by Harrington, who made a last ditch defense of personal union. Accusing the opposition of inconsistency, he averred

> that the dominions of Great Britain and Hanover are distinct and independent of each other, has often been asserted and asserted with truth . . . I hope those who so studiously separate their interest on all other occasions will not now unite them only to reflect maliciously on the conduct of His Majesty.[121]

Harrington's charge was unfair. Opposition figures may have believed personal union to be the only satisfactory relationship with Hanover, but they had rarely believed it actually pertained. For years, they had perceived a more imperial relationship, while disagreeing about the seat of empire.

A good example of the opposition's perspective on personal union can be found in James Ralph's articles for *The Champion*. Writing as 'Lilbourne', he described Britain and Hanover as 'divided sovereignties'. Ralph picked up William Arnall's comparison of dynastic union to that between Sweden and Hesse-Cassell. Ralph praised Sweden's conduct with respect to Hesse-Cassell,

> by which it is evident that the head is the same, the bodies continue separate . . . the prejudices of the king in favor of his native country find no admittance into the senate . . . the king is ever to be found *resident* in his capital city at the head of the *commonwealth*, and *Sweden* is always at liberty to exert her whole

---

118 [Ralph], *The Groans of Germany*, p. 11.
119 Cobbett, ed., *The Parliamentary History*, xii, col. 257.
120 Cobbett, ed., *The Parliamentary History*, xii, col. 260.
121 Cobbett, ed., *The Parliamentary History*, xii, col. 284.

force in support of her own interest without fear of, or concern for, what may be the consequence to her sister by political marriage, *Hesse-Cassel*.

By contrast, the Act of Settlement ('a sort of second *Magna Charta*') had been violated during the Northern War, by 'repeated, expensive, foreign voyages', and by the recent Hanoverian idyll of Britain's foreign mercenaries.[122] Personal union had been vitiated by Hanoverian interest.

A similar ambivalence was revealed by the anonymous author of *A Letter from a Member of the Last Parliament to a New Member of the Present*. Echoing Chesterfield's acceptance of Hanover's status as a British ally, he criticized the neutrality on the grounds that it 'robbed us of the assistance of that very ally that was the dearest and most inseparable from us . . . the electorate of Hanover'.[123] But the same author undercut his own position in another passage, wherein he fervently wished to distance Britain from Hanover. He claimed that by dynastic union with that electorate, '*England* . . . has come to be placed, and design'd to be attacked, as if it were part of the continent. The great benefit of being an island, and not to be attacked by *France* or any other enemy, has been lost to us'.[124] Although the maritime argument was by no means incompatible with personal union, it more often criticised British empire over Hanover. Another anonymous journalist simply concluded that 'we must immediately bid adieu to H----r'.[125]

As it happened, Walpole had the same idea, and belatedly considered the dissolution which he had wistfully envisioned with Hervey. Arthur Onslow, the speaker of the house of commons, later remembered:

a little while before Sir Robert Walpole's fall, and as a popular act to save himself . . . he took me one day aside and said, 'What will you say, speaker, if this hand of mine shall bring a message from the king to the house of commons declaring his consent to having any of his family after his own death, to be made by act of parliament incapable of inheriting and enjoying the crown and possessing the electoral dominions at the same time'? My answer was, 'Sir, it will be as a message from heaven'. He replied, 'It will be done'. But it was not done, and I have good reason to believe it would have been opposed and

---

[122] *The Champion, or the Evening Advertiser* no. 342 (19 Jan. 1742), p. 1.

[123] *A Letter from a Member of the Last Parliament to a New Member of the Present Concerning the Conduct of the War with Spain* (London, 1742), p. 51.

[124] *A Letter from a Member of the Last Parliament*, p. 50. See also Bolingbroke to Marchmont, 6 Apr. 1742, published in Sir George Henry Rose, ed., *A Selection from the Papers of the Earls of Marchmont* (3 vols., London, 1831), ii, pp. 276–7.

[125] *A Letter to a Right Honourable Member of Parliament Demonstrating the Absolute Necessity of Great Britain's Assisting the House of Austria* (London, 1742), pp. 53–4. Another call for dissolution can be found in *The Champion, or the Evening Advertiser* no. 342 (19 Jan. 1742), p. 1.

rejected at that time because it came from him, and by the means of those who had always been most clamorous for it.[126]

Walpole's brainstorm represented a craven retreat from his previous doctrine, in which personal union prevented both Britain and Hanover from hurting one another. It might have comforted Walpole to think that Hanover, and not his person, was at issue in the winter of 1741–2. But he had identified himself so closely with the electorate during 1730 and 1731 that, as Onslow recognized, much of its unpopularity derived from his own. But where Walpole resigned in February 1742, the Hanoverian relationship persisted impervious to political vagaries.

Befitting a famously unimperial minister, Walpole preferred to discuss Hanover in terms of personal union rather than empire. While Walpole himself was relatively consistent, his publicity machine was not; some of his scribes nevertheless endorsed the idea of British empire over Hanover. But Walpole's opponents were equally divided, unsure of whether the empire they criticized was based in Britain or Hanover. The neutrality ended both these inconsistencies. It proved Hanover's independence, confuting the opposition critique of British empire over the electorate. But it also damaged personal union, demonstrating that it could work to Britain's disadvantage as well as to its profit. Britons were now divided between those who wanted to reassert control over the wayward electorate and those who wanted nothing to do with it.

---

126 Coxe, *Memoirs of the Life and Administration of Sir Robert Walpole*, ii, pp. 571–2.

# 4

# The War of Austrian Succession

The 1740s, during which Britain's assistance to Maria Theresia displaced its naval war against Spain, might seem to exemplify the distinction between overseas empire and continental diplomacy.[1] But while few historians have questioned the distinction between continental and maritime policy,[2] contemporaries perceived no such difference. Many British contemporaries would have preferred an empire free of European commitments. But the continental reality remained imperial, whether Hanover sought empire over Britain or vice versa. Further, the latter scenario of British empire over the electorate made great advances in government circles. Hanoverians also began to see advantages in British empire, which had once occasioned only apprehension. Few voices in either country argued for the existence of personal union, which had been discredited by Hanover's neutrality of 1741. Yet for all that most Britons and Hanoverians could agree that their countries' relationship was imperial, they differed over its desirability. This was particularly true of Britain, which staged its greatest debate over Hanover during the early 1740s.[3]

The revival of British imperialism towards Hanover was exemplified by the new government's dominant personality, Lord Carteret. The new secretary of state for the northern department had been a protégé of Stanhope, the last minister to represent such a view. Carteret had negotiated the Treaty of Stockholm for Stanhope, securing Sweden's official cession of Bremen and Verden to Hanover. The expansionist perspective had further informed his opposition to the Walpole's policy of personal union, especially after the 1741 neutrality. Carteret entered office in 1742 determined to undo it, and to impose British influence over the electorate. He told the Hanoverian

---

[1] Richard Pares, 'American versus Continental Warfare, 1739–63', *English Historical Review* 51 (1936), pp. 429–65; Jeremy Black, *America or Europe? British Foreign Policy, 1739–63* (London, 1998).
[2] For an exception, see Richard Harding, *Amphibious Warfare in the Eighteenth Century: The British Expedition to the West Indies 1740–1742* (London, 1991), pp. 185–97.
[3] See Frauke Geyken, ' "The German Language Is Spoken in Saxony with the Greatest Purity", or English Images and Perceptions of Germany in the Eighteenth Century', in Joseph Canning and Hermann Wellenreuther, eds., *Britain and Germany Compared: Nationality, Society and Nobility in the Eighteenth Century* (Göttingen, 2001), pp. 58–69.

minister in London, Ernst von Steinberg, that 'the distinction between His Majesty as king and as elector must cease'.[4] Although this comment was clearly incompatible with personal union, it did not specify the seat of empire. This Carteret confided to his secretary, who informed the British ambassador at The Hague 'that he stakes his whole on keeping the elector an Englishman'.[5] To sweeten the deal for Hanoverians, Carteret hinted at a British military subsidy.[6] War had strained Hanoverian finances, and the neutrality had foreclosed the possibility of British subventions.[7]

A subsidy would also at least partially redress the electoral vulnerability which would necessarily result from abrogating neutrality. It was part of the assistance Carteret promised, in case of an attack upon the electorate. Although this policy functioned similarly to Walpole's, its rationale was quite different. Walpole's assistance to Hanover only applied when the electorate was attacked because of British policy, and was therefore a defense of personal union and the two countries' consequent independence from one another. Conversely, Carteret likened Hanover to a British dominion when promising assistance to Steinberg.[8] The king's parsimony and belligerence overrode his amour propre, and he allowed the neutrality to lapse over the course of 1742.[9]

The government's move towards empire over Hanover occurred in secret. The first to express it publicly was the dean of Durham and provost of Eton, Henry Bland. Bland was a school friend of Walpole's,[10] and published a vindication of *The Conduct of the Late Administration with Regard to Foreign Affairs* in April 1742.[11] While British empire over Hanover had been an afterthought of Walpolean publicity, Bland now elevated it to the status of leitmotif. Equating the importance of dynastic union with that of the Protestant succession, he wrote that

---

4   Quoted and translated by Uriel Dann, *Hanover and Great Britain 1740–1760: Diplomacy and Survival* (Leicester, 1991), p. 45.

5   Weston to Trevor, 19/30 Mar. 1742, London, published in Historical Manuscripts Commission (HMC), *The Manuscripts of the Earl of Buckinghamshire, the Earl of Lindsey, the Earl of Onslow, Lord Emly, Theodore J. Hare, Esq., and James Round, Esq., M. P.* (London, 1895), p. 82.

6   Dann, *Hanover and Great Britain*, p. 45.

7   Gert Brauer, *Die hannoversch-englischen Subsidienverträge 1702–1748* (Aalen, 1962), pp. 119–23.

8   Dann, *Hanover and Great Britain*, p. 45.

9   Dann, *Hanover and Great Britain*, pp. 46–7.

10   For Bland, see Nicholas Carlisle, *Collections for a History of the Ancient Family of Bland* (London, 1826), pp. 107–14.

11   For the attribution, see *The Late Minister Unmask'd, or an Answer to a Late Pamphlet Entitled The Conduct of the Late Administration with Regard to Foreign Affairs* (London, 1742), passim.

a minister can never act up to the spirit of the *Revolution*, nor answer the ends of it, unless he have a constant eye to the defeating all secret as well as open attempts in favor of the *pretender*, and the supporting and even extending the power and influence of our present royal family in *Germany*. They are points so absolutely necessary towards strengthening the *Protestant* interest.[12]

Walpole's publicists may have advocated British influence over Hanover, but they never extended this to assisting the electorate's territorial expansion. Bland even celebrated its controversial purchase of Bremen and Verden. 'His late Majesty's acquisition of the duchies of *Bremen* and *Verden*', he remarked, 'render his royal heirs, in quality of electors, more useful to *Great Britain* than all other *Protestant* allies.'[13] Walpole's publicist James Pitt had also hitched dynastic union to the cause of the Protestant interest. But while Pitt had described Britain as irresolute, Bland restored it to the natural leadership of European Protestantism ascribed to it by Toland in *Anglia libera*.

Maillebois' presence in Westphalia delayed the Hanoverian subsidy until his departure for Bohemia later in 1742 freed the electoral army for service with the British army in Flanders. George II dispensed with the formality of negotiating with himself, and simply approved a contract hiring 16,000 Hanoverian mercenaries. Hanover received 167,079 florins more per month than it would have under its previous subsidy treaty with England of 1702,[14] although this apparent advantage was doubtless qualified by inflation. But Carteret was happy to hazard financial losses for the strategic coup of Hanover's return to quasi-belligerence.

Carteret had pursued an intellectually coherent policy on Hanover, one which he had impressed upon his ministerial colleagues, the king, and electoral officials. But consistent with the motto 'give any man the crown on his side, and he can defy everything',[15] Carteret felt less obliged to court public opinion; Bland's publication of similar views derived from ideological realignment rather than ministerial initiative. Where Walpole had usually saluted parliamentary sessions with a pamphlet, Carteret waited until parliament had already convened to pronounce his new theory of dynastic union – orally, in the house of lords. He noted that the Act of Settlement

> provided that this nation shall not be engaged in war in the quarrel of Hanover. But I see no traces of a reciprocal obligation, nor can discover any

---

[12] [Henry Bland], *The Conduct of the Late Administration with Regard to Foreign Affairs from 1722 to 1742, wherein That of the Right Honble the Earl of Orford (Late Sir Robert Walpole) Is Particularly Vindicated* (London, 1742), pp. 11–12.

[13] [Bland], *The Conduct of the Late Administration with Regard to Foreign Affairs*, p. 13.

[14] Brauer, *Die hannoversch-englischen Subsidienverträge*, p. 133.

[15] Horace Walpole to Mann, 26 Nov. 1744, published in W. S. Lewis, ed., *The Yale Edition of Horace Walpole's Correspondence* (48 vols., New Haven, 1937–83), xviii, p. 535.

clause by which we are forbidden to make use in our own cause of the alliance of Hanover, or by which the Hanoverians are forbidden to assist us.[16]

It is true that Carteret described Hanover as an ally, which implied its independence from Britain within personal union. But the argument was no less than the familiar imperialist perspective which held that Britain should manipulate Hanover through the mechanism of its absolute government.

Unfortunately for Carteret, some opposition peers did not share his Olympian indifference to public opinion. The earl of Chesterfield was the animating spirit of a redoubled whig opposition to dynastic union, despite his marriage to George I's natural daughter by his German mistress. His hostility to Hanover as ambassador to The Hague had greatly contributed to Britain's desertion of it during the negotiation of the Second Treaty of Vienna in 1731.[17] And after moving into opposition, he ridiculed dynastic union from the pages of *Common Sense*. The polemical thrust of these anti-Hanoverian articles had been, however, greatly diminished by their thick irony. Certainly, Chesterfield had celebrated aspects of dynastic union which he knew would actually alarm his readers. Chesterfield's assertion that 'instead of being a clog or encumbrance upon *England*, *Hanover* maintains more troops than *England* itself, which . . . may even be of use here if by groundless fears of mistaken frugality we should ever reduce our own military establishments too low' played into long-established fears of electoral invasion. But in establishing his expertise, Chesterfield had inadvertently exposed truths which flattered Hanover. He added, 'nor is it an absolute government and . . . can give our princes neither a taste of nor relish for unlimited power. The people have liberties and privileges and, the better to secure them, there are states composed of wise and grave persons'.[18] Perhaps drawing on information from his German wife, Chesterfield was the first Briton to acknowledge the Hanoverian estates' existence since the anonymous author of *British Advice* in 1715. But Chesterfield's slip changed British impressions of Hanoverian politics no more than its predecessor.

By 1742, Chesterfield still maintained his ironic perspective on Hanover when in private. For instance, he joked that 'if we have a mind effectually to prevent the pretender from ever obtaining this crown, we should make him elector of Hanover, for the people of England will never fetch another king

16 William Cobbett, ed., *The Parliamentary History of England* (36 vols., London, 1806–20), xii, col. 848.
17 See Chesterfield's letters to Harrington in William Coxe, *Memoirs of the Life and Administration of Sir Robert Walpole* (3 vols., London, 1798), iii, pp. 32–94, passim.
18 *Common Sense, or the Englishman's Journal* no. 14 (7 May 1737), p. 1. I base the attribution of this article upon stylistic similarities with another ascribed to Chesterfield in Matthew Maty, ed., *Miscellaneous Works of the Late Philip Dormer Stanhope, Earl of Chesterfield* (2 vols., London, 1777), i, pp. 104–8.

from there'.[19] But his public pronouncements were considerably more alarmist, reflecting perhaps the perspective of his collaborator the member of parliament Edmund Waller. He joined with Waller to publish *The Case of the Hanover Forces in the Pay of Great Britain Impartially and Freely Examined* immediately before the commons debate of 10 December on the Hanoverian troops.[20] Chesterfield was undeterred by the commons' subsequent approval of Carteret's design. He instigated a lords' protest to be debated on 1 February 1743,[21] which he and Waller again anticipated with a *Vindication* of their previous effort. And when this scheme failed in its turn, Chesterfield helped found a newspaper which attacked dynastic union on a weekly basis. He contributed an inaugural essay for *Old England, or the Constitutional Journal*, which was coedited by James Ralph and William Guthrie.[22] In so doing, Chesterfield made dynastic union a cause célèbre for the first time in its history.[23]

Chesterfield and Waller were not entirely opposed to Carteret's programme of extending British empire to Hanover. Indeed, their *Vindication* even commented that if the Act of Settlement had remained inviolate, 'time would insensibly have worn out those prejudices which divide the interests of the two dominions, and the lesser would have been, according to all true policy, absorbed in the greater'.[24] The conditional tense effectively overruled Toland, who had believed the Act of Settlement would guarantee British empire over Hanover in the absence of an electoral equivalent. But Chesterfield and Waller also questioned the desirability of British supremacy in the electorate. Firstly, maritime considerations continued to make empire on the European continent appear positively disadvantageous. *The Case of the Hanover Forces* paraphrased its namesake, *The Case of the Hessian Forces* (1731), observing that '*Hanover* robbed us of the benefit of being an island and was actually a pledge for our good behavior on the continent'.[25] Chesterfield and Waller perceived little else in Hanover that would outweigh its strategic liabilities. The earl of Sandwich echoed them when describing it to

[19] Horace Walpole to Mann, 9 Dec. 1742, London, published in Lewis, *The Yale Edition of Horace Walpole's Correspondence*, xviii, pp. 123–4.

[20] See William B. Todd, 'The Number, Order, and Authorship of the Hanover Pamphlets Attributed to Chesterfield', in *The Papers of the Bibliographical Society of America* 44 (1950), pp. 224–38.

[21] See Chesterfield to Marchmont, 5. Jan. 1743, published in Sir George Henry Rose, ed., *A Selection from the Papers of the Earls of Marchmont* (3 vols., London, 1831), ii, p. 290.

[22] Robert Harris, *A Patriot Press: National Politics and the London Press in the 1740s* (Oxford, 1993), pp. 39–41.

[23] 'Hanover's role in the war . . . remained at, or near to, the forefront of popular and press concern for most of this period [1742–44].' Harris, *A Patriot Press*, p. 177.

[24] [Philip Dormer Stanhope, 4th earl of Chesterfield, and Edmund Waller], *A Vindication of a Late Pamphlet Intitled the Case of the Hanover Troops Considered* (London, 1743), p. 42.

[25] [Philip Dormer Stanhope, 4th earl of Chesterfield, and Edmund Waller], *The Case of the Hanover Forces in the Pay of Great Britain Impartially and Freely Examined* (London, 1743), p. 27.

the lords as a 'petty dominion . . . which was, perhaps, only suffered to retain the appearance of a separate sovereignty because it was not worth the labor and expense of invasion, because it would neither increase riches nor titles, nor gratify either avarice or ambition'.[26]

Sandwich's statement appeared to ratify the existence of personal union between Britain and Hanover, which Chesterfield himself had endorsed while opposing parliament's 1741 guarantee of Hanover. In his inaugural essay for *Old England*, Chesterfield wrote that

> the people settled the crown upon the family of *Hanover* . . . [not] from their being persuaded that the crown of this kingdom, in right of blood, belonged to that house, but because they thought that the government of those princes bade fairest to make themselves happy. They thought that princes of that house having fewer connections with any interest upon the continent, destructive to that of *Great Britain*, would be more *independent* and less encumbered with any *foreign concern*, and consequently more at liberty to act for the interest of this nation.[27]

This was revisionist history, to say the least. The British succession had devolved upon the house of Hanover because it had a better hereditary claim than any other Protestant family. And in underestimating the electorate's continental commitments, Chesterfield overcompensated for Toland's exaggeration of them. Inaccuracies notwithstanding, the passage's wistful tone indicated that Chesterfield's allegiance to personal union had died during the uproar over Hanoverian neutrality.

The one remaining diagnosis, that which Chesterfield and Waller accepted, was that of Hanoverian empire over Britain. In this, they drew heavily upon James Ralph. They adopted his historical perspective, demonstrating at great detail how 'the British empire was . . . steer'd by the Hanover rudder'[28] since 1714. Ralph repaid the compliment by quoting extensively from their historical analysis in his *Critical History of the Administration of Sir Robert Walpole*, which he published in March 1743.

The first manifestation of Hanover's purported empire over Britain was the electorate's attempt to engage Britain in its territorial expansion. Chesterfield and Waller presented a plausible explanation for this in their *Vindication*, where they wrote

> as our security arises from our being an island, the danger of *Hanover* arises from its being upon the continent and surrounded by princes infinitely more powerful. *Hanover* views them with fear and envy. They view *Hanover* with

---

26 Cobbett, ed., *The Parliamentary History*, xii, col. 1077.

27 *A Collection of Letters Publish'd in Old England, or the Constitutional Journal* (London, 1743), p. 3. For the attribution, see Maty, ed., *Miscellaneous Works of the Late Philip Dormer Stanhope, Earl of Chesterfield*, i, p. 110.

28 [Chesterfield, and Waller], *The Case of the Hanover Forces*, p. 10.

some jealousy . . . *Hanover* wants to extend itself in order to be nearer a match for its neighbors, which they are determined to prevent if they can. These circumstances must eternally for the future, as they have done for the time past, fatally involve us in all the affairs of the continent.[29]

There was, of course, the familiar episode of Bremen and Verden, but also what Chesterfield and Waller whimsically termed the affair 'of the *Prussian bearskin*'.[30] During the winter of 1741, George II had contemplated an Austro-Hanoverian partition of Prussian territory. He abandoned these plans sometime before requesting the Austrian subsidy of April 1741.[31] But they were 'inadvertently disclosed in early 1742 through the inadequate censorship of diplomatic papers placed before parliament on the eve of Walpole's fall'.[32] Chesterfield and Waller implied that the electorate had been forced 'to empty its sacred coffers' in preparation for the abortive partition of Prussia, and had taken 'the first favorable opportunity to replenish them' by renting its soldiers to Britain.[33]

Chesterfield and Waller complained in their *Vindication* that, by the employment of Hanoverian mercenaries, 'we are now to enrich the dominions we cannot enlarge'.[34] They continued further, saying that 'the extraordinary sum demanded for these *Hanover* troops . . . plainly proves that all we are now doing upon the continent is only a pretence to give that very sum'.[35] Chesterfield elaborated upon this argument in the lords, where he said that

> the long stay of the troops in Flanders, a place where there is no enemy to encounter . . . is a sufficient proof that there is nothing more designed than that the troops of Hanover shall loiter on the verge of war and receive their pay for feasting in their quarters and showing their arms at a review, and that they in reality design nothing but to return home with full pockets, and enjoy the spoils of Great Britain.[36]

Of course, the employment of Hanoverian mercenaries was merely the latest measure suspected of diverting British specie to the electorate. Another opposition whig peer, the duke of Bedford, alleged that British specie had converted Hanover into a latter-day El Dorado. 'The state of the country', he told the lords, 'has, since the accession of its princes to this throne, been

29 [Chesterfield, and Waller], *A Vindication of a Late Pamphlet*, pp. 26–7.
30 [Chesterfield, and Waller], *The Case of the Hanover Forces*, p. 26.
31 Dann, *Hanover and Great Britain*, pp. 27–31.
32 Harris, *A Patriot Press*, p. 147.
33 [Chesterfield, and Waller], *The Case of the Hanover Forces*, p. 27.
34 [Chesterfield, and Waller], *A Vindication of a Late Pamphlet*, p. 41.
35 [Chesterfield, and Waller], *A Vindication of a Late Pamphlet*, p. 43.
36 Cobbett, ed., *The Parliamentary History*, xii, col. 1144.

changed without any visible cause. Affluence has begun to wanton in their towns and gold to glitter in their cottages without the discovery of mines or the increase of their trade.'[37] This was fanciful but logical, if one believed that specie (still considered the best index of wealth) had been transported to the electorate for almost thirty years. According to the perspective which detected Hanoverian empire over Britain, the subsidy resembled imperial tribute which threatened to make the latter 'a money-province to that electorate'.[38]

War secretary Sir William Yonge assured the commons that the Hanoverians' 'march into Flanders is a manifest proof that this measure was not calculated for the enriching of Hanover because the money we pay to them will not be spent in Hanover, but in Flanders'.[39] Waller conceded to the commons that much British specie would wind up in Flanders rather than Hanover. But he asked 'will not the maintaining of 16,000 men, which must otherwise have been maintained by the electorate itself, be an advantage to it?'[40] Indeed, this had been George II's rationale.

Waller furthermore noted Britain's payment of levy and recruitment money, which would be spent in Hanover. This observation inspired at least two members of parliament to examine the Hanoverian contract of 1742 in a comparative framework. John Philipps, a Welsh Jacobite, remarked that the levy money was 'to be paid for forces that were not raised for our service, but had been long on foot'. He further noted that the levy money 'amounts to near four times as much as the subsidy we pay for the Hessians'.[41] James Stanley, Lord Strange, an independent member for Lancashire, commented that Britain had not paid levy money to Hanover the last time it had hired Hanoverian mercenaries in 1702. Strange added that Britain had never before paid recruitment money to any mercenary prince – 'an article of expense which was never allowed even to our own army because this service is always provided for out of the savings that necessarily happen every year by men's' dying, deserting, or being killed'.[42] Such comparisons led Strange to conclude that 'the elector of Hanover may ask what he pleases for his troops, and his British ministers . . . have complaisance enough to agree to all his demands'.[43]

All this recalled the association of dynastic union with British political corruption. The veteran Jacobite member of parliament Sir John St Aubyn considered that Carteret 'had flattered his master's passions to secure his own

37 Cobbett, ed., *The Parliamentary History*, xii, col. 1090.
38 [Chesterfield, and Waller], *The Case of the Hanover Forces*, p. 83.
39 Cobbett, ed., *The Parliamentary History*, xii, col. 945.
40 Cobbett, ed., *The Parliamentary History*, xii, col. 956.
41 Cobbett, ed., *The Parliamentary History*, xii, col. 1016.
42 Cobbett, ed., *The Parliamentary History*, xii, col. 1007.
43 Cobbett, ed., *The Parliamentary History*, xii, col. 1009.

power and had taken advantage of a virtuous quality in his prince, a love for his native country, to persaude him to a thing which might be a prejudice both to that country and this'.[44] As had Drake's in 1702, St Aubyn's ostensibly sympathetic approach to royal favoritism for Hanover nonetheless damned with faint praise. Its emphasis upon birth in the formation of national loyalties advantaged the British-born pretender over a king who had actually spent far more time in the country.

Other opposition whigs were not so generous. Another literary nobleman, Chesterfield's friend the earl of Marchmont, alleged in the anonymously published *Present Interest of the People of Great Britain at Home and Abroad* that 'the king of *Great Britain*, as possess'd of absolute power in *Hanover*, must look upon all the advantages of a good bargain to that electorate as accruing to his own pocket'.[45] Marchmont probably felt vindicated when he later heard that George II had justified his visits to the electorate by likening it to a British country seat.[46] If the king was enriching what amounted to a private estate, he was just as venal as his ministers. Jacobites had accused elector-kings of transporting British specie to Hanover for self-interested reasons since early 1715. But Marchmont was the first opponent of dynastic union to explain this explicitly in terms of his absolute rule of the electorate.

Marchmont was typical of the near-consensus prevailing in Britain that George II governed Hanover absolutely. But Britons rarely paused to consider the bases of his absolute rule in the electorate. One who did was St Aubyn, who pronounced in the commons that

> the elector of Hanover, as elector of Hanover, is an arbitrary prince; his electoral army is the instrument of that power. As king of Great Britain, he is a restrained monarch . . . the hearts of the British soldiery are as yet free and untainted, yet I fear that too long an intercourse may beget a dangerous familiarity, and they may hereafter become a joint instrument . . . to invade our liberties.[47]

[44] Stephen Taylor and Clyve Jones, eds., *Tory and Whig: The Parliamentary Papers of Edward Harley, 3rd Earl of Oxford, and William Hay, M. P. for Seaford 1716–1753* (Woodbridge, 1998), p. 187.

[45] [Hugh Hume Campbell, 3rd earl of Marchmont], *The Present Interest of the People of Great Britain at Home and Abroad, Considered in a Letter to a Member of Parliament* (London, [1742]), p. 22. For the attribution, see Allen T. Hazen, *A Catalogue of Horace Walpole's Library* (3 vols., New Haven, 1969), i, p. 449.

[46] George II 'said . . . that the people here were angry at his going to Hanover when they went all out of town to their country seats, but it was unjust, for Hanover was his country seat and he had no other'. Sir George Henry Rose, ed., *A Selection from the Papers of the Earls of Marchmont* (3 vols., London, 1831), i, p. 54. For another such comparison by George II, see Jeremy Black, *The Hanoverians: The History of a Dynasty* (London, 2004), p. 193.

[47] Cobbett, ed., *The Parliamentary History*, xii, col. 952.

St Aubyn retailed the pretender's secular account of Hanoverian despotism, which had been articulated so well in 1717 by Shippen and *The Necessity of a Plot*.

St Aubyn left the details of how the electoral mercenaries might 'invade our liberties' to other parliamentary speakers. His fellow Jacobite John Philipps revived Drake's republican fear that Hanover might impoverish Britain to reduce its capacity to resist tyranny. The Hanoverian mercenaries, he said, 'must suck the blood and vitals of this kingdom. And as they drain us they must necessarily tend to enslave us, and to deprive us of that power of resistance which every Englishman is entitled to whenever his property shall happen to be invaded.'[48] But other opposition figures favored a straightforward invasion scenario. Marchmont worried in *The Present Interest* that Hanoverian mercenaries differed from those from other countries, whose

> natural masters will not agree to their acting but in consequence of the design and upon the principles for which they were hir'd . . . How very different is this from the case where both principals and auxiliaries own the same prince as their natural head? For then in case of any arbitrary views he may entertain upon the rights and the liberty of that part of his dominions which is free, he is sure of being assisted with the forces of the other part where he is absolute and who are paid by the very people whom he may design to suppress.[49]

Marchmont was careful not to be more specific. But the corporation of London had already instructed its members of parliament to withhold supply, in part because 'the people are not a little alarmed that an army of *Hanoverians* has been brought so near them as *Flanders*'.[50] Opposition whigs reclaimed the invasion thesis from the Jacobites who had been its primary exponents since 1705.

How could dynastic union's opponents sustain the invasion thesis in the face of Hanover's manifest military weakness? Hanover's vulnerability after 1725 had led opposition whigs to borrow the pretender's charge that Hanover was 'inconsiderable', while ignoring the possibility of electoral invasion. Opposition whigs did not sacrifice their low estimation of Hanover during the winter of 1742–43, but the Hanoverian troops' presence in Flanders called out for vigilance. Marchmont attempted to reconcile these seemingly incompatible positions, writing that 'the forces of H----- in themselves are too weak' to invade Britain, but wondered what they might be capable of 'when join'd on the continent by a body of mercenaries in our own pay'.[51]

Chesterfield and Waller elaborated and spread a complex argument for

48 Cobbett, ed., *The Parliamentary History*, xii, col. 1017.
49 [Marchmont], *The Present Interest of the People of Great Britain*, pp. 21–2.
50 *A Letter to My Lord Mayor Vindicating the Late Instructions from the City of London for Postponing the Subsidies to the Redress of Grievances* (London, 1742), p. 14.
51 [Marchmont], *The Present Interest of the People of Great Britain*, p. 22.

the existence of Hanoverian empire over Britain, to which they also proposed a solution. As had John Barnard in 1730, they regretted 'that by the Act of Settlement the *Hanover* dominions were not originally separated from those of *Great Britain*'. And as had Barnard in 1731, they moved from nostalgia to programme. Just as he had seconded Aston's recommendation that the electorate be put under the duke of Cumberland, Chesterfield and Waller urged that Hanover be 'willingly parted with to a younger branch of the royal family'.[52] Chesterfield's and Waller's anti-union programme became general among opposition whigs from this point.

Carteret was temperamentally unfit to orchestrate publicity in the manner of Chesterfield. But limited intellectual options after personal union's self-destruction in 1741 partially remedied the lack of leadership from Carteret, by imposing its own form of discipline. Supporters of government hewed entirely to arguments for British primacy over Hanover. Lord Chancellor Hardwicke confessed,

> why the hire of troops of any particular country should be considered as an act of submission to it or of dependency upon it, I cannot discover . . . To hire foreigners, of whatever country, only to save the blood of Englishmen is, in my opinion, an instance of preference which ought to produce rather acknowledgments of gratitude than sallies of indignation.[53]

And despite his earlier promise to assist Hanover in case of attack due to British policy, Carteret himself reassured the lords that it would be unnecessary 'to endeavor the preservation of dominions which their own sovereign is inclined to hazard'.[54] In doing so, he even further distanced himself from his predecessor's policy respecting dynastic union.

More specifically, supporters of government attempted to show that the subsidy was in fact more advantageous to Britain than the opposition had claimed. Pro-Hanoverians argued, for example, that dynastic union actually made electoral mercenaries more rather than less attractive.[55] The pro-union *Letter to a Friend in the Country* noted that 'we pay only for the forces, and no subsidy' such as Britain would ordinarily have to pay other German princes.[56] Aside from economics, there was also a republican logic for the Hanoverians' hire. Alluding to the notorious unreliability of mercenaries in general, Lord Bathurst informed the lords that

> there was . . . no objection against the troops of Hanover that was not of equal strength against all foreign troops, and there was at least one argument in their

---

[52] [Chesterfield, and Waller], A *Vindication of a Late Pamphlet*, p. 42.
[53] Cobbett, ed., *The Parliamentary History*, xii, col. 1179.
[54] Cobbett, ed., *The Parliamentary History*, xii, col. 1085.
[55] See Taylor and Jones, eds., *Tory and Whig*, p. 184.
[56] A *Letter to a Friend in the Country upon Occasion of the Many Scurrilous Libels Which Have Been Lately Publish'd* (London, 1743), p. 47.

favor: that they were subjects of the same prince, and that therefore we could have no reason to fear their defection or to suspect their fidelity.[57]

Bathurst was a tory who had criticized the Hanoverian neutrality[58] before joining the court after Walpole's fall.[59] Interestingly, the other members of parliament to make the same argument – Stephen Fox's younger brother Henry and John, Lord Perceval[60] – also had recent opposition backgrounds. Perhaps they were better prepared than government time-servers to refute republican arguments on their own terms.

The appeal of British empire over Hanover even won over former exponents of personal union, most notably Horatio Walpole. In the face of the ministry's active discouragement,[61] he published a defense of union entitled *The Interest of Great Britain Steadily Pursued*. Answering Chesterfield's and Waller's account of the Hanoverian acquisition of Bremen and Verden, Walpole frère remarked that

> whether it be most for the interest of *Great Britain* that those countries which command the navigation of the *Elbe* and *Weser*, the only inlets from the *British* seas in *Germany*, and which in case of any disturbance in the *North* are most capable of protecting or interrupting the *British* trade to *Hamburg*, should remain in the hands of *Denmark*, who has frequently formed pretensions to that City, or of *Sweden*, who molested our commerce in the *Baltic*, rather than be annex'd for ever to the king's electoral dominions is a question which can easily be decided by a bare inspection into the map of *Europe*.[62]

This was, of course, the very same argument advanced by 1717's *Some Considerations*.

*The Interest of Great Britain* was answered, predictably enough, by *The Interest of Hanover Steadily Pursued since the A------n*. The pamphlet has traditionally been ascribed to Chesterfield, but William Todd questioned this attribution in his study of Chesterfield's Hanoverian pamphlets.[63] Todd's textual analysis was shoddy,[64] and overlooked passages which almost

---

57 Cobbett, ed., *The Parliamentary History*, xii, col. 1099.
58 Cobbett, ed., *The Parliamentary History*, xii, col. 286.
59 Linda Colley, *In Defiance of Oligarchy: The Tory Party 1714–60* (Cambridge, 1982), p. 239.
60 For their comments, see Cobbett, ed., *The Parliamentary History*, xii, cols. 1031, 1045–6.
61 For this, see Harris, *A Patriot Press*, p. 36.
62 [Horatio Walpole], *The Interest of Great Britain Steadily Pursued* (London, 1743), pp. 12–13.
63 Todd, 'The Number, Order, and Authorship of the Hanover Pamphlets Attributed to Chesterfield', pp. 233–4.
64 Todd's reading of the passage, 'you were answering . . . as fast a friend as any in the nation to our present happy settlement', was that the author of *The interest of Hanover* was a friend of the author of *The Case of the Hanover Forces*. But it is obvious that the author meant 'a friend . . . to our present happy settlement'.

perfectly copied sections of Chesterfield's and Waller's *Vindication*.[65] This could have resulted from another journalist's plagiarism, but there is little reason in any case to disqualify Chesterfield as its author. In any case, Horatio Walpole's revival of *Some Considerations'* case for Hanoverian possession of Bremen and Verden prompted the author of *The Interest of Hanover* to complain that

> he cannot look upon His Majesty's having *German ports* which open into the *British* seas any additional security to his *freedom* . . . Suppose any [future elector-king] should take a whim of being as absolute here as at *Hanover*, and should think it a proper season to become so when he should see us reduced by *poverty* and spirit-broken by a multitude of legal restraints . . . could anything facilitate the execution of such a scheme of *slavery* so much as the having ports of his own, where he might order as many foreign troops to be embark'd as he should think necessary for fitting us with manacles by means of these ports, these outlets from *Germany*.[66]

This was nothing less than Toland's invasion scenario, leavened by Drake's fear that export of wealth would reduce British resistance to tyranny.

The battle of Dettingen, fought in summer 1743, intensified the British furor over dynastic union. Dettingen is most famous as the last battle in which a British monarch personally led his troops in battle. But its contemporary significance was as a symbol of dynastic union.[67] Indeed, Dettingen provided the union's opponents with their most vivid iconography yet. Its events and personalities translated easily into the relatively accessible forms of popular ballads and prints. As Ranke observed, 'the question of the relation of Hanover to England . . . became at this moment the most important of all questions'.[68]

The British commander, Lord Stair, led his army from Flanders to Germany during the spring of 1743. George II joined it in the Main river valley, where it subsequently defeated a French army on 16/27 June. In retrospect, Dettingen seems a strange battle to have celebrated. Technically, British troops were not principals but auxiliaries in the service of Maria Theresa. But part of the British public cheered Dettingen anyway, as the nation's first military triumph since the capture of Porto Bello in 1739. The

---

[65] Compare, for example, pp. 29–30 of *The Interest of Hanover* with p. 41 of the *Vindication*.

[66] [Philip Dormer Stanhope, 4th Earl of Chesterfield], *The Interest of Hanover Steadily Pursued since the A-------n* (London, 1743), pp. 38–9.

[67] Sebastian Küster, *Vier Monarchien – Vier Öffentlichkeiten: Kommunikation um die Schlacht bei Dettingen* (Munster, 2004), pp. 333–448.

[68] Leopold von Ranke, *A History of England Principally in the Seventeenth Century*, trans. C. W. Boase, W. W. Jackson, H. B. George, H. F. Pelham, M. Creighton, A. Watson, G. W. Kitchin, A Plummer (6 vols., Oxford, 1875), p. 408.

government fed this appetite with a burst of triumphalist literature. And while the publicity directly relating to the battle took no overt notice of dynastic union, the battle did occasion the most detailed defense of the government's employment of Hanoverian mercenaries. This was *Faction Detected*, written by Egmont's son John, Lord Perceval.

Opposition whigs were not above turning a victorious battle against dynastic union. *Old England* noted Cumberland's heroics (he was wounded in the leg) in its issue of 17 September 1743, and proposed rewarding him with the electorate of Hanover. This was, of course, the same expedient proposed by Aston in 1731. But where most opponents of union believed that its end would be a benefit in and of itself, *Old England* argued that Britain would especially profit from its devolution to Cumberland.

> it [might] be urg'd that His Royal Highness *the duke*, when once elector of *Hanover*, might, as many princes have done before him, forget his connection with *England* and all ties of blood and pursue his separate electoral interests only, and that consequently we might lose the many benefits we now enjoy by the union of *Hanover* with *England* in the same person. As to the first I beg leave to say that I have many reasons and *some experience* for thinking that His Royal Highness's possession of and residence at *Hanover* will rather endear *England* the more to him, and that his natural partiality for the country he was born in will prevail over all little political considerations whatsoever, and that we might then upon all occasions depend upon the *unsubsided* assistance of the Hanoverian forces.[69]

Just as the victory had temporarily forced the opposition to commend the duke, it also encouraged them to pay ironical lip service to Carteret's idea of British empire over the electorate. The author insinuated, by means of the italicized phrase 'some experience', that natal bias would incline Cumberland to British advantage just as had that of his father and grandfather to electoral interests.

Rumors of royal partiality towards the Hanoverian auxiliaries, related in the correspondence of British officers and politicians in Germany,[70] spared the opposition any further acknowledgments of Dettingen's glory. These rumors became public after Stair's resignation, which was announced by *Old England* in its issue of 24 September. In a memorial to the king which was later published, the general complained of the disregard he considered he suffered. Ominously, Stair was already in the confidence of Chesterfield, to whom he sent an early draft of the memorial.[71] Stair did not explicitly

---

[69] *Two Letters Publish'd in Old England, or the Constitutional Journal* (London, 1743), p. 6.
[70] For this, see Brauer, *Die hannoversch-englischen Subsidienverträge*, pp. 143–5.
[71] Eliga Gould, 'War, Empire, and the Language of State Formation: British Imperial Culture in the Age of the American Revolution' (Ph. D. dissertation, Johns Hopkins, 1992), p. 39 (note).

complain about pro-Hanoverian favoritism in his memorial. But the opposition reported it nevertheless. A *True Dialogue* published in November 1743 alleged that after the king's arrival, Hanoverian generals had 'govern'd everything, and neither the earl of *Stair* nor any *E----sh* officer was ever consulted'.[72]

Hanoverian primacy at Dettingen reinforced British suspicions of electoral empire over Britain. *Old England* opined,

> something . . . seems to be due to the rank of the *English* as a nation . . . something to the friendly, generous, charitable, disinterested part they have been induced to act in the present GERMAN WAR, and something to their being *pay-masters* to these very *Hanoverians*, who . . . are thus playing the part of *Jacob* and cheating them of their *birthright*. For wages imply both subordinacy and subjection, and nothing can be more absurd than that he who covenants to be my servant should take my money and not only refuse to obey my commands but insist on doing all the honors of my house.[73]

This passage demonstrated how Hanover supposedly masked its mastery of Britain behind outward inferiority, but did not explain how the electorate achieved a degree of influence so disproportionate to its modest geopolitical status.

The answer was, as usual, royal bias. The opposition press construed George II's active interest in the Hanoverians' provisions as favoritism.[74] Journalists dwelt upon alleged disparities in Hanoverian and English rations. The *True Dialogue* reported that Hanoverians 'had their bellies full while we were starv'd, and the *English* could have nothing till the *H--------ns* were first serv'd'.[75] One popular drinking song, the *H-n---r Scrubs, or a Bumper to Old England – Huzza*, even claimed that the Hanoverians were too well-fed to fight during the battle at Dettingen:

> Their bellies so full, too unwieldy to fight,
> For decency they stepp'd aside for to sh--e.[76]

In such representations, provisioning at Dettingen became a microcosm of the economic imperialism opposition figures suspected Hanover of exercising over Britain.

---

72 A *True Dialogue between Thomas Jones, a Trooper Lately Return'd from Germany, and John Smith, a Serjeant in the First Regiment of Foot-Guards* (London, 1743), p. 4.
73 *Old England, or the Constitutional Journal* no. 36 (8 Oct. 1743), p. 1.
74 For George II's solicitude, see Brauer, *Die hannoversch-englischen Subsidienverträge*, pp. 134–8.
75 A *True Dialogue*, p. 3.
76 *Beef and Butt Beer against Mum and Pumpernickle; H-n---r Scrubs, or a Bumper to Old England – Huzza* (London, 1743), p. 7.

Their supposed voracity was not the only reason the opposition press deemed the Hanoverians to have fought disgracefully at Dettingen. Opposition politicians had already questioned the bravery of Hanoverian soldiers during the parliamentary debates of the previous winter.[77] Dettingen now amplified these allegations. The first instance of supposed Hanoverian cowardice came before the battle, when most of the electoral troops brought up the army's rear. This position could well have been more exposed had the French harried the British army, which was retreating at the time. But as it happened the Hanoverians were spared the brunt of the onslaught when the French instead decided to attack the British vanguard. The question was whether George II had anticipated French tactics or not – in other words, whether he had intended to sacrifice or shield his electoral troops. Ultimately, either interpretation served the purposes of *Old England* equally well. The paper observed that 'whether this disposition of the *Hanoverian mercenaries* [in the rear] was made to do them honor or provide for their security, either way PARTIALITY must have been the motive'.[78]

The opposition was more certain of Hanoverian cowardice in an individual case. A Hanoverian general, one Thomas Eberhard von Ilten, supposedly refused Stair's order to pursue the retreating French after the battle. *Old England* introduced Ilten to the British public in its issue of 24 September 1743. Ilten, it said 'had posted himself . . . very *advantageously* behind a tree, and urg'd in excuse for his conduct that it was his duty to PRESERVE the king's troops, which procured him the droll title of His M-----y's CONFECTIONER'.[79] Grotesque satire, such as that which also lampooned his countrymen in the collective, was particularly unkind to Ilten. A popular ballad entitled *The Yellow Sash, or H-----r Beshit* recalled that

> The bold *English* call'd out who can now be afraid?
> What a question to ILTEN then quaking for fear;
> Who behind a great tree was then running full speed,
> Letting fly as he went a discharge from his rear.[80]

In British satire, Ilten came to personify his own corps. The accusations of cowardice prompted at least one member of parliament who had voted for the Hanoverians in December 1742, Vere Poulett, to retract his support for their employment in January 1744.[81]

Ilten's inaction revealed the Hanoverians' true motivation, wrote opposition publicists. The *True Dialogue* observed that 'they were only to be paid,

---

[77] See, for example, Sandwich's speech in Cobbett, ed., *The Parliamentary History*, xii, col. 1077.
[78] *Old England, or the Constitutional Journal* no. 41 (12 Nov. 1743), p. 2.
[79] *Two Letters Publish'd in Old England, or the Constitutional Journal*, p. 16 (note).
[80] *The Yellow Sash, or H-----r Beshit* (London, 1743), p. 6.
[81] William Cobbett, ed., *The Parliamentary History of England* (London, 1812), xiii, col. 485.

and not expos'd'.[82] With this in mind, other opposition journalists suggested that Hanoverian soldiers had deliberately sabotaged the victory, so that France would not have to sue for peace. *The Westminster Journal* wrote in its 'Chronicle and Lamentation for the Year 1743':

> this was the reasoning of the *Ha-------ns* when they communed together: do we not receive *E----sh* pay? Wherefore then should we at once put an end to the war, and be sent home to eat up our farmers and burghers? Surely the *k---* desireth it not, for he loveth his people.[83]

According to this interpretation, cowardice also profited the electorate at Britain's expense.

The opposition further insinuated that Hanover had prolonged the war in another context, and for other motives. Carteret had capitalized upon Dettingen by discussing peace with the Emperor's surrogate, Prince Wilhelm of Hesse-Cassel, at Hanau in July 1743. But the negotiations had foundered upon Austrian demands for an equivalent of Silesia. Edmund Waller, speaking to the commons in December 1743, detected Hanoverian machinations behind the failure to conclude peace:

> if France . . . had offered some bishopric, or some additional territory, to Hanover at the same time that she offered to withdraw her troops from Germany, the project of giving an equivalent to the queen of Hungary would never have been set up by our ministers, and the tranquility of Europe, or at least of Germany, would have been restored before this time.[84]

The bishoprics which Hanover was suspected of demanding were the adjacent territories of Hildesheim and Osnabrück, the latter of which alternated in the electoral family according to the Peace of Westphalia but which was currently ruled by a Catholic bishop. Waller's accusation was completely unfounded,[85] but allowed the opposition to continue its allegations of Hanoverian territorial, as well as pecuniary, greed.

But most of all, Ilten's purported recalcitrance at Dettingen afforded opposition publicists another opportunity to skewer the royal prejudice for Hanover. The *True Dialogue* explained that British troops would have chased the French without the Hanoverians, but that 'just as they were going *somebody* in a *yellow scarf* came up and forbid 'em saying, *there was blood enough spilt already* and that he wou'd have no more'.[86] That somebody was

---

82 A *True Dialogue*, p. 5.
83 *The Westminster Journal, or New Weekly Miscellany* no. 100 (22 Oct. 1743), p. 1.
84 Cobbett, ed., *The Parliamentary History*, xiii, col. 235.
85 'It is difficult to see how Hanoverian interests were directly affected by either the acceptance or the rejection of the Hanau propositions'. Sir Richard Lodge, 'The So-Called "Treaty" of Hanau of 1743', *The English Historical Review* 38 (1923), p. 399.
86 A *True Dialogue*, p. 6.

George II. Dettingen may have been the last battle personally directed by a British king, but George II identified more as the elector of Hanover by wearing a yellow rather than red sash. Uriel Dann has speculated that the yellow sash was 'of no more significance to the king than a sentimental memory. [It] was his accouterment at the battle of Oudenarde thirty-five years before, when he had charged against the French as electoral prince'.[87] But whatever the king's motives, his yellow sash reinforced British stereotypes of Hanover. Yellow was, of course, the color of cowardice. *The Yellow Sash* contrasted it with the British red:

> From the blood which the brave spend so freely in fight,
> The bold SCARLET hath *England* assum'd as her own;
> While from that I'll not name cowards drop in their fright,
> Is the color peculiar to *H------* known.[88]

Color assumed such a political significance in late 1743 that *Old England* reported with satisfaction in December that British ladies preferred red garments to yellow ones.[89]

George II became so identified with his electorate, that he actually personified it in one remarkable illustration. The 1743 print, 'An Actual Survey of the electorate, or Face of the Country whereon Hanover Stands', appeared at first glance to be a pastoral landscape. Depictions of manufactures producing boar's heads and pumpernickel bread, as well as one of beggars, reinforced the caricature of Hanoverian rural poverty. But the geographical formations in the background constituted a profile of George II, which was more easily visible when viewed from the print's right side.[90] The print proved to be the most effective conflation of elector and electorate.

The opposition accepted that dynastic unions were functionally unequal, irrespective of legal conceit. The anomaly, it observed, was that Hanover enjoyed empire over Britain rather than vice versa. *Old England* wrote that

> if now it could be presum'd that true policy would always have the ascendancy at court, it must be presum'd likewise that the interest of the great power would always weigh down the less. Whence it would follow that, without being legally connected with the crown of *E-----d*, *H-----r* would nevertheless be so influenc'd by it that we should have no more reason to complain of that *e--------e* now than of our *French* dominions formerly.[91]

---

[87] Dann, *Hanover and Great Britain*, p. 53.
[88] *The Yellow Sash*, p. 7.
[89] *Old England, or the Constitutional Journal* no. 47 (24 Dec. 1743), p. 1.
[90] See Frederic George Stephens and Mary Dorothy George, eds., *Catalogue of Political and Personal Satires Preserved in the Department of Prints and Drawings in the British Museum* (11 vols., London, 1870–1954), iii, p. 467.
[91] *Old England, or the Constitutional Journal* no. 44 (3 Dec. 1743), p. 1.

An Actual Survey of the Electorate, or Face of the Country whereon Hanover Stands (1743)
© Copyright the Trustees of the British Museum

As had previous opposition writers, this author displayed no maritime bias against British empire on the continent. Problems only arose when continental possessions exerted empire over Britain.

The question was, of course, why the king instituted Hanoverian ascendancy over Britain. *Old England* located George II's preference in the monarch's lust for dominion. It wrote,

> such . . . is the perverse disposition of man that he had rather be *fear'd* than *lov'd*, he had rather be undone by following his own ridiculous caprice than be ador'd by complying with the wholesome advices of others. It would be scarce a wonder therefore if a prince who was arbitrary in a petty dominion should be more fond of being the tyrant of that dominion than of being the head of a mighty empire where the laws were his superior, and where he was tied up from acting unjust by his not being permitted to act at all.[92]

Hanover's heraldic device, the white horse, was just as unfortunate in this context as its color yellow had been in the debate over its troops' bravery. Opposition journals contrasted the horse, a beast of burden, with the British lion, a symbol of untamed independence. *The Westminster Journal* imagined a conversation between the two symbolic animals, in which the horse pointedly told the lion, 'I, without *serving* and only by dint of my *dutiful* and *respectful behavior*, have procured, of MERE GRACE, that *nourishment, protection*, and *indulgence* for which you BARGAIN'D.'[93]

But as Marchmont had proposed the previous winter, George II might have also had venal reasons for preferring an electorate which he governed absolutely. *Old England* continued,

> sovereigns are not less govern'd by their interests than private men. Now though the whole *executive power* of this kingdom is vested in the k---, the gains which may arise from a wise and honest use of it belong to the *people*. But with regard to *H------*, 'tis far otherwise. All acquisitions there are the *sole property* of the e------. Whence it is easy to imagine into what channel a *selfish* prince would turn the whole current of his favors, and how very effectually this *executive power* of the k-----m might be apply'd to enrich the e--------e.[94]

*Old England* ended this discourse with a repeated plea to dissolve dynastic union.

*Old England* also feared that the elector-king might not be content to restrict his absolute rule to Hanover.

> he that govern'd by *will* and *pleasure* in one country would be apt to think himself extremely unlucky that he could not do the same in another, and other

---

[92] *Old England, or the Constitutional Journal* no. 44 (3 Dec. 1743), p. 1.

[93] *The Westminster Journal, or New Weekly Miscellany* no. 102 (5 Nov. 1743), p. 1.

[94] *Old England, or the Constitutional Journal* no. 44 (3 Dec. 1743), p. 1.

than continue thus unhappy he would endeavor to introduce and establish, if not exactly his own arbitrary system, something that might answer his ends almost as well. And this might be easily and safely done by his dodging between the two capacities of k--- and e------'.[95]

Union's opponents scarcely tried to reconcile their historical fear that Hanoverian regulars might help to establish absolute rule in Britain with allegations of their cowardice. But *Old England* did observe, with reference to the Hanoverian occupation of Mecklenburg earlier in the century, that 'it is one thing to be a dexterous *collector* and another to be a good *soldier*'.[96] And in a subsequent issue, it indicated that absolute rule had domestic antecedents as well. One way 'to break the spirit of a nation [is] by breaking the spirit of their *national troops*'.[97] According to this interpretation, George II calculatedly snubbed his British troops in Germany with the intent of weakening resistance to absolute rule in Britain.

But opponents of union also affected sympathy for the king's natal sentiments, in a tradition stretching back to James Drake. The most eloquent exposition of this perspective yet came from Chesterfield, speaking to the lords in December 1743:

> our case [is] at present very singular. Other nations generally suffer by ministers parasitically indulging the vices and private passions of their sovereign, but we may suffer by ministers parasitically indulging the virtues and public affections of our king. The love of one's native country is one of the most virtuous and useful affections of the human mind, and as His Majesty is endowed with that as well as every other laudable affection, it is the duty and ought to be the business of his ministers to take care that his natural partiality towards the people of his electorate shall extend no farther than is consistent with the interest and happiness of the people that freely and generously made him a king.[98]

*Old England*, the paper with which Chesterfield was so intimately linked, elevated this sentiment the following day when it honored George II with 'the most distinguished appellation of *Roman* virtue . . . that of *pater patriæ*, which being literally translated signified *the father of* HIS NATIVE *country*'. It went on to compare the king's behavior during the Hanoverian neutrality with the famous caution of Fabius during the Punic Wars.[99] Although it thereby reflected upon Hanoverian bravery, *Old England* genuinely represented George II and his Hanoverian retainers as republican heroes.

95 *Old England, or the Constitutional Journal* no. 44 (3 Dec. 1743), pp. 1–2.
96 *Old England, or the Constitutional Journal* no. 36 (8 Oct. 1743), p. 1.
97 *Old England, or the Constitutional Journal* no. 39 (29 Oct. 1743), p. 1.
98 Cobbett, ed., *The Parliamentary History*, xiii, cols. 339–40.
99 *Old England, or the Constitutional Journal* no. 45 (10 Dec. 1743), p. 1.

Whether George II's bias for Hanover reflected good or ill upon his person, it was a betrayal of his royal office in its utility to corrupt British politicians. Parliamentary opponents of union once again charged that Britain's employment of the Hanoverian mercenaries 'was the scheme of one infamous flagitious minister, intoxicated with power, who got and maintained his power by flattering the passion of his master in this point'.[100] This was obviously Carteret, whom a young William Pitt dubbed the 'Hanover troop minister'.[101] Other opponents of union charged that Carteret aimed not only at the maintenance, but at the expansion, of his political power. Once again, Hanover proved the model as well as the tool for the achievement of absolute rule in Britain. The anonymous author of *The Detector Detected* wrote in response to *Faction Detected*, 'there is *a faction* amongst us who, under pretence of supporting the prerogatives of the crown, are for introducing slavery – the very worst sort of slavery – *corrupt* Hanoverian *slavery*'.[102]

Government ministers were by no means insensitive to these charges. Like Chesterfield, Newcastle also had distraught correspondents in the British army who related all the perceived slights of the campaign.[103] Newcastle scuttled Carteret's negotiations at Hanau, grumbling to Walpole (now the earl of Orford) about 'German politics, German measures, and (what perhaps is near as bad as either) German manners'.[104] By early November 1743, he had resolved to support the dismissal of Hanoverian mercenaries from within government.[105] In a letter to Hardwicke, he even endorsed *Old England*'s interpretation of Dettingen,[106] and concluded that 'to think of going on without either representing against, or by our measure putting a stop to, the late Hanover partialities is impossible'.[107] But Orford persuaded the cabinet to retain the soldiers in British pay,[108] and rallied the government's parliamentary supporters to reject the opposition calls to cashier them.[109]

Not all government figures were as susceptible as Newcastle to opposition argument respecting Hanover. But they recognized the threat it posed to

---

100 Taylor and Jones, eds., *Tory and Whig*, p. 189.
101 Cobbett, ed., *The Parliamentary History*, xiii, col. 465 (note).
102 *The Detector Detected, or the Danger to Which Our Constitution Now Lies Exposed Set in a True and Manifest Light* (London, 1743), p. 61.
103 For this, see Brauer, *Die hannoversch-englischen Subsidienverträge*, pp. 143–5; 148.
104 Quoted in Lodge, 'The So-Called "Treaty" of Hanau of 1743', p. 400.
105 Newcastle to Hardwicke, 7 Nov. 1743, Claremont, published in William Coxe, *Memoirs of the Administration of the Right Honourable Henry Pelham* (2 vols., London, 1829), i, p. 107.
106 Newcastle to Hardwicke, 7 Nov. 1743, Claremont, published in Coxe, *Memoirs of the Administration of the Right Honourable Henry Pelham*, i, p. 108.
107 Newcastle to Hardwicke, 7 Nov. 1743, Claremont, published in Coxe, *Memoirs of the Administration of the Right Honourable Henry Pelham*, i, p. 109.
108 John B. Owen, *The Rise of the Pelhams* (London, 1957), p. 187; Brauer, *Die hannoversch-englischen Subsidienverträge*, p. 152.
109 Owen, *The Rise of the Pelhams*, pp. 210–11.

Carteret's theory of British empire over the electorate. Realizing that the imputation of cowardice damaged Hanover's perceived utility as a British strategic pawn, Carteret moved swiftly to defuse it. Respecting the Hanoverians' position in the rear of the British army, Carteret argued that 'if they kept that post, if they refused to advance without orders, it proceeded not from their cowardice, but from what is more necessary and more useful in an army than courage . . . a strict observance of military discipline'.[110] He continued,

> the courage or cowardice of troops depends entirely upon their discipline and the nature of the government they live under. The people of Hanover are naturally a robust, hardy people, and no government in the world is better calculated for forming good soldiers than that government has been under the reigns both of his majesty and his father, for courage and military knowledge have been almost the only qualifications whereby a man could expect to raise himself to any supereminence in his country.[111]

This was entirely consistent with the tradition whereby Hanover's absolute government provided Britain with a mechanism for the electorate's manipulation.

The government also attempted to neutralize the other controversy which threatened to disprove Britain's imperial domination of Hanover, that relating to the supposed discrepancy between British and electoral provisions at Dettingen. The disparity was confirmed by Solicitor General William Murray, a former Jacobite who was now a Pelham lieutenant and later achieved fame as Lord Mansfield the chief justice.[112] But Murray told the commons that the Hanoverians' logistical edge 'proceeded from their commissaries and proveditors being better acquainted with the country and more masters of the language, perhaps more masters of their business too, than those that were employed as commissaries and proveditors for the British troops'.[113] The argument that better organization on the Hanoverians' part accounted for the divergent provisioning tended to distract attention from the alleged royal bias in their favor.

And yet ministers spoke with many voices when addressing the general issue of the king's partiality. Carteret denied it outright,[114] while Newcastle largely conceded it.[115] Murray came closest to a synthesis, saying that 'any trifling predilection must be only temporary and die with the present genera-

---

110 Cobbett, ed., *The Parliamentary History*, xiii, col. 287.

111 Cobbett, ed., *The Parliamentary History*, xiii, cols. 286–7.

112 For Murray's Jacobite youth, see J. C. D. Clark, *Samuel Johnson: Literature, Religion, and English Cultural Politics from the Restoration to Romanticism* (Cambridge, 1994), p. 92.

113 Cobbett, ed., *The Parliamentary History*, xiii, col. 251.

114 Cobbett, ed., *The Parliamentary History*, xiii, col. 353.

115 Cobbett, ed., *The Parliamentary History*, xiii, cols. 608–9. For Pelham's private agree-

tion'. In the meantime, he argued, the Act of Settlement sufficed to prevent abuse of the dynastic union.[116] There was no mistaking the pro-union camp's confusion about royal partiality.

Supporters of union were similarly confused about what the ideal balance of power in the dynastic union should be. Carteret reiterated his belief that he had seized the preponderant influence within dynastic union for Britain. At the time of the Hanoverian neutrality, he argued, 'England was subservient to Hanover. But Hanover is now subservient to England. The electorate is regulated by our measures and is, not without the utmost danger, engaged in a war which might have been easily declined.'[117] Carteret's imperialism remained the government position on Hanover, but only just. An anonymously written pamphlet vindicating *The Present Measures* questioned whether inequality must inhere to all dynastic unions. *The Present Measures* observed that 'when two countries are under one prince and their interests become the same, it is in the power of any man to say this takes the lead or that, though in effect neither [do], both being guided by the common good'.[118] If it had not presumed unity between Britain and Hanover, *The Present Measures* would have been close to personal union.

But this was the closest someone could come to belief in personal union during the early 1740s. Another example was provided by Henry Fox, who told the commons,

> if Hanover had . . . got some addition to her dominions, could it have been of any disadvantage to this kingdom? On the contrary, I think we should study her advantage more than that of any other ally . . . because we can at all times depend more certainly upon her assistance. And the more the intrinsic power of that electorate is increased, the more able it will be to defend itself, and consequently the less assistance it will stand in need of from us, should it at any time be attacked on our account, which it will certainly be, as often as we are at war with any nation that can carry the war into that electorate.[119]

Fox referred to Hanover as an ally, but implied imperial influence rather than legal equality. Repeating Bland's call for electoral territorial expansion, he held that it would simultaneously increase Britain's power while decreasing the responsibilities necessitated by Hanoverian vulnerability.

Imperial designs upon Hanover were even more evident in an anonymously published *Letter to a Friend Concerning the Electorate of Hanover*. The

---

ment with Newcastle's public assessment, see Brauer, *Die hannoversch-englischen Subsidienverträge*, p. 151.

[116] Cobbett, ed., *The Parliamentary History*, xiii, col. 468 (note).

[117] Cobbett, ed., *The Parliamentary History*, xiii, col. 583.

[118] *The Present Measures Proved to Be the Only Means of Securing the Balance of Power in Europe, as Well as the Liberty and Independency of Great Britain* (London, 1743), pp. 21–22.

[119] Cobbett, ed., *The Parliamentary History*, xiii, col. 213.

*Letter*, whose origin in Cirencester suggests Bathurst as its author, justified Hanover's relationship to Britain in terms which could easily have applied to more obviously British outposts in Europe such as Gibraltar and Minorca.

> it is known to everybody of what consequence maritime forts and harbors are to the trade of this nation, even though they should require a very heavy expense to keep them up . . . I do not see why the same arguments may not in some degree hold good with respect to our having a naturalized tenure among the *Germanic* body on the continent.[120]

This generalized the economic argument for union which 1717's *Some Considerations* (and, more recently, Horatio Walpole) had applied to Elbe and Weser river basins.

The Elbe/Weser argument was repeated in perhaps the most remarkable pamphlet to follow Dettingen. Entitled *Popular Prejudice Concerning Partiality to the Interests of Hanover*, its anonymous author claimed to be Ilten himself. This might well have been true, for Ilten had previously lived in Britain and was doubtless acquainted with its journalism.[121] Significantly, most opposition publicists accepted his authorship of the pamphlet. The pamphlet parried charges of cowardice not only in Ilten's defense, but to reinforce Carteret's notion of British empire over Hanover. *Popular Prejudice* even echoed the minister's belief that George II had left 'his *German* dominions exposed to reinforce the E-----h army',[122] as well as the older Elbe/Weser thesis.[123] But the latter was only an entrée into a more general theory of British advantage from Hanoverian expansion. *Popular Prejudice* considered that '*Hanover* is as much an accession to the power of *England* as *Ireland*, and therefore every acquisition to the territories of that electorate must be of advantage to *England*'.[124] It was therefore the first pamphlet since Tindal's *Remarks* of 1714 to reprise Toland's theory that wealth in dynastic unions must flow to the court of the common monarch.[125]

But while *Popular Prejudice* played to British interests, it simultaneously aired distinctively Hanoverian dissent which prevented its publication in the

---

120 [Allen, 1st Baron Bathurst], *A Letter to a Friend Concerning the Electorate of Hanover* (London, 1744), pp. 20–1.

121 Eduard Bodemann, 'Jobst Hermann von Ilten: Ein hannoverscher Staatsmann des 17. und 18. Jahrhunderts', *Zeitschrift des historischen Vereins für Niedersachsen* (1879), p. 162.

122 [Thomas Eberhard von Ilten], *Popular Prejudice Concerning Partiality to the Interests of Hanover, to the Subjects of That Electorate, and Particularly to the Hanoverian Troops in British Pay, Freely Examined and Discussed* (London, 1743), p. 16.

123 [Ilten], *Popular Prejudice*, p. 54.

124 [Ilten], *Popular Prejudice*, p. 53.

125 [Ilten], *Popular Prejudice*, p. 14.

electorate. Following contemporary economic theory, it linked Britain's imperial profit with colonial disadvantage, writing that 'Irish . . . wealth and power must necessarily add to the power of England. In like manner must all additions to the wealth and power of this electorate be an increase of the power of that nation that envies us our poverty.'[126] Popular Prejudice was the first pro-union tract to advertise Hanoverian privation, weakening its claim that Britain profited from empire over the electorate. But it also highlighted one of the central contradictions in the anti-union case, by which Hanover robbed Britain of its specie but remained poor. Attacking theorists of Hanoverian empire over Britain, the pamphlet reiterated the traditional Hanoverian lamentation at the electoral absence:

> there are no benefits accruing to us, there can be none from our sovereign's being king of a powerful nation at so great a distance from us. But had his kingdoms been nearer, as their laws stand, we can never benefit by his royalty. We are forever excluded from the advantages we might reasonably hope for by the greatness of our prince. We are shut out from all employments, emoluments and honors among our new fellow-subjects, though we were made believe by some of themselves that all disqualifications should be removed in time.[127]

The ill economic effects of the elector's absence in Britain might have eased, were British offices opened to Hanoverian candidates. But they were not, allowing Popular Prejudice to conclude that 'we are losers by the accession of royalty to our august family'.[128] The German experience dovetailed more closely with British than with Hanoverian empire.

Aside from economics, Popular Prejudice attacked the thesis of Hanoverian empire on the related grounds of political liberty. It minimized Hanover's threat to British liberty, even though the latter sometimes shocked its German sensibilities. Its author was astonished, for example, by George II's inability as king to censor anti-Hanoverian literature.[129] And while its opponents saw political corruption as dangerous to liberty, Popular Prejudice indelibly associated the two in its portrait of George I. In the first Hanoverian admission that British political corruption had continued beyond 1714, it considered that George I

> knew the nation, was no stranger to their behavior to their k---s, knew their levity and unsteadiness, their propensity to faction, to opposition, and corruption, and probably it was their bias to corruption which alone determined him to comply with their request. He might think that, by means of corruption, there would be a chance of governing a headstrong, untractable people.[130]

126 [Ilten], Popular Prejudice, p. 15.
127 [Ilten], Popular Prejudice, pp. 51–2.
128 [Ilten], Popular Prejudice, p. 51.
129 [Ilten], Popular Prejudice, p. 2.
130 [Ilten], Popular Prejudice, p. 26.

But where *Popular Prejudice* condemned Britain's libertarian excesses, it credited Hanover with its historical political achievement. The English, it observed, 'owe the best of their customs and laws and their very constitution to their Saxon ancestors – that is to us, who are the same people with the Saxons'.[131] This idea was later confirmed by the controversial argument of Hannover's mayor, Christian Ulrich Grupen, that the ancient Saxons who conquered England in the fifth century had come overwhelmingly from the lands which came to constitute the electorate of Hanover.[132] Although *Popular Prejudice* intended to reassure Britons that his electorate posed no threat to their liberty, its remarks also reflected Hanover's evolving image of Britain.

*Popular Prejudice* was harder pressed to demonstrate how Britain's surfeit of political freedom brought about a corresponding Hanoverian deficit, as it had done in the case of economics. But the pamphlet did indicate that metropolitan freedom was entirely compatible with coercion on the imperial periphery. *Popular Prejudice* complained of the English that

> they treat even their own fellow-subjects of *Ireland* and *Scotland* with as great inhumanity and imperiousness as they do foreigners. They plume themselves not only upon their being *free* themselves, but being the assertors and bulwarks of liberty all over *Europe*. And they vilify most of the nations on the continent, but particularly ours, for beings slaves, as they call us. But yet I defy them to point out any nation in *Europe* kept in more abject slavery and dependence than the *Irish* are by themselves.[133]

It thereby recalled Bernstorff's sympathy for Ireland and Scotland, and his fear that Hanover might someday suffer the same dependence upon Britain. According to this perspective, Britain endangered Hanover's freedoms rather than vice versa. So while *Popular Prejudice* repeatedly justified Hanoverian independence, it sensed that it was already dissipating.

Despite its critique of dynastic union with Britain, *Popular Prejudice* never envisioned its dissolution. The first Hanoverian to do so was George II himself who, surprised by the backlash against his triumph at Dettingen, asked his Hanoverian privy council to consider separation from Britain. Two ministers – Gerlach Adolf von Münchhausen, the leading minister in

---

[131] [Ilten], *Popular Prejudice*, pp. 12–13.

[132] Grupen first expressed this idea in his 'Anmerkung, daß Holdenstedt, wo Kayser Carl der Grosse Ao. 804 sein Lager geschlagen, im Fürstenthume Lüneburg, Amts Moisburg belegen, nicht aber Holstein, noch ein Ort im Holsteinischen sey', *Hannoversche Gelehrte Anzeigen* 1 (1751), p. 823. He subsequently developed it at length in 'Anmerkung von der Sachsen Uebergang in Britannien aus Altsachsen', *Hannoversche Gelehrte Anzeigen* 2 (1752), pp. 65–162 and in his book *Observationes rerum et antiquitatum germanicarum et romanarum oder Anmerkungen aus den teutschen und römischen Rechten und Alterthümern* (Halle, 1763).

[133] [Ilten], *Popular Prejudice*, p. 13.

Hanover, and Karl Philipp von Diede zum Fürstenstein, his foremost adviser in matters of foreign policy[134] – produced memoranda. Although these succumbed to World War II bombing, their content can be reconstructed from Richard Drögereit's 1937 paraphrasis. Moreover, the privy council's joint memorandum has survived. The ministers' memoranda were not polemical, as those of their predecessors pressing Georg Ludwig to accept the British succession had been. The ministers' attempt to balance consider-ations for and against union gave the 1744 memoranda a rather more equiv-ocal tone.

The ministers largely echoed *Popular Prejudice*'s sense that Hanover was now subordinate to Britain, but interpreted this more benignly. Indeed, they repeatedly demonstrated how the electorate assisted British policy on the European continent. The privy council considered that dynastic union had weakened Britain's enemy France in that it 'freed those German princes, who wish to conclude treaties of alliance and subsidy with Great Britain, from the fear of swift oppression which could not be averted in timely fashion from Britain itself'.[135] Similarly, British allies in Scandinavia could expect 'the quickest assistance, or a commensurate diversion, from the electoral lands' in any quarrel with French allies in the region.[136] Münch-hausen illustrated Britain's need for continental leverage with reference to Pufendorf's account of Cromwellian designs upon the duchy of Bremen,[137] just as Stanhope had when Hanover acquired the duchy several decades earlier. The ministers also relied upon Britain for protection, writing that

> the assistance Great Britain can proffer through alliances will be all the more crucial to Your Majesty's electoral lands as they are not safe from Prussian invasion. The power wielded by a mere elector of Brunswick-Lüneburg is insufficient, and we would fear violence and injustice from not only Prussia but France in the event of a separation.[138]

Hanoverian deference to Britain was far more marked than in earlier commentaries upon union.

Hanoverian dependence upon Britain was expressed in terms of the

---

[134] For Diede and his relationship to Münchhausen, see Walther Mediger, *Moskaus Weg nach Europa: Der Aufstieg Russlands zum europäischen Machtstaat im Zeitalter Friedrichs des Grossen* (Braunschweig, 1952), pp. 414–15.

[135] Privy council's memorandum, 7 Feb. 1744, Hannover, Niedersächsisches Haupt-staatsarchiv (NHStA), Hann. 92 Nr. 70, f. 10.

[136] Privy council's memorandum, 7 Feb. 1744, Hannover, NHStA, Hann. 92 Nr. 70, f. 11.

[137] Richard Drögereit, 'Das Testament König Georgs I. und die Frage der Personalunion zwischen England und Hannover', *Niedersächsisches Jahrbuch für Landesgeschichte* 14 (1937), p. 153.

[138] Privy council's memorandum, 7 Feb. 1744, Hannover, NHStA, Hann. 92 Nr. 70, f. 15.

latter's supposed maintenance of the European balance of power. 'Your Majesty's German lands', the ministers intoned, 'contribute to the support of the imperial system and the balance of power, and therefore to English interests.'[139] The ministers assumed the intersection of British interest and balance of power, saying only that 'if the balance should collapse it . . . will suffer principally'.[140] But they were much more emphatic about Hanover's dependence upon the status quo, writing that 'Your Majesty's electoral lands share in the benefit which derives from these measures of the English crown, in as much as their preservation and security principally depends upon the imperial system and Austrian power.'[141] The ministers also considered dynastic union secured Britain's defense of the Protestant interest.[142]

While the balance of power theory had long provided Hanover's rationale for union with Britain, it now changed to reflect the electorate's greater deference. Hanover had once been Britain's conscience, compelling it to keep the peace in Europe as the emperor did in Germany. But the memories of Stuart waywardness which had justified this role had mostly lapsed by 1744. Ministers furthermore believed that 'the English nation's commerce extends so far, and is so crucial to the preservation of its state, that it is obliged to take part in foreign affairs'.[143] This being so, Hanover was free to assume a more submissive position. The ministers even stated that, in the event its interest should clash with Britain's, 'matters could be managed so that the smaller yields to the greater. The experience of 1741 well deserves to be cited as an example of this, for Your Majesty set aside the appearance of advantages for Your German interest from Prussia or France to follow England's public-spirited system.'[144] Ministers discreetly neglected the separate peace of the same year. Deference to Britain's defense of the balance of power could occasion expansionism as well as self-abnegation, as the ministers' 1745 plea to London for acquisitions in Westphalia to blunt French expansion showed.[145] But the situation was nonetheless new; Hanoverians' faith in the European balance of power had gone from supporting empire over Britain to the opposite.

Britain's supposed defense of international liberty could still reflect well

---

[139] Privy council's memorandum, 7 Feb. 1744, Hannover, NHStA, Hann. 92 Nr. 70, f. 13.

[140] Privy council's memorandum, 7 Feb. 1744, Hannover, NHStA, Hann. 92 Nr. 70, f. 12.

[141] Privy council's memorandum, 7 Feb. 1744, Hannover, NHStA, Hann. 92 Nr. 70, ff. 9–10.

[142] Privy council's memorandum, 7 Feb. 1744, Hannover, NHStA, Hann. 92 Nr. 70, f. 16. See also Drögereit, 'Das Testament König Georgs I.', p. 154.

[143] Privy council's memorandum, 7 Feb. 1744, Hannover, NHStA, Hann. 92 Nr. 70, f. 12.

[144] Privy council's memorandum, 7 Feb. 1744, Hannover, NHStA, Hann. 92 Nr. 70, f. 13. See also Drögereit, 'Das Testament König Georgs I.', p. 154.

[145] Mediger, *Moskaus Weg nach Europa*, pp. 401–9.

on its civil liberties, the doubts of *Popular Prejudice* notwithstanding. The young Justus Möser enthused in 1746 that

> we who have the recognized luck to live in His Majesty's German states can pride ourselves on a British liberty because of this monarch's philanthropy. We have the right to be human beings, and our king, instead of aspiring to a vain idolatry, holds it to be his greatest happiness to be a human being and likewise to rule over human beings and not over machines. England therefore has a greater guarantee of its rights in his royal manner of thinking than in all laws.[146]

While Möser was to become famous for championing political particularism, he here repeated the familiar argument of Britain's and Hanover's constitutional affinity for one another. He furthermore did so on the basis of the natural-law argument exemplified by Leibniz's letter to Burnet, instead of the rather more specific ancient constitution which the great philosopher had revived in the *Anti-Jacobite*.

The British debate about union maintained its high pitch well beyond 1743, but few new ideas surfaced after Christmas. One exception appeared in an anonymously published pamphlet of January 1744, *The English Nation Vindicated from the Calumnies of Foreigners*, which attempted to explain the economic paradox of Hanoverian empire over Britain. It wrote that 'notwithstanding the immense sums supposed to have been transported to *Hanover* the people there may be as poor as ever, for without *circulation* the vastest treasure is of no benefit to the public'.[147] *The English Nation Vindicated* left no doubt as to who was blameworthy in the failure to circulate British coin in Hanover. Its author remarked that he knew 'not whether the subjects of the electorate be richer or poorer now than at the accession, but am sure the elector is or ought to be richer by far.'[148] The elector-king now joined his courtiers in Hornby's 1722 accusation of hoarding, which defied the economic imperative to circulate currency.

Opponents of union feared that British reserves of specie were not infinite. William Pitt warned Hanover in the commons in December 1743 that if Britain's credit collapsed, 'neither Hanover nor any other foreign state would be able to draw a shilling more from us'.[149] Pitt continued, wondering

> what might be the consequences of the pretender's being landed among us at the head of a French army. Would not he be looked upon by most as a third

---

[146] Justus Möser, 'Anrede eines Weltbürgers an alle seine Mitbürger', *Ein Wochenblatt* no. 33 (31 Aug. 1746), reprinted in *Justus Mösers Sämtliche Werke* (14 vols., Oldenburg and Berlin, 1943–90), i, p. 189.

[147] *The English Nation Vindicated from the Calumnies of Foreigners* (London, 1744), p. 25.

[148] *The English Nation Vindicated from the Calumnies of Foreigners*, p. 63.

[149] Cobbett, ed., *The Parliamentary History*, xiii, col. 167.

savior? Would not the majority of the people join with him in order to rescue the nation from those that had brought it into such confusion?[150]

Pitt anticipated developments in the mid-1740s, which would see events – and the Jacobite threat – increasingly drive the union debate at the expense of new ideas.

As it happened, the Stuart court was planning just such a descent upon Britain. If the controversy surrounding dynastic union factored less in the pretender's calculations than war and the prospect of French assistance, he exploited it nonetheless. In a declaration of 23 December 1743, James Stuart remarked,

> we have seen the treasures of the nation applied to satiate private avarice, and lavished for the support of *German dominions* . . . We have since seen . . . a great body of *Hanoverians* taken into the *English* pay and service in a most extraordinary manner, and at a most expensive rate. Nor could we behold without indignation the preference and partiality shown on all occasions to these *foreigners*, and the notorious affronts put on the *British* troops.[151]

In the end, bad weather crippled the French troop convoys which were outfitting in Dunkirk for an invasion of Britain in February/March 1744. But France had revealed itself, and formally declared war on both Britain and Hanover.

Jacobites relished the French invasion attempt not only because it aimed at a Stuart restoration but because it presented another chance to decry the relationship with Hanover; the earl of Orrery complained that the government paid 'so close attention to the great and important territory of Hanover that they have totally neglected the defence of this insignificant island'.[152] But the invasion scare reduced the consternation with Hanover,[153] juxtaposing as it did Catholic absolute rule with its supposed Protestant counterpart. It did not vanish altogether, remaining more conspicuous than it had ever been before 1742. But while denunciations of Hanoverian empire over Britain maintained their shrillness, they ceased to innovate ideologically.[154]

---

150 Cobbett, ed., *The Parliamentary History*, xiii, col. 168.

151 James Francis Edward Stuart, *His Majesty's Most Gracious Declaration* (n. p., 1743), p. 2.

152 Orrery to Lady Orrery, 4 Feb. 1744, Westminster, published in Emily Charlotte Boyle, countess of Cork and Orrery, *The Orrery Papers* (2 vols., London, 1903), ii, p. 181.

153 Harris, *A Patriot Press*, p. 163.

154 One notable exception was James Ralph's addition of a maritime dimension to his Swedish analogy: 'that a people may preserve themselves independent of all foreign interests, however they may be connected with those of their sovereign, is evident from the late and present conduct of the *Swedes* . . . We find the *Swedes* taking no part in the present commotions in *Germany*, we hear of no troops they pay or send, or no engage-

The public's preoccupation with union further declined after the Pelhams forced the resignation of Carteret (by now the earl of Granville) on 24 November 1744.[155] The Pelhams' increasing disaffection with Hanover undoubtedly played a role in the coup. When Newcastle first envisioned an ouster of Carteret in June, he made clear to his brother Henry that

> that which particularly at this time makes it, in my opinion, impracticable to go on with him is that his chief view in all he does or proposes to do is the making court to the king by mixing with or preferring Hanover considerations to all others. By this method he secures the closet whether his schemes succeed or not.[156]

Newcastle realized, of course, that Carteret was not the ultimate source of Hanoverian favoritism. For this reason, he added that

> if the king would remove Lord Carteret tomorrow and make an administration just as we ourselves would have it, I will not on any account take a part in it without having it first explain'd that this Hanover complaisance is no longer to influence all our conduct. There is the sore, there the grievance. This preserved the peace, this made the war.[157]

Murray went even further in an October conversation with Marchmont, in which he – perhaps drawing upon his Jacobite background – confided that 'Hanover was a millstone about our necks . . . and that this was an admirable opportunity to separate Hanover from England.'[158] But the Pelhams would scarcely have acted had union not also contributed to the parliamentary disaffection which, in the event, dictated Granville's removal.[159] This was borne out by the subsequent preferment of Chesterfield, along with a host of others who had denounced dynastic union – Bedford, Sandwich, Sir John

---

ments they have entered into for the defense of *Hesse*. But if they should take any part in the present affairs of *Germany*, it might not indeed be *prudent*, but it might be *defensible*. They live upon the same continent, some of their possessions are contiguous to certain powers now in arms, and they have no concerns in trade to deter them. But has G---t B-----n any such excuses to plead? No. Yet we see her venturing her last shilling; the sword is at the throats of her troops and allies . . . as an island and an independent people, we have no more to do with the present war, than we could have in a war betwixt *Kublai Khan* and *Prester John*.' Old England, or the Constitutional Journal no. 86 (22 Sept. 1744), p. 1.

[155] Harris, A *Patriot Press*, p. 178.
[156] Newcastle to Pelham, 10 June 1744, Claremont, British Library (BL), Add. MS 32703, f. 108.
[157] Newcastle to Pelham, 10 June 1744, Claremont, BL, Add. MS 32703, ff. 109–10.
[158] Rose, ed., A *Selection from the Papers of the Earls of Marchmont*, i, p. 59.
[159] Owen, *The Rise of the Pelhams*, pp. 230–1; 238.

Philipps, George Grenville, George Bubb Dodington, and Edmund Waller. Ralph and Guthrie received government pensions.[160] Delighted by the change in personnel, *Old England* confidently proclaimed that 'henceforward . . . it may be presum'd that the door will be for ever shut on every foreign interest'.[161]

Carteret's fall did not discredit his arguments for empire over Hanover, but seems rather to have amplified them. The anonymously published *Advantages of the Hanover Succession and English Ingratitude Freely and Impartially Considered and Examined* was the most spectacular example of this trend. It reprised the economic case for Hanover's annexation of Bremen and Verden, first articulated by *Some Considerations* in 1717. To this, the *Advantages* added the wholly new contention that Bremen and Verden might actually foil, rather than facilitate, an invasion of Britain. 'In case of invasions from *France* or elsewhere', it noted, Britain 'can be more certainly succor'd from *Hanover* by means of the port of *Bremen* than from any other quarter'.[162] The *Advantages* even defended Carteret's bogey, the 1741 neutrality, for preserving 'the electorate, which gives *England* so great weight on the continent'.[163] It even paraphrased Bland's notion that 'every acquisition to the electorate of *Hanover* is an addition to the power of *England*'.[164]

Yet in its rush to detect profit in the Hanoverian connections, the *Advantages* risked confirming its opponents' detection of electoral empire over Britain. The *Advantages* claimed that Hanoverian investment rescued British credit after the tory ministry of 1710–14. Acknowledging Hanoverians' relative material deprivation, it insisted that their contribution had been moral more than financial: 'they came in the first with all the weight of their wealth to support the money'd credit of England, and by setting the example were more serviceable in that respect than far richer nations'.[165] This was of course wholly imaginary, but individual Hanoverians' later notorious involvement in the South Sea Bubble made it seem plausible enough. The question remained, however, why richer foreign nations would follow the Hanoverians' putative example. The *Advantages* remarked that

> so soon as the world saw [Britain] associate with a nation the most prudent, steady, and honest of any on the continent, the public opinion was alter'd. The credit of *Englishmen* was retriev'd by the opinion conceiv'd of the probity

160 Harris, *A Patriot Press*, pp. 39–40.
161 *Old England, or the Constitutional Journal* no. 87 (8 Dec. 1744), p. 1.
162 *Advantages of the Hanover Succession and English Ingratitude Freely and Impartially Considered and Examined* (London, 1744), p. 29.
163 *Advantages of the Hanover Succession*, p. 68.
164 *Advantages of the Hanover Succession*, p. 29.
165 *Advantages of the Hanover Succession*, p. 25.

of *Hanoverians*. And the giddiness and infidelity of the first was overlooked on account of the known steadiness and sincerity of the latter, insomuch that the *English* gained no less by *Hanoverians* in point of character than wealth.[166]

As it happened, the *Advantages* believed that dynastic union had actually imparted some of the Hanoverian national character to Britain. It remarked upon the increasing refinement of British society, and observed that 'all nations are more or less polish'd as their several courts are so, and their courts fall in necessarily with the humor and passions of the prince. Are the English more polite, affable, courteous, less stiff and ceremonious than they were, to whom are they indebted but to Hanoverians?'[167] The *Advantages* finally fulfilled the potential of Toland's and Addison's earlier commentaries upon Hanoverian politeness, by discovering a dynastic mechanism for its transmission to Britain.

But Hanover's supporters knew their British readers were unlikely to respond favorably to electoral influence, however beneficial. Another pamphlet returned to the theme of Hanover's utility to British empire. The anonymously published *Plain Reasoner* wrote,

> if it be true, as our minor politicians say, that our business [in Germany] is only to defend *Hanover*, I hope there will always be a *Hanover* there . . . so the *French* may be always kept in *Germany* at the hazard of the ruin of *France*. And I conceive that if there was neither a *Hanover* nor a house of *Austria* in *Germany*, yet one would contrive to find something else, to keep them employed on that side to keep them in a perpetual waste of wealth and strength rather than that they should come with their whole force and vigor to our own doors.[168]

The *Plain Reasoner* showed that the best antidote to maritime argumentation was its application to France as well as Britain.

Such arguments notwithstanding, the ministers moved to dismiss the Hanoverian troops many of them had come to oppose during Granville's ministry. But they wished neither to alienate the king, nor to damage the allied war effort. The government decided to continue supporting 14,000 of the Hanoverian troops in the form of a £200,000 subsidy to Maria Theresia, who would then assume the role of their nominal employer. That the plan was nothing more than bureaucratic slight of hand is revealed by the fact that Britain paid its 'Austrian' subsidy directly to Steinberg in London.[169] The measure's audacity was breathtaking. Stephen Poyntz cynically observed, 'I don't find the newcomers have stipulated any exemption but that of not

---

166 *Advantages of the Hanover Succession*, pp. 25–6.
167 *Advantages of the Hanover Succession*, pp. 30–1.
168 *The Plain Reasoner, wherein the Present State of Affairs Are Set in a New but Very Obvious Light* (London, 1745), pp. 50–1.
169 Brauer, *Die hannoversch-englischen Subsidienverträge*, pp. 168–70.

swallowing their own words for retaining the Hanover troops in the immediate pay of Great Britain.'[170]

The Austrian subsidy drew criticism in the commons, both from the remnants of the old opposition and Granville's supporters. One of the latter, Lord Doneraile, predictably complained that the 'Hanoverians would be less under our command whilst they were in the queen's pay'.[171] And Lord Strange kept the old opposition alive, observing that

> the court of Hanover have a mind to have £200,000 of our money. And since they find they cannot come at it directly, they are resolved to make use of the queen of Hungary as the cat's paw for drawing that sum out of the pockets of the people of England, which is a piece of low legerdemain that princess would scorn to submit to if she did not know that if she refused she must expect no more assistance from this nation.[172]

Strange concluded by attacking the familiar, and linked, bugbears of royal favoritism for Hanover and ministerial corruption.[173] Strange's vitriol eventually found its way into the pages of the opposition press. Its relationship with Chesterfield over,[174] *Old England* fumed that

> during the last m------y, a H--------n spirit might have been easily enough smelt throughout all our c-----ls. But then it was simple, it was undisguis'd, and the antidote to it was ready and easy. But the H----------sm of this m------y is double distill'd. It is refin'd from all savor of B----sh spirit; even the vessels which are to export it are foreign.[175]

This compared Pelham's policy to the covert Hanoverian favoritism under Walpole.

The Austrian subsidy, as well as another imminent royal visit to Hanover, caused *The Westminster Journal* to call for an eventual dissolution of union on George II's death. It added,

---

170 Poyntz to Trevor, 9 Jan. 1745, London, published in HMC, *The Manuscripts of the Earl of Buckinghamshire*, pp. 109–10.
171 Cobbett, ed., *The Parliamentary History*, xiii, col. 1176 (note).
172 Cobbett, ed., *The Parliamentary History*, xiii, cols. 1194–5.
173 'It is our present misfortune that our king has a foreign dominion where he and his ancestors have reigned for many ages. There he was born, there he was brought up, there he was married and became the father of several children before he ever saw this kingdom. It is but natural, it is highly commendable, in him to have a love for his native country. And we have many reasons to suspect that this commendable passion has been too much indulged by his ministers.' Cobbett, ed., *The Parliamentary History*, xiii, col. 1199.
174 Harris, *A Patriot Press*, p. 44.
175 *Old England, or the Constitutional Journal* no. 106 (20 Apr. 1745), p. 1.

though *Hanover* be not yet sufficient either in power or interests . . . to domi-
neer it over *Britain*, if she goes on increasing according to her efforts and drawing after her all that strength and influence which ought to act only in defense
of our own trade and honor, can we tell how soon she may presume herself in
possession of this *sufficiency*? Should other *Bremens* and *Verdens* be added for
the enlargement of this favorite state till at last the common sovereign should
think it the *most desirable part* of his dominions and make it the place of his
*ordinary residence*, what could then secure us from becoming a mere *money
province* , a conduit to supply the demands not of the prince only but a succession of rapacious *viceroys?*[176]

The *Westminster Journal* later wrote that Hanover would come to govern
Britain just as the latter did Ireland, a country which remained subject
despite its advantageous maritime situation.[177] The fear that Britain would
lose its maritime invulnerability and wealth to Hanover directly echoed
Drake's *History* (1702).

The defeat at Fontenoy in May further embittered the opposition to
Hanover. The electoral auxiliaries apparently redeemed their honor, so
soiled at Dettingen; a British cavalry officer even considered that 'by the
behavior of the Hanoverians they may henceforth justly be styl'd of the same
nation'.[178] But opposition journalists still cherished the notion that Hanover
guided British policy, and held it culpable for the diplomatic context in
which Fontenoy occurred. Noting Prussia's defection from the coalition
which had opposed Louis XIV before dynastic union, *The Westminster
Journal* expanded the sentiment, first uttered by Gyllenborg in 1716, that
'H-----r hinders Gr--t B-----n from having her natural interest among the
*Protestant powers*.'[179] As French troops captured the Flemish ports in the
aftermath of Fontenoy, it grimly joked that 'even *Hanover* and *Bremen* may
be at last of some use to *England*, if it be only a way to bring home our
troops'.[180]

The diagnosis of Hanoverian empire remained strong enough that
Jacobites used it to justify Charles Stuart's insurrection of autumn 1745.
Much Jacobite publicity was familiar; the pretender's declaration of 23
December 1743, which was composed during the uproar over Dettingen, was

176 *The Westminster Journal, or New Weekly Miscellany* no. 177 (20 Apr. 1745), p. 1.
177 'The same trade that is now carried on upon the *Thames* may . . . when it shall please
superior wisdom to remove entirely the seat of our government, be quite as commodiously
transfer'd to the *Elbe* or the *Weser*. As *England* deprives *Ireland* of her natural Advantages,
may not another country in the same manner deprive *England* whenever she has full
power. The favor of the prince, in all confederacies of *government*, will at last fix the
general seat.' *The Westminster Journal, or New Weekly Miscellany* no. 188 (6 July 1745), p.
1.
178 Quoted in Stephen Conway, 'War and National Identity in the Mid-Eighteenth-
Century British Isles', *The English Historical Review* 116 (2001), p. 887.
179 *The Westminster Journal, or New Weekly Miscellany* no. 185 (15 June 1745), p. 1.
180 *The Westminster Journal, or New Weekly Miscellany* no. 195 (24 Aug. 1745), p. 1.

widely circulated. But some Jacobites did advance new variants of old themes. Anonymously authored *Considerations Addressed to the Publick* recapitulated the argument that Britain bled specie to Hanover during the royal visits to the electorate. But where traditional accounts had fingered the king and his German retainers as the agents of transportation, the *Considerations* also fingered the British courtiers who accompanied them. The author described Hanover as 'the annual resort of its duke attended by multitudes of *Englishmen*, where the expenses run so high that to use good economy is looked on as unpardonable'.[181]

The *Considerations* also revived an old explanation for the king-elector's preference for Hanover, which it linked to the royal family's unpopularity in Britain. 'The more the cry has been against foreign concerns', it observed, 'the more he has attended to them; the more the dissatisfaction at sending money abroad, the more he has practiced it.' This was, of course, one Jacobite explanation for the king's pro-Hanoverian bias which had originated in the spring of 1715. The *Considerations* urged its readers to transfer their allegiances to the Stuarts, 'princes who neither have nor can have any foreign concern, who have no way to send money out of the kingdom, and whose security must depend on the affection of their people, as they have no way of retreat nor any foreign territory to take shelter in'.[182]

Another supporter of the '45, the Scottish Jacobite William Harper, focused less on Hanover's enrichment than its potential role in the establishment of absolute rule in Britain. Harper's *Advice of a Friend to the Army and People of Scotland* claimed that the government had gone to war to deplete the British army 'that, being stripp'd of your defense, you may the easier be conquered by the next invasion from *Germany* – that is, so soon as the *Hanoverians, Hessians,* and *Dutch* now in your pay can be brought over [for] that purpose'.[183] Yet he also acknowledged that the Stuarts might also establish absolute rule in Britain should they be successful. Harper recapitulated Lockhart's preference for the Stuart variant of absolute rule, above that of Hanover:

> I declare sincerely, I love no arbitrary government; but was I under the unhappy necessity of submitting to one and had my choice, I would prefer the *French* to the *German* yoke. For the first has a frankness and generosity to temper, to qualify and soften it: but a *German* despotism, being grafted on a stock of a sullen, sour, morose, bitter nature congenial to the nation, is by far the more dangerous and dreadful of the two.[184]

---

181 *Considerations Addressed to the Publick* (n. p., 1745), p. 7.
182 *Considerations Addressed to the Publick*, p. 10.
183 [William Harper], *The Advice of a Friend to the Army and People of Scotland* (n. p., c. 1745), p. 22.
184 [Harper], *The Advice of a Friend*, p. 31.

It was a wholly fatuous distinction, but one which illustrates how far Germanophobia could hamstring Jacobite political strategy.

The Jacobite uprising naturally encouraged the government's rehire of Hanoverian troops. And the government needed to conciliate George II, who resented the Pelhams' successive ultimata of November 1744 and February 1746. Thus the cabinet recommended, and the parliament approved, the employment of 18,000 Hanoverians in April 1746. One anonymously published pamphlet, *An Examine of the Expediency of Bringing over Immediately the Body of Hanoverian Troops Taken into Our Pay*, applauded the resolution from Granville's imperialist perspective. It repeated his former government's argument from 1742–3 that dynastic union made the Hanoverians more reliable than other mercenaries.[185] It also repeated the 1744 *Advantages'* argument for Hanover's possession of Bremen and Verden, whence Britain could be assisted in case of invasion,[186] and recommended the new mercenaries' deployment in Britain. The implications were clear when the author wrote that

> as we are governed by the same prince, the interest of both nations should be inseparable . . . Once cleared of prejudice and jealousy . . . all distinctions will vanish, and we shall look upon *Hanover* to be as much a part of our political body as *Ireland*, and *Hanoverians* to be as much entitled to our care and esteem as either the *Scots* or *Irish*.[187]

It is perhaps unsurprising that the Jacobite '45 inspired the most exuberant praise of the Hanoverian union in British history.

It repeated much of the 1744 *Advantages* verbatim, including its argument that Hanover had rescued Britain's credit and established national politeness.[188] But it avoided any further overtones of Hanoverian cultural imperialism by refuting traditional fears of Hanoverian invasion, writing

> nor are we to suppose . . . that *Hanoverian* troops any more than native would be instrumental in curtailing the liberties of these nations. Their being entitled to no freedom in their own country, but at the will of the sovereign, could be no reason for them to contribute to the loss of ours. I should think, on the contrary, that the sensibility of their own loss would wean them from making attempts for setting us on the level with themselves. For as none can be so sensible of the value of freedom as they who want it, we cannot suppose that our foreign brethren would endeavor to reduce us to a condition which they themselves must so much lament to be reduced to.[189]

---

[185] *An Examine of the Expediency of Bringing over Immediately the Body of Hanoverian Troops Taken into Our Pay* (London, 1746), pp. 39–40.
[186] *An Examine of the Expediency*, pp. 20–1.
[187] *An Examine of the Expediency*, p. 21.
[188] *An Examine of the Expediency*, pp. 14–15.
[189] *An Examine of the Expediency*, pp. 40–1.

This was the first time the thesis (first articulated in different ways by Drake and Tindal) that dynastic union could contain both free and absolute governments had been taken so far as to justify the presence of Hanoverian troops in Britain. The government nevertheless ignored this particular suggestion, preferring to keep the Hanoverian troops in Flanders.

The *Examine* and other publications blamed the '45 on the anti-Hanoverian clamor of the early 1740s.[190] This did not entirely stop denunciations of Hanoverian empire in 1746. Indeed one pamphlet, entitled *The Peace Offering*, expanded upon Chesterfield's whimsical proposal of 1742 that the electorate be ceded to the pretender, claiming that only this *démarche* on the part of George II could prevent further insurrections. And *The Westminster Journal* expressed a veiled wish for dynastic union to end.[191] Anti-union sentiment bubbled along until the war's end. There were calls for Cumberland to assume the electoral cap in 1748,[192] and at least one pamphlet termed the Treaty of Aix-la-Chapelle a Hanoverian peace.[193]

But just as anti-Hanoverian publicity endured, so did the opinion that Hanover advantaged the British empire. It was during this time that David Hume penned his essay, 'Of the Protestant Succession', in which he allowed that ideally,

> it were much to be wished that our prince had no foreign dominions, and could confine all his attention to the government of this island. For not to mention some real inconveniencies that may result from territories on the continent, they afford such a handle for calumny and defamation as is greedily seized by the people, always disposed to think ill of their superiors. It must, however, be acknowledged that Hanover is, perhaps, the spot of ground in Europe the least inconvenient for a king of Great Britain. It lies in the heart of Germany at a distance from the great powers which are our natural rivals, it is protected by the laws of the empire as well as by the arms of its own sovereign, and it serves only to connect us more closely with the house of Austria our natural ally.

> In the last war, Hanover was of service to us by furnishing us with a considerable body of auxiliary troops the bravest and most faithful in the world . . . And ever since the accession of that family, it would be difficult to show any harm that we have ever received from the electoral dominions except that short disgust in 1718 with Karl XII who, regulating himself by maxims very different from those of other princes, made a personal quarrel of every public injury.[194]

190 *An Examine of the Expediency*, pp. 34–5. See also Harris, *A Patriot Press*, pp. 80, 177.
191 *The Westminster Journal, or New Weekly Miscellany* no. 236 (7 June 1746), p. 1.
192 *The Westminster Journal, or New Weekly Miscellany* no. 336 (6 May 1748), p. 2; *The Preliminaries Productive of a Premunire, or Old England Caught in a Trap* (London, [1748]), pp. 23–4, 29–30, 34.
193 *Pasquin and Marforio on the Peace* (London, [1748]), p. 36.
194 David Hume, *Essays Moral, Political, and Literary*, ed. T. H. Green and T. H. Grose (2 vols., London, 1898), i, pp. 477–8 (text and note).

Hume composed a compelling argument for Hanover's strategic value to Britain. But to what ends might it be deployed? John Robertson has plausibly connected David Hume's definition of British interest to his concern for the European balance of power.[195] Yet like other British supporters of union during the 1740s, he declined to link it explicitly to the balance after the example of earlier theorists. This could have been a legacy of the 1741 neutrality, when Hanover had appeared to desert it. But Hume could just as well have considered Hanover useful to Britain's commercial rivalry with France, which, as Robertson notes, he only questioned later in his career.[196]

A study of Britain's relationship to Hanover during the 1740s confutes the commonplace that contemporary grand strategy distinguished between transoceanic empire and the European continent. Britons agreed that their connection with the continental electorate was imperial, differing only over the disposition of sovereignty within it. The imperial flavor of the period furthermore colors the entire duration of the British-Hanoverian relationship, in that the early 1740s marked the apogee of British interest in the electorate in terms of both quantity and intensity. Almost as noteworthy was the absence of such debate in Hanover. Although the British uproar revealed Hanoverian deference to British imperial leadership, Germans declined to match it in terms of either scale or quality. This would begin to change during the Seven Years' War, which confronted Hanover with the dual challenge of French occupation and a British-born elector.

[195] John Robertson, 'Universal Monarchy and the Liberties of Europe: David Hume's Critique of an English Whig Doctrine', in Nicholas Phillipson and Quentin Skinner, eds., *Political Discourse in Early Modern Britain* (Cambridge, 1993), p. 354.
[196] Robertson, 'Universal Monarchy and the Liberties of Europe', in Phillipson and Skinner, eds., *Political Discourse in Early Modern Britain*, pp. 369–71.

# 5

# *The Seven Years' War*

Continental Europe (and thereby Hanover) became less important to the British Empire during the Seven Years' War. This was perhaps natural, given that the war originated in North America. It nevertheless spread to Europe, where it quickly surpassed the destructiveness of its transatlantic antecedent. France extended its imperial rivalry with Britain to Hanover, which it occupied in 1757. Hanover's vulnerability revived interest in personal union, both in Britain and the electorate. But it also prompted Britain to send an army to Hanover, seemingly substantiating imperial interpretations of their relationship. This was the policy of William Pitt the elder, whose maritime credentials have been greatly exaggerated.[1] His association with Hanover meant that it was his resignation in 1761, and not the death of George II in 1760, that demoted the European continent in British grand strategy. Pitt's fall freed the British-born George III to pursue a more purely maritime vision of empire.[2] But if the new king's hatred of Hanover had derived solely from the electorate's association with his grandfather, it might have ended soon after the death of the latter. George III's hostility lasted longer because of Hanover's connection with Pitt, who represented continuity with the policies and personnel of the previous reign.

Hanover resumed its former significance in British politics during the mid-1750s, when it was once again endangered by royal policy. Prussia menaced the electorate in 1753, after British creditors protested its default on loans to indemnify East Frisian losses to British privateers.[3] And once tensions with Prussia subsided, France threatened to extend its North American conflict with Britain to Hanover. Newcastle, by now the first minister, reverted to

[1] Marie Peters, 'The Myth of William Pitt, Earl of Chatham, Great Imperialist; Part I: Pitt and Imperial Expansion 1738–1763', *The Journal of Imperial and Commonwealth History* 21 (1993), pp. 31–74.
[2] Jeremy Black, 'The Crown, Hanover, and the Shift in British Foreign Policy in the 1760s', in Jeremy Black, ed., *Knights Errant and True Englishmen* (Edinburgh, 1989), pp. 113–34.
[3] Mitchell D. Allen, 'The Anglo-Hanoverian Connection: 1727–1760' (Ph. D. dissertation, Boston University, 2000), pp. 210–11. Friedrich II's charge that British grievances masked electoral designs upon East Friesland is given too much credit by Uriel Dann, *Hanover and Great Britain 1740–1760: Diplomacy and Survival* (Leicester, 1991), pp. 84–5.

the language of personal union. Newcastle reassured Holdernesse, the British secretary of state accompanying George II in Hanover, that 'any necessary support for the king's German dominions is founded on justice and declaration of parliament, and is the necessary consequence of our measures at sea and North America'.[4] Indeed his government prompted the commons to renew the previous resolutions of 1726 and 1741. The commons proclaimed itself

> bound in justice and gratitude to assist His Majesty against insults and attacks that may be made upon any of His Majesty's dominions, though not belonging to the crown of Great Britain, in resentment of the part His Majesty has taken in a cause wherein the interests of this kingdom are immediately and so essentially concerned.[5]

Such pronouncements emphasized Hanover's independence from Britain, as they imputed injustice to British enemies who would seek redress in Germany. Yet Newcastle had never been consistent on the subject of Hanover's constitutional relationship with Britain, and contradicted himself even now. He echoed Carteret's imperial attitude when he told George Bubb Dodington that 'if Hanover was attacked for the sake of England, it ought to be looked upon as England'.[6] And though Dodington was in opposition, he agreed. He had already told the dowager princess of Wales that he 'was as ready to defend Hanover as Hampshire if attacked on our account, thought it no encumbrance if properly treated, and the only difference between me and the ministers was not about the thing but the manner'.[7] Such ambiguity augured poorly for the short-term future of the personal union thesis.

Although Britain endangered Hanover as it had under Walpole, both countries were more diplomatically isolated than they had been then. George II's electoral ministers attempted to remedy this by proposing that it subsidize a grandiose continental alliance based upon Austria and Saxony.[8] Newcastle was by now committed to continental strategies such as this,[9] but the unprecedented scale and cost of the American war forced him to veto the Hanoverian idea. He wrote that 'the enormous expenses which we presently furnish for our navy, for our operations in America and to protect His Majesty's kingdoms from any insult . . . render us unable to sustain the burden

---

4  Newcastle to Holdernesse, 11 July 1755, Claremont, British Library (BL), Add. MS 32857, f. 41.
5  William Cobbett, ed., *The Parliamentary History of England* (36 vols., London, 1806–20), xv, cols. 539–40. See col. 535 for the equivalent resolution in the lords.
6  John Carswell and Lewis Arnold Dralle, eds., *The Political Journal of George Bubb Dodington* (Oxford, 1965), p. 332.
7  Carswell and Dralle, eds., *The Political Journal of George Bubb Dodington*, p. 316.
8  Dann, *Hanover and Great Britain*, p. 92.
9  See H. M. Scott, ' "The True Principles of the Revolution": The Duke of Newcastle and the Idea of the Old System', in Jeremy Black, ed., *Knights Errant and True Englishmen: British Foreign Policy 1660–1800* (Edinburgh, 1989), pp. 55–91.

of a war on the continent'.[10] Newcastle implored his Hanoverian counter-parts to eschew 'so general and extended a plan' and 'to confine our views and efforts for the present to the sole defense of the king's dominions'.[11] Britain had just secured 8,000 Hessian mercenaries which might be applied to this purpose,[12] and later negotiated an additional 55,000 men from Russia.[13] Newcastle then used the Russian subsidy to bring Prussia to terms in the Convention of Westminster, signed in January 1756.[14] Although the Prussian alliance was calculated to protect Hanover, the electoral government was understandably ambivalent about its rapprochement with the unpredictable Friedrich II. The Convention of Westminster was manifestly a British initia-tive, in which ministers sought to prevent hostilities from spreading to Europe. To characterize it as an electoral measure which was the true cause of Hanoverian vulnerability, as Jeremy Black has done, is to blame the victim.[15]

These measures revived British anti-Hanoverianism, which the failure of Earl Poulett's lords address against George II's visit to the electorate had shown to be dormant as recently as the spring.[16] The most serious opposition came from within Newcastle's own government. The chancellor of the exchequer, Henry Bilson Legge, declined to sign the warrant for the Hessian troops.[17] He had already acted a pro-Hanoverian part as envoy to Prussia in 1748[18] but was now willing to do the opposite to harass Newcastle, who had systematically marginalized him in government.[19] Legge's secretary, Samuel Martin, drew up a memorandum which was later published as *Deliberate Thoughts on the System of Our Late Treaties with Hesse-Cassell and Russia in Regard to Hanover*.[20] Martin appeared to accept the existence of a personal union when he admitted a moral obligation, bounded by practicality, to

[10] Newcastle to G. A. von Münchhausen and Steinberg, 18 July 1755, London, BL, Add. MS 32857, f. 199.
[11] Newcastle to G. A. von Münchhausen and Steinberg, 18 July 1755, London, BL, Add. MS 32857, ff. 201–2.
[12] Carl William Eldon, *England's Subsidy Policy towards the Continent during the Seven Years' War* (Philadelphia, 1938), p. 31.
[13] Eldon, *England's Subsidy Policy*, pp. 38–9.
[14] D. B. Horn, 'The Duke of Newcastle and the Origins of the Diplomatic Revolution', in J. H. Elliott and H. G. Koenigsberger, eds., *The Diversity of History: Essays in Honour of Sir Herbert Butterfield* (London, 1970), p. 262; Karl W. Schweizer, *Frederick the Great, William Pitt, and Lord Bute: The Anglo-Prussian Alliance, 1756–1763* (New York, 1991), pp. 15–17.
[15] Jeremy Black, *The Continental Commitment: Britain, Hanover, and Interventionism 1714–1793* (London, 2005), p. 37.
[16] For Earl Poulett's motion, see Cobbett, ed., *The Parliamentary History of England*, xv, cols. 520–3.
[17] J. C. D. Clark, *The Dynamics of Change: The Crisis of the 1750s and English Party Systems* (Cambridge, 1982), p. 496.
[18] Sir Richard Lodge, 'The Mission of Henry Legge to Berlin, 1748', *Transactions of the Royal Historical Society* fourth ser. vol. 14 (1931), pp. 1–38.
[19] Clark, *The Dynamics of Change*, p. 167.
[20] Dann, *Hanover and Great Britain*, p. 91.

defend the electorate when attacked in a British cause.[21] But he also feared the consequences of such a policy, detailed in imaginary advice from Newcastle to George II:

> if the interests of your island were disconnected from the rest of *Europe*, the *French* would have no resource to counteract our operations except an attempt to invade us . . . They would contend against all chances, aiming to transport an army across the sea in spite of a stronger navy . . . Nothing remains but to cast their eyes upon the continent of *Europe*. There indeed we have a precious pledge, justly precious to Your M------, . . . which, if the *French* can wrest it from us, will cast the balance in the account of war entirely in their favor . . . Pitiful and ungrateful would be the *British* m------r who could hesitate to sur-render all these lesser *American* advantages . . . for the sake of regaining a terri-tory so important to Your M------'s personal interest and so essential to your figure and greatness in the eyes of all *Germany* . . . Necessity seems to point out to the *French* this plan of operation to wound *Great Britain* through the sides of H-----r.[22]

Martin complained that an absolute obligation to Hanover transformed that electorate from an independent country into a British imperial liability upon the continent.

Legge's dissent inspired another minister in a somewhat similar position, William Pitt.[23] Pitt had, of course, first earned political prominence as a vitriolic critic of dynastic union. But he had defended it to the commons since joining government in 1746, a change of heart which had not gone unnoticed by the opposition press.[24] Pitt found himself in the same uncertain position as Legge in 1755, and once again turned a critical eye towards dynastic union. Lord Chancellor Hardwicke related a private conversation, wherein Pitt attacked Newcastle's policy:

> the maritime and American war he came roundly into, though very onerous, and allowed the principle and the obligation of honor and justice as to [Hanover's defense], but argued strongly against the practicability of it; that subsidiary treaties would not go down, the nation would not bear them; that they were a chain and connection and would end in a general plan for the con-tinent, which this country could not possibly support . . . that if any misfortune should happen to Hanover (which he hoped not) it could only be temporary; [that it] might be made the quarters of French or Prussian troops for a time, but there was no danger of the king or his family finally losing it; and he thought that England ought never to make peace without restitution and a full

21 [Samuel Martin], *Deliberate Thoughts on the System of Our Late Treaties with Hesse-Cassell and Russia in Regard to Hanover* (London, 1756), p. 5.
22 [Martin], *Deliberate Thoughts*, pp. 8–10.
23 Stanley Ayling, *The Elder Pitt, Earl of Chatham* (London, 1976), pp. 164–5.
24 Peters, 'The Myth of William Pitt, Earl of Chatham, Great Imperialist; Part I', p. 65; Robert Harris, *A Patriot Press: National Politics and the London Press in the 1740s* (Oxford, 1993), pp. 77–8.

dédommagement to the king on that account; that he was for treating the king's German dominions with the same support and regard as even a foreign dominion belonging to the crown of Great Britain, so situated, should in prudence be treated; and [that] he had rather concur in giving the king five millions by ways of dédommagements at the end of the war than undertake the defense of it by subsidies.[25]

This point of view, which argued for the restitution rather than defense of Hanover on maritime grounds, had already been expressed by Sir John Barnard, the member of parliament from London who had been one of the first whigs to oppose dynastic union in 1730–31.[26] But with Pitt, it entered the government. As a practical politician, Pitt was willing to dilute his principle and endorse one of the subsidy treaties in exchange for a promotion.[27] This being impossible for Newcastle, both Legge and Pitt opposed the Hessian and Russian treaties in parliament when it opened in mid-November 1755 and consequently lost their offices. But by that time, the debate about dynastic union had already become public.

During the summer, the debate over Hanover was restricted to whig, governing circles. But once the Hessian and and Russian treaties became public in the fall, the tories finally demonstrated their capacity for criticism of union. *The Monitor*, an opposition journal founded by the London tories Richard and William Beckford,[28] offered a maritime interpretation of the Act of Settlement in its issue of 18 October.[29] One of the earliest writers for *The Monitor* was the self-styled physician John Shebbeare,[30] whose intellectual development over the course of 1755 epitomized that of anti-Hanoverians. His novel *Lydia*, which began appearing in June, had satirized George II and anti-Hanoverians alike.[31] But like Chesterfield before him, Shebbeare abandoned ridicule for alarmism in early November's *Second Letter to the People of England*. Echoing James Drake's comparison of Hanover with the crown's medieval possessions in France, Shebbeare wrote that 'the people of this nation have owed their increase in riches to the single circum-

---

[25] Hardwicke to Newcastle, 9 Aug. 1755, London, published in Philip C. Yorke, *The Life and Correspondence of Philip Yorke, Earl of Hardwicke, Lord High Chancellor of Great Britain* (3 vols., Cambridge, 1913), ii, pp. 231–2.
[26] Newcastle to Holdernesse, 11 July 1755, Claremont, BL, Add. MS 32857, f. 45.
[27] Clark, *The Dynamics of Change*, pp. 178, 185.
[28] For the Beckfords and *The Monitor*, see Marie Peters, *Pitt and Popularity: The Patriot Minister and London Opinion during the Seven Years' War* (Oxford, 1980), pp. 6–16.
[29] 'To take foreign troops into British pay on condition only to cover or make a diversion in favor of any dominions on the continent without the consent of Parliament carries the appearance of a war within the prohibition of the Act of Settlement.' *The Monitor, or British Freeholder, from August 9 1755 to July 31 1756, Both Inclusive* (London, 1756), p. 86.
[30] For Shebbeare's association with *The Monitor*, see Peters, *Pitt and Popularity*, p. 13 (note).
[31] [John Shebbeare], *Lydia, or Filial Piety* (4 vols., London, 1755), ii, pp. 68–9; iii, p. 185.

stance of being once detached from continental possessions' between 1558 and 1688.[32] So far, this was merely the maritime language of the previous months. But Shebbeare linked it to another argument from the dynastic union's past. He wrote that after the Revolution,

> the unspeakable disadvantage which this nation had suffered form their sovereigns being possessed of dominions in *France* returned with double fury. *Holland* and *Germany* were yoked to this nation. The last, like an enormous wen fixed to a beautiful body, has grown luxuriant by draining the vital juices which should have been distributed through this realm, and emaciated its natural strength, beauty, and vigor.[33]

Although Shebbeare criticized 'territories which, though belonging to our kings, were independent of *England*',[34] he actually targeted de facto empire over continental principalities without dignifying Newcastle's alternative claims for the existence of personal union.

The more Shebbeare wrote, the more he converted Hanover from Britain's imperial dependency into its master. In his *Third Letter*, he claimed that British wealth was squandered 'to fatten the sterile soil and fill the empty purses of more favorite subjects' in Hanover.[35] And Shebbeare even suggested that 'that immense sum which has been so long hoarding up in [Hanover], . . . those millions which E-----d has already squandered for the advantage of H-----r', was the true reason for French designs upon the electorate.[36] Thus was the blame for Hanover's vulnerability shifted from Britain to the electorate itself. Shebbeare believed Hanover governed Britain through the political corruption of George II and Newcastle. His *Third Letter* wrote that corruption rested upon 'the outrageous love for foreign nations in one' and 'the inextinguishable hunger after rapine in the other and in his profligate adherents'.[37] This consideration encouraged Shebbeare in an oblique opposition to union. 'The interest of this island', he wrote, 'will no more permit the sovereigns of it to possess plurality of realms than the Christian religion plurality of wives. It cannot suffer this kingdom to be

---

32 [John Shebbeare], *A Second Letter to the People of England on Foreign Subsidies, Subsidiary Armies, and Their Consequences to This Nation* (London, 1755), p. 40.

33 [Shebbeare], *A Second Letter to the People of England*, p. 41.

34 [Shebbeare], *A Second Letter to the People of England*, p. 43.

35 [John Shebbeare], *A Third Letter to the People of England on Liberty, Taxes, and the Application of Public Money* (London, 1756), p. 24.

36 [John Shebbeare], *A Full and Particular Answer to All the Calumnies, Misrepresentations, and Falsehoods Contained in a Pamphlet Called a Fourth Letter to the People of England* (London, 1756), p. 39. See also p. 26. For the attribution, see James R. Foster, 'Smollett's Pamphleteering Foe Shebbeare', *Publications of the Modern Language Association* 57 (1942), p. 1079.

37 [Shebbeare], *A Third Letter to the People of England*, p. 48.

wedded for her wealth, subservient to another more favorite wife taken for love alone.'[38]

Opposition to union resurfaced during the 1755–56 parliamentary session. Pitt's brother-in-law Earl Temple opposed the Hessian and Russian treaties, complaining that Britain had 'become an insurance office to Hanover'.[39] And Pitt himself criticized the treaty with Prussia by echoing the Jacobite author of *To Robert Walpole, Esq*:

> defending Hanover by subsidies . . . would in a few years cost us more money than the fee-simple of the electorate was worth, for it was a place of such inconsiderable note that its name was not to be found in the map. He ardently wished to break those fetters which chained us, like Prometheus, to that barren rock.[40]

But neither was the first to revive opposition to union. That was William Beckford, who in a commons debate of 1755 revived the suggestion that George II devolve Hanover upon the duke of Cumberland.[41] Even the war secretary, Lord Barrington, 'owned he wished the royal family had been a younger branch', but noted that this would have deprived Britain of George II's great benevolence as king.[42]

But sympathizing with the opposition did not help the government, which needed positive arguments for its policy of assistance to Hanover. For these they may have turned to the very individual, Marchmont, who had in 1742 offered a particularly unflattering explanation for George II's 'outrageous love' of which Shebbeare now spoke. Marchmont was by 1755 a government supporter in the lords, where he and the duke of Marlborough moved the resolution to defend Hanover.[43] His change of heart was pronounced enough that Horace Walpole believed him to have been the anonymous author of pro-Hanoverian *Reflections upon the Present State of Affairs at Home and Abroad*.[44] It appealed to justice in arguing for the defense of an independent country held accountable for Britain's North American policy,[45] implying the existence of a personal union. The *Reflections* even described Hanover as an ally, considering that

---

38 [Shebbeare], *A Third Letter to the People of England*, p. 23.
39 Horace Walpole, *Memoirs of King George II*, ed. John Brooke (3 vols., New Haven, 1985), ii, p. 94.
40 Cobbett, ed., *The Parliamentary History*, xv, col. 704.
41 Horace Walpole, *Memoirs of King George II*, ed. John Brooke, ii, p. 68.
42 Horace Walpole, *Memoirs of King George II*, ed. Brooke, ii, p. 102.
43 Horace Walpole, *Memoirs of King George II*, ed. Brooke, ii, p. 66.
44 Allen T. Hazen, *A Catalogue of Horace Walpole's Library* (3 vols., Newhaven, 1969), i, p. 471.
45 [Hugh Hume Campbell, 3rd earl of Marchmont], *Reflections upon the Present State of Affairs at Home and Abroad, Particularly with Regard to Subsidies and the Differences between Great Britain and France* (London, 1755), pp. 40–1, 47, 51.

a happy circumstance for *Great Britain* is that (independent of the consideration of any connections with her) she has an ally in *Germany* so able as His Majesty is to maintain that balance which it is always her interest should prevail there, for upon the preservation of that in *Germany* depends . . . the preservation of the trade of *Great Britain* all over *Europe*.[46]

Although Hanover was technically independent, it was a pawn to be manipulated in Britain's imperial interest. This was of course *Anglia Libera*'s argument for the Act of Settlement, whose purpose the *Reflections* believed 'most certainly was to secure the liberties of *England* by concurring to support those of *Europe*'.[47] The *Reflections* was the first pro-Hanoverian tract which reverted to the balance of power since the 1741 neutrality had turned the idea over to critics of Hanoverian imperialism.

Lord Chancellor Hardwicke agreed, in his comments to the lords, with the *Reflections*' optimistic assessment of the Hanoverians' strength:

> we are obliged to protect them because they maintain 20 or 30,000 good troops which have always, without any subsidy, been and always will be at our command when we have occasion for them, which must give us a greater weight at all the courts upon the continent than we could expect had we no such body of troops at our command.[48]

In making a case for British empire over Hanover, Hardwicke also anticipated and refuted traditional criticisms of that objective. He continued that

> our resolution to defend Hanover against any unjust attack will never make France think of extorting any unjust concessions from this nation by threatening to invade Hanover because a war upon the continent, in which this nation is heartily engaged, will always be of more dangerous consequence to France than it can be to us.[49]

Hardwicke tacitly took up *The Plain Reasoner*'s 1745 suggestion that Hanover would be useful to Britain in seducing France away from a maritime strategy of its own.

But in 1756, France appeared to be conducting a more effective maritime policy than Britain. For example, Shebbeare blamed Hanover for the loss of Minorca during the summer. In his *Fourth Letter*, he asked

> why was *H-----r* fortified and secured by treaties with *Russians*, *Prussians*, *Hessians*, and *Holsteiners* purchased by profusion of *E-----sh* treasure – *H-----r*, which has already proved so fatal in exhausting the riches of *E-----d* – and

---

[46] [Marchmont], *Reflections upon the Present State of Affairs*, p. 37.
[47] [Marchmont], *Reflections upon the Present State of Affairs*, p. 25.
[48] Cobbett, ed., *The Parliamentary History*, xv, col. 650.
[49] Cobbett, ed., *The Parliamentary History*, xv, cols. 651–2.

*Minorca*, though not the source of your wealth the protection of it when drawn from other fountains, totally disregarded? What reason can be assigned for this inverted behavior but that, having lavished millions in consequence of those treaties and the safeguard of *German* dominions, there remained not supplies sufficient to protect *Minorca*?[50]

Critics also juxtaposed Hanover with Britain's American colonies. Yorkshire instructed its members of parliament that 'if a continent must be supplied [and] our spoils be shared, let AMERICA partake rather than ungrateful Germany, the sepulchre of British interest'.[51] Contrasting Hanover with Britain's Mediterranean and American colonies, maritime theorists sought to define continental Europe as an inappropriate forum for British empire.

If the Hessian and Prussian treaties, and the fall of Minorca, provoked critics of British empire over Hanover, then the government's deployment of Hanoverian mercenaries at home raised suspicions of electoral empire over Britain. This episode was preceded by an interesting exchange, prompted by the complaint that employment of (non-Hanoverian) foreign officers contravened the Act of Settlement. Horace Walpole warned the commons that 'this country had experienced how little even English kings could resist practicing against English liberty; a race of German princes, accustomed to arbitrary government, was still more likely to grasp at arbitrary power'.[52] But he continued that George II had only given

> one instance which, in the most strained construction could make the most jealous suspect that His Majesty meditated even to surprise us into subjection; and that was by governing Hanover with so parental a hand as if he meant to insinuate to Englishmen that they might be the happiest subjects in the world, though under an arbitrary prince.[53]

George II's reaction to Walpole's speech – that 'I try to make my people at Hanover as happy as I can, and they deserve it of me'[54] – seemed to vindicate the description of Hanoverian government as absolute. The king struck a similar tone some months earlier, when delaying his return to Britain from Hanover. The king then held that 'there are kings enough in England; I am nothing there. I am old and want rest, and should only go to be plagued and

---

50 [John Shebbeare], *A Fourth Letter to the People of England on the Conduct of the M------rs in alliances, Fleets, and Armies since the First Differences on the Ohio to the Taking of Minorca by the French* (London, 1756), pp. 46–7 or pp. 92–3, depending on the edition.

51 *The Voice of the People, a Collection of Addresses to His Majesty and Instructions to Members of Parliament by Their Constituents upon the Unsuccessful Management of the Present War Both at Land and Sea, and the Establishment of a National Militia* (London, 1756), p. 35.

52 Horace Walpole, *Memoirs of King George II*, ed. Brooke, ii, p. 129.

53 Horace Walpole, *Memoirs of King George II*, ed. Brooke, ii, p. 130.

54 Horace Walpole, *Memoirs of King George II*, ed. Brooke, ii, p. 132.

teased there about that d----d house of commons'.[55] Although the Hanoverian example tempted George II to withdraw from British public life, Britons feared he intended to emulate it in London. This fear, and the concomitant dread of Hanoverian empire, revived after the Hanoverians' arrival in spring of 1756.

The Convention of Westminster had prompted France to redirect its offensive from Hanover to Britain itself.[56] Girding for a cross-Channel invasion with parliament's assent, the government imported 8,000 Hanoverian mercenaries, in addition to the 8,000 Hessians hired the previous summer.[57] Despite its obvious resonance for republicans, as the first occasion on which electoral regulars set foot on British soil, this operation was in fact generally welcomed. The opposition member of parliament Thomas Potter informed Pitt that 'Hanover treaties and Hanover troops are popular throughout every country. The almost universal language is, opposition must be wrong when we are ready to be eat up by the French.'[58] As late as August, unfounded rumors of the Germans' imminent withdrawal contributed to riots in Warwickshire.[59] The forces' popularity may have stiffened Newcastle's resolve to keep them in Britain when the king was subject to a loss of nerve.[60] George II vainly conveyed the pleas of his electoral privy council, which wanted the troops back in an increasingly unstable Germany.[61]

Pitt made unusual alliance with the Hanoverian ministers, anticipating their objections by several months. He rose from his sickbed in April to tell the commons that 'he feared we should advise His Majesty's involving another country of his in equal or worse peril than our own'.[62] Critics of dynastic union had occasionally affected sympathy for Hanover, in order to detach it from Britain. But this strategy did not take off in the public imagination until Pitt revived it in 1756. Shebbeare later extended this analysis, in his *Fourth Letter*, to the alliance with Prussia, which, he said, encouraged a French invasion of the electorate by antagonizing Russia and Austria.[63] Sympathy for Hanoverian subjects, as opposed to Hanoverian rulers, was to be a hallmark of 1750s opposition.

---

[55] Holdernesse to Newcastle, 3 Aug. 1755, Hanover, BL, Add. MS 32857, ff. 553–4.

[56] Richard Middleton, *The Bells of Victory: The Pitt-Newcastle Ministry and the Conduct of the Seven Years' War, 1757–1762* (Cambridge, 1985), p. 4.

[57] Eldon, *England's Subsidy Policy*, pp. 67–9. See also *The Gazetteer and London Daily Advertiser* no. 4543 (17 Mar. 1756), p. 1.

[58] Potter to W. Pitt, 4 June 1756, Bath, published in *Correspondence of William Pitt, Earl of Chatham* (4 vols., London, 1838), i, p. 161.

[59] Willes to Newcastle, 21 Aug. 1756, Warwick, BL, Add. MS 32867, f. 6.

[60] 'The necessity of keeping the king's German troops here . . . made the king yesterday very uneasy.' Newcastle to Hardwicke, 28 Aug. 1756, Claremont, BL, Add. MS 32867, ff. 115–16.

[61] See Allen, 'The Anglo-Hanoverian Connection', p. 239.

[62] Horace Walpole, *Memoirs of King George II*, ed. Brooke, ii, p. 140.

[63] [Shebbeare], *A Fourth Letter to the People of England*, pp. 22, 25, 51 or pp. 44–5, 50, 102, depending on the edition.

Another distinctive feature of the 1750s was the revival of opposition to Hanover's alleged religious imperialism. *The Monitor* argued against the importation of Hanoverians from another perspective which was equally idiosyncratic. It feared that the Hanoverian mercenaries might be 'permitted by our superiors in the church to exercise Lutheranism in one of our cathedrals, though it must be confessed this toleration is not so blamable as [the Pelhams' attempted] naturalization of the Jews'.[64] This fear rested on the traditional tory elision of Lutheran with Catholic doctrine. A popular ballad on the subject of the Hanoverian mercenaries made that clear, reporting that

> In *Luther's* whims the *Hanoverians* hope,
> Or else believe the errors of the pope.[65]

Tories felt free to stigmatize Hanoverian error, once the pretender's cause had irrevocably declined. Nevertheless, the secular critique of Hanoverian empire which the pretender had promoted remained in rude health.

Hanover's supposed imperialism was best expressed in *England's Warning*, a letter which purported to come from an electoral soldier stationed in Britain. It revealed that 'we . . . shall always tarry here unless H------ be attacked, to prevent any insurrection that may arise on the account of so much of their money being spent in our defense whilst . . . [Britain's] affairs are but little minded'.[66] The republican pedigree of this argument was evident in *The Monitor's* defense of Britain's mixed constitution; the Hanoverian mercenaries, the paper claimed, were 'straining our constitution and giving too great a power to one part thereof' – the monarchy.[67]

The opposition press also highlighted parallels with the Saxon invasion of antiquity, a staple of republican argument against Hanover since John Toland's *Limitations*. *German Cruelty* reprised the familiar tale of how Britain's ancient luxury had necessitated the importation of Saxon mercenaries, who eventually betrayed and defeated their effete employers. But where the propagation of ancient German liberties had conferred a silver lining on that earlier conquest, Britons expected nothing so good from modern German values. The earl of Bath's chaplain, John Douglas, joked in *A Serious Defense of Some Late Measures of the Administration* that the government intended to

---

64 *The Monitor, or British Freeholder, from August 9 1755 to July 31 1756, Both Inclusive*, p. 424.

65 *A Lamentation for the Departure of the Hanoverians, Being an Epistle from an English Maiden to Her German Sweetheart* (London, [1757]), p. 5.

66 *England's Warning, or the Copy of a Letter from a H--------n Officer in England to His Brother in H-----r Found near Canterbury and Faithfully Translated from the German, together with a Letter to the Author of the Citizen* (n. p., [1756]), p. 4.

67 *The Monitor, or British Freeholder, from August 9 1755 to July 31 1756, Both Inclusive*, p. 346.

remedy the sorry state of British manhood by breeding the Hanoverian and Hessian soldiers with British women. He wrote,

> *German* solidity, which some have maliciously termed stupidity, being once brought into our constitutions, will in time extinguish a troublesome race of mere *Englishmen*, some of whom at present, though happily their number is small, by the vivacity of their genius clog the wheels of government and distress the administration by unseasonable oratory and obstinate opposition in both houses of parliament. Blessed days when the influence of *Germanic* phlegm shall extend itself o'er our public councils, when the pertness of *English* eloquence shall be checked, and our senates nod assent without one lord or commoner to rail at *subsidies*, and to recommend *militias*![68]

Douglas deplored, of course, that Britons should acquire martial attributes – stolidity, obedience, etc. – more appropriate to Germans (and Hanoverian empire) than Britons.

In mentioning the militia, Douglas promoted the British alternative to Germanic militarization. British republicans had called for a volunteer force ever since the young pretender had caught the professionals flatfooted in 1745.[69] Now it buttressed two arguments against Hanoverian empire. *The Monitor* first considered that Hanoverian considerations doomed the militia bill, observing that 'a German prince who traffics in human flesh, and has no other market but Great Britain, might with great propriety interest himself against such a resolution'.[70] Just as had Marchmont's *Present Interest* thirteen years earlier, *The Monitor* argued that George II's personal greed and absolute power as elector combined to foster a similar status in Britain. *The Monitor* later moderated this traditional image of absolute government in Hanover, hoping that Britain might take inspiration from Hanover's own militia.[71] It reported that

> we have been told from Hanover that the militia there were with the utmost assiduity learning the art and exercise of arms as the *properest* and *most natural* defense against an invasion. Why should not the same step which is thought prudent to be taken in His Majesty's electorate be thought prudent also in His Majesty's kingdom?[72]

---

[68] [John Douglas], *A Serious Defence of Some Late Measures of the Administration, Particularly with Regard to the Introduction and Establishment of Foreign Troops* (London, 1756), pp. 17–18.

[69] See Eliga H. Gould, 'To Strengthen the King's Hands: Dynastic Legitimacy, Militia Reform and Ideas of National Unity in England 1745–1760', *The Historical Journal* 34 (1991), pp. 329–48.

[70] *The Monitor, or British Freeholder, from August 9 1755 to July 31 1756, Both Inclusive*, p. 417.

[71] For the Hanoverian militia, see Allen, 'The Anglo-Hanoverian Connection', pp. 212–13.

[72] *The Monitor, or British Freeholder* no. 59 (11 Sept. 1756), pp. 350–1.

Yet this concession to electoral political freedom simply reinforced suspicions of Hanoverian empire among Britons.

Although the traditional republican distrust of British regulars certainly informed its support for a militia, the opposition certainly trusted them more than their Hessian or Hanoverian counterparts.[73] Of the latter, *The Monitor* inquired

> are they within the limitations and conditions under the restrictions, penalties, and punishments of the mutiny bill? If they are not, what dependence can there be on their service in case of national danger? May they not refuse to act under the command of our sovereign? Can they be punished for desertion? Yet this is not the worst reflection that arises from this measure. May it not be a cause of great disgust in the soldiery of this realm to be supplanted by a foreign army, to be sent abroad like felons to America to make room for Hessians and Hanoverians to eat the bread of idleness in old England?[74]

*The Monitor* clearly placed more urgency on the latter consideration, that weakening the morale of British regulars and shipping them to America might facilitate a Hanoverian conquest of Britain. But it was the former question of the legal extraterritoriality of Hanoverian troops which was to prove most prescient.

The discontent over the Hanoverian troops' presence in Britain came to a boil after 13 September 1756, when a Maidstone shopowner named Christopher Harris accused a Hanoverian soldier from the nearby encampment of stealing two silk handkerchiefs worth eight shillings.[75] Horace Walpole later absolved the soldier, one Wilhelm Schröder, of criminal intent, saying that he had been 'buying four handkerchiefs [and] took by mistake the whole piece, which contained six'.[76] Nevertheless, Harris brought his case before the mayor and another justice of the peace, who jailed Schröder on a felony charge to be tried later.[77] Schröder's commanding officer, Count Kielmansegg, applied to the mayor on the following day for his discharge on the (specious) grounds that 'it was expressly stipulated by treaty that no Hanoverian soldier was to be tried by the laws of England during their stay here'.[78] The town's deputy recorder advised the mayor to deny Kielmansegg's request, whereupon the Hanoverian officer 'talked of making use of force' to

---

73 Gould, 'To Strengthen the King's Hands', p. 336.
74 *The Monitor, or British Freeholder, from August 9 1755 to July 31 1756, Both Inclusive*, p. 424.
75 *The London Evening Post* no. 4507 (25–28 Sept. 1756), p. 1.
76 Horace Walpole, *Memoirs of King George II*, ed. Brooke, ii, p. 175.
77 *The London Evening Post* no. 4507 (25–28 Sept. 1756), p. 1.
78 *The London Evening Post* no. 4505 (21–23 Sept. 1756), p. 4.

free Schröder.[79] But Kielmansegg instead decided to petition George II for the soldier's release.

Schröder's arrest caused George II great consternation. Newcastle reported to Hardwicke that 'His Majesty was very angry, and said he must send away his troops if they were to be subject to our laws . . . to be tried by *themselves*.'[80] The elector-king may have therefore been trying to use the Maidstone incident as a pretext for their return. But the king's agenda did not yet coincide with that of Newcastle, who still wanted the Hanoverian troops in Britain. Murray drafted a warrant for Schröder's release, which Holdernesse signed and dispatched to Maidstone. Schröder's transfer from British to Hanoverian custody did not immediately end his legal travails, for he was still subject to Hanoverian court martial. England's medieval statute against praemunire apparently deterred Harris from testifying in the Hanoverian case.[81] Schröder nevertheless received three hundred lashes, while Kielmansegg was removed from his post.[82]

By personalizing previously abstract considerations, the events in Maidstone crystallized British fears of Hanoverian empire. Anti-Hanoverian sentiment focused upon the 'treaty' Kielmansegg claimed provided for Hanoverian extraterritoriality. *The London Evening Post* initially doubted its existence,[83] but later recanted. It opined,

> there is too much reason to fear that some such cruel and unconstitutional treaty is really subsisting, a treaty . . . that, by presupposing their committing the crimes of murder, robbery, etc. on the subjects of Great Britain and providing that they should not be imprison'd or punish'd for the same by the laws of England, seems to me to bespeak an intention of allowing these mercenaries to commit such atrocious crimes here.[84]

According to such thought, Hanoverian extraterritoriality opened the door to military occupation. Anti-Hanoverian publicity fanned this suspicion, emphasizing Kielmansegg's threat to free Schröder by violence.[85]

Interestingly, journalists sympathetic to Hanover made the same progression from skepticism to credulity respecting the 'treaty'. *The Gazetteer's* commentator considered that

> as to the treaty in question, I doubt whether any such act could be made in *due form*, as one prince is sovereign of both countries. Therefore I can only suppose that when a body of the electoral troops was drafted for England, in

---

[79] *The London Evening Post* no. 4505 (21–23 Sept. 1756), p. 4.

[80] Newcastle to Hardwicke, 18 Sept. 1756, London, BL, Add. MS 32867, f. 328.

[81] *The Gazetteer and London Daily Advertiser* no. 4704 (9 Oct. 1756), p. 1.

[82] Horace Walpole, *Memoirs of King George II*, ed. Brooke, ii, p. 176.

[83] *The London Evening Post* no. 4507 (25–28 Sept. 1756), p. 1.

[84] *The London Evening Post* no. 4513 (9–12 Oct. 1756), p. 1.

[85] *England's Warning*, p. 5.

consequence of the addresses of both houses of parliament to His Majesty, the regency of the electorate might stipulate before these forces embarked that they should not be subject to the *forms* of the English laws during their abode in this island and yet be punishable for any crimes or disorders they might commit here . . . by sentence of their own court martial. And if they did make such stipulations before they would march or embark, they were certainly in the right as we wanted them on that emergency and they well knew how little they were liked by the [British] people in general.[86]

*The Gazetteer's* contention that Hanoverian law would protect Britons from electoral regulars did not address the argument against Hanoverian empire, wherein electoral authorities harbored dangerous ambitions. It did however discredit the element of Newcastle's argument which relied upon personal union. Once again, George II's inability to contract with himself hamstrung the theory of mutual independence under international law.

The Maidstone incident not only featured in public debate, but also in the Newcastle administration's desperate overture to Pitt during October 1756. Pitt condemned Schröder's release as 'the most atrocious act of power and the grossest attempt to dispense with the laws of England . . . since the days of Lord Strafford' and demanded the Hanoverian troops's departure from Britain as a condition of entering government.[87] While Newcastle nominally presided over the decision to repatriate the electoral regulars during the waning days of his government, it was his successor Pitt who received the credit.[88] Pitt seemed to justify this opinion when he threatened not to take office if the commons approved a resolution similar to that of the lords thanking George II for bringing over the Hanoverian troops.[89]

Much as Carteret's resignation had done twelve years earlier, Newcastle's fall in late 1756 appears to have invigorated proponents of British empire over Hanover. Their first salvo was *The Gazeteer's* re-publication of David Hume's case for British influence over Hanover.[90] Then the political economist Malachy Postlethwayt seconded Hume's assessment that Hanover was strategically useful to Britain. In *Great Britain's True System*, he termed it an 'ally',[91] implying its independence from Britain. But Postlethwayt nevertheless also likened Hanover to British dependencies like Gibraltar and Minorca. He asked,

is the preservation of *Holland* and *Hanover* of less concernment to *Great Britain* than [Minorca and Gibraltar] as well as in relation to our commerce as the

86 *The Gazetteer and London Daily Advertiser* no. 4704 (9 Oct. 1756), p. 1.
87 Quoted in Clark, *The Dynamics of Change*, p. 271.
88 *A Lamentation for the Departure of the Hanoverians*, p. 4.
89 Horace Walpole to Mann, 8 Dec. 1756, published in W. S. Lewis, ed., *The Yale Edition of Horace Walpole's Correspondence* (48 vols., New Haven, 1937–83), xxi, pp. 30–1.
90 *The Gazetteer and London Daily Advertiser* no. 4738 (18 Nov. 1756), pp. 1–2.
91 Malachy Postlethwayt, *Great Britain's True System* (London, 1757), p. cxxxvi.

annoyance of the enemy in time of war? If we are by the event of war losing of valuable possessions in one part of the world that have promoted our trade, should not this put us the more on our guard not to lose those allies on whom our security and our commerce in other channels great depend?[92]

As Postlethwayt made clear, his argument was as much economic as military. To this end, he revived the argument of 1717's *Some Considerations*, which had championed Hanover's strategic position astride British shipping lanes in the Elbe and Weser rivers.[93]

Postlethwayt had no doubt that Hanover economically benefited Britain in other ways. He wrote that

> instead of *English* money being sent to *Hanover*, I am convinced the fact is quite otherwise . . . If His Majesty's household is supported in *England*, have we not the benefit of his royal residence and that of his council? And by His Majesty's general abode here, can we suppose that the interest of his *German* dominions has not been thereby neglected to serve that of *Great Britain*?[94]

This was, of course, the economic case for empire over Hanover, by which the elector-king's residence in Britain supposedly attracted electoral wealth. The argument was venerable, having first been proposed by John Toland in *Anglia Libera*, although only Ilten had revived it since 1714. Of course, the argument required proof that Hanover possessed riches worthy of British interest. Postlethwayt furnished this by writing a breathless survey of the Hanoverian economy that was indebted to, but more extensive than that of, Guy Miège's *Present State of His Majesty's Dominions in Germany* (1715).

But because he believed that Hanover suffered in dynastic union with Britain, Postlethwayt defended the king's care for the former. This he further located in George II's personal interest. Postlethwayt observed,

> the royal house of *Hanover* has no competitor to their electoral dominions. Can any sensible man expect that a prince would absolutely neglect or wholly abandon certain patrimonial territories whose right is indisputable and never called in question for the sake of those, though much greater, which others make pretensions to and have often endeavored to wrest out of his royal hands?[95]

Postlethwayt strongly hinted at Hanover's importance to the dynasty as a refuge in case of Jacobite revolution in Britain. He was the first pro-

---

[92] Postlethwayt, *Great Britain's True System*, p. cxxxix.
[93] 'The King of *England's* dominions in *Germany* are not disadvantageously situated for trade and commerce, and . . . have been greatly instrumental to promote and advance the trade and commerce of *Great Britain*.' Postlethwayt, *Great Britain's True System*, p. cviii.
[94] Postlethwayt, *Great Britain's True System*, pp. cxxxiv–v.
[95] Postlethwayt, *Great Britain's True System*, p. cxxxv.

government theorist to take up the idea, first conceived by the Jacobites in 1715 as an explanation for George I's Hanoverian favoritism.

Although Postlethwayt pitied Hanover for its economic disadvantages with relation to Britain, its strategic subsidiarity was more dangerous to the electorate. George II remarked to Earl Waldegrave during early 1757 that 'we were angry because he was partial to his electorate, though he desired nothing more to be done for Hanover than what we were bound in honor and justice to do for any country whatsoever when it was exposed to danger entirely on our account'.[96] This was, of course, the justice-based rhetoric of personal union. Never had calls for British assistance to Hanover been more apposite, as deterrence of France's cross-Channel assault had caused it to target the electorate once again.

The monarch's logic had an effect upon Pitt. Pitt had foreshadowed a pragmatic complaisance with respect to the electorate when he hinted to Madame von Walmoden (by now the Countess of Yarmouth) that 'Hanover might not lose *all* its friends' once he supplanted Newcastle in government.[97] He then addressed Hanover's persistent vulnerability, which was increasing in inverse relation to Britain's. A Pittite journal, *The Con-Test*, prepared its readers for his possible pliancy in November, when it opined that 'an *accidental* or *immediate* exigency may render a regard for a *foreign* interest a probable security for the preservation of our own'.[98] Pitt eventually provided for the electorate's defense in February 1757, when he obtained a parliamentary grant of £200,000 to Friedrich II. Pitt contrasted his supposed modesty in Hanover's defense with the profligacy of previous administrations, noting that 'instead of paying the Hanoverians as we did through all the last war, His Majesty engages to pay all the present 36,000 himself'.[99] But Pitt realized that his measure would not be compared to those of Carteret and Pelham as much as they would be to his own statements against the treaties of 1755–6. This he attempted to preempt, saying that he 'was never against granting moderate sums of money to the support of a continent war as long as we did not squander it away by millions'.[100] The negotiations of 1755 attest to the truth of this statement, but it nevertheless confronted the public's perception that his opposition to continental subsidies had been categorical.

Pitt's apparent volte face was eased by the support of *The Monitor* and William Beckford, who irreversibly attached himself to the former upon his entry into government.[101] But Pitt's rival Henry Fox pointed out Pitt's inconsistency, telling the commons that 'he had been told indeed that the

96   J. C. D. Clark, ed., *The Memoirs and Speeches of James, 2nd Earl Waldegrave* (Cambridge, 1988), p. 207.
97   Horace Walpole, *Memoirs of King George II*, ed. Brooke, ii, p. 183.
98   *The Con-Test* no. 1 (23 Nov. 1756), p. 3.
99   Quoted in Clark, *The Dynamics of Change*, p. 327.
100  Quoted in Clark, *The Dynamics of Change*, p. 328.
101  Peters, *Pitt and Popularity*, p. 12.

German measures of last year would be a millstone about the neck of the minister. He hoped *this German* measure would be an ornament about the minister's neck'.[102] Pitt's conversion to support for dynastic union ironically weakened his position in government. His £200,000 subsidized a German army of observation in Westphalia, which Fox's patron Cumberland was to command. Cumberland made his service contingent upon Pitt's dismissal, which he easily obtained; Horace Walpole asked, 'could His Majesty hesitate between an unwelcome servant and a favorite dominion?'[103] Pitt's dismissal was only temporary, and he formed one of Britain's greatest war ministries three months later with the duke of Newcastle.

Opponents of Hanover were slow to abandon the thesis of Hanoverian empire, despite the electorate's apparent weakness. *The Monitor*, its vigilance sharpened by Newcastle's resurrection, opined in July that the government should not 'show too great an attachment to the interest of the electorate of Hanover, or a readiness to enter into any scheme for enlarging the dominions or pursuing the resentment of that electorate'.[104] Territorial enlargement had long been a bogey of those who feared Hanoverian imperialism. But *The Monitor* simultaneously admitted Hanover's vulnerability to British enemies, writing that

> to perform our engagements with the electorate of Hanover is our duty. But except the Protestant powers on the continent join heartily with us, we ought not in common prudence to venture our blood and treasure in a defense which . . . would deprive us of the means to fight our own battles.[105]

This, of course, amounted to a maritime critique of British empire over Hanover. The latter analysis gathered more momentum after the French defeated Cumberland at Hastenbeck and occupied much of the electorate. A correspondent who pretended to be Hanoverian urged *The Monitor's* readers to hew to a maritime strategy.[106]

Yet rather than admitting Hanover's prior submission to Britain, critics of Hanoverian empire welcomed Hastenbeck as if it had been a liberation. One poet considered Cumberland's dilemma as the custodian of his father's electoral 'house', writing

> Oh, the house of his father, his father's fine house,
> That a million *per* year out of E-----d did chouse,
> And made the *lean Briton* sh-t small as a mouse,
> Pray was it not, looking you, a plentiful house?[107]

---

102  Horace Walpole, *Memoirs of King George II*, ed. Brooke, ii, p. 214.
103  Horace Walpole, *Memoirs of King George II*, ed. Brooke, ii, pp. 246–7.
104  *The Monitor, or British Freeholder* no. 106 (30 July 1757), p. 635.
105  *The Monitor, or British Freeholder* no. 106 (30 July 1757), p. 636.
106  *The Monitor, or British Freeholder* no. 111 (3 Sept. 1757), p. 676.
107  *A New Historical, Political, Satyrical, Burlesque Ode on That Most Famous Expedition of All Expeditions Commonly Called the Grand Secret Expedition* (London, 1757), p. 5.

The anonymous poet declined to detail when and how Hanover swindled Britain of its specie, but another humorist made clear that the royal trips to the electorate had been the occasion and method for the crime. The anonymous author of *The Book of Lamentations, Being the Soliloquy of an Old Man for the Loss of His House* described Newcastle and Harrington as competing for who could present more lavish entertainments during their (separate) voyages to Hanover in the capacity of secretaries of state.[108] Once again, the royal voyages to Germany appeared as an economic mechanism for Hanoverian empire over Britain.

Hanover's capitulation was the consummation of royal fears since 1725. Distraught, George II authorized Cumberland to conclude a separate peace with France. But while his British government kept official silence on the matter, they privately communicated their opposition to another Hanoverian neutrality.[109] Pitt and Newcastle provided the electorate with £100,000 from a credit voted by parliament in May – a vote which Pitt himself (during his short period in opposition) had resisted on the grounds that some of it might be diverted to Hanoverian ends.[110] His government's actions in the fall of 1757 revealed that Pitt had recognized and accepted British influence over Hanover. Pitt's change of heart sparked another one in George II, who now directed Cumberland that 'a separate peace would be incompatible with his obligations as king of England'.[111] The king's volte face was too late, however; unbeknownst to him, Cumberland had already signed a cease-fire at Kloster Zeven which dispersed the army of observation and consented to France's continued occupation of the electorate. An angry monarch recalled Cumberland from his command.

Supporters of British empire over Hanover joined *The Gazeteer* in blaming Kloster Zeven on 'a timorous spirit in the regency of the electorate',[112] but at least one Hanoverian minister disavowed it. Philip Adolf von Münchhausen second-guessed his older brother's handiwork from the comfortable remove of London, where he had succeeded Steinberg as electoral minister. Meeting at the younger Münchhausen's initiative,[113] the British cabinet considered that

> the king's servants do not conceive themselves anyways founded to offer their humble advice to His Majesty with regard to the safety and welfare of his electoral dominions. But in case His Majesty as elector shall, on the advice of his electoral ministers, judge proper to consider the convention concerning His

---

108 *The Book of Lamentations, Being the Soliloquy of an Old Man for the Loss of his House* (London, [1757]), p. 6.
109 Middleton, *The Bells of Victory*, p. 35.
110 Eldon, *England's Subsidy Policy*, p. 97.
111 Middleton, *The Bells of Victory*, p. 36.
112 Quoted in *The Gentleman's Magazine and Historical Chronicle* 27 (1757), p. 515.
113 Horace Walpole, *Memoirs of King George II*, ed. Brooke, ii, pp. 281–2.

Majesty's army of observation as broken and annulled and in consequence thereof shall put the said troops again into activity, their lordships are humbly of opinion that, the electoral revenues being entirely cut off, the pay and charge of the said troops ought in justice and in honor be supplied from hence from the day that they shall recommence the operations of the war against he forces of France in concert with the king of Prussia.[114]

Yet despite the resolve, both royal and ministerial, to change Hanoverian policy at the earliest possible instance, circumstances were initially unfavorable. In the meantime, government bore the brunt of public anger at Kloster Zeven.

Kloster Zeven confirmed opponents of British empire over Hanover in their position. They observed that empire came with responsibilities which might neutralize advantages. *The Monitor* insinuated that the government had sabotaged its own naval descent on Rochefort (which in reality failed for purely tactical reasons) to procure the cease-fire.[115] This suspicion led an anonymous poet to observe that

> The fleet was so large, so fine and so brave,
>     To frighten all France it was their intention;
> Which they might have done, I'll bet two to one,
>     Hadn't it been for a d---'d c-nv--t--n.[116]

As they had in 1741, critics suspected that British naval passivity spared Hanover the worst of French ravages.

There were, however, publicists who still focused upon what they took to be Hanover's (admittedly now, pre-Hastenbeck) empire over Britain. They were epitomized by John Shebbeare, who wrote in a *Sixth Letter* that

of *England's* revenues . . . [British ministers] were lavish in extreme to sustain *German* interests; of the *Hanoverian*, of which the elector was absolute master, they were equally parsimonious, though necessary for the preservation and advantage of his subjects; thus whilst your ministers were ruining this nation by a profusion of supplies squandered in *German* measures, the *Hanoverians* were oppressed by a criminal parsimony, scarce possessing without the electoral coffers money sufficient for the common necessaries of life. And each action, the extravagance and avarice, manifested an utter insensibility to the miseries of human kind – proofs incontestable that this rapacious appetite after *English* treasure sprung not from the palliating motive of rendering the *Hanoverians* more free and happy, but from the ministerial thirst which, like that of *German* princes after increasing dominions and the number of slavish subjects, was forever craving and insatiate.[117]

114 Quoted in Dann, *Hanover and Great Britain*, p. 116.
115 *The Monitor, or British Freeholder* no. 117 (15 Oct. 1757), p. 712.
116 *A New Historical, Political, Satyrical, Burlesque Ode*, p. 4.
117 [John Shebbeare], *A Sixth Letter to the People of England on the Progress of National*

This was an amplification of an argument put forward in *The English Nation Vindicated from the Calumnies of Foreigners* (1744), which had explained Hanover's modest economic performance in the face of inflows of British specie in terms of the monarch's failure to circulate the latter more widely.

Shebbeare provided a motive for elector-king's behavior beyond simple venality. He further explained that

> *George* [I] at his accession to the crown was naturally agitated by the suspicion of being dethroned in preference to the house of *Stuart*. It was therefore as natural for him to attempt increasing his *German* dominions at your expense, that at least his coming to this kingdom might prove of some advantage to him. Which maxim being adopted by his ministers to procure themselves stability and conciliate favor, it so fell out that, by the time the apprehension of instability on this throne from the interest of the *Stuarts* was almost vanished, so many transactions had been completed to the advancement of *Hanover* and the ruin of *England* that these had created a secondary and new dread of being displaced by a people so egregiously injured on the account of *German* predilection. This then still kept alive the same fear of being dethroned on that account so strong in the illustrious family, and therefore the same propensity of subjecting *England* to the views of *Hanover*.[118]

Shebbeare reclaimed the conception of Hanover as dynastic insurance policy from Postlethwayt's pro-union argument. Shebbeare then contradicted himself by implying that the pretender was no longer a viable option. He nevertheless, compared the latter favorably with the house of Hanover, outrageously claiming that the drafters of the Act of Settlement 'believed . . . that the danger of converting the kingdom to the Catholic religion by the return of the *Stuarts* was not an object to be dreaded equal with your being chained to *German* interests'.[119] This polemical excess effectively ended Shebbeare's run of anti-Hanoverian publicity, consigning him as it did to both prison and pillory.[120]

As they suffered French requisitoning and quartering, Hanoverians were shocked to see Kloster Zeven faulted by their relatively fortunate British counterparts. British criticism pushed Hanoverian resentment, probably substantial anyway given France's North American calculations, into the press. It revitalized Hanoverian interest in personal union, which had been largely dormant since George I's will had provided for it as a halfway house on the way to complete independence.

*Ruin, in which It Is Shewn That the Present Grandeur of France and Calamities of This Nation are Owing to the Influence of Hanover on the Councils of England* (London, 1757), pp. 117–18.

[118] [Shebbeare], *A Sixth Letter to the People of England*, pp. 58–9.

[119] [Shebbeare], *A Sixth Letter to the People of England*, p. 37.

[120] Foster, 'Smollett's Pamphleteering Foe Shebbeare', pp. 1088–9.

London's *Literary Magazine* published the first Hanoverian grievances in a 'Letter from a Member of the Regency of Hanover'. As with *Popular Prejudice* in 1743, there can never be certainty that the 'Letter' actually came from the pen of an electoral official. But its tone was genuinely Hanoverian. The author followed Ilten's example in publishing candid reflections on the British-Hanoverian relationship in London's relatively open press rather than in the electorate, where French censorship now supplemented that of the local authorities. But unlike *Popular Prejudice*, the 'Letter' appeared in Frankfurt and Leipzig.[121]

The 'Letter' demonstrated the collapse of Hanoverian justifications of the relationship with Britain, which had hitherto referred to the European balance of power. Interestingly, the English 'Letter' omitted a phrase from its German version which indicated that the electoral absences were 'merely to uphold the balance'.[122] The adverb 'merely' indicated a new ambivalence towards the balance of power in Hanoverian political discourse. This resulted in part from a purely intellectual antecedent, for the iconoclastic Göttingen police commissioner Johann Heinrich Gottlob von Justi had just attacked the idea of a European balance in *Staatswirthschaft* (Political Economy).[123] Most Hanoverians were unwilling to part company with the idea altogether. But as they surveyed the damage around them in 1757, they must have considered that the balance of power was ailing. Their anger fell squarely upon Britain, which they had long considered to be the custodian of the balance. The disillusion was palpable when the author of the 'Letter' described Hanover's historical expectation that Britain's 'government, founded as it is upon revolution principles, would not abandon them at a crisis so interesting not only to all Protestants but to all the unenslaved part of Europe'.[124] This was the traditional Hanoverian faith that Britain had committed itself in 1688 to European as well as British freedom, an orientation Hanover had sacrificed its elector to maintain. But the 'Letter' complained that British assistance in 1757 had been inadequate, consisting only of 'an army of observation whose numbers were sufficient to provoke, but not to repel, an invasion'.[125] Its author believed that British derogation

---

121 *Schreiben eines Hannoveraners an einen Milord in England, bey Gelegenheit der Kloster-zevenschen Convention* (Frankfurt and Leipzig, 1757), published in *Teutsche Kriegs-Canzley auf das Jahr 1758* 2 (Frankfurt and Leipzig, 1758), pp. 922–38.
122 *Schreiben eines Hannoveraners*, p. 929.
123 See Johann Heinrich Gottlob von Justi, *Staatswirthschaft, oder Systematische Abhandlung aller Oekonomischen und Cameral-Wissenschaften, die zur Regierung eines Landes erfodert werden* (Leipzig, 1755), pp. 64–6.
124 'Letter from a Member of the Regency of Hanover Relating to the Convention between His R---- H------- the D--- of C--------- and the French of September 8th and October 6th and the State of Affairs in Germany', *Literary Magazine* 2 (1757), p. 483.
125 'Letter from a Member of the Regency of Hanover', p. 484.

had, as in 1712–13, precipitated a breakdown in the balance of power, complaining to his (imaginary?) correspondent that

> some of your present ministry, my Lord, have, it seems, struck into a new and an opposite system of policy and by loudly declaring against all continental connections have wrought themselves into popularity. If this, my Lord, is the case in England, has not Hanover as good a right to declare against all *insular* connections?[126]

Dynastic union's failure to prevent British recidivism discredited it altogether.

The balance of power's collapse sharpened Hanoverian qualms about the electoral absence, which it had traditionally alleviated. Replying to British charges of pro-Hanoverian favoritism, the 'Letter' considered that

> no advantages resulting to our electoral family in our country can make amends for the prejudice we sustain by their absence from ours. Nor, my Lord, is it in His Majesty's power – let his partiality in our favor be ever so great – to make us amends for the privation of that residence of sovereignty amongst us which alone can give spirit to a people, success to trade, life to manufactures, and encouragement to industry of any kind.[127]

Hanoverians still believed that dynastic union, by necessitating the elector's absence in Britain, interfered with his ability to improve his electorate by example and by enlightened initiatives. They ranked the French occupation high on the list of problems exacerbated by the electoral absence. 'We could have no recourse', the author wrote, 'to our own sovereign, whose situation in another country did not permit him to come to the safety of this.'[128] Finally, the 'Letter' seemed to echo George I's fear that princely residence would correlate with political sovereignty – thereby rendering absence synonymous with dependence.

If the diagnosis of the 'Letter' resembled that of George I, so did its prescription. Its author was the first since the late monarch to advocate something resembling personal union between Britain and Hanover. It defended Kloster Zeven with reference to the Act of Settlement's war clause, asking 'does not the reason on which it is founded operate equally for Hanover as for England, and have not the Hanoverians as good a right as the English have to demand that their country shall not pour forth either her blood or treasure in foreign quarrels?'[129] The Act of Settlement had always been a favorite motif of British personal union theorists, as it seemed to

---

126 'Letter from a Member of the Regency of Hanover', p. 482.
127 'Letter from a Member of the Regency of Hanover', p. 481.
128 'Letter from a Member of the Regency of Hanover', p. 484.
129 'Letter from a Member of the Regency of Hanover', p. 480.

establish independence from Hanover. But this was the first time a Hanoverian had laid claim to equivalent rights, rights which admittedly derived more from justice than positive law.

The argument that Hanover possessed an implicit equivalent of the Act of Settlement's war clause dovetailed nicely with the tradition that its constitution closely resembled Britain's. Yet strangely, the author did this from Leibniz's natural-law perspective on dynastic union rather than from the institutional one better supported by the Act of Settlement. The 'Letter' dismissed the British belief that Hanover was ruled absolutely, observing to a noble correspondent that

> there are constitutions in Europe where the prince *may be* arbitrary, but I know of none where he *is so*. An arbitrary prince is one who . . . makes nothing but his own will the measure of his conduct. But this, my Lord give me leave to say, is what nothing but a madman will ever do.[130]

Significantly, 'madman' was the English translation of 'person . . . bereft of all reason' – the phrase which appeared in the letter's German version, *Schreiben eines Hannoveraners*.[131] The use of 'reason' indicated a sense of constitutional affinity based upon natural law. The author proved this with the specific example of the royal veto, which allowed him to make the case that British liberty still depended upon princely reason.[132] The author concluded that 'our elector is no more arbitrary than your king, and we expect to be govern'd by the same salutary maxims as you are – that is, we expect that our master and elector will not to our destruction make his own will the sole measure of his government'.[133] Comparisons of Hanoverian to British governance now resisted British influence as well as the insults which had first inspired them earlier in the eighteenth century.

If the author of the 'Letter' was in fact a Hanoverian minister, then it probably resulted from a renewed query by George II about the feasibility of dissolving dynastic union. This time seven ministers wrote individual memoranda, which constitute one of the most important Hanoverian sources for dynastic union. As they had in 1744, the memoranda provided a balanced analysis of union's advantages and disadvantages, which gave them a peculiarly ambivalent tone.

Some ministers still argued for Hanoverian empire over Britain, which supposedly anchored Britain to a European balance resembling the Holy

---

130 'Letter from a Member of the Regency of Hanover', p. 481.

131 *Schreiben eines Hannoveraners*, p. 927.

132 'Give me leave without offence to ask whether you have in your constitution any principle that can communicate the executive powers to a law or a measure agreed upon by both houses of Parliament if your king should take it in his head that he is *arbitrary* too, and without giving any reason but his own *will* refuse his assent. I am afraid, my Lord, *constitutionally* you have not.' 'Letter from a Member of the Regency of Hanover', p. 481.

133 'Letter from a Member of the Regency of Hanover', p. 481.

Roman Empire in macrocosm. Although he was the youngest privy councillor, Burchard Christian von Behr made the antiquated argument that separation from Britain would 'be highly disadvantageous to the Protestant interest and the freedom of the Empire and all Europe, which would find themselves in the greatest danger of French hegemony if they were not upheld from now on from here'.[134] Behr implicitly conceded that the balance of power had temporarily failed, but still believed it might be restored.

Other ministers followed the memoranda of 1744 in detecting a more submissive posture to Britain, though relying less upon the balance of power. Gerlach Adolf von Münchhausen endorsed Hanoverian deference, writing that 'these lands are surrounded by powerful neighbors, and have therefore hitherto needed English protection for our conservation'.[135] But Levin, Baron Hake, considered that Britain endangered the electorate more than it protected it. He wrote that

> the interest of the crown may often conflict with that of the electorate, in which case the latter will be subordinated to the former. Since England's interest is directed at maintaining maritime superiority and above all at weakening France's power, the latter may seek to revenge itself upon the German states during every war if it does not consider itself a match for England.[136]

Hake weakened the force of this apprehension with the argument that France would never again repeat its occupation of the electorate 'because of the associated costs'.[137] Johann Clamor August von dem Bussche seconded this, writing that 'France may become convinced that it weakened its army through its invasion of our lands without winning the least [concession] from the English nation, and will probably refrain from the same foolish venture in the future.'[138] But dependence upon France's future restraint was scarce comfort for Bussche, whose Hannover townhouse now accommodated the French commander.[139]

Obviously the Hanoverians preferred to rely upon British assistance. In a passage recalling his colleagues' 1744 description of the electorate's advantages to British empire, Steinberg argued that Hanoverian services deserved compensation. He wrote that

---

134 Behr's memorandum, 19 Oct. 1757, Stade, Niedersächsisches Hauptstaatsarchiv (NHStA), Hann. 92 Nr. 70, f. 53.
135 Münchhausen's memorandum, 12 Oct. 1757, Hannover, NHStA, Hann. 92 Nr. 70, f. 29.
136 Hake's memorandum, 12 Oct. 1757, Hannover, NHStA, Hann. 92 Nr. 70, f. 56. See also Schwicheldt's memorandum, 20 Oct. 1757, Stade, NHStA, Hann. 92 Nr. 70, f. 47.
137 Hake's memorandum, 12 Oct. 1757, Hannover, NHStA, Hann. 92 Nr. 70, f. 59.
138 Bussche's memorandum, 12 Oct. 1757, Hannover, NHStA, Hann. 92 Nr. 70, f. 63.
139 Eberhard Jürgen Abelmann, *Hannover im Siebenjährigen Krieg*, ed. Hans Hartmann (Hameln, 1995), p. 97.

a separation would hardly be thinkable now, because Your Royal Majesty protected England from a descent by sending over a part of your German troops and thereby obliged the enemy to bring the war into your German lands in order to carry out its design against England. English help is therefore to be expected so that the already totally ruined German lands can recover somewhat, and it would be very hard if England should deny this help and detach itself from the same by a separation.[140]

Steinberg declined to specify what form British assistance might take, but other ministers seem to have envisioned renewed subsidies. Diede feared that dissolution might prompt Britain to cut them off,[141] although he admitted that Hanover had also received subsidies before dynastic union.[142] Diede also conceded that there were times under the dynastic union in which Hanover had not received subsidies from Britain. He wrote that 'the acquisition of Bremen and Verden, as well as the decrease in expenses formerly required by [the elector's] permanent presence in the land, contributed to the fact that the military not only remained in its former condition but strengthened after [British] subsidies ceased'.[143] But Hanoverians knew how controversial Bremen and Verden were in Britain. The episode caused Schwicheldt to argue that dynastic union impeded the Hanoverian interest in territorial expansion. He held that 'the interest of the English crown has not allowed the growth of the electorate' under dynastic union.[144] Referring to the Act of Settlement, he noted that 'England fears becoming involved in disputes which it regards as foreign to England the more that the elector, who is at the same time king, expands the borders of his hereditary lands.'[145] This was somewhat unfair, as some British observers had evinced far more enthusiasm for the acquisition of Bremen and Verden than their Hanoverian equivalents.

As usual, strategic considerations were linked to the electoral absence they had once legitimated. And while complaints about Hanover's leadership vacuum were by now familiar, they were now joined to a new economic anxiety. For the first time, Hanoverians feared losing specie to Britain, in a manner analogous to long-standing British anxieties concerning the reverse. Münchhausen reinforced the impression of British empire over Hanover, warning that

commonly a country is in a bad way if it is not ruled according to its own interest and state maxims, but those of that land upon which it is dependent. It becomes poorer when expenditures decrease and surplus revenues go out of the

---

140 Steinberg's memorandum, 19 Oct. 1757, Stade, NHStA, Hann. 92 Nr. 70, ff. 35–6.
141 Diede's memorandum, 20 Oct. 1757, Stade, NHStA, Hann. 92, Nr. 70, ff. 77–8.
142 Diede's memorandum, 20 Oct. 1757, Stade, NHStA, Hann. 92, Nr. 70, f. 71.
143 Diede's memorandum, 20 Oct. 1757, Stade, NHStA, Hann. 92, Nr. 70, f. 72.
144 Schwicheldt's memorandum, 20 Oct. 1757, Stade, NHStA, Hann. 92 Nr. 70, f. 50.
145 Schwicheldt's memorandum, 20 Oct. 1757, Stade, NHStA, Hann. 92 Nr. 70, f. 51.

country, as the Hessian lands have experienced to their great cost in their union with Sweden.[146]

Münchhausen's account of the Hessian-Swedish relationship differs enough from James Ralph's to merit some attention. It probably rested upon the infrequency of Fredrik I's visits to Hesse-Cassell, a fact which would have endeared him as much to Ralph as it would have troubled Münchhausen.

The Hanoverian ministers hastened to exempt George II from their critique of British empire. Hake believed that its ill effects had been mitigated by George II's Hanoverian birth, considering that

> nature effects a partiality for the land where one was born and raised. Your present Majesty as well as your father of glorious memory were born and raised in these German lands, from which circumstance derives the excellent partiality the German lands have enjoyed and still enjoy under these two rulers.[147]

Thanks to this bias, the electoral absence had actually benefited the Hanoverian economy in certain respects. Bussche noted that 'the revenues of these lands . . . stay in them, since their rulers contented themselves with the [British] crown revenues and applied the income of the electoral lands solely to the inner improvement of the same'.[148] Hake added that these monies could go to reconstruction following a French withdrawal.[149] Schwicheldt also thanked George II for ensuring that his absence was as economically painless as possible, writing that

> Your Majesty has most graciously condescended not only to keep up your entire royal household as if you were constantly present, but also conserved a numerous army wherein so many subjects – especially the nobility – find a respectable employment. It can therefore hardly be feared of Your Majesty that you take money from your German provinces to England.[150]

This was, of course, the anxiety first addressed by George I's will, which had required his successors to maintain the Hanoverian court in their absence.

But the Hanoverian ministers recognized that they would lose this sentimental advantage upon the death of George II. When Prince Frederick had died in 1751, the British diplomat Sir Charles Hanbury Williams had reported that

---

146 Münchhausen's memorandum, 12 Oct. 1757, Hannover, NHStA, Hann. 92 Nr. 70, ff. 29–30.
147 Hake's memorandum, 12 Oct. 1757, Hannover, NHStA, Hann. 92 Nr. 70, f. 55.
148 Bussche's memorandum, 12 Oct. 1757, Hannover, NHStA, Hann. 92 Nr. 70, f. 62.
149 Hake's memorandum, 12 Oct. 1757, Hannover, NHStA, Hann. 92 Nr. 70, ff. 58–9.
150 Schwicheldt's memorandum, 20 Oct. 1757, Stade, NHStA, Hann. 92 Nr. 70, ff. 41–2.

the grief at Hanover for the death of the late prince of Wales is very great. They look upon themselves (and I hope with reason) as likely to become in reality a province subservient to the interests of Great Britain, and it is high time they should be so . . . for time impossible that a prince not born there can possibly like such a poor scrubby town and such barren and melancholic country'.[151]

This anxiety informed the contribution of Diede, who wrote that the heir apparent

will have to leave the direction of the most important government business to his ministers, being unable to appoint well qualified persons to ministries and other offices according to his own experience. If the authority of English ministers acquires too much influence in the government affairs of his German lands, the latter will be disadvantaged.[152]

The advantage of the elector-king's birth would end with George II's death, whereupon it would become an advantage for imperial Britain.

Despite these visions, Hake attempted to identify the benefits a British-born elector might bring. He wrote that 'an absent prince can often learn the condition of his land and the behavior of his advisers more reliably than one who is present, for truth then finds a more secure way to his throne'.[153] Hake did not explain how this was so, but imagined that the electorate would be able to outbid Britain for the affection of a British-born elector.

the successors to the crown will exhibit their respect and care for a land which centuries ago gave rise to their race, where subjects are not accustomed to exaggerated freedom but to an excellent love, loyalty and obedience to their ruler and to good orderliness and manners, which forms a significant part of Germany, which confers the electoral dignity, which supports a respectable corps of troops, and offers every possible sensory delight to a ruler present there.[154]

Although he criticized Britons' freedom, Hake also sympathized with their jealousy of it. He wrote that 'it is to be expected of a wise king that he will observe the same [restraint] in his electorate, thereby giving the English nation a reliable proof of good inborn characteristics'.[155] Once again,

---

[151] Quoted in Jeremy Black, *The Hanoverians: The History of a Dynasty* (London, 2004), p. 202.
[152] Diede's memorandum, 20 Oct. 1757, Stade, NHStA, Hann. 92, Nr. 70, f. 69.
[153] Hake's memorandum, 12 Oct. 1757, Hannover, NHStA, Hann. 92 Nr. 70, f. 57.
[154] Hake's memorandum, 12 Oct. 1757, Hannover, NHStA, Hann. 92 Nr. 70, f. 57.
[155] Hake's memorandum, 12 Oct. 1757, Hannover, NHStA, Hann. 92 Nr. 70, f. 58.

Hanoverians hoped that dynastic union with Britain would reinforce and improve their own constitutional freedoms.

Whatever its speculative contributions to Hanoverian civil liberty, Britain did help liberate the electorate from its French masters. Friedrich II's victory at Rossbach in November 1757 enabled George II to reconstitute the army of observation under Prince Ferdinand of Brunswick, for whom Pitt secured a grant of £100,000. Harassed by Ferdinand and weakened by an exceptionally cold winter,[156] the French finally evacuated Hannover in February 1758. But while the enemy had departed, it left behind economic deprivation and concomitant bitterness at the British empire.

David Georg Strube expressed this mood in a 1758 pamphlet entitled *Die gerechte Sache Großbritanniens und Churhannovers* (The Just Case of Great Britain and Hanover). He blamed Britain's American disputes with France for starting the war, writing that

> the Hanoverians never promised to stand for that which their elector does as king. Acadia concerns them no more than Monomotapa. If he undertakes something respecting his German lands, they must approve it and suffer for it if need be, but not for that which he performs for the good of the English nation, which they can join no more than it deems itself obliged to help them if not promised in particular acts of parliament limited to certain cases.[157]

By now Hanover's top legal officer, Strube presented a broader vision of electoral power than he had as a young man. But the elector's remit did not extend, he emphasized, to involving Hanover in British quarrels. Like the author of the 'Letter', Strube held that Hanover tacitly possessed the same rights Britain had enumerated for itself in the Act of Settlement. Out of this sentiment evolved Pütter's construct of personal union, which characterized Hanover's relationship to Britain as dynastic accident without legal relevance.

Ironically, the British ministry which Hanoverians blamed for their condition was to be criticized in its own country for being too favorable to them. William Pitt the elder determined British perceptions of dynastic union more than any other official since Sir Robert Walpole. But where Walpole had actively identified himself with Hanover at one point, Pitt's association with it was, by contrast, unpremeditated. As John Brewer has shown more generally, Pitt the practical politician was captive to his rhetorical history;[158] his flamboyant attacks upon Hanover from the opposition encouraged his

---

156 For the cold, see Abelmann, *Hannover im Siebenjährigen Krieg*, ed. Hartmann, p. 98.

157 [David Georg Strube], *Die gerechte Sache Großbritanniens und Churhannovers gegen Frankreich und Oesterreich* (Hannover, 1758), published in *Teutsche Kriegs-Canzley auf das Jahr 1758* 1 (Frankfurt and Leipzig, 1758), p. 963.

158 John Brewer, *Party Ideology and Popular Politics at the Accession of George III* (Cambridge, 1976), pp. 96–111.

enemies to accuse him of complaisance when in government. Although he had already experienced such scrutiny in 1746 and 1757,[159] it became virtually permanent after his decision to supplement Ferdinand's army with British regulars during the summer of 1758. Nothing could be further from the truth than the proposition that 'continental interventionism . . . was . . . dissociated from the charge of Hanoverianism . . . in 1758'.[160] From then on, important British politicians considered Pitt to be a creature of Hanover. This was true even of the prince of Wales, whose accession as George III hastened the end of Pitt's successful war ministry. 'For George III', Lewis Namier has written, 'Hanover, Germany, and the continental war were indissolubly bound up with the person of George II; he gloried in the name of "Britain" primarily because that distinguished him from his grandfather, and he talked of Hanover as "that horrid electorate" because it was his grandfather's home.'[161] This was only half true; George III also loathed Hanover because of its association with William Pitt the elder.

Kloster Zeven had reconciled Pitt to British empire over Hanover. He obtained William Beckford's support for a January payment to Ferdinand with the argument that 'the troops were now under British direction and could be used for British purposes'.[162] And when Pitt concluded the vastly more expensive Convention of London with Prussia in April, the earl of Denbigh said in parliament that 'he was glad the elector of Hanover was included in it, that he might not desert the king of England'.[163] The subsidies of early 1758 were, according to this perspective, a mechanism to reassert British primacy over Hanover within dynastic union. Although some supported the policy from a personal union viewpoint emphasizing justice,[164] the government sought to manipulate Hanover to Britain's advantage.

Pitt's inconsistency had its mirror image in the opposition press, which opposed Kloster Zeven's abrogation as much as they had the original convention. The anonymous author of *The Political Freethinker* asked,

> must posterity be mortgaged for a G-rm-n war in which we are not concerned? H-----r is out of the question now a *neutrality* is obtained for it. And however ridiculous may have been the measure that produced it, we should be much to blame if we did not turn it the most to our advantage.[165]

---

159  For the precedent of 1746, see Harris, *A Patriot Press*, pp. 77–8.

160  Black, *The Continental Commitment*, p. 119.

161  L. B. Namier, *England in the Age of the American Revolution* (London, 1930), p. 354.

162  Peters, *Pitt and Popularity*, p. 104.

163  Horace Walpole, *Memoirs of King George II*, ed. John Brooke (3 vols., New Haven, 1985), iii, p. 16.

164  'The Concluding Speech upon the Prussian Treaty', *Literary Magazine* 3 (1758), p. 244. William Cobbett misdated this debate in his *Parliamentary History* to February 1757.

165  *The Political Freethinker, or a Real and Impartial Enquiry into the Causes of Our Late Miscarriages and Our Present Melancholy Situation* (London, 1757), p. 24.

*The Political Freethinker* further feared that the convention's rejection might lead the French to carry out even worse exactions on the electorate than they already had.[166] The Exeter tory George Coade further developed the argument that British engagement on the continent would only worsen Hanover's position. In *A Letter to the Right Honourable W. P., Esq.* which he composed during spring 1757 and published a year later, Coade wrote that 'the more we interfere in continental affairs, the more we add to the hazard and danger of these dominions. And the less we have to do on the continent, the more we add to their real safety and security.'[167] Both these pamphlets used Pitt's former arguments against him, in particular his professions of sympathy for an electorate when Britain had requisitioned 8,000 troops to protect against France's projected 1756 invasion. Pitt's inconsistency was much more dangerous to him than was that of his comparatively unknown opponents to themselves.

Pitt further exposed himself to his enemies by avowing that subsidies would be the limit of his government's engagement upon the continent. Pitt declared to the commons in December 1757 that 'he had never been against continental measures when practicable, but would not now send a drop of our blood to the Elbe to be lost in that ocean of gore'.[168] In fact, he had been contemplating a British continental force ever since Kloster Zeven had presented the specter of Hanoverian neutrality.[169] Pitt prudently waited until parliament's prorogation to dispatch British regulars to Germany in the summer of 1758.[170]

*The Monitor* angrily attacked British military intervention on the continent. Some of its arguments drew heavily upon traditional fears of Hanoverian empire over Britain. Where Shebbeare had blamed electoral vulnerability upon Hanoverian avarice, *The Monitor* attributed it to Hanoverian expansionism.

> it is to the Hanoverians' abuse of their connection with Britain that they ought to impute their misfortunes. Had the electorate been content with its original mediocrity, there would have been no temptation nor jealousy to expose her to invasions. But the parental foible of aggrandizing a darling child, giving the preference to its co-estates in all contracts for mercenary troops, increasing its dominion and power, and making it a party in most of the treaties, negotiations, and transactions with Great Britain placed it in a light too conspicuous to be neglected by its neighbors in time of danger or to remain unmolested by the enemies of Great Britain.[171]

---

166 *The Political Freethinker*, p. 26.
167 [George Coade], *A Letter to the Right Honourable W. P., Esq.* (Exeter, 1758), p. 75.
168 Horace Walpole, *Memoirs of King George II*, ed. Brooke, iii, p. 3.
169 Middleton, *The Bells of Victory*, p. 57.
170 Peters, *Pitt and Popularity*, p. 116.
171 *The Monitor, or British Freeholder* no. 158 (29 July 1758), p. 957.

The last sentence indicated, however, that *The Monitor* could not deny that Britain bore a greater responsibility for Hanoverian suffering. Accordingly, *The Monitor's* analysis transformed into a critique of British empire over the electorate. *The Monitor* claimed that Britons

> are desirous to retaliate the oppressions and desolation with which the French overran the electoral dominions by carrying the seat of war into the heart of the enemy's country and never to sheath the sword 'til the damages they have sustained on the account of Britain shall be repaired by the terms of peace. Any other method . . . would fall short of its relief and deprive this island of its advantageous situation. To go farther than this measure would be to connect the interest of a foreign state with our own, which is deviating from the true intention of the Act of Settlement and, instead of serving either, must be the destruction of both.[172]

*The Monitor* displayed the increasing tendency to promote a maritime view of British empire while sympathizing with Hanoverian losses.

*The Monitor's* criticism of British empire over Hanover was further developed by an anonymously-published pamphlet entitled *Things as They Are*, which also expanded upon *The Political Freethinker's* case against a rejection of Kloster Zeven. It wrote that Britain's complicity in that act was not only dishonorable,[173] but contrary to its own, and Hanover's, national interests. *Things as They Are* considered Kloster Zeven had been a missed opportunity, asking 'whether, in short, the fairest of occasions was not missed of [Britain] untwisting with a country, the connection with which had never but cost her more than it was worth?'[174] The anonymous author contended that Hanover was equally useless to the French, whose retreat proved that 'those parts [are] of themselves not the most fruitful'.[175] And he excoriated that retreat, writing that 'the ridding Hanover of [the French] might be a merit to Hanover. The quickening their march and seeing them safe home was not of much disservice to the French. But in what could Britain benefit by the return of those forces so much nearer home?'[176] Here again was the inverted maritime ideology wherein dynastic union was useful to Britain for keeping France preoccupied in Germany, except that now it was employed for the first time by dynastic union's critics.

*Things as They Are* displayed its debt to *The Monitor*, and three years of tory argumentation. But speculation about its authorship centered exclu-

---

172 *The Monitor, or British Freeholder* no. 158 (29 July 1758), p. 958.
173 [John Perceval, 2nd earl of Egmont], *Things as They Are* (London, [1758]), pp. 75–6.
174 [Egmont], *Things as They Are*, p. 73.
175 [Egmont], *Things as They Are*, p. 78.
176 [Egmont], *Things as They Are*, p. 79.

sively on whigs. The pamphlet was widely attributed to the earl of Egmont, who disowned it in a letter to the member of parliament Sir John Cust.[177] If Egmont was really the author, then his speculation as to the pamphlet's sincerity on dynastic union illustrated his own motivation. It was true that he had previously supported union, to the point of defending the employment of Hanoverian mercenaries in his famous pamphlet *Faction Detected* (1743). But Egmont directed Cust's attention to other suspected authors: Fox, Dodington, Ralph, and Marchmont. All of these were whigs, and three – Dodington, Ralph, and Egmont himself – were alumni of the Leicester House oppositions conducted by the late Prince Frederick and his widow Princess Augusta. So while *Things as They Are* still followed the tory lead, it anticipated a new criticism of British empire over Hanover which would gradually replace that dominated by the tories.

One of the suspected authors of *Things as They Are*, George Bubb Dodington, published an *Examination of a Letter* in which he anticipated that an eventual peace might require Britain to part once again with Cape Breton, which it had just captured, as the Treaty of Aix-la-Chapelle had in 1748. This fear originated in *The Monitor*, just as some made in *Things as They Are* had.[178] The difference was that Dodington's *Examination* concluded that 'those very orators . . . will, by their fatally connecting us with Prussia and by their bringing on us the odium of abetting the breach of the Hanoverian convention, [who] have created the necessity of such a cession'.[179] Dodington's orator was obviously Pitt. Remarkably, given such pressures, Pitt refused to rule out cession of Cape Breton. Speaking before parliament in December 1758, he avowed that 'he would not give up an iota of our allies for any British consideration'.[180] In his next effort, a pamphlet which he misleadingly entitled *The Honest Grief of a Tory*, Dodington reported that 'Mr. P--t shamelessly declar'd that he would sooner part with [Cape Breton] than forego one single iota belonging to the electorate of Hanover.'[181] Dodington connected this attack on British empire over Hanover to a criticism more often associated with the reverse, political

---

[177] Egmont to Cust, 17 Aug. 1758, London, published in Lionel Cust, ed., *Records of the Cust Family, Series III: Sir John Cust, Third Baronet, P. C., M. P. for Grantham 1742–1770, Speaker of the House of Commons 1761–1770* (London, 1927), p. 171.

[178] 'Should this island be, under any pretences, drawn again into a continental war . . . perhaps Cape Breton and Senegal [would be] given up for the evacuation of some German principality.' *The Monitor* no. 162 (26 Aug. 1758), p. 982.

[179] [George Bubb Dodington], *Examination of a Letter Published under the Name of L--------t G-----l B--gh and Addressed to the Hon. W-----m P--t, Esq.* (London, 1758), p. 25. For the attribution, see Horace Walpole, *Memoirs of King George II*, ed. Brooke, iii, p. 38.

[180] Quoted in Peters, *Pitt and Popularity*, p. 133.

[181] [George Bubb Dodington], *The Honest Grief of a Tory, Expressed in a Genuine Letter from a Burges of ----- in Wiltshire to the Author of The Monitor, Feb. 17 1759* (London, 1759), pp. 15–16. For the attribution, see Hazen, *A Catalogue of Horace Walpole's Library*, i, p. 474.

corruption; he termed the employment of British regulars in Germany 'to be the last excess of ministerial compliance with the sovereign'.[182] In Dodington, who had been sympathetic to Hanover when close to office in 1755, Pitt's inconsistency had its mirror image.

William Beckford and *The Monitor* had, by now, closed ranks behind Pitt's policy, and disputed Dodington's argument. The newspaper asked,

> can you deem this aid a sacrifice of flattery to the E-----r of H-----r, or even to his cousin the king of Prussia? . . . Has Britain no interest in the preservation of a bulwark to arbitrary power and universal monarchy on the continent? Look at our exports: examine the extent of our trade to Germany. Should the Rhine, the Elbe, the Weser, the Oder, and the whole navigation of Germany be reduced under the power of France, our manufactures and merchandize, our colonies and settlements would feel their loss severely.[183]

A year and a half after Pitt, Beckford and *The Monitor* converted to British empire over Hanover. But in so doing, they forfeited criticism of the reverse to Dodington and kindred spirits.

One of those kindred spirits was the prince of Wales. Prince George's minority, and the opportunity it presented his grandfather to interfere in his affairs, had only heightened the insecurity endemic to adult heirs apparent. He sought support from politicians both inside his junior court at Leicester House, such as his tutor the earl of Bute, and at Westminster. Pitt had featured prominently in the latter category until he declined to communicate the decision to deploy British regulars in Germany to Leicester House.[184] Prince George denounced their 'wavering friend' and worried that 'if this unhappy measure should be taken we shall be drawn deeper in a continent war than ever'.[185] Bute echoed this criticism twice during October.[186] And when Pitt omitted to consult Leicester House on the renewal of the Prussian subsidy in December, the prince complained to Bute that 'he treats both you and me with no more regard than he would do a parcel of children. He seems to forget that the day will come when he must expect to be treated according to his deserts.'[187] Dodington gradually replaced Pitt in Leicester House's graces.[188]

Pitt's enemies renewed their criticism in summer with an anonymously

---

[182] [Dodington], *The Honest Grief of a Tory*, p. 21.

[183] *The Monitor, or British Freeholder* no. 190 (10 Mar. 1759), p. 1149.

[184] James Lee McKelvey, *George III and Lord Bute: The Leicester House Years* (Durham, NC, 1973), p. 76.

[185] George, Prince of Wales, to Bute, c. 2 July 1758, published in Romney Sedgwick, ed., *Letters from George III to Lord Bute 1756–1766* (London, 1939), p. 11.

[186] McKelvey, *George III and Lord Bute*, p. 77.

[187] George, Prince of Wales, to Bute, c. 8 Dec. 1758, published in Sedgwick, ed., *Letters from George III to Lord Bute 1756–1766*, p. 18.

[188] McKelvey, *George III and Lord Bute*, pp. 77–8.

published *Letter from the Duchess of M-r------gh in the Shades to the Great Man*. The pamphlet was yet another opposition whig rejection of Pitt, to whom the late duchess had bequeathed £10,000 for his supposed incorruptibility.[189] It attacked empire over Hanover, from the rejection of Kloster Zeven to the subsequent deployment of British regulars in Germany. The *Letter* observed that 'the very man who had fulminated against continental connections . . . plunged over head and ears into them, new-cemented one of the most obnoxious and the most dangerous of them with P--ss-a, and renewed another with H-----r, etc., which had been fortunately broken off of itself'.[190] A *Defence of the Letter* noted the irony that Hanover was 'endangered by [George II's] great tenderness for it',[191] observing that 'if Britain has been the sacrifice, Hanover has already been . . . the idol and victim'.[192] But such sympathy was lost on Prince George, who nevertheless complained about 'the partiality ---- has for that horrid electorate which has always liv'd upon the very vitals of this poor country'.[193] The prince's pessimism went unrewarded; news of Prince Ferdinand's spectacular victory at Minden soon arrived, increasing expectations of an advantageous peace.

Accusations to the contrary aside, Pitt was not uniformly complaisant to George II on Hanoverian issues. The king had been demanding territorial indemnification for the French occupation of Hanover, at least since October 1758.[194] Pitt told Newcastle that

> in no situation could he, or would he, consent to it. He thought it destruction both to the king as king and as elector . . . He hazarded he might lose his popularity to a degree by the immense sums given for the support of the war upon the continent and the king's Hanover dominions, that he thought it right and so far he risked his popularity. But then he had the comfort to think that people would see that that was done for the sake of the whole, and not to aggrandize or promote any acquisition for Hanover.[195]

The minister's talk of the 'whole' implicitly included Hanover within the British empire, but was grudging – as a later episode revealed. When informed that the government could not support Hanoverian enlargement,

189 Peters, *Pitt and Popularity*, p. 154 (note).
190 *A Letter from the Duchess of M-r------gh in the Shades to the Great Man* (London, 1759), pp. 16–17.
191 *A Defence of the Letter from the Dutchess of M---------h in the Shades to the Great Man* (London, 1759), p. 11.
192 *A Defence of the Letter from the Dutchess of M---------h*, p. 34.
193 George, Prince of Wales, to Bute, 5 Aug. 1759, published in Sedgwick, ed., *Letters from George III to Lord Bute*, p. 28.
194 See Newcastle to Hardwicke, 5 Oct. 1758, Kensington, published in Philip C. Yorke, *The Life and Correspondence of Philip Yorke, Earl of Hardwicke, Lord High Chancellor of Great Britain* (3 vols., Cambridge, 1913), iii, pp. 230–1.
195 Newcastle to Hardwicke, 31 Oct. 1759, Claremont, published in Yorke, *The Life and Correspondence of Philip Yorke, Earl of Hardwicke*, iii, pp. 241–2.

the king petulantly responded that 'since you will do nothing for me, I hope you will agree to separate my electorate from this country'. The king envisioned a dissolution by act of parliament, which would leave Britain to the prince of Wales and Hanover to the duke of York. Pitt 'most heartily wish'd that the thing could be done',[196] but continued to act as if it couldn't. The Great Commoner's common denominator was a distaste for personal union.

Pitt's opponents continued to attack British empire over Hanover. The anonymously published *Political Thoughts* complained that 'the attachment of Hanover to the crown of England . . . has brought upon us all the expenses and perplexity of continual wars upon the continent'.[197] Maritime grand strategy still furnished the most compelling argument against continental empire. The author of *Political Thoughts* expressed a 'wish that the renunciation of Hanover had taken place instantly upon the accession' of the Hanoverian dynasty in 1714,[198] but admitted the historical unfeasibility of proceeding thus. He continued that 'in former days, I could not decently have avowed a wish for the expulsion of a family from this crown without securing to them a peaceable and prosperous retreat to their undisputed dominions from whence they were invited by us for the support of the Protestant cause'.[199] This analysis of royal favoritism for Hanover derived, of course, from Leslie and the Jacobites. Although they were precisely the reason the *Political Thoughts* was so forgiving of dynastic union's early abuses, the Jacobites' prospects had since declined markedly. The anonymous author considered that after

> the precise period from which we may account the succession to have been established in perfect security . . . the ministers of the crown are without excuse whenever they may have advised, concerted, or not opposed any such Hanoverian measures as may not have been consistent with the dignity and interests of this country. This their condemnation is founded in the letter of the Act of Settlement.[200]

For this reason, *Political Thoughts* proposed dissolving dynastic union as part of a comprehensive European peace. Prussia would cede Silesia to Austria, securing peace in the Empire. Prussia would in turn be compensated with Hanover, thus severing Britain's dynastic connection with that electorate. Finally, Austria would relinquish its provinces in the Netherlands to an 'independent prince' under British influence.[201]

George II's death, on 25 October, quite naturally prompted further

---

196 Newcastle to Hardwicke, 21 Nov. 1759, London, BL, Add. MS 32899, ff. 6–7.
197 *Political Thoughts* (n. p., 1760), p. 14.
198 *Political Thoughts*, p. 37.
199 *Political Thoughts*, p. 38.
200 *Political Thoughts*, p. 38.
201 *Political Thoughts*, pp. 48, 68.

analysis of Britain's relationship with Hanover. Edmund Burke, the young Irish-born editor of *The Annual Register*, was surprised at the failure of Hanoverian empire over Britain. Burke wrote that

> it would perhaps be impossible to exhibit a more pleasing picture than that which might be formed from a just view of His late Majesty's conduct to these two so differently constituted parts of his dominions. His virtue was proved by two of the greatest trials to which the nature of man is liable: the trust of absolute and unbounded power, and the most exalted station limited by the strictest laws. For these two so very different situations, very different and almost opposite tempers and talents have been always thought necessary. But that king had a mind perfectly adapted to both, for whilst in England he kept the liberties of his people inviolate and like a wise magistrate was satisfied to make his authority cooperate with law and his will freely subservient to the wisdom of ages, in Hanover like an indulgent father acting only from the sentiments of a paternal heart his affection and his equity supplied the want of law and constitution.[202]

George II's ability to quarantine Hanover's supposedly absolute government suggested the existence of personal union, which prevailed despite the king's preference for the electorate. Burke wrote that

> it is true that during his whole life he had shown a remarkable affection to his Hanoverian subjects, yet the last act of it demonstrated that they were far from engrossing the whole of his regard, and that in reality his German possessions held no other place in his consideration than what their relative importance to the rest of his dominions naturally claimed.[203]

Considering Hanover in its relative importance to Britain's vast empire necessarily subordinated the former to the latter.

Whatever George II's Hanoverian policy had been, that of his successor was less clear. *The Monitor* expected the threat of Hanoverian empire to diminish observing that

> however just, wise, and good that prince may be who is a stranger and an alien born, his government never gives that thorough satisfaction as under a native king whose interest and love cannot be supposed to be divided as his must be, who rules over nations of diverse interests and of different constitutions.
>
> But there is the greatest reason to expect that our continental connections will become more constitutional, that no interest nor errors of a German

---

[202] *The Annual Register, or a View of the History, Politicks, and Literature for the Year 1760* (London, 1764), pp. 41–2.

[203] *The Annual Register, or a View of the History, Politicks, and Literature for the Year 1760*, p. 41.

government will evermore influence the councils of a BRITON, that a due regard will be paid to every clause in the Act of Settlement . . .

The sovereign who glories in the name of Briton will glory in every measure that is conducive to the glory of his country, and in discouraging and rejecting every connection that shall tend to diminish that glory or to oppress his people for the advantage of a foreign state . . . He will have no thought to seek protection and defense from foreign auxiliaries, the terror of a free people, and not to be accounted for in any other way than in that timidity and jealousy which a stranger born cannot shake off.[204]

The account of intrinsic royal favoritism for Hanover which had subsisted since Drake suggested it, evaporated in the face of a British-born king.

Indeed, the king had encouraged such thinking. In his first speech to parliament, he had self-consciously differentiated himself from his foreign-born predecessor by announcing, 'born and educated in this country, I glory in the name of Briton'.[205] George III thereby recalled Anne's speech fifty-eight years earlier, wherein she had avowed that 'I know my heart to be entirely English.'[206] The evolution of 'English' into 'Briton' led some to suspect that George III had exchanged the pro-Hanoverian bias of his sires for an affection for the native Scotland of his tutor Bute. Yet there is little question that the king himself meant, like Anne, to distance himself from his foreign-born predecessor. Bute had, after all, instructed him four years earlier that 'he is not a foreigner, but a prince born and bred in the country . . . He will have no predilection for any other country, nor any prejudices of foreign politics.'[207]

But if George III's anti-Hanoverianism had been simply a matter of filial rebellion, it would have dissipated soon after his grandfather's death – just as it had in the case of the latter in 1727. But the king maintained it for his struggle with Pitt, who was as identified with Hanover as Walpole had been thirty-three years earlier. Each day Pitt continued in office delayed the king's eventual reconciliation with Hanover. This was evinced by their conflict over his first speech to privy council, which was to be widely published. Drafted by Bute, the speech originally had the king vow that 'as I mount the throne in the midst of a bloody war, I shall endeavor to prosecute it in the manner most likely to bring an honorable and lasting peace'. Pitt managed to replace the adjective, 'bloody', with the phrase 'expensive, but just and necessary', and obtained the addition of a promise to seek peace 'in concert with our allies'.[208] Hanover was an important subtext of these differences, and remained an issue as long as Pitt remained in office.

---

[204] *The Monitor, or British Freeholder* no. 280 (29 Nov. 1760), pp. 1690–1.
[205] Cobbett, ed., *The Parliamentary History*, xv, col. 982. The words were George III's.
[206] Edward Gregg, *Queen Anne* (London, 1980), p. 152. The words were those of her uncle, Rochester.
[207] Quoted in McKelvey, *George III and Lord Bute*, p. 86.
[208] John Brooke, *King George III* (London, 1972), p. 75.

The fact that George II's death did not immediately alter British attitudes towards Hanover was illustrated by the publication, in November 1760, of Israel Mauduit's critical *Considerations on the Present German war*. The pamphlet sold over 5,000 copies in five editions, making it one of the age's most successful publications.[209] Horace Walpole recorded that Mauduit, a dissenting woolens merchant,[210] published his pamphlet with Hardwicke's 'countenance'.[211] Hardwicke may have been Mauduit's patron, but it was telling that the *Considerations'* foremost parliamentary exponent in December 1760 was Sir Francis Dashwood,[212] a political ally of Bute's who had supported Earl Poulett's motion against George II's last visit to Hanover in 1755.[213] Bute later condescended to award Mauduit a place in his government, along with a pension.[214]

As Marie Peters has said of the *Considerations*, 'there was little new . . . Rather, Mauduit gave new cogency to well-established arguments.'[215] Indeed, the *Considerations* furnished a classic maritime critique of British empire over Hanover. Mauduit did not categorically rule out involvement with the continent, indeed he considered 'the Act of Settlement . . . was itself a continental connection and a very happy one, though intended perhaps to be not quite so great a one'.[216] The latter phrase indicated Mauduit's discomfort with the imperial responsibilities which had arisen from the Hanoverian succession. Noting France's military superiority on land, he complained that British defense of Hanover 'is giving up all the advantages of our situation and joining our island onto the continent, by finding for our enemy a field to beat us in. It is giving up all the benefit of our naval superiority for the sake of a distant land war'.[217] Kloster Zeven, by which Hanoverian ministers had 'renounc[ed] all their English connections', was mourned in particular. Mauduit observed that 'since the H--------ns by themselves were content to sign a neutrality and let the French stay in their country, we need not put ourselves to the annual expense of four to five millions to keep them out'.[218] This comment reflected the economic premise of maritime strategy, that continental warfare drained wealth from Britain.

---

209 Karl Schweizer, 'Israel Mauduit: Pamphleteering and Foreign Policy in the Age of the Elder Pitt', in Stephen Taylor, Richard Connors, and Clyve Jones, eds., *Hanoverian Britain and Empire: Essays in Memory of Philip Lawson* (Woodbridge, 1998), p. 200.

210 Robert J. Taylor, 'Israel Mauduit', *New England Quarterly* 24 (1951), p. 209.

211 Horace Walpole, *Memoirs of the Reign of King George III*, ed. Derek Jarrett (4 vols., New Haven, 2000), i, p. 25.

212 Rigby to Bedford, 22 Dec. 1760, London, published in Lord John Russell, ed., *Correspondence of John, Fourth Duke of Bedford* (3 vols., London, 1843), ii, p. 426.

213 Clark, *The Dynamics of Change*, pp. 157–8.

214 K. W. Schweizer, 'A Note on Israel Mauduit's *Considerations on the Present German war*', *Notes and Queries* 225 (1980), p. 46.

215 Peters, *Pitt and Popularity*, p. 182.

216 [Israel Mauduit], *Considerations on the Present German War* (London, 1760), p. 102.

217 [Mauduit], *Considerations on the Present German War*, p. 128.

218 [Mauduit], *Considerations on the Present German War*, p. 28.

Indeed Mauduit estimated that 'the income of the whole electorate would not be worth . . . one half of the value of Martinique',[219] a British objective in the French West Indies. Denying Hanover's wealth discredited some arguments for British empire over the electorate, as well as some for Hanoverian empire over Britain.

Another traditional argument recast by Mauduit was that of sympathy for the Hanoverian people. He embroidered upon the previous disclaimer of *The Observations on the Treaty of Seville Examined* (1730), writing of the Hanoverians that

> I would always consider them as our fellow subjects and our fellow Protestants. I wish that Hanover could be joined to this island, that we might consider them as our countrymen. But 'til then it is for the interest of both that they keep the distance which nature has placed them at.[220]

The geographic determinism of the last sentence revealed the insincerity of the foregoing. Mauduit was more convincing when assailing British imperialism's effects upon the electoral populace. Mauduit wrote

> by thus considering a distant country as a part of Britain and discovering too great a fondness for it, we expose the poor people of it to continual broils and misery and entail perpetual ignominy on B----n by attempting to defend them. They may justly come within our compassion. But for that very reason we ought to separate our cause from theirs, because they are far removed out of our protection.[221]

Of course, this familiar stance drew upon forbears such as Barnard, Coade, and even Pitt himself.

Mauduit argued for a maritime war, followed by unspecified indemnification for Hanover at the peace.[222] Dodington supported at least the first proposition, suggesting to Bute that George III declare 'that this way of defending Hanover would ruin this country without defending that, and [he] therefore would no longer expose his regal dominions to such hardships for fruitless attempts to defend his electoral ones, but would leave them in his enemies' hands'.[223] A sympathetic pamphlet entitled *The Plain Reasoner* went even farther.[224] Its anonymous author believed that as Britain's troubles 'resulted from our honorary connection with Hanover, it should seem very reasonable that some means be found to sever this connection.'[225] *The Plain Reasoner*

---

219 [Mauduit], *Considerations on the Present German War*, p. 122.
220 [Mauduit], *Considerations on the Present German War*, p. 127.
221 [Mauduit], *Considerations on the Present German War*, p. 44.
222 [Mauduit], *Considerations on the Present German War*, pp. 57, 128.
223 Carswell and Dralle, eds., *The Political Journal of George Bubb Dodington*, p. 411.
224 For its authorship, see Peters, *Pitt and Popularity*, p. 185 (note).
225 *The Plain Reasoner, or Farther Considerations on the German War* (London, 1761), p. 33.

was the first pamphlet to flatter a British monarch by suggesting dissolution of dynastic union.

*The Plain Reasoner* shared, of course, its name with the 1744 pamphlet which had introduced the inverted maritime policy to the dynastic union. The difference was that the new pamphlet's inspiration, Israel Mauduit, followed *Things as They Are* in deploying the argument against, rather than for, Hanover. Mauduit wrote that France's campaigns in Germany had been foolish, exposing its troops in distant, poor territories.[226] But the inverted maritime theory was still congenial to pro-Hanoverians too. *A Vindication of the Conduct of the Present War* wrote that 'by employing almost the whole power of *France* [in Germany], we have diverted them from objects of higher import. In other words . . . by throwing this *Hanover*, this tub, to the whale, the ship we swim in has been less endangered'.[227] The inverted maritime argument for Hanover had never sat comfortably with imperial designs upon Hanover, in that it saw the electorate as indirectly useful rather than desirable for itself. Indeed, the *Vindication* seemed to hint more at personal union when it invoked the Walpolean language of justice. If self-interest were not reason enough for Britain's engagement in Germany, the *Vindication* further asked, 'would not the ties of honor, gratitude, and justice bind us to endeavor the rescue of a wretched people suffering all the calamities of war from an insolent foe merely on our account?'[228]

A *Full and Candid Answer* to the *Considerations* also articulated the fairness argument. It refuted Mauduit's argument that 'Great Britain has, in the least, contributed to make that electorate the seat of war. It was unjustly attacked by France, and all the sophistry of mankind cannot pretend that Great Britain has not acted a just and therefore a wise part in endeavoring to protect that electorate.'[229] This notwithstanding, British empire over Hanover retained its charms. The *Full and Candid Answer* detailed Hanover's utility to British policy, asking

> can it be supposed that King William and the patriots who formed that Act [of Settlement] did not foresee all the inconveniences that have arisen, or can arise, from making an elector of Hanover king of Great Britain? They, without all manner of doubt, saw that the electorate of Hanover would always be considered by France as a deposit for the conduct of Great Britain. But that consideration rather confirmed them in than deterred them from their resolution. They kept their eye upon one great object, which was that of maintaining the liberties of the Germanic body, or they thought that their having a German

---

226 [Mauduit], *Considerations on the Present German War*, p. 24.

227 *A Vindication of the Conduct of the Present War in a Letter to ******* (London, 1760), pp. 15–16.

228 *A Vindication of the Conduct of the Present War*, p. 13.

229 *A Full and Candid Answer to a Pamphlet Entitled Considerations on the Present German War* (London, 1760), pp. 30–1.

elector to be king of Great Britain strengthened the common cause. They were not deceived.[230]

As both James Pitt and Marchmont had before it, the *Full and Candid Answer* linked Walpolean justice to the concern for European liberty, which had motivated the actors in 1701.

Yet William Pitt's sponsorship of Hanover had limits. His war aims for Hanover changed little since 1759, for he again informed Newcastle in April 1761 that 'he would *make war* to save or regain Hanover, *or rather continue*, but that he would never consent to give up the acquisitions that he thought necessary for this country to keep for the sake of Hanover'.[231] But where he had once threatened to resign over the related principle of a territorial indemnification for Hanover,[232] he offered the French envoy Bussy Guadeloupe for the evacuation of Göttingen several months later.[233] When Pitt ultimately did resign in October 1761, it was over his government's failure to declare war on Spain.

Although Pitt's resignation had nothing to do with Hanover, the ensuing retrospection refocused the public's attention on the electorate. *The Conduct of a Rt. Hon. Gentleman in Resigning the Seal of His Office Justified by Facts* defended his support for Hanover according to the Walpolean justice-based formula:

> a people who fail in the points of honor and gratitude must soon stand by themselves, a situation which a commercial people, of all others, ought to endeavor to avoid. Hanover had been engaged in the war and involved in all the distresses she suffered merely on account of the generous sacrifice her elector made of her security to the interest of Great Britain.[234]

That this was not incompatible with Britain's interest was illustrated by Pitt, who famously informed the commons that 'America had been conquered in Germany'[235] – the ultimate expression of the inverted maritime strategy.

But Pitt's enemies crucified him on Hanover. No one put the case against

---

230 *A Full and Candid Answer to a Pamphlet Entitled Considerations on the Present German War*, pp. 50–1.
231 Peter D. Brown and Karl W. Schweizer, eds., *The Devonshire Diary* (London, 1982), p. 92.
232 Brown and Schweizer, *The Devonshire Diary*, p. 29.
233 Karl W. Schweizer, 'Lord Bute, William Pitt, and the Peace Negotiations with France', in Karl W. Schweizer, ed., *Lord Bute: Essays in Re-Interpretation* (Leicester, 1988), p. 45; Black, 'The Crown, Hanover, and the Shift in British Foreign Policy in the 1760s', p. 122.
234 *The Conduct of a Rt. Hon. Gentleman in Resigning the Seals of His Office Justified by Facts, and upon the Principles of the British Constitution* (London, 1761), p. 8.
235 Horace Walpole, *Memoirs of the Reign of King George III*, ed. Jarrett, i, p. 65. See also pp. 70–1 for Pitt's assertion that 'as Germany had formerly been managed, it had been a millstone about our necks; as managed now, about that of France'.

him better than Fox's protégé Philip Francis in his *Letter from a Right Honourable Person and the Answer to It Translated into Verse*. Francis wrote that

> the late king, whose love for his native country may justly be numbered among his virtues must have certainly been highly satisfied with a minister who so largely gratified his favorite passion, who poured forth the blood and treasures of Great Britain into Hanover with a profusion which no other minister durst have ventured.[236]

Here was the old complaint that Pitt was just as corrupt as his predecessors in indulging George II's electoral favoritism, an argument which was further developed by Israel Mauduit's *The Parallel, Being the Substance of Two Speeches Supposed to Have Been Made in the Closet by Two Different Ministers Some Time before a Late Demise*. Not even Pitt's most distinctively patriotic measures escaped the vigilance of Hanover's critics. Drawing upon the widespread unpopularity of militia service,[237] *An Impartial Enquiry into the Conduct of a Late Minister* depicted the Militia Act of 1757 as a scheme 'to smuggle away more British troops to Hanover'.[238] The vulnerable electorate appeared as a British imperial dependency, but one vastly privileged out of all proportion.

Opponents of British empire over Hanover still waxed nostalgic for Kloster Zeven, which they considered a lost opportunity. The anonymous author of *A Letter to the Right Honourable William Pitt, Esq.* reproached the former minister with Hanover's suffering: 'all she now retains is a mere phantom of independency, without money, without means, and without nerves to support it . . . Those calamities, Sir, are owing to your policy, which prevented her embracing neutrality'.[239] Pitt's critics believed Britain would have also benefited from Kloster Zeven, had it been allowed to stand. The anonymously published *Case of the British Troops Serving in Germany* asked, 'if the defense of Hanover was given up by that ministry themselves, was the British ministry to undertake it at an expense the most monstrous that any war we ever were engaged in cost?'[240] This was naturally the conventional maritime critique of continental empire, but *The Case of the British Troops*

---

236 [Philip Francis], *A Letter from a Right Honourable Person and the Answer to It Translated into Verse as Nearly as the Different Idioms of Prose and Poetry Will Allow* (London, 1761), p. 18.

237 Eliga H. Gould, *The Persistence of Empire: British Political Culture in the Age of the American Revolution* (Chapel Hill, 2000), pp. 72–105.

238 *An Impartial Enquiry into the Conduct of a Late Minister* (London, 1761), p. 10.

239 *A Letter to the Right Honourable William Pitt, Esq., on the Present Negotiations for a Peace with France and Spain* (London, 1762), p. 45.

240 *The Case of the British Troops Serving in Germany Humbly Submitted to the Consideration of Parliament, with Occasional Remarks on the Fallacy of the French Historical Memorial* (London, 1761), p. 18.

also availed itself of the inverted variant thereof. It wrote that 'it is against common sense to imagine that France, . . . were she at this very time possessed of Hanover, could be able to keep it for six months without expending ten times more than the whole electorate is worth'.[241] By this analysis, it was Britain's interest to sanction Kloster Zeven and leave France to fester in its occupation of Hanover. At least two pamphlets would have preferred redeeming Hanover at the peace to defending it during war,[242] following a suggestion made by Pitt himself in 1755.

In all this attack upon British empire in Hanover, at least one anonymously authored pamphlet, *Letters to Two Great Men*, recalled the arguments against its reverse. Its epistle to Bute avoided the prevailing impression of Hanoverian poverty, writing that

> the electorate of *Hanover* . . . had been enriched exceedingly since the beginning of the present century. The city itself, the capital, from being little better than *Old Brentford upon Thames* raised its head and became one of the finest in *Lower Saxony* – it even vied with *Munich* or *Dresden*. Many new streets had been added to it, stately and lofty palaces had adorned these. The courts were spacious and beautiful, and the gardens of *Herrenhausen* were but little inferior to those of Lord *Burlington* at *Chiswick* or even those of *Versailles*.
>
> The brilliancy of the most numerous and splendid court in *Europe* every second year tended to enrich the tradesman, the peasant, and the mechanic so that, at the time when the marquis *d'Armentières* by a feint crossed the *Weser* with 14,000 men and ten pieces of cannon on the 25th of July 1757, they entered the best-cultivated, the richest, and most flourishing country in the *German* Empire.[243]

This was consistent with the economic critique of the royal visits to Hanover, and the bountiful vision of Hanover first articulated by the duke of Bedford in 1743. A second letter to Pitt's successor, the earl of Egremont, criticized favoritism to Hanoverians in Ferdinand's army in tones which recalled reports from Dettingen.[244] But the apprehension of Hanoverian empire over Britain was by now far less pronounced than that of British power over the electorate.

Bedford was indeed poised to reenter the fray over dynastic union. He supported a withdrawal of British regulars from Germany from within government, as lord privy seal. Importantly, he knew Bute and George III were of his opinion. Bute, who was now secretary of state, broached the issue in an exploratory fashion on 6 January 1762 before the cabinet, whose

---

[241] *The Case of the British Troops*, pp. 57–8.
[242] *An Impartial Enquiry into the Conduct of a Late Minister*, p. 22; *Constitutional Queries Humbly Addressed to the Admirers of a Late Minister* (London, [1762]), p. 6.
[243] *Letters to Two Great Men: The First to the Earl of E******t, the Second to the Earl of B\*\*e* (London, [1762]), pp. 36–7.
[244] *Letters to Two Great Men*, pp. 25–6.

ambivalence put the measure on hold.[245] Yet George III registered his disappointment, telling Bute that

> though I have subjects who will suffer immensely whenever this kingdom withdraws its protection from [Hanover], yet so superior is my love to this my native country over any private interest of my own that I cannot help wishing that an end was put to that enormous expense by ordering our troops home.[246]

The king's personal sentiments probably contributed to Bedford's 5 February motion in the house of lords to withdraw the British troops from Germany.[247]

Bedford and his allies attacked what they considered to be British empire over Hanover, from both the British and Hanoverian perspectives. Hardwicke's notes indicate that the duke declared 'England now engaged for the cause of Hanover; Hanover and Hesse destroyed and wasted by it'.[248] The earl of Shelburne was more vitriolic. A veteran himself of the war in Germany, he observed that

> the happy situation and peculiar advantages of Britain render it wholly independent upon the continent, and consequently render continental connections unnecessary. It will appear from history that a partiality to continental states has always been destructive to the interest of this country. The partiality of King William to his native country brought on disadvantages which we feel at this day, and since the Hanoverian Succession the national debt has increased 70 millions from [the] same cause – an oppressive load under which we are sinking and under which we must sink if some means are not speedily found to lessen its weight, which a continuation of continental measures must still increase. Everybody knows how much pains were taken in a late reign to enthrall us in continental fetters which, though all felt to be galling, none have had spirit to break. Hanover in the beginning of this war was our first object on the continent, and Hanover drew us again into the ruinous measure of burying our men and money on the continent after the treaty of Kloster Zeven. After the two great battles of the king of Prussia, he became the object of our attention still for the sake of Hanover. He was the invincible prince before whom the French nation was to sink into nothing, and we exerted ourselves for Hanover under a pretence of assisting him to destroy the French as enemies of Great Britain. And thus have we been led on step by step, our strength dissipated, and our credit put on the rack 'til we are on the brink of ruin.[249]

---

245 K. W. Schweizer, 'The Bedford Motion and House of Lords Debate 5 February 1762', *Parliamentary History* 5 (1986), p. 108.
246 George III to Bute, 6 Jan. 1762, published in Sedgwick, ed., *Letters from George III to Lord Bute*, p. 78.
247 Schweizer, *Frederick the Great, William Pitt, and Lord Bute*, p. 220.
248 Cobbett, ed., *The Parliamentary History*, xv, col. 1217 (note).
249 Schweizer, 'The Bedford Motion', p. 116.

Like Bedford, Shelburne was confident of royal favor. Several weeks earlier, his protégé Colonel Isaac Barré had complained to the commons that 'in the late king's reign we had been governed by solely Hanoverian measures and councils', but celebrated that 'the present king . . . was so English that he did not believe he had looked into the map for Hanover'.[250]

Shelburne's violence alienated his friend Bute,[251] who opposed Bedford's motion as too precipitate. From a policy point of view, the victor of 5 February was the duke of Newcastle. He professed

> great concern to hear his old master blamed for continental connections or a partiality for Hanover. He said Hanover was always a sufferer on account of the quarrels of Great Britain and was never the cause of such quarrels; that if it was not for its connection with this kingdom, it might enjoy peace and tranquillity under the protection of the Empire like other small states; that the Hanoverians and Hessians were now fighting our battles and ours only, by drawing the attention of the French to that quarter and giving us an opportunity of making the conquests we had already made and were continuing to make.[252]

Just as he had done as sole minister, Newcastle combined personal union with British empire over Hanover to argue for the status quo.

Newcastle's victory was short-lived, for the Prussian subsidy's cancellation in April heralded the movement towards peace. Newcastle chose to resign, writing of his ministerial adversaries that 'they think, but . . . may be mistaken, that the abandoning Germany, the king's electoral dominions, and our allies in this scandalous manner will make them popular, and those that are on the contrary side of the question the reverse'.[253] Bute's publicity as Newcastle's successor merely confirmed this suspicion. He considered authoring a maritime criticism of George II's rejection of Kloster Zeven, but omitted explicit mention of Hanover.[254] This he left to his countryman and publicist, Tobias Smollett.[255] Smollett had already satirized Shebbeare's intemperate opposition to the electorate in the character of Mr. Ferret in the *Life and Adventures of Sir Launcelot Greaves*,[256] but Greaves' reflection that

250 Horace Walpole, *Memoirs of the Reign of King George III*, ed. Jarrett, i, p. 72.
251 Schweizer, 'The Bedford Motion', p. 110.
252 Schweizer, 'The Bedford Motion', p. 117.
253 Newcastle to Sir Joseph Yorke, 14 May 1762, London, published in Yorke, *The Life and Correspondence of Philip Yorke, Earl of Hardwicke*, iii, p. 358.
254 K. W. Schweizer, 'The Draft of a Pamphlet by John Stuart, 3rd Earl of Bute', *Notes and Queries* 232 (1987), pp. 343–5.
255 For their association, see Lewis Mansfield Knapp, *Tobias Smollett: Doctor of Men and Manners* (Princeton, 1945), p. 245.
256 Margaret E. Avery, 'Toryism in the Age of the American Revolution: John Lind and John Shebbeare', *Historical Studies* 18 (1978–9), p. 26.

Ferret 'mixed some melancholy truths with his scurrility' indicated political if not personal sympathy.[257] Smollett now wrote for Bute's *Briton* that

> I hope the elector of H-----r will never again have influence enough with the K--g of G---t B-----n to engage him in a war for retrieving it that shall cost his kingdom annually for a series of years more than double the value of the country in dispute.[258]

Bute continued to posture against Pitt's continental empire, even with the latter out of office.

This was because anti-Hanoverianism was an important rhetorical resource for Bute, who was defending himself from a tidal wave of English Scotophobia. A pseudonymous correspondent in *The Gazetteer* responded to *The Monitor's* attacks on Bute, writing

> you insinuate as if His Majesty's employing a noble lord, born in North Britain, as a minister is the cause of people's being afraid of a bad peace. You mistake the cause, it is . . . our connection with Germany by possessing territories there, and whoever is minister as long as we resolve to defend H-----r never can make a good peace.[259]

This argument was based entirely upon a maritime criticism of continental empire, whereby France supposedly stood to regain some of its overseas territories by retaking and ransoming Hanover. *The Gazetteer* concluded that 'there is but one way to save this country from ruin by these foreign dominions, viz. to give them to some younger branch of the royal family, and to take care that the same person shall not possess both'.[260] The peculiar situation, in which a journalist could attempt to flatter an elector-king by suggesting he forfeit Hanover, continued. *The Gazetteer* even endorsed its correspondent's proposal, adding that 'we believe the Hanoverians would be as glad of the change as ourselves, for the their connection with us has occasioned all their troubles, so that the advantage of a separation will be reciprocal to the inhabitants at least of both nations'.[261]

One measure of Pitt's failure to win the debate was the degree to which some of his supporters abandoned his position. The member of parliament John Wilkes preferred to use Bute's arguments against himself in *The North Briton*, writing that

---

257 [Tobias Smollet], 'The Life and Adventures of Sir Launcelot Greaves', *British Magazine* 1 (1760), p. 515.
258 *The Briton* no. 7 (10 July 1762), p. 40.
259 *The Gazetteer and London Daily Advertiser* no. 10,411 (3 Sept. 1762), p. 1.
260 *The Gazetteer and London Daily Advertiser* no. 10,411 (3 Sept. 1762), p. 1.
261 *The Gazetteer and London Daily Advertiser* no. 10,411 (3 Sept. 1762), p. 1.

since the accession of our present most gracious sovereign, it does not appear that there has been any change in the *German* system. I rather fear that the nation will believe the present ministry is more *germanized* than any this country has ever had because their greatest efforts have been made, and their real strength pointed, to save *Hanover* and *Hesse*, in which they have succeeded. But for want of timely and adequate succors, [they] have lost almost all *Portugal*, an object of infinitely greater importance to this *commercial* kingdom.[262]

Wilkes anticipated an ancillary theme of his later campaigns to reenter parliament.[263] But the administration's coolness to Hanover made his position untenable, at least in the short term. No longer a symbol of government corruption, Hanover receded from prominence in the British press.

Aside from corruption, Hanover had also represented the European continent. Here too it began to fade in importance, because George III and Bute had finally resolved the decades old controversy between continental and maritime imperialists in favor of the latter. They risked killing the overseas empire with kindness, and the American Revolution kept interest in Hanover alive in so far as the electorate might be compared to the colonies. But while Hanover had mostly been discussed in terms of empire during the Seven Years' War, Britons now preferred the language of personal union. Indeed, this was the period in which Göttingen professor Johann Stephan Pütter first invented the term 'personal union' and applied it to the British relationship with Hanover. This was partly a response to the hardships of the Seven Years' War, which the Hanoverians felt they might have avoided by better articulating their independence from the British empire.

---

[262] *The North Briton* no. 25 (20 Nov. 1762), p. 157.
[263] Paul Kléber Monod, *Jacobitism and the English People, 1688–1788* (Cambridge, 1989), p. 41.

# 6

# *The American Revolution*

The shift in British emphasis from European to extra-European empire, already visible at the end of the Seven Years' War, arguably caused the American Revolution and certainly intensified during it. If Hanover did not 'fall back into political irrelevance' during this period,[1] it did move from intrinsic to extrinsic importance in that it tended to feature as a point of comparison for publicists more interested in Britain's American empire. Nevertheless, their passing references to Hanover shed light on the nature of its relationship to Britain. Increased references to personal union during the 1760s and 1770s bespeak nostalgia for the Walpole era, one also suggested by Edmund Burke's famous paean to 'salutary neglect'. Although the Hanoverian professor Johann Stephan Pütter coined the term 'personal union' and applied it to Britain during this period, Hanover's relationship to the empire attracted far more attention from Pütter's Anglo-American contemporaries. Given the prominence (though by no means dominance) of natural law in American political discourse,[2] it is not surprising that Hanover should feature in arguments against metropolitan sovereignty. But parliament's supporters also resorted to the personal union thesis, if only to restrict its pertinence to Britain's relationship with Hanover. Accordingly, the personal union thesis (at least as applied to Hanover) experienced fleeting consensus among British commentators. But this popularity abated once Americans resolved to separate from Britain altogether, and began to identify with Hanover's supposed status as an exploited imperial possession. And even though Hanover's personal union did not necessarily depend upon the American parallel, the decline of the latter reacquainted Britons with their old skepticism about the ability of personal unions in general to prevent imperial exploitation.

---

1 Frauke Geyken, *Gentlemen auf Reisen: Das britische Deutschlandbild im 18. Jahrhundert* (Frankfurt, 2002), p. 133.
2 See J. C. D. Clark, *The Language of Liberty 1660–1832: Political Discourse and Social Dynamics in the Anglo-American World* (Cambridge, 1994), pp. 46–140; T. H. Breen, *The Lockean Moment: The Language of Rights on the Eve of the American Revolution* (Oxford, 2001).

*

Imperial constructions of Britain's relationship with Hanover proved their durability in America's reaction to the Stamp Act. Metropolitan Britons already paid a tax on legal and commercial paper, which was stamped to indicate compliance. But in 1765 parliament extended this tax to the empire in an attempt to defray the cost of the standing army which would garrison Britain's new American conquests. Additionally, Britain hoped the revenue would pay down the debt it had incurred in the Seven Years' War. Americans noted ruefully that they were footing the bill for the wartime defense of Hanover, which the parliament had not taxed.[3] This was the old lament that Hanover was an overly privileged component of Britain's imperial periphery. Identification with Britain in opposition to Hanover made sense so long as Americans opposed the Stamp Tax with reference to their right as 'Englishmen' to consent to taxation.

But if American constituencies were admitted to the British parliament, they would have paid even more taxes. So American patriots simultaneously distanced themselves from metropolitan Britain. Some argued that parliament could not levy excises within individual colonies, but could only impose tariffs so as to regulate trade within the empire. Others denied parliament a coordinating role within the empire altogether, a power they reserved for the king. It was now that Americans began to covet, rather than criticize, Hanover's supposed privileges. In March 1766, an anonymous columnist for *The Boston Gazette* informed Americans that 'the people of England could have no more political connection with them or power of jurisdiction over them than they now have with or over the people of Hanover, who are also subjects of the same king'.[4] This was the first assertion that both the American colonies and Hanover were in personal union with Britain.

Although it is possible that *The Boston Gazette*'s anonymous journalist coined the parallel himself, he may have drawn upon the authority of Oxford jurist William Blackstone. Blackstone had only just published the first volume of his *Commentaries on the Laws of England*, which was an instant sensation on both sides of the Atlantic.[5] Blackstone reminded Americans that at least one territory was subject to George III, but not to parliament, when he wrote that

3  See for example *The Boston Gazette and County Journal* no. 540 (5 Aug. 1765), p. 1.
4  *The Boston Gazette and County Journal* no. 572 (17 Mar. 1766), p. 1.
5  For Blackstone's reception in America, see Gerald Stourzh, 'William Blackstone: Teacher of Revolution', *Jahrbuch für Amerikastudien* 15 (1970), pp. 184–200; Dennis R. Nolan, 'Sir William Blackstone and the New American Republic: A Study of Intellectual Impact', *New York University Law Review* 51 (1976), pp. 731–68; Beverly Zweiben, *How Blackstone Lost the Colonies: English Law, Colonial Lawyers, and the American Revolution* (New York and London, 1990), pp. 117–48; Craig Evan Klafter, 'The Americanization of Blackstone's *Commentaries*', in Elisabeth A. Cawthon and David E. Narrett, eds., *Essays on English Law and the American Experience* (College Station, 1994), pp. 42–65.

the territory of Hanover and His Majesty's other property in Germany . . . do not in any ways appertain to the crown of these kingdoms, they are entirely unconnected with the laws of England, and do not communicate with this nation in any respect whatsoever. The English legislature had wisely remarked the inconveniences that had formerly resulted from dominions on the continent of Europe from the Norman territory which William the Conqueror brought with him and held in conjunction with the English throne, and from Anjou and its appendages which fell to Henry the Second by hereditary descent.[6]

In thus accounting for the Act of Settlement, Blackstone followed the very first British proponent of what came to be the personal union thesis – James Drake. But because Blackstone advanced his theory in a popular reference work rather than a polemic, it reached and convinced many more readers – including, perhaps, an anonymous journalist in Boston.

It would be wrong to emphasize Blackstone overmuch, as the tory jurist would have denied any substantive similarity between Hanover and the American colonies. During the 1760s, most British observers who addressed the comparison explicitly rejected it. In a manuscript first written in 1766, the Scottish portraitist Allan Ramsay complained that 'at one time an American claims the rights of an Englishman. If these are not sufficient he drops them and claims the rights of an Irishman. And when those do not fully answer his purpose, he expects to be put upon the footing of a Hanoverian.'[7] It was for literary services such as these, as well as for his art, that George III appointed Ramsay principal painter to the king in the following year.[8]

Ramsay's manuscript had to await publication for three years, as imperial tensions temporarily subsided after the repeal of the Stamp Act in 1766. But it eventually appeared in 1769, after parliament imposed tariffs on glass, lead, paint, and tea entering the American colonies. These duties bore the name of the minister who conceived them, Charles Townshend, who called the American bluff that parliament was entitled to raise external taxes. Some Americans objected that tariffs should yield regulation rather than revenue, but others again denied parliament's authority to institute them at all. One was of these was Pennsylvania's agent in London – Benjamin Franklin. Franklin was unusually knowledgeable about Hanover for an American (or, for that matter, a Briton), having visited that electorate during the summer of 1766.[9] Franklin made the parallel with America public

6  William Blackstone, *Commentaries on the Laws of England* (4 vols., Oxford, 1765–9), i, p. 106.
7  [Allan Ramsay], *Thoughts on the Origin and Nature of Government Occasioned by the Late Disputes between Great Britain and Her American Colonies* (London, 1769), p. 51.
8  For Ramsay, see Alastair Smart, *The Life and Art of Allan Ramsay* (London, 1952).
9  See Hans Walz, 'Benjamin Franklin in Hannover', *Hannoversche Geschichtsblätter* new series 21 (1967), pp. 61–5.

as early as 1768,[10] but he saved his best formulations for his marginalia in Ramsay's pamphlet. There, he averred that the American colonies were 'parts of the king's dominions as the provinces in France were, as Scotland was before the union, as Jersey, Guernsey, and Hanover are still, to be governed by the king according to their own laws and constitutions and not by acts of the British parliament'.[11] Just as James Drake had used the personal union thesis to distance England from Hanover, Franklin used it to distinguish America from Britain.

Just as they had during the Stamp Act crisis, Britons denied any similarity between the American colonies and Hanover. In his 1770 pamphlet recommending the admission of colonial representatives to parliament, Francis Maseres belatedly conceded the American position of 1765. But Maseres, a former attorney general of Quebec, attacked the more current notion that the British empire consisted of 'separate states independent of and coordinate with each other, and connected together by no other tie but that of owing an allegiance to the same sovereign, which is no other than the relation in which Hanover has stood to Great Britain ever since the accession of the present royal family'.[12] As it happened, it was not Maseres' plan but the simultaneous repeal of every Townshend duty but that on tea which quieted the second imperial crisis.

Hanover did not come into its own as a constitutional illustration until the third pre-revolutionary controversy. In 1773, the prime minister Lord North poured salt into an old wound by allowing the East India Company to market tea directly to American colonists. Americans once again protested, but this time they met with retaliation rather than conciliation. After Bostonians destroyed company tea, North closed the port and revoked Massachusetts' charter. Americans expressed solidarity with Massachusetts by convening a continental congress at Philadelphia in 1774. The Hanoverian comparison once again became alluring to American patriots and their British sympathizers.

The most distinguished advocate of the Hanoverian parallel during the prelude to revolution was the British dissenter and scientist Joseph Priestley. In a 1774 pamphlet which Franklin encouraged him to write, Priestley wrote that 'to say that *America was subject to England* would have been considered as equally absurd with saying that it was subject to Ireland or to Hanover, that is, the subject of subjects, all being equally subject to one king who is

---

10 *The Gentleman's Magazine and Historical Chronicle* 38 (1768), p. 7. For the attribution, see Leonard W. Labaree, William B. Willcox, Claude A. Lopez, Barbara B. Oberg, and Ellen R. Cohn, eds., *The Papers of Benjamin Franklin* (36 vols., New Haven, 1959– ), xv, p. 38.
11 Labaree et al., *The Papers of Benjamin Franklin*, xvi, p. 325.
12 [Francis Maseres], *Considerations on the Expediency of Admitting Representatives from the American Colonies into the British House of Commons* (London, 1770), p. 5.

himself subject to the laws'.[13] Ireland, Britain, and Hanover formed a network of personal unions, which Priestley termed a 'common empire'.

Priestley was refuted by Josiah Tucker, the dean of Gloucester and celebrated political economist. Tucker believed the extension of the personal union thesis to the American colonies was dishonest or ignorant because, unlike the Americans, neither

> the *Hollanders* [under William III] nor the *Hanoverians*, notwithstanding their being the subjects of the same prince, were ever reputed to be *Englishmen*. For 'til acts of parliament were passed in *England* for naturalizing the *Scotch* and similar laws enacted in Scotland for naturalizing the *English*, the two nations were as much aliens and foreigners to each other as if they had been a thousand leagues asunder. Moreover, as to the *Hollanders* and *Hanoverians*, they neither were nor are a jot the nearer to be invested with the rights and privileges of *English* subjects than if they had been so many *French* or *Spaniards*. They are still aliens, still incapable of enjoying any one privilege or immunity, any one dignity or honor, any one office, place, or preferment peculiar to the subjects of the British empire.[14]

Although Tucker failed to mention *Calvin's Case*, the English court case which had naturalized Scots born after 1603, its subsequent application was inconsistent enough to warrant his characterization. Tucker used the Scottish example to show that the personal union thesis was more appropriate to the history of European state-building than to the history of British empire in America. But Tucker proposed to meet American mendacity with resignation rather than repression, arguing that Britain should cut its losses by abandoning its wayward colonies. And here, he also mentioned Hanover. Supposing the Anglo-Saxons to have originated in what had become modern Hanover, Tucker wrote in a 1774 pamphlet,

> nor can we with any color of reason pretend to complain that even the *Bostonians* have treated us more indignantly than we have treated the *Hanoverians*. What then would have been the case if the little insignificant electorate of *Hanover* had presumed to retain a claim of sovereignty over such a country as *Great Britain*, the pride and mistress of the ocean? And yet I believe that in point of extent of territory the present electoral dominions, insignificant as they are sometimes represented, are more than a moiety of *England* exclusive of *Scotland* and *Wales*, whereas the whole island of *Great Britain* is scarcely a

---

[13] [Joseph Priestley], *An Address to Protestant Dissenters of All Denominations on the Approaching Election of Members of Parliament with Respect to the State of Public Liberty in General and of American Affairs in Particular* (London, 1774), p. 11.
[14] Josiah Tucker, *Tract V. The Respective Pleas and Arguments of the Mother Country and of the Colonies Distinctly Set Forth and the Impossibility of a Compromise of Differences or a Mutual Concession of Rights Plainly Demonstrated* (Gloucester, 1775), p. 15.

twentieth part of those vast regions which go under the denomination of *North America*.[15]

For Tucker, Hanover was more similar to Britain than to any of the American colonies, although his comparison rested more on ancient conquest than on contemporary dynastic union.

Although other supporters of parliament disagreed with Tucker's radical solution to Britain's problems with America, they fell behind his objections to the Hanoverian parallel. This was no longer a ridiculous sophistry, but a scary possibility. The Massachusetts loyalist Daniel Leonard, writing under the pseudonym of 'Massachusettensis', supported Britain's repressive policy with the prediction that

> if this opportunity of reclaiming the colonies and reducing them to a sense of their duty is lost, they in truth will be dismembered from the empire and become as distinct a state from Great Britain as Hanover. That is, although they may continue their allegiance to the person of the king, they will own none to the imperial crown of Great Britain.[16]

He returned to this critique a month later, comparing the patriots' purported constitution to Hanover and to the Anglo-Scottish union of crowns before 1707.[17] This elicited studied diffidence from the man who was by now his journalistic rival, John Adams. Writing as 'Novanglus', Adams considered that 'there is no need of being startled at this consequence . . . distinct states may be united under one king'.[18]

The problem for American patriots was, of course, that their king supported parliament against them. As George III became less popular, the personal union thesis became less attractive. Americans began to compare their colonies to Hanover – not in its capacity as an independent state, but as an oppressed imperial periphery. This perspective was first evident in a 1774 pamphlet by Charles Lee, an Englishman of Irish descent who settled in America and became an active opponent of parliament. Lee feared that Britain might fight a future war against America with electoral mercenaries, but consoled himself with a vision of Hanoverian opposition. He pondered whether

> the state of Hanover would consent to such a draining of their country? . . . His most excellent Majesty GEORGE the third . . . is not very popular in the

15 Josiah Tucker, *Four Tracts together with Two Sermons on Political and Commercial Subjects* (Gloucester, 1774), p. 154.
16 *The Massachusetts Gazette and the Boston Post-Boy and Advertiser* 903 (5–12 Dec. 1774), p. 2.
17 *The Massachusetts Gazette and the Boston Post-Boy and Advertiser* 907 (2–9 Jan. 1775), p. 1.
18 *The Boston Gazette and County Journal* 1038 (6 Mar. 1775), p. 3.

electorate of Hanover. These people . . . think it hard that two hundred and twenty thousand pounds should annually be drawn from them for the purposes (as they conceive it) of corrupting the members of St. Stephen's chapel [the house of commons] in order to support the power and authority of . . . men who from the beginning have been enemies to the succession of the Hanover line.[19]

Lee's criticism of Hanoverian conscription drew upon the professions of sympathy for Hanoverians which had punctuated the opposition tracts of the Seven Years' War. But his allegation that Britain drew money from Hanover had more in common with Münchhausen's fear, voiced in 1757, that the accession of a foreign elector might deprive Hanover of currency. And Lee's allegation that Hanoverian funds corrupted British politics was utterly novel. In the past, corruption had been deemed to funnel money *away from* Britain *to* Hanover. Lee's argument respecting corruption anticipated that of Hanoverian anglophobes by a quarter century.

Sympathy for Hanover's supposed prostration grew along with Americans' desire for independence from Britain, especially after the outbreak of war in April 1775. Another British-born revolutionary, Tom Paine, hearkened to Lee's perspective in his famous argument for American independence – *Common Sense*. Paine feared that membership in the empire exposed the American colonies to attack by Britain's European rivals, adding 'the miseries of Hanover [during the] last war ought to warn us against connections' with Britain.[20] American revolutionaries no longer wanted to emulate Hanover's relationship to Britain, which they increasingly regarded as subordinate.

Josiah Tucker welcomed *Common Sense*, not simply because it seemed to vindicate his own call for American independence (albeit on different grounds) but because he considered it a more honest expression of American opinion than the personal union thesis had been. Quoting from Paine's pamphlet, he wrote that

> our junction with *Hanover* was far from . . . a blessing to either country. For . . . the innocent inhabitants of that electorate have been involved for our sakes in all the calamities of war whilst we ourselves enjoyed no sort of advantage from their misery – unless the lavishing of our blood and treasure in defense of a country not to be defended can be called an advantage.[21]

---

[19] [Charles Lee], *Strictures on a Pamphlet Entitled a Friendly Address to All Reasonable Americans on the Subject of Our Political Confusions* (Philadelphia, 1774), p. 8.
[20] [Thomas Paine], *Common Sense Addressed to the Inhabitants of America* (Philadelphia, 1776), p. 33.
[21] Josiah Tucker, *A Series of Answers to Certain Popular Objections against Separating from the Rebellious Colonies and Discarding Them Entirely* (Gloucester, 1776), p. 56.

But for Tucker, Hanover's inconveniences were not on the order of those which militated for separation from the American colonies. He continued,

> Hanover is but a little way off and is indeed but a little country if compared to America, nor can it ever be a greater. But . . . the mass of the inhabitants of that electorate have . . . been instructed in . . . notions . . . of submission and obedience. Whereas *America* is an immense country, the nearest part of which is 3,000 miles distant from *Great Britain*. And the *Americans* in general are described by their own friends and advocates as some of the most litigious, turbulent, and ungovernable people upon Earth . . . *Hanover* can never wrest from *England* the seat of empire . . . Whereas it has been the unanimous opinion of the *North Americans* for these fifty years that the seat of empire ought to be transferred from the lesser to the great country, that is from *England* to *America*.[22]

Tucker's praise of Hanoverians' supposed servility echoed earlier British advocates of empire over the electorate. Indeed he was increasingly skeptical about the viability of personal union, even when restricted to Europe. He wrote that 'the genius of the *English* is peculiarly unfit to be joined with any other people upon an equal footing or in a coordinate state, of which their behavior towards the *Scotch* and *Irish* as well as towards the *Hanoverians* is too striking an example'.[23] Of course in 1776, personal union was historic in the Scottish case and euphemistic in the Irish case; by juxtaposing them with Hanover, Tucker further undermined the personal union thesis.

The decline of the personal union thesis' application to America was manifest in a contribution from Richard Price, the Welsh dissenter. In his controversial pamphlet, *Observations on the Nature of Civil Liberty, the Principles of Government, and the Justice and Policy of the War with America*, Price attacked the old argument that America owed Britain taxes in return for services rendered during the Seven Years' War. He asked, 'how much has been done by this kingdom for *Hanover*? But no one will say that on this account we have a right to make the laws of *Hanover* or even to draw a single penny from it without its consent.'[24] Perhaps Price extended the personal union thesis to America this obliquely because he recognized its diminished currency. Without American patriots favoring independence, the constituency for compromise had dwindled to the minority of Britons who shared Price's sympathy for American grievances.

But opponents of the parallel between Hanover and America were still confident, as evidenced by the number of attacks on this particular component of Price's argument. One of them issued from Hanover's old opponent,

---

22  Tucker, *A Series of Answers*, pp. 58–9.
23  Tucker, *A Series of Answers*, p. 57.
24  Richard Price, *Observations on the Nature of Civil Liberty, the Principles of Government, and the Justice and Policy of the War with America* (London, 1776), p. 26.

John Shebbeare. Given his past, Shebbeare had to concede that 'much has been done for *Hanover*, but not in this reign. It was the work of whigs and dissenters in the preceding reigns.' But he held that, unlike America,

> *Hanover* is *not* subject to the crown of *Great Britain*. It is as virtually the dominion of *another prince* as if it appertained to *another person*. All that has been done for it was by *treaty* and therefore we have no more right to make laws for *Hanover* than for *Japan*, nor draw from thence a single penny because the *British* legislature neither has extended nor can extend its power over that state.[25]

The accession of a British-born elector had alleviated most of Shebbeare's fears with respect to Hanover.

But George III did not repair the constitutional deficiencies of personal union for another of Price's opponents, who complained that its application to America 'would be making a dozen more HANOVERS, all DEAD WEIGHTS upon this nation and mere patrimonies of the reigning prince . . . Infinitely better would it be to cut them off forever from being members of the British empire'.[26] The Scottish economist Adam Smith agreed, remarking that

> we used to complain that our connection with Hanover deprived us of the advantages of our insular situation and involved us in the quarrels of other nations with which we should otherwise have had nothing to do. But we surely have had much more reason to complain upon the same account of our connection with America. If in those days it was the general wish of the people that Hanover might some time or other be separated from the Crown of Great Britain, it ought to be much more their wish now that America should be so.[27]

Personal union, whether with Hanover or the American colonies, functioned to saddle Britain with all the responsibilities of an imperial metropolis, while conferring none of the benefits.

The response to Price's enunciation of the Hanover parallel cowed its next exponent, the British radical John Cartwright. In a 1778 publication, Cartwright rehearsed the conventional argument that the Americans had been 'only the subjects of the *king*, not of the British *parliament*, for they had

---

[25] John Shebbeare, *An Essay on the Origin, Progress, and Establishment of National Society* (London, 1776), pp. 102–3.

[26] [James Stewart], *A Letter to the Rev. Dr. Price, F. R. S., wherein His Observations on the Nature of Civil Liberty, the Principles of Government, &c. Are Candidly Examined* (London, 1776), p. 42.

[27] Adam Smith, 'Thoughts on the State of the Contest with America, February 1778', published in Ernest Campbell Mossner and Ian Simpson Ross, eds., *The Correspondence of Adam Smith* (Oxford, 1987), p. 382.

legislatures of their own. Their allegiance to the king did not make them *British* subjects for, were that so, then would the Hanoverians be British subjects.'[28] But he qualified this position in a footnote, where he denied any intention 'to insinuate that Great Britain's connections with British America and with Hanover were of the same nature because I know that they agreed only in the sole circumstance of the respective countries having the same sovereign'.[29] Comparing the American colonies to Hanover was more difficult for anti-war Britons once the Americans themselves had abandoned the argument to pursue outright independence.

The decline of personal union and consequent revival of the imperial sensibility with respect to Hanover was evident in a pamphlet of 1782. Originally submitted to the Rockingham administration as a manuscipt memorandum, *The Recovery of America Demonstrated to be Practicable* proposed to sacrifice Hanover in return for the rebellious American colonies. The anonymous author recognized that one of Britain's disabilities during the recent war had been the lack of a European war which might divert the energies of the United States' principal allies, France and Spain, away from the Atlantic theater. He suggested that Britain attack Prussian commerce, inducing Friedrich II to seize Hanover in retaliation. The author hoped that Prussia's self-aggrandizement in Germany would encourage Emperor Joseph II to return to the British alliance his mother had forsaken in 1756. As for the hapless electorate, which 'is risked for the reinstatement of the British, it should be guaranteed at the expense of Great Britain, which it is expected may be done without British troops upon a subsidy of money'.[30] Why France and Spain should be tempted into an Austro-Prussian war when they had remained aloof from the earlier War of Bavarian Succession, the author did not say. It was an utterly far-fetched and unrealistic plan, in both its European and American assumptions. But it illustrated an increased willingness to think about Hanover's strategic advantages, even if these were only secondary to those of North America. The author particularly recalled the argument of mid-century British imperialists who had stressed Hanover's capacity to divert French energies away from competition for overseas empire.

One result of the American Revolution was that Hanover loomed larger in its elector's consciousness. The Revolution brought an end to the long government of Lord North, and political instability ensued. For two years, George III and parliament struggled to agree on a government. When parliament procured the king's reluctant appointment of the Fox-North coalition

---

28 John Cartwright, *A Letter to the Earl of Abingdon Discussing a Position Relative to a Fundamental Right of the Constitution* (London, 1778), p. 5.
29 Cartwright, *A Letter to the Earl of Abingdon*, pp. 5–6 (note).
30 *The Recovery of America Demonstrated to Be Practicable by Great Britain upon Principles and Deductions that Are Clear, Precise, and Convincing* (London, 1782), p. 17.

in early 1783, the king contemplated abdication. Although he never sent it, George III drafted a message to parliament in which he pronounced himself 'resolved to resign my crown and all the dominions appertaining to it to the prince of Wales . . . and to retire to the care of my electoral dominions, the original patrimony of my ancestors'.[31] Had the king actually abdicated, he would have suspended the dynastic union of Britain and Hanover. George's increased sympathy for Hanover lasted into the mid-1780s, when the electorate's participation in the Prussian-led Fürstenbund undercut British overtures to Austria.[32] Divergent policies were, of course, justified with reference to the personal union thesis.

But British criticism of Hanoverian policy showed how far personal union had fallen in popularity. Now in opposition, Charles James Fox asked the house of commons, 'could the British troops act against those of Hanover?'[33] This being the implication of personal union, Fox argued that Britain should reign in the independent electorate. He argued that

> the regency of Hanover ought neither to form laws nor enter into any treaties which might prove injurious to Great Britain. Consequently it behooved the ministers of this country to have prevented their entering into any alliances which might involve serious consequences to the interests of England. If Hanover, through this mistaken policy, should sustain a detriment, it naturally followed that Great Britain must become her guarantee.[34]

Fox extended his campaign against George III's independence even to his Hanoverian patrimony, implicitly preferring some form of British empire over that country.

The prime minister, William Pitt the younger, put aside his personal pique at the king's actions as elector to defend them against Fox's imprecations. He highlighted the central inconsistency in his opponent's argument, arguing

> it was difficult to reconcile the caution of the right hon. Gentleman to prevent this country being on any occasion embroiled for Hanover with his attempt to make the ministers of Great Britain responsible for the government and politics of that country. If that were done, it would become a limb and member of the British empire, and as such would be entitled to demand protection.[35]

---

[31] George III, 'Draft of a Message from the King to Parliament', [28 Mar. 1783], published in Sir John Fortescue, ed., *The Correspondence of King George the Third from 1760 to December 1783* (6 vols., London, 1927–8), vi, p. 317.

[32] T. C. W. Blanning, ' "That Horrid Electorate" or "ma patrie germanique"? George III, Hanover, and the Fürstenbund of 1785', *The Historical Journal* 20 (1977), pp. 311–44.

[33] William Cobbett, ed., *The Parliamentary History of England* (36 vols., London, 1806–20), xxv, col. 1025.

[34] Cobbett, ed., *The Parliamentary History of England*, xxv, cols. 1019–20.

[35] Cobbett, ed., *The Parliamentary History of England*, xxv, col. 1027.

But personal union was not as persuasive as it had been during the American Revolution. *The Times* reproached Pitt by recalling his father's famous analogy of Britain and Hanover to Prometheus and the rock.[36] It seemed that Pitt's passivity had conjured up the very scenario he had wished to avoid.

This confusion over which country, Hanover or Britain, should have the upper hand can be illustrated in an anonymously authored pamphlet of 1787, *Sentiments on the Interests of Great Britain*. Its author expressed fears of Hanoverian empire over Britain in republican language, posing the familiar scenario of a Hanoverian army conquering Britain. The author assumed the existence of personal union, but noticed that Hanoverians 'certainly have as *much right* to invade this country as we theirs'.[37] Should such a conquest succeed, the king could 'proclaim himself the *absolute monarch of these realms by right of conquest*'.[38]

The author of the *Sentiments* vastly preferred a form of British empire over the electorate, considering that

> the same monarch is equally the sovereign of Hanoverians and Briton – they are both his people – and as the latter greatly exceed the former in number and their territory is proportionally more extensive, it follows that, though the king should even sacrifice the immediate interests of Hanover, yet if it is beneficial to Britain, he would still be pursuing the conduct of a philanthropist and father of his people because acting for the *general* benefit of his subjects.[39]

The *Sentiments* grounded British empire over Hanover in utilitarian terms, so that numbers overruled constitutional distinctions. Interestingly, the utilitarian philosopher Jeremy Bentham was not so sanguine about the benefits of British empire over Hanover. He lamented that the Act of Settlement 'did not prevent Hanover from being paved with English gold and bedewed with English blood by the first Pitt; it will as little prevent it being paved and fertilized in the same manner by the second'.[40] Bentham's condemnation upon political corruption was as republican as it was utilitarian.

Dynastic union was becoming more unpopular during the 1780s, even among those who declined to locate a seat of empire. Declaring that 'the union is most undoubtedly prejudicial to both' Britain and Hanover,[41] the

---

36 *The Times* 318 (31 Dec. 1785), p. 2.
37 *Sentiments on the Interests of Great Britain, with Thoughts on the Politics of France and on the Accession of the Elector of Hanover to the German League* (London, 1787), p. 96.
38 *Sentiments on the Interests of Great Britain*, pp. 99–100.
39 *Sentiments on the Interests of Great Britain*, pp. 81–2.
40 Bentham Papers, University College London, XXV.107, Col. 7. For the context of the Fürstenbund, see Stephen Conway, 'Bentham versus Pitt: Jeremy Bentham and British Foreign Policy 1789', *The Historical Journal* 30 (1987), pp. 791–809. I wish to thank David Armitage for referring me to these sources.
41 John Horne Tooke, *A Letter to a Friend on the Reported Marriage of His Royal Highness the Prince of Wales* (London, 1787), p. 13.

veteran radical John Horne Tooke hoped that the prince of Wales' secret marriage to Maria Fitzherbert might cut Hanover adrift. Horne Tooke was correct that the marriage could break up Britain and Hanover, but wrong about the mechanism. Hoping that Britain would retain the whiggish prince, Horne Tooke believed that Mrs. Fitzherbert would prove too common for Hanover. But it was Britain which restricted its rulers more, forbidding them to marry Catholics such as Mrs. Fitzherbert; the prince of Wales' Hanoverian rights were more secure. In the end, the marriage was annulled as contrary to the Royal Marriages Act of 1772. But Horne Tooke's joy at the prospective end of Britain's relationship with Hanover showed that personal union was more unpopular than it had been in over twenty years.

Although the historians of personal union have never proposed Hanover's inclusion in the history of British empire, there is ample reason to try. Recent work stressing the looseness of Britain's eighteenth-century empire enables an imperial analysis of Hanover,[42] even if the paradigm of personal union defined the electorate's relationship to Britain during the late 1760s and early 1770s. Furthermore, the willingness of American patriots and their British supporters to compare the American colonies' relationship to Britain with the personal union facilitates Hanover's incorporation into imperial history. But of course, the natural law parallel between Hanover and America eventually yielded to a more overtly imperial comparison as American aims shifted from constitutional reform to independence. The argument that America and Hanover shared a history of imperial exploitation by Britain was first advanced by two British-born revolutionaries, Charles Lee and Tom Paine, and gradually filtered across the Atlantic to their homeland. Although Britons sympathetic to America continued to compare it to Hanover in terms of personal union, they were increasingly embattled. Most Britons were once again disillusioned with personal unions, whether in America or Hanover.

---

[42] See Jack P. Greene, *Peripheries and Center: Constitutional Development in the Extended Polities of the British Empire and the United States 1607–1788* (Athens, GA, 1986), pp. 1–150.

# 7

# The French Revolution

The French Revolution ended a period in which Britain had concentrated on its extra-European empire, and placed the continent at the top of its agenda for the first time since 1760. Similarly, British debate about Hanover reverted to the arguments of mid-century; the electorate was once again intrinsically important, if not mentioned as frequently as before. Strangely, the French Revolution did not introduce an egalitarian strain into British debate over Hanover. There is corroborating evidence for continuity across the watershed of 1789;[1] British radicals followed their predecessors in arguing that Hanover hurt their countrymen irrespective of station. Their omission accentuated Britain's discursive disconnect with Hanover, where the burgeoning press increasingly examined Britain through a social prism. Initially, reformers hoped that dynastic union might facilitate the introduction of British social mobility to the electorate. But Britain's employment of Hanoverian mercenaries against France threatened to reinforce inequality at home and abroad. By the end of the decade, Hanoverian dissidents argued that Britain maintained its empire over Hanover by building up a compliant oligarchy.

Complaints about aristocratic privilege were nothing new in Hanover. But Hanoverians believed the elector was the only political force competent to address it, at least until the late 1780s.[2] But by then, Hanover had been ruled for nearly thirty years by a foreign elector who never visited it. Hanoverians began to imagine that homegrown institutions, such as the

---

1  J. G. A. Pocock, 'The Varieties of Whiggism from Exclusion to Reform', in J. G. A. Pocock, *Virtue, Commerce, and History* (Cambridge, 1985), p. 282; Paul Kléber Monod, *Jacobitism and the English People 1688–1788* (Cambridge, 1989), p. 220; James Vernon, *Politics and the People: A Study in English Political Culture, c. 1815–1867* (Cambridge, 1993), p. 307; James A. Epstein, *Radical Expression: Political Language, Ritual, and Symbol in England 1790–1850* (Oxford, 1994), p. 9; Murray G. H. Pittock, *Inventing and Resisting Britain: Cultural Identities in Britain and Ireland, 1685–1789* (New York, 1997), pp. 168–9.
2  See for example Tönnies Dreves, *Allerunnerdanigste un fraiden-vulle niee Jahrs Wunsch an usen allergnädigsten Herrn Könje van Grohten Britanjen* (Buxtehude, 1720); Albrecht von Haller, *Alfred König der Angel-Sachsen* (Göttingen and Bern, 1773), book 4. Although the latter was set in historical England, it was an obvious allegory about eighteenth-century Hanover.

estates, might redress the grievances with privilege. This may seem odd, since the estates embodied privilege. But they had recently received a fillip from Göttingen professor Ludwig Timotheus Spittler, who had rhetorically amplified the opinions of Treuer and Strube in his 1786 *Geschichte des Fürstenthums Hannover* (History of the Principality of Hanover). Spittler, a Stuttgarter who tended to support the influential Swabian estates against the duke of Württemberg, presented a traditionally dualistic analysis of Hanoverian politics in which the estates moderated princely excesses.[3] While he did not address aristocratic privilege per se, his description of the Hanoverian estates as 'representatives of the nation'[4] encouraged others to ascribe them a remit for its reform. Even while France witnessed aristocrats' reluctance to part with their privileges, Hanoverians reposed great faith in their estates' capacity for self-abnegation. Some even believed that the estates' historic purpose had been to defend the people as much from the excesses of privilege as from those of the prince. One Hanoverian publicist actually asserted in 1789 that 'it was formerly the principal duty' of the knighthood (the official name for the estate of the nobility) 'to protect the oppressed and defenseless'.[5] Such claims were unprecedented, for the estates had formerly been seen as a constitutional check upon princely abuses of power. Hanoverians first mentioned Britain in their debate about privilege with respect to an issue which had also raised popular passions in France – the right to hunt.

In eighteenth-century Hanover, as well as the rest of Europe, the right to hunt was a privilege which had been granted to particular corporations and families by the elector. The converse of this arrangement, namely that the rest of the population was not entitled to hunt, was deeply unpopular. Peasants may have wanted to eat game, but also wanted to prevent wild animals from damaging their crops. Crop failure was an ominous threat to the Hanoverian electorate, whose economy was overwhelmingly agricultural. The issue was thought to be critical enough that the estates of Calenberg and Göttingen in 1788 attempted to reconcile the just cause of the aggrieved peasants with the electoral government's obvious inability to compensate all cases of marauding wildlife. It clarified exactly what sort of damage was redeemable, and established a regimen of inspections by the elector's gamekeepers to ascertain the validity of claims.

---

[3] For a study of the estates which emphasizes cooperation with the prince, see Horst Kruse, *Stände und Regierung – Antipoden? Die calenbergisch-göttingschen Landesstände 1715–1802* (Hannover, 2000).

[4] Ludwig Timotheus Spittler, *Geschichte des Fürstenthums Hannover seit den Zeiten der Reformation bis zu Ende des siebzehnten Jahrhunderts* (2 vols., Göttingen, 1786), i, pp. 209–10.

[5] 'Beytrag zu den Materialien eines Normal-Gesetzes wegen Erstattung des Wildpret-Schadens im Hannöverschen', *Journal von und für Deutschland* 6 (1789), p. 442.

Some Hanoverians criticized the estates' conflict of interest. They pointed out that the new hunting regulation had been drafted by the estates' standing committee, which was charged with handling the estates' permanent business while the majority of the members were in recess. The anonymous author of a 'Beytrag' (Contribution) on the subject noted that fourteen of the committee's twenty deputies 'coincidentally' represented seigneuries or corporations entitled to hunt, and had therefore produced an ordinance which was exceptionally favorable to hunters' interests.[6] He argued that experts, rather than interests, should formulate policy. Hanover should, he continued, emulate Britain, where 'hundreds of merchants are examined either at the bar or in parliament or by a committee when a trade bill is drafted, so that [members of parliament] may properly inform themselves of all doubts and reasons for or against the new law'.[7] These calls for the Hanoverian imitation of British institutions were without precedent.

An anonymous pastor developed this invitation to British empire in a response to the 'Beytrag'. In order to ascertain the manner in which British institutions might be productively copied, the author first had to show how 'the *English* state experienced several changes before it raised itself to its present perfection'.[8] He believed that the British parliament and Hanoverian estates shared the same antecedent, medieval representative bodies which consisted of those 'whose persons and lands were to be made happy by such laws. And their advice appeared all the more important in as much as they were interested [in the laws] on account of their possessions.'[9] The pastor was clear: the legislature should consult landowners on legislation affecting their property. During the middle ages, 'the *peasant* was naturally not summoned because he had no property under *serfdom*'.[10] But after serfdom's demise in both countries, 'fairness seemed to require that the peasant be consulted as though he henceforth constituted an autonomous estate'.[11] Although it was hardly practical to expect the corresponding 'sacrifice of time' from the peasants,[12] British and Hanoverians institutions nonetheless altered to represent the peasant's viewpoint virtually. The author wrote that 'this was the larger number of country towns and market villages in England, and the introduction of voting by estate in Calenberg', where the clergy was mostly of bourgeois origin.[13] These differing solutions to the representation of peasants constituted the first significant discrepancy between the British and Hanoverian constitutions.

---

6  'Beytrag zu den Materialien', p. 412.
7  'Beytrag zu den Materialien', p. 438.
8  'Vergleichung der englischen und hannoverschen Landschaftsverfassung und ihres beyderseitigen Patriotismus', *Journal von und für Deutschland* 7 (1790), p. 356.
9  'Vergleichung der englischen und hannoverschen Landschaftsverfassung', p. 355.
10  'Vergleichung der englischen und hannoverschen Landschaftsverfassung', p. 355.
11  'Vergleichung der englischen und hannoverschen Landschaftsverfassung', p. 359.
12  'Vergleichung der englischen und hannoverschen Landschaftsverfassung', p. 359.
13  'Vergleichung der englischen und hannoverschen Landschaftsverfassung', p. 359.

The pastor opined that Britain's and Hanover's different mechanisms for representing peasant viewpoints performed equally until the establishment of the estates' standing committee in Calenberg during the late seventeenth century.[14] All estates business had previously been conducted during session (Landtag), which usually lasted two or three days.[15] Sessions lasted ever longer after the formation of the standing committee, and normally went on for many months by 1788.[16] Few members of the estates could afford to attend sessions for anything less important than the election of new deputies to the standing committee.[17] Thus were the affairs of the Calenberg estates in the hands of individuals who resided for long stretches at Hannover, where they gradually lost touch with their rural neighbors and tenants.

The pastor proposed to replace the Calenberg estates with a unicameral body modeled after the British house of commons. The Calenberg estates in their totality already resembled the house of commons in that the bulk of their members represented either municipal corporations or rural constituencies.[18] The author compared the two bodies' respective compositions:[19]

|  | England and Wales | Calenberg and Göttingen |
|---|---|---|
| abbeys | 0 | 9 |
| 'knights' | 92[20] | 163[21] |
| large towns | 50[22] | 4 |
| small towns | 339[23] | 15 |
| privileged ports | 16[24] | 0 |
| universities | 4 | 0 |

[14] 'Vergleichung der englischen und hannoverschen Landschaftsverfassung', p. 359.

[15] 'Vergleichung der englischen und hannoverschen Landschaftsverfassung', p. 359.

[16] 'Beytrag zu den Materialien', p. 412.

[17] 'Vergleichung der englischen und hannoverschen Landschaftsverfassung', p. 360.

[18] The author denied that Calenberg had an analogue to the British house of lords, whose bishops and peers he compared to the imperial bishops and nobles represented in the Regensburg Reichstag. He believed that the Hanoverian noble was really more comparable to the British member of parliament elected from county constituencies – both were, after all, formally 'knights'. 'Vergleichung der englischen und hannoverschen Landschaftsverfassung', p. 357.

[19] The following statistics on British and Hanoverian representation come from 'Vergleichung der englischen und hannoverschen Landschaftsverfassung', pp. 357–9.

[20] Each of England's forty counties elected two 'knights of the shire' to represent it at Westminster. Welsh counties elected one each.

[21] 163 seigneuries were entitled to representation in the Calenberg 'knighthood'.

[22] 25 cities sent two deputies each.

[23] 167 English boroughs sent two deputies each. Five English and twelve Welsh corporations sent only one.

[24] Eight privileged ports sent two deputies each to Westminster.

But while the two representative bodies were comparable in terms of their constituent elements, they differed markedly in these elements' proportions relative to each other. The pastor advocated matching the British rate of municipal representation in Calenberg as a way of indirectly amplifying peasants' viewpoints in the estates. The author suggested in particular that 17 market villages be admitted to the estates,[25] and that every town or village elect two deputies in the British fashion. But his plan depended as much upon the reduction of the noble 'knights' in the estates. The author calculated that each of the 92 English 'knights of the shire' represented a little more than 31 square miles, a ratio of land to knight which, if applied to the Calenberg estates, would have supported little more than two of the 163 knights otherwise entitled to sit there.[26] These calculations put the estates 'on an English footing':[27]

| | |
|---|---|
| deputies from abbeys | 3 |
| 'knights' | 3 |
| deputies from large towns | 8 |
| deputies from small towns | 30 |
| deputies from market villages | 34 |
| deputies from the university of Göttingen | 2 |

The pastor admitted that his reform slighted the Hanoverian nobles' traditional right to attend sessions of the estates. 'But what good is a right', its author queried, 'which he can no longer [practically] exercise after the introduction of endless sessions?'[28] But while he sympathized with nobles who were functionally disenfranchised by the standing committee, his particular concern remained the enfranchisement of the peasantry.

Schemes to adapt Britain's constitution to other states did not always presuppose a dynastic union with it. Indeed, the pastor's project was in many ways emblematic of its time. French revolutionaries had only just considered an anglomorphic constitution. Their rejection of it exemplified a recklessness which the pastor contrasted with 'the most felicitous peace and quiet' in Britain.[29] But despite the propitious timing for an anglophile constitutional reform, dynastic union lay behind it. The pastor's proposal seemed all the more practical when its author considered that 'the union of both states under one scepter, under one *monarch* whose most ardent wish is to make his subjects happy, excuses this' imitation of British representation on a much

---

25 These would have been Nörten, Adelebsen, Bodenfelde, Lauenförde, Lauenstein, Hemmendorf, Eyme, Saltzhemmendorf, Wallensen, Duingen, Grohnde, Polle, Ertzen, Lauenau, Gehrden, Wiedensahl, and Erichshagen. 'Vergleichung der englischen und hannoverschen Landschaftsverfassung', p. 358.
26 'Vergleichung der englischen und hannoverschen Landschaftsverfassung', pp. 358–9.
27 'Vergleichung der englischen und hannoverschen Landschaftsverfassung', p. 358.
28 'Vergleichung der englischen und hannoverschen Landschaftsverfassung', p. 363.
29 'Vergleichung der englischen und hannoverschen Landschaftsverfassung', p. 353.

smaller scale.[30] Like the author of the 'Beytrag', he was open to British empire on the understanding that it would promote civil equality in Hanover.

This anglophilia was typical of the Hanoverian mood during the 1770s and 80s. The ascension of a British-born elector may have inspired an elevated degree of identification with Britain, or an increased desire to flatter the land of his birth. Alternatively, admiration of Britain may have simply been a Hanoverian variant of the anglophilia which could be found independently of dynastic union in other German countries.[31] Whatever the reason, Hanoverians were more willing than ever to concede British superiority. Spittler wrote that 'we here are happy to be half-Englishmen, not only in clothing, mores, and fashion, but also in character.'[32]

Spittler also conceded Hanoverian inferiority to the British constitution of the late seventeenth century. Spittler condemned George I's two immediate Hanoverian predecessors, Duke Johann Friedrich and Elector Ernst August, for introducing servility and luxury into the principality with 'almost despotic energy'.[33] Spittler concluded that dynastic union with Britain had rescued Hanover from this plight:

> it is only thanks to the British sense of freedom, personal thanks to the glorious *Georges*, that the historian of the principality of Hanover must seek the *consummated* history of this un-German revolution, the beginning of which manifested itself under *Johann Friedrich* and *Ernst August*, in other German provinces.[34]

Ernst Brandes, a Hanoverian official and intellectual, very likely drew upon Spittler when expressing a similar view to Edmund Burke in 1796.[35]

But, unlike the anglophilic pastor, Spittler refused to defer to the present

---

[30] 'Vergleichung der englischen und hannoverschen Landschaftsverfassung', p. 354.
[31] For this, see Michael Maurer, *Aufklärung und Anglophilie in Deutschland* (Göttingen, 1987).
[32] Spittler, *Geschichte des Fürstenthums Hannover*, ii, p. v.
[33] Spittler, *Geschichte des Fürstenthums Hannover*, ii, p. 268.
[34] Spittler, *Geschichte des Fürstenthums Hannover*, ii, p. 269.
[35] 'There is however now a compensation of very great moment remaining for the loss of the presence of the sovereign and it is this: the race of our monarchs, having been born and educated in England, must have imbibed there from their infancy much larger and more liberal notions of government than they could have done in any other country. And though the constitutions of England and Hanover are different and every country must be governed according to the true genius of its constitution, yet the Hanoverians have felt and continue to feel the blessings which large and liberal notions of government inherent to their princes can bestow.' Brandes to Burke, 29 Oct. 1796, Hannover, published in Stephan Skalweit, 'Edmund Burke, Ernst Brandes, und Hannover', *Niedersächsisches Jahrbuch für Landesgeschichte* 28 (1956), pp. 39–40.

British constitution. Indeed, he considered that Hanover's had reverted to a superiority within dynastic union. Spittler wrote that

> when King George III wants to levy a new tax upon the eight million subjects on his island, the consent of merely a single parliament is necessary, and the approval of only one of the two estates which compose this assembly of national representatives is required. But when he desires a new general tax from all of his German subjects, who number approximately the tenth part of his islanders, it must be negotiated with six different parliaments. And each of these six different parliaments consists of several classes of provincial estates with equally important rights and equally guaranteed privileges, all of which must be asked for their free acquiescence no matter how different their prerogatives are otherwise.[36]

When speaking of the Hanoverian parliaments, Spittler meant the six estates of Calenberg and Göttingen, Grubenhagen, Lüneburg, Bremen and Verden, Lauenburg, and Hoya. Unlike his predecessors Strube and Treuer, who had implied equality between the British and Hanoverian constitutions, Spittler lionized the latter at the former's expense.

But ominously, Spittler became more anglophobic as the campaign against aristocratic privilege moved from game law to the poll tax. This was a flat tax upon adults, which was instituted in 1766 with a view to paying the debts ensuing from the French occupation of the Seven Years' War. The poll tax appeared fair enough at first, in that it tapped noble wealth which had been otherwise exempt from taxation. But it was also regressive, affecting poor taxpayers' consumption disproportionately. The egalitarian atmosphere of the French Revolution encouraged unprecedented scrutiny of the poll tax, and the British connection which had necessitated it. It was in this environment that Spittler criticized the poll tax, and suggested its replacement with a graduated tax in which wealthy subjects paid more than poor subjects. His analysis was largely domestic, but did prompt one embittered reflection upon dynastic union's role behind the poll tax. Spittler wished that Britain had paid the debt Hanover had undertaken on its account, writing that 'Acadian border disputes and hostilities on the Ohio river caused this enormous misery of the Leine; the Calenberger suffered for the Englishman. One could have all the more reliably importuned the king's generosity'.[37] Once again, British empire over Hanover seemed more harmful than benign.

---

36 Spittler, *Geschichte des Fürstenthums Hannover*, i, pp. 1–2.
37 Ludwig Timotheus Spittler, 'Geschichte des Kopf-Geldes im Fürstenthum Calenberg', *Göttingisches Historisches Magazin* 6 (1790), pp. 331–2.

*

In Britain, imperial interpretations of the relationship with Hanover were already on the rise before the French Revolution. But while Edmund Burke did not mention Hanover in his famous *Reflections* on the French Revolution, francophiles seized upon the electorate in their rebuttals. In 1790, the dissenting minister Joseph Towers complained that the Prussian alliance of 1788 had been concluded for

> the preservation of the electorate of Hanover which, if a war should take place, may possibly be attacked and which a king of Prussia . . . may have it in his power to defend. The electorate of Hanover has been considered . . . as the private patrimony of the king, and therefore British ministers have found it beneficial to themselves and that it tended to keep them in favor and power to pay a particular attention to the real or suppose interests of that electorate in order to gratify the private views or attachments of their royal master.[38]

Towers believed this was contrary to the war clause of the Act of Settlement, which – he argued – should have required George I to forfeit Hanover upon accepting the British succession.[39] Although he clearly saw the electorate as a continental liability, Towers precluded British empire over Hanover by considering it as a private patrimony of George III. If the electorate had commandeered the British state for its own advantage, it instead revealed Hanoverian empire over Britain.

In his best-selling *Rights of Man*, Tom Paine agreed that the Act of Settlement ought to have required the renunciation of Hanover. Abandoning his earlier diagnosis of British empire over Hanover, Paine denounced Hanoverian empire over Britain:

> a German elector is, in his electorate, a despot. How then could it be expected that he should be attached to principles of liberty in one country, while his interest in another was to be supported by despotism? The union cannot exist, and it might easily have been foreseen that German electors would make German kings.[40]

In what did German despotism consist? Paine's recalled that, during the American Revolution, a prisoner of war from Brunswick had told him, 'in my country, if the prince say "eat straw", we eat straw'.[41] The military context hints at the influence of the old republican case against Hanoverian empire over Britain. Although Paine abandoned the mixed constitution for natural

---

[38] Joseph Towers, *Thoughts on the Commencement of a New Parliament* (London, 1790), pp. 28–9.
[39] Towers, *Thoughts on the Commencement of a New Parliament*, pp. 30–2.
[40] Thomas Paine, *The Rights of Man, Being an Answer to Mr. Burke's Attack on the French Revolution* (London, 1791), pp. 133–4.
[41] Paine, *The Rights of Man*, p. 124.

law,[42] he retained other features of old-fashioned republicanism.[43] Perhaps natural law was disqualified in the case of Hanover because of its proximity to personal union and its defense of the status quo.

Personal union's capacity to defend the status quo was revealed by one response to Paine, that of *A Rod in Brine, or a Tickler for Tom Paine*. Its anonymous author upheld the personal union thesis, writing that

> the Act of Settlement is our defense, a barrier of strength sufficient to protect us against all mischief. But to add to our happiness, neither Geo. 1st nor either of his descendents have ever made any efforts . . . to invade our rights. What the German electors are in their own country it is not our business to inquire; it is enough for us to know that THE PRESENT KING upon our throne is a mild and merciful prince.[44]

The *Rod in Brine* accepted Paine's contention that George III was absolute in Hanover. But Paine's greatest rival, Edmund Burke, questioned this detail too. In his *Appeal from the New to the Old Whigs*, Burke emphasized that the electorate had

> a free constitution in which the states of the electorate have their part in the government. And this privilege has never been infringed by the king or, that I have heard of, by any of his predecessors. The constitution of the electoral dominions has indeed a double control, both from the laws of the Empire and from the privileges of the country.[45]

Declarations of constitutional affinity with Hanover were exceedingly scarce in eighteenth-century Britain. Remarks about the importance of the Hanoverian estates were still rarer: Burke's only predecessor in this respect had been the anonymous author of *British Advice* and the earl of Chesterfield. Indeed, Burke reversed the earlier argument he had made for constitutional difference between electorate and kingdom in *The Annual Register* for 1760. Burke may have learned something about Hanoverian politics in the intervening years from his friend Brandes. But the exhaustive letter about the electorate which Brandes wrote to Burke in 1796 would seem to indicate previous ignorance on the part of the latter. It is more likely that Hanover benefited from Burke's increased sympathy for other European constitutions

---

[42] Blair Worden, 'The Revolution of 1688–9 and the English Republican Tradition', in Jonathan I. Israel, ed., *The Anglo-Dutch Moment: Essays on the Glorious Revolution and Its World Impact* (Cambridge, 1991), p. 273.

[43] Pocock, 'The Varieties of Whiggism', p. 288; Worden, 'The Revolution of 1688–9', p. 275.

[44] *A Rod in Brine, or a Tickler for Tom Paine* (Canterbury, 1792), pp. 81–2.

[45] [Edmund Burke], *An Appeal from the New to the Old Whigs, in Consequence of Some Late Discussions in Parliament Relative to the Reflections on the French Revolution* (London, 1791), p. 93.

of the ancien régime, a sentiment which had already found expression in the *Reflections* and which would develop further during the 1790s.[46]

Burke did not quiet Paine, who returned to the subject of Hanover in the second part of *The Rights of Man*. This installment was even more revolutionary than the first, but Paine failed to follow the example of his Hanoverian counterparts in tying the issue of dynastic union to social inequality. Instead he reiterated the republican case against Hanoverian empire over Britain, remembering that 'George the first . . . bought the duchy of Bremen . . . at the expense of England [and] added it to his Hanoverian dominions for his own private profit.'[47] This reference to corruption was distinctively republican, but in the mould of the Renaissance rather than the Enlightenment.

British radicals initially followed Paine's lead, using Hanover as an incitement to radicalism. As the Holy Roman Empire prepared for war with France, the London Corresponding Society resolved menacingly that 'we view the elector of Hanover join his troops with traitors and robbers. But the king of Great Britain will do well to remember that the country is not Hanover – should he forget this distinction we will not.'[48] After Britain itself went to war with France using Hanoverian auxiliaries, the electorate might have become even more unpopular. But after the execution of Louis XVI shocked British opinion, Hanover actually gave radicals an opportunity to prove their moderation. At the treason trial of Thomas Hardy, Edward Gosling testified that the Shoreditch silversmith John Baxter had argued that 'he did not wish the king or any of his family to lose their lives, but he thought they might go to Hanover'.[49]

The critique of Hanover naturally persisted after Britain hired electoral mercenaries in spring 1793, which revived sensitivity about money. Apart from paying the Hanoverians' costs, Britain also compensated the electorate for deaths. The issue of compensation featured later that year in a famous conversation between two members of the London Corresponding Society, the satirist Charles Pigott and Dr. William Hodgson.[50] Discussing a British defeat at the London Coffee House, Hodgson told Pigott that 'it would be an expensive business for England . . . although beneficial to the elector of Hanover from the great number of Hanoverians destroyed on the occasion'.[51] The remark linked suspicion of payments to the electorate with that

---

46  David P. Fidler and Jennifer M. Welsh, eds., *Empire and Community: Edmund Burke's Writings and Speeches on International Relations* (Boulder, 1999), pp. 47–9.

47  Thomas Paine, *Rights of Man Part the Second* (London, 1792), pp. 116–17 (note).

48  T. B. Howell and T. J. Howell, eds., *A Complete Collection of State Trials* (34 vols., London, 1809–28), xxiv, p. 523. I wish to thank Torsten Riotte for referring me to this source.

49  Howell and Howell, eds., *A Complete Collection of State Trials*, xxiv, p. 717.

50  See John Barrell, 'Coffee-House Politicians', *Journal of British Studies* 43 (2004), pp. 217–25.

51  William Hodgson, *The Commonwealth of Reason* (London, 1795), p. viii.

sympathy for ordinary Hanoverians which had characterized the opposition of the 1750s. It was controversial enough that fellow patrons demanded that Hodgson and Pigott drink the king's health. When Hodgson toasted the French republic instead, they were arrested. While a grand jury declined to indict Pigott, Hodgson was eventually tried and sentenced to two years' imprisonment.

Further military setbacks reminded radicals of Hanover's other danger: that far from being powerful enough to subvert British liberty, the electorate was fatally weak and represented an undesirable responsibility. During his short (but fatal) imprisonment, Pigott wrote a *Political Dictionary* which said of Hanover,

> from the year 1740 to 1756, it was a place not to be found in the map, *a poor, pitiful electorate*. But being the patrimonial territory and the electoral dominions of our most SERENE SOVEREIGN, [it] must be preserved as a millstone about the neck of England, the ruin of our treasury and the grave of Britons.[52]

Pigott obviously sought to wound the prime minister, William Pitt the younger, through his father. He not only contrasted Pitt the elder's early indictment of British empire over Hanover with his son's supposed complaisance, but with his own later apostasy. Tom Paine channeled Pitt the elder with much the same effect in his *Letter to the People of France* (1797).[53] He added that

> it is from this mischievous compound of elector and king that originates a great part of the troubles that vexed the continent of Europe. And with respect to England, it has been the cause of her immense national debt, the ruin of her finances, and the insolvency of her bank. All intrigues on the continent, in which England is a party . . . are generated by and act through the medium of this Anglo-Germanic compound. It will be necessary to dissolve it. Let the elector retire to his electorate and the world will have peace.[54]

Paine had seemingly moved from an old-fashioned republican case against Hanoverian empire over Britain to the maritime argument against the reverse scenario of British empire over Hanover. It may be that his audience necessitated a volte face, for the French would never be as receptive to the notion of Hanoverian empire over Britain as Paine's fellow Britons. But Paine could have simply been returning to his original opinion on Hanover, as expressed to Americans in *Common Sense*.

---

[52] Charles Pigott, A *Political Dictionary Explaining the True Meaning of Words* (London, 1795), p. 57.

[53] Thomas Paine, *Letter to the People of France and the French Armies* (New York, 1798), pp. 22–3 (note).

[54] Paine, *Letter to the People of France*, p. 21.

Hanover became more popular among opponents of war when it acceded to the Treaty of Basel (1795), in which Prussia removed northern Germany from the anti-French coalition.[55] The government of Pitt the younger was clearly disappointed, and its publicists initially criticized the electoral neutrality from a position of British empire over Hanover.[56] But while this came close to George III's personal sentiments, airing them looked bad; eventually the ministerial press had to uphold the personal union thesis which had enabled Basel. *The Times* found a silver lining in the fact that 'the political interest of the ELECTOR of HANOVER and KING of GREAT BRITAIN *should be totally distinct*. Had such an opinion always prevailed, great would have been the saving of English blood and English treasure.'[57] In return, the peace lobby reminded *The Times* that the current war had cost Britain more than 'the fee simple of Hanover a hundred times over'.[58]

The problem with personal union was that it made the king look inconsistent or hypocritical. The whig *Morning Chronicle* considered that the monarch

> must be convinced as elector of Hanover that France has a government capable of maintaining the accustomed relations of peace and amity. It is therefore to be hoped that as king of Great Britain he will convince his ministers of this important fact and thereby remove the grand obstacle to negotiations for peace.[59]

Sarcasm simultaneously allowed the opposition to posture as royalists, striving to free the king from Pitt's restraints. The playwright Richard Sheridan told the house of commons that 'jealousies were commonly entertained of the introduction of Hanoverian troops into this country. But . . . he should have no objection to import the whole Hanoverian council and install them in the office of His Majesty's present ministers.'[60] Sheridan only jokingly advocated a form of Hanoverian empire over Britain, but the very utterance was testimony to the quiescence of republican fears of Hanoverian empire during the 1790s.

The Hanoverian neutrality owed much to an official of the Calenberg and Göttingen estates, Friedrich Ludwig von Berlepsch.[61] Abandoning his fellow

---

55 For Basel, see Guy Stanton Ford, *Hanover and Prussia 1795–1803: A Study in Neutrality* (New York, 1903), pp. 53–103.
56 See the citation in *The Morning Chronicle* no. 8111 (20 Oct. 1795), p. 2.
57 *The Times*, 26 Oct. 1795, p. 2.
58 *The Morning Chronicle* no. 8117 (27 Oct. 1795), p. 2.
59 *The Morning Chronicle* no. 8106 (14 Oct. 1795), p. 3.
60 William Cobbett, ed., *The Parliamentary History of England* (36 vols., London, 1806–20), xxxii, col. 159.
61 For Berlepsch, see Heiko Leerhoff, *Friedrich Ludwig v. Berlepsch, hannoverscher Hofrichter, Land- und Schatzrat und Publizist 1749–1818* (Hildesheim, 1970).

nobles, Berlepsch had supported the government's reform of the poll tax. But he then aligned with the nobility to oppose the government's military cooperation with Britain. The common denominator driving this apparently inconsistent behavior was anglophobia, a desire to mitigate the legacy of occupation endured for Britain's sake and to prevent another. In 1793, he argued that the king of Britain's employment of Hanoverian troops in fulfillment of his treaties with the United Provinces could not substitute for his imperial obligations as elector. And in 1794, Berlepsch complained that George III had not consulted the estates adequately about the war.[62] Needless to say, the electoral government hardly accepted that the estates possessed oversight of its foreign policy.

But French victories in 1794 prompted Berlepsch to fear a repetition of 1757. In August, he proposed that the estates remonstrate with George III for the troops' return from the low countries.[63] Berlepsch went still further on 20 November, when he moved that the estates declare 'that they in no way approve the measures and arrangements which their prince has unilaterally, and therefore unconstitutionally, undertaken with the English crown'.[64] In language befitting a friend of Spittler,[65] Berlepsch suggested further that the estates should declare the full neutrality of 'the Calenberg and Göttingen nation' – without George III's assent if need be.[66] He justified the latter course of action with reference to a precedent from 1626, in which the estates had opted for neutrality in the face of Tilly's Imperial army despite the duke's treaty with Denmark.[67] Berlepsch renewed his call for neutrality in December, when he pronounced Hanover to be 'in a political emergency . . . unconstitutionally occasioned by our prince for the advantage of the English . . . whereby he has brought the hate and vengeance of the French nation upon himself' and his Hanoverian lands.[68] Berlepsch's opposition contributed to the Hanoverian government's accession to Basel, and the attendant position of personal union.

But Berlepsch could not savor the neutrality, for he was losing his offices in the electoral judiciary and estates. After Berlepsch's motion of 20 November 1794 appeared in a Danish journal at the end of 1795, the government dismissed him from his position in the provincial estates in 1796.[69] The electoral government's right to remove Berlepsch from an elec-

---

62 Leerhoff, *Friedrich Ludwig v. Berlepsch*, p. 62.
63 Leerhoff, *Friedrich Ludwig v. Berlepsch*, p. 65.
64 'Votum des Herren Hofrichters Berlepsch als calenbergischen Land- und Schatzraths', *Der Genius der Zeit* no. 10 (1795), p. 161.
65 They belonged to the same masonic lodge in Göttingen. For this, see Joist Grolle, *Landesgeschichte in der Zeit der deutschen Spätaufklärung: Ludwig Timotheus Spittler* (Göttingen, 1963), pp. 48–9.
66 Berlepsch, 'Votum', pp. 162–3.
67 Berlepsch, 'Votum', pp. 164–5.
68 Quoted in Leerhoff, *Friedrich Ludwig v. Berlepsch*, p. 66.
69 Leerhoff, *Friedrich Ludwig v. Berlepsch*, p. 110.

tive position within the estates was doubtful, so he turned to his fellow deputies for vindication. Berlepsch arranged for some favorable publicity to
appear before the next Landtag met in February 1797. For his champion, he
selected Carl Friedrich Häberlin, a Helmstedt professor well versed in the
historical constitution. In *Ueber die Rechtssache des Herrn Hofrichters, auch
Land- und Schatzraths, von Berlepsch* (On the Case of Herr von Berlepsch,
Justice and Treasury Councilor), Häberlin portrayed Berlepsch as a traditional defender of the estates' rights against the elector and his British
empire.

Häberlin presented the most detailed German attack on dynastic union
yet. He reversed Spittler's theory that dynastic union had arrested princely
despotism in Hanover, arguing that it actually engendered it. Häberlin wrote
that the first Hanoverian to perceive this danger was Ludolf Hugo, the
eminent jurist. Hugo supposedly marked the Act of Settlement's passage in
1701, informing Elector Georg Ludwig that 'I heartily welcome this news for
your person and your house *but I cannot as a patriot.*'[70] Häberlin believed
Hugo's purported observations relied upon European experience of dynastic
unions. But he contended further that Hugo's fears had already been realized
when Georg Ludwig in 1700 borrowed 300,000 Reichstaler from the
standing committee of the Calenberg estates without the rank-and-file
deputies' knowledge or assent. Although Georg Ludwig probably needed the
loan to replace the English subsidies which had ceased with peace in 1697,[71]
Häberlin and Berlepsch assumed it was destined to bribe parliament to
include the electoral family in the Act of Settlement.[72] This was the first
Hanoverian echo of Charles Lee, who had been the first to allege that
Hanoverian monies corrupted British politicians. It would not be the last.

Yet before 1760, Häberlin wrote, the 1700 loan remained a solitary index
of British empire. George I and George II may have spent more time in
Britain, but they

> had spent their best years in Hanover, they knew the land, its rights, and con-
> stitution, as well as the loyal character of its inhabitants. They knew how
> much they owed to Hanoverian money, and it almost appears as if they took
> pains to redeem the constitutional trespass George I had allowed himself. In
> short, their care for the land, which they truly loved, appeared to double . . .
> Although the actual court went to London, its well-organized apparatus
> remained in Hanover as before. Palaces and gardens were maintained with
> care, and greater sums were spent for the administration and good of the coun-
> try than before.

---

70 Carl Friedrich Häberlin, *Ueber die Rechtssache des Herrn Hofrichters, auch Land- und
Schatzraths, von Berlepsch* (Berlin, 1797), p. 17.
71 Georg Schnath, *Geschichte Hannovers im Zeitalter der neunten Kur und der englischen
Sukzession 1674–1714* (4 vols., Hildesheim, 1938–82), iii, p. 34.
72 Häberlin, *Ueber die Rechtssache*, pp. 13–15.

Money, therefore, did not leave the country. On the contrary, new inflows opened themselves to Hanover because George II often graced his dear fatherland with his presence. Foreign ambassadors followed him to Germany, where German princes or their representatives also visited him to tender their respect. How much money entered circulation, thereby increasing Hanover's wealth?[73]

Häberlin's analysis of dynastic union under the first two Georges was undistinguishable from that of the ministers in 1757, who had also considered continued expenditure on court institutions under dynastic union as evidence of electoral good will.

But the ministers had also feared the accession of a British-born elector. Had Häberlin known of their memoranda, he would have considered that history had justified their anxiety. George III's unfamiliarity with Hanover and its constitution, he wrote, exposed him to counsels which exaggerated electoral prerogative in order to harness the electorate to Britain's commercial imperatives. Häberlin wrote that Hanover

> does not enjoy the presence of its prince, who is perpetually absent, who becomes ever more ignorant of and estranged from his own land and its constitution, who rules a large foreign kingdom, and who can therefore be easily moved to sacrifice the interest of the relatively small land to that of the greater kingdom. The ignorance of the English in geography and statistics is famously great, and it is just as well known that they consider the German states of the king a farm. Such views may be instilled in a young prince, who may sacrifice the welfare of his German lands in the course of imperial adventures designed to make himself popular with his nation.[74]

Häberlin agreed with Berlepsch that George III's treaties with Britain of 1793 and 1794 were unconstitutional, in that the elector had not communicated them to the estates.[75] Häberlin ominously commented that if the estates should lose their right to consent in electoral foreign policy, 'the Hanoverian lands will become involved in all wars which Great Britain wages for its commercial advantage'.[76]

Indeed, Häberlin considered this had already been the case under George III, beginning with Britain's employment of Hanoverian mercenaries in the Mediterranean and India during the American Revolution. This event, he recalled, 'entailed loss for the country without it drawing the slightest use from the treaty of subsidy, which was concluded for Great Britain's advantage'.[77] Collaboration with Britain during the American Revolution served

---

[73] Häberlin, *Ueber die Rechtssache*, pp. 18–19.
[74] Häberlin, *Ueber die Rechtssache*, p. 186.
[75] Häberlin, *Ueber die Rechtssache*, pp. 27, 69.
[76] Häberlin, *Ueber die Rechtssache*, pp. 200–1.
[77] Häberlin, *Ueber die Rechtssache*, p. 24.

as a precedent for the later engagement against revolutionary France, which had indirectly precipitated the Berlepsch controversy. Examining the difficult conscription of 1793, Häberlin asked 'why . . . was the land robbed of its men, and thereby of its protection and defense? To defend Holland, whose preservation may be very important to England but was highly indifferent to Hanover.'[78] He further noted that Hanoverian service in the British army not only left the electorate defenseless, but had exposed it to French resentment. 'Everyone knows that the French hated no one more than the king of England', Häberlin observed, 'and the harder it is to attack the king in his kingdom, the more likely they were to do so in his German lands.'[79] Here was the thesis, previously restricted to British imperialist propaganda, by which Hanover served as a continental bait which distracted France from maritime conflict.

The electoral government did not let Häberlin go unanswered; its anonymously authored *Actenmäßige Darstellung der Sache des Herrn von Berlepsch* (Documentary Account of the Case of Mr. von Berlepsch) appeared in early February, days before the Landtag was scheduled to consider Berlepsch's case. The author was August Wilhelm Rehberg, a protégé of Justus Möser and bureaucratic colleague of Ernst Brandes. Rehberg knew, and probably already disliked, Berlepsch from transactions with the estates in his role overseeing the electoral excise.[80] Although a reformer himself, he balked at the scope of Berlepsch's proposals. And Rehberg decidedly disapproved of Berlepsch's passivity in the face of French military advances. Addressing the estates, Rehberg revealed Berlepsch had petitioned the government in 1793 for a unilateral abolition of the poll tax.[81] But Rehberg nonetheless limited the estates' role to that of an electoral helpmeet. While not denying Berlepsch's contention that the estates had mutinied against princely foreign policy in 1626, he considered this precedent to have become obsolete after the Treaty of Westphalia.[82]

Even so, Rehberg conceded the truth of Häberlin's and Berlepsch's argument that George III had committed constitutional irregularities during the war with revolutionary France. But he denied that George III had ever sacrificed the Hanoverian interest to that of Britain.[83] Rehberg scorned the notion that furnishing military assistance to Britain might expose the electorate to French attack, since the latter 'learned in the Seven Years' War that they could not compel the English crown to peace by invading

---

[78] Häberlin, *Ueber die Rechtssache*, p. 65.
[79] Häberlin, *Ueber die Rechtssache*, p. 66.
[80] Leerhoff, *Friedrich Ludwig v. Berlepsch*, p. 125.
[81] [August Wilhelm Rehberg], *Actenmäßige Darstellung der Sache des Herrn von Berlepsch* (Hannover, 1797), pp. 29–31.
[82] [Rehberg], *Actenmäßige Darstellung*, p. 48.
[83] [Rehberg], *Actenmäßige Darstellung*, p. 18.

Hanover'.[84] This was, of course, an idea which Bussche and Hake had advanced during the selfsame occupation. Yet Rehberg believed France capable of threatening Hanover out of revolutionary fervor, if not dynastic resentment. For this reason, he judged that Hanoverian and British interests had converged in the failed attempt to defend the United Provinces.[85] Although Rehberg believed Britain's parliament to be more widely representative (its members having long since forfeited their aristocratic privileges)[86] than the Hanoverian estates, he entreated the latter to emulate its indulgence of constitutional oversights made in the national interest. He wrote,

> no people is so partial to its constitution and its freedom as the English, no assembly so jealous of its rights as the lower house of parliament. But there has been, and will be, no war in which the minister does not admit to having overstepped the authority of the crown on occasion. But the parliament authorizes faits accomplis and thereby repairs the errors in form. If this happens, and must happen, even in that constitution, it is unavoidable in the relations of our estates in which, unlike there, the ruler's first advisers and servants do not lead the deliberations themselves, do not propose, defend, and justify their plans themselves.[87]

Britain further differed from Hanover in that its ministers were drawn from members of parliament. Yet Rehberg had not entirely departed from the tradition emphasizing the two countries' common constitutional heritage, for he still believed that the estates might profitably imitate the parliament. Indeed, Rehberg also compared the noble estate's imminent consideration of Berlepsch's dismissal to an impeachment trial in Britain's house of Lords.[88] He thereby broke with the anonymous pastor, who had considered the Hanoverian 'knighthood' to be more analogous to the rural component of the house of commons. Rehberg hoped that British empire over Hanover might foster a more moderate degree of political reform.

According to Rehberg, the 1700 loan of 300,000 Reichstaler to Georg Ludwig was just such a constitutional irregularity, justified by policy. Despite its implausibility, he accepted Häberlin's and Berlepsch's judgment that Georg Ludwig spent the 300,000 Reichstaler in a massive bribe to the English parliament. But Rehberg argued again that it had enriched Hanover. He likened it instead to a recent British loan to the Emperor, which parliament had approved of as 'unlawful, but highly meritorious'.[89] Its merit was to have facilitated dynastic union with Britain, which Rehberg insisted had

---

84 [Rehberg], *Actenmäßige Darstellung*, p. 57.
85 [Rehberg], *Actenmäßige Darstellung*, pp. 56–7.
86 Ursula Vogel, *Konservative Kritik an der bürgerlichen Revolution: August Wilhelm Rehberg* (Darmstadt, 1972), p. 154.
87 [Rehberg], *Actenmäßige Darstellung*, p. 5.
88 [Rehberg], *Actenmäßige Darstellung*, p. 86.
89 [Rehberg], *Actenmäßige Darstellung*, p. 9.

returned Hanover's investment tenfold during the reigns of George I and George II.[90] He wrote that the

> powerful influence of the English crown acquired Bremen and Verden [for Hanover] . . . so that the lands of Brunswick-Lüneburg attained a [territorial] consistency which is of tremendous value to domestic and foreign policy. The union with England put these lands in a position to fight wars, some of which inevitably involved them, without ruin, indeed in such a way that their welfare often increased. Since the accession to the throne, sums were applied to public matters which in other small countries go to court expences and other needs entailed by the prince's residence.[91]

Rehberg's remarks on war were peculiar. Not only had Hanover suffered greatly during the Seven Years' War despite (and because of) union, but it had received British subsidies years before it could have been foreseen. But he was certainly in the right on the two other issues of territorial expansion and court expense. Rehberg accepted Häberlin's argument that Britain wielded empire over Hanover, but argued that this was benevolent rather than exploitative. Rehberg's propaganda contributed to the estates' eventual rejection of Berlepsch's petition.[92]

Berlepsch was undeterred by this setback. He immediately appealed his case to the Reichskammergericht in Wetzlar, which in January 1798 ordered Hanover to reinstate him in his offices. But he did not rely entirely upon his judicial victory. Berlepsch also turned to the court of public opinion, publishing a *Mémoire addressé à l'auguste congrès à Rastadt* (Memoir Addressed to the August Congress of Rastatt) under his own name. The *Mémoire* asked diplomats negotiating peace between the Empire and France to adopt an article '*which guarantees the Hanoverian nation against all the influence of British government*'.[93] In an attempt to win sympathy, Berlepsch emphasized the importance of Hanover's North Sea coast to the participants at Rastatt. He reminded the Germans that it furnished Britain with a beachhead for invasion of the Empire, and the French that it facilitated the embarkation of Hanoverian troops to foment civil war in France or to defend Britain.[94] Although Berlepsch repeatedly referred to the relationship between Britain and Hanover as a 'personal union',[95] it was clear that he considered this to be the ideal rather than reality.

---

90 [Rehberg], *Actenmäßige Darstellung*, p. 9.
91 [Rehberg], *Actenmäßige Darstellung*, pp. 7–8.
92 Leerhoff, *Friedrich Ludwig v. Berlepsch*, pp. 129–30.
93 Friedrich Ludwig von Berlepsch, *Memorial Delivered at Rastadt against His British Majesty as Elector of Hanover*, ed. and trans. [F. A. Winzer] ([Hamburg], 1798), pp. 53–4.
94 Berlepsch, *Memorial*, p. 13.
95 Winzer translated this into 'personal combination', but the German was 'persönliche

Berlepsch's *Mémoire* was, in one sense, an overdue response to Rehberg and his government. But he did not overplay their significance, 'the ministers of Hanover being merely the organ of the will of an *English prince*'. Berlepsch laid his blame squarely upon George III, observing bluntly that 'it is the interest of Great Britain alone which has actuated and guided His Serene Highness the elector of Hanover'. He based this observation on the war against revolutionary France, which he still believed had exposed Hanover to the resentment of Britain's enemies. Although Berlepsch hinted ominously that George III might be withdrawing Hanoverian specie for British purposes,[96] his only specific complaint was that the 1793 treaty had contained no subsidy. 'Hence *Monseigneur* the elector of Hanover at the expense of the Hanoverian country', Berlepsch lamented, 'made *a present* of *above* twenty thousand soldiers, native Hanoverians, to the king of Great Britain without consulting the interests of his electorate.'[97] This was common practice under the dynastic union, but had never been criticized in Hanover until now. Not even Hanover's present neutrality mollified Berlepsch, who believed that an '*express* and *real* accession' to the Treaty of Basel, such as the elector had avoided semantically, would have been 'the only efficacious means to *detach* Monseigneur the elector of Hanover from the English interest'.[98]

Despite their rejection of his claims, Berlepsch nonetheless reassumed the guise of the estates' champion in the face of princely constitutional abuses. He heatedly denied that the Peace of Westphalia had altered the Hanoverian constitution[99] so as to revoke the precedent of 1626 which had established the estates' right to consent in foreign treaties, still less that a change could have occurred after the onset of dynastic union with Britain. Berlepsch argued that

> the national representation of Hanover has very justly remarked that the *personal* combination of the elector of Hanover with the king of Great Britain did absolutely require some counterpoise for the security of the people of Hanover. Thus it never abdicated any of its constitutional, inalienable, imprescriptible rights of the country.[100]

Berlepsch even claimed that this right obviated the need for a Hanoverian equivalent of the clause in the British Act of Settlement mandating parliamentary consent for war on behalf of foreign dominions ruled by the king.[101]

Verbindung'. See Friedrich Ludwig von Berlepsch, *Mémoire addressé à l'auguste congrès à Rastadt* (Rastatt, 1798), passim.

96 Berlepsch, *Memorial*, p. 15.
97 Berlepsch, *Memorial*, p. 23.
98 Berlepsch, *Memorial*, p. 33.
99 Berlepsch, *Memorial*, p. 7.
100 Berlepsch, *Memorial*, p. 11.
101 Berlepsch, *Memorial*, pp. 7, 9.

In this he developed the argument of the 1757 'Letter', which had considered that Hanover possessed a tacit equivalent to the war clause in the British Act.

But after the estates supported the electoral government's expulsion of a judicial official attempting to enforce the Reichskammergericht's verdict in his favor, Berlepsch turned against his former colleagues in a supplement to his *Mémoire*. He warned that the action demonstrated 'that His Britannic Majesty and the oligarchical party of the States of Hanover persist in their oppressive conduct on the liberty and independence of the Hanoverian nation'.[102] Taking up the campaign against privilege for the first time since becoming the estates' champion in 1793, Berlepsch now linked it to the British empire which he had been fighting ever since. He again requested that the Congress of Rastatt issue a decree which

> defends the constitution of the country of Hanover against all influence of the British government, a decree which guarantees the liberty and independence of a good and brave people, which loudly calls for the first of all political rights – a right not to be betrayed by a faction of its representatives, which have no other motive than to sacrifice them to a foreign interest and to surrender them (its reigning prince being always absent and inaccessible to his German subjects, and consequently ill informed) to the most abominable despotism – to that of an aristocratical oligarchy intermixed with a most vile collegial regency of Hanover.[103]

To illustrate George III's physical inaccessibility to his German subjects, Berlepsch flourished decrees of 30 September 1763 and 7 May 1778 which forbade Hanoverians from travelling to London to present their grievances.[104] He also hinted at two symbiotic variants of oligarchy – nobles within the estates colluded with politically ambitious officialdom in order to safeguard their historical privilege.

Once again, the Hanoverian government answered Berlepsch's accusations. The great Göttingen jurist, Georg Friedrich von Martens, was in Rastatt and published *Betrachtungen über das Memoire* (Observations on the Memoir). Martens reiterated Rehberg's arguments, including that which posited the prince's primacy in post-1648 foreign policy.[105] He also agreed with Rehberg that George III's absence economically benefited the electorate, arguing against Berlepsch's vague insinuation that George III withdrew specie from Hanover. Martens wrote that electors 'have always

---

102 Berlepsch, *Memorial*, p. 67.
103 Berlepsch, *Memorial*, pp. 69, 71.
104 Berlepsch, *Memorial*, p. 71 (note).
105 Georg Friedrich von Martens, *Betrachtungen über das Memoire vom 1sten Februar und den dazu gehörigen Nachtrag vom 19. März 1798, welche Herr Friedrich Ludwig von Berlepsch an den Congreß zu Rastadt gerichtet hat*, trans. J. F. W. von Duve (n. p., 1798), p. 42.

dedicated the considerable revenues of their *demesnes* and the sums which the maintenance of a sizable court demands, which they saved by their absence, to the necessities and advantage of the electorate'.[106] But where Rehberg had assumed a modicum of British empire over Hanover, Martens defended the personal union thesis.

As an international lawyer, Martens preferred the tradition of Grotius, Pufendorf, and Pütter. Repeatedly using Berlepsch's formulation of the term 'personal union' (*persönliche Verbindung*), Martens wrote that

> all courts know that different ambassadors lead the negotiations which con-
> cern the two states, because their political interest is different . . . Courts are
> furthermore so convinced by the real separation of interest between these two
> states that, during wars with England in which the electorate takes no part,
> they allow the elector's ambassador to remain while that of England must
> depart.[107]

Martens particularly illustrated the latter case with reference to the American Revolution, when Hanoverian representatives had remained at the courts of Britain's European enemies.[108] Hanover's acquiescence in the Treaty of Basel showed even better 'how much the king took it upon himself to save the Brunswick-Lüneburg lands from the scourge of war without regard for Great Britain's political system'.[109] Thus did the concept of 'personal union', which had grown during the effort to distance Hanover from Britain after the Seven Years' War, defend against the further disassociation proposed by Berlepsch in the 1790s.

But personal union did not rule out international cooperation between Britain and Hanover. Martens argued that 'the political interest of both states has been the same more than once in history, when their union has been correspondingly natural. This would have also happened if the elector were totally different from the king of England.'[110] He remembered that this had been the case before the union, during the Nine Years' War and the War of Spanish Succession.[111] In particular, Martens believed dynastic union strengthened regional security. 'England's help confers upon the electorate the weight which the political balance of northern Germany requires, without being of the same use to the former.'[112] Here was a faint echo of the Hanoverian imperial ethos which had declined along with belief in a balance of power. Yet even Martens, who had included the balance of power

---

106  Martens, *Betrachtungen über das Memoire*, trans. Duve, p. 81.
107  Martens, *Betrachtungen über das Memoire*, trans. Duve, pp. 76–7.
108  Martens, *Betrachtungen über das Memoire*, trans. Duve, p. 77.
109  Martens, *Betrachtungen über das Memoire*, trans. Duve, p. 69.
110  Martens, *Betrachtungen über das Memoire*, trans. Duve, p. 78.
111  Martens, *Betrachtungen über das Memoire*, trans. Duve, p. 78 (note).
112  Martens, *Betrachtungen über das Memoire*, trans. Duve, p. 80.

in his works on international law,[113] paid tribute to Hanoverians' general skepticism about the issue, wondering whether 'it is still permissible to speak of a political balance'.[114]

Martens' were the last government-sponsored reflections upon the Berlepsch affair. But this was not because Berlepsch's interest in publicity flagged. Indeed, the next years were to witness his best work. In mid-1798, he published anonymous *Gedanken eines teutschen Patrioten* (Thoughts of a German Patriot).[115] Like the *Mémoire* it purported to review, the *Gedanken* addressed extra-Hanoverian constituencies. These were foremost the French and Prussian governments, the latter of which had been authorized by the Reichskammergericht to enforce its verdict in Berlepsch's favor. The *Gedanken* accordingly focused upon dynastic union's international profile. Then in early 1799, he published a *Pragmatische Geschichte* (Pragmatic History) of the finances of Calenberg and Göttingen. A classic of German statecraft,[116] it nonetheless addressed the Hanoverian domestic concerns which had been naturally downplayed in the *Gedanken*. Taken together, the two works represent Berlepsch's mature argument against dynastic union.

Although he again used the term 'personal union',[117] Berlepsch made clear his belief that 'Hanover's state interest is . . . subordinated to Britain's.'[118] Berlepsch refuted the notion, propounded by Rehberg and others, that advantages might accrue from British empire. Denying that the British empire could protect Hanover, he wrote that

> the Hanoverian lands can expect no protection and no advantages from Great Britain, any more than another territory of the Empire. Experience fully supports this fact. As soon as other political considerations interceded, England pulled back its land-forces and left Hanover to its own fate. The relationship functions so that Great Britain has *everything* from Hanover, but the latter can expect *nothing* from the former.[119]

Instead, Berlepsch went on to emphasize that British empire positively disadvantaged the electorate.

---

113 In his *Précis du droit des gens moderne de l'Europe* (Göttingen, 1789), Martens forwarded a modest version of the balance of power idea which attempted to reconcile Justi's criticisms with the traditional account (pp. 142–6). 'The example of England' remained central to his analysis (p. 145).

114 Martens, *Betrachtungen über das Memoire*, trans. Duve, p. 80.

115 For the attribution, see Leerhoff, *Friedrich Ludwig v. Berlepsch*, p. 157 (note).

116 For the larger historical significance of the *Pragmatische Geschichte*, see Leerhoff, *Friedrich Ludwig v. Berlepsch*, p. 168.

117 Alternatively 'personelle Verbindung', 'Personalverbindung', 'persönliche Verbindlichkeit', and 'persönliche Verbindung'.

118 Friedrich Ludwig von Berlepsch, *Pragmatische Geschichte des landschaftlichen Finanz- und Steuerwesens der Fürstenthümer Calenberg und Göttingen* (Frankfurt and Leipzig, 1799), p. 199 (note).

119 Berlepsch, *Pragmatische Geschichte*, p. 95.

Berlepsch returned to the story of Georg Ludwig's illegal loan, which he had related to Häberlin in the first place. But in his hands, the illegal loan was more than a story of Hanoverian tribute to British political corruption; it related how dynastic union exacerbated Hanoverian social inequality. Berlepsch implied that the standing committee's approval of the loan was eased by an increase in the salaries of its members.[120] Thus did British political corruption beget an analogue. At least the members of the standing committee paid towards the amortization of the loan, through the bushel- and tenth-tax levied upon nobles. But they excused themselves from paying for the British succession when the estates abolished the bushel- and tenth-tax partially in 1738 and fully in 1749.[121] Berlepsch wrote that thereafter the non-noble 'countryside and small towns had to bear, and still bear, the enormous burden of the English succession of the house of Brunswick-Lüneburg'. He omitted the large towns from this account, because they had not incurred the debt of 1700 in the first place.[122] British empire amplified Hanover's civil inequality.

The precedent of the illegal loan convinced Berlepsch that Britain's political corruption sucked money from Hanover. He fretted that Hanoverian moneys could be 'diverted to the king of England's civil list in order to lighten the English nation's taxes or to make members of parliament *willing* to burden the latter with newly invented taxes'. Berlepsch was short on concrete examples of this, although he spread a rumor that Hanoverian money had recently gone to pay off the prince of Wales' debts.[123] Berlepsch's accusations respecting corruption would influence future critics of British empire.

Berlepsch believed that Hanover subsidized Britain's commerce as well as its politics. He wrote that 'the honest peasant and the industrious townsman, the unhappy coolies of the state . . . must . . . sacrifice life, health, all domestic joys . . . and finally their purse – the product of their sweat . . . to appease proud islanders and preserve their commercial despotism'.[124] Universal monarchy had acquired an economic component during the 1660s, when English royalists feared Dutch maritime hegemony.[125] But Britain found the model turned against it after the War of Austrian Succession, by France.[126] Berlepsch first referred to Britain's 'monopoly on trade

---

120 Berlepsch, *Pragmatische Geschichte*, p. 79.

121 Berlepsch, *Pragmatische Geschichte*, p. 105.

122 Berlepsch, *Pragmatische Geschichte*, p. 103.

123 [Friedrich Ludwig von Berlepsch], *Gedanken eines teutschen Patrioten über das zu Rastadt übergebene von Berlepsche Memoire und seinen Anhang* (Frankfurt and Leipzig, 1798), p. 23.

124 Berlepsch, *Pragmatische Geschichte*, p. 223 (text and note).

125 See Steven C. A. Pincus, *Protestantism and Patriotism: Ideologies and the Making of English Foreign Policy, 1650–1668* (Cambridge, 1996), pp. 256–68.

126 Daniel A. Baugh, 'Withdrawing from Europe: Anglo-French Maritime Geopolitics, 1750–1800', *The International History Review* 20 (1998), pp. 13–14.

and shipping' in the *Gedanken*,[127] but it was only in the following year that he realized its consequences for Hanoverians. He thereby transformed an argument for Hanoverian empire over Britain into an argument against British empire over Hanover.

Berlepsch agreed with Häberlin that the illegal loan of 1700 remained dynastic union's singular abuse for a long time. But his account of when abuse became systematic deviated from Häberlin's chronology. Where Häberlin had traced it to the American Revolution, Berlepsch detected it as early as the Seven Years' War. He avoided impugning the sainted George II by blaming Pitt the elder for British empire over Hanover. Apparently ignorant of Pitt's opposition to the measure, Berlepsch criticized Britain's importation of Hanoverian mercenaries during the French invasion scare of 1756. But he rightly saddled Pitt with the 1758 deployment of British regulars in Hanover.[128] Berlepsch even paraphrased his villain, remembering how 'England took *Canada* from the French in Hanover' during the Seven Years' War.[129] All of this had been immensely costly to Hanover, which incurred enormous debts under French occupation. Berlepsch highlighted Britain's failure to compensate the electorate for its losses under French occupation, writing that 'the English cheated [Hanoverians] out of the reparations from the Seven Years' War which they paid to other powers such as Hesse because their elector did not allow them to make their demands to the British parliament, lest he become unpleasant to it'.[130] Not only did British empire bring ruin to Hanover, but it withheld restitution for the resulting costs. In lieu of British assistance, Calenberg and Göttingen had been forced to adopt a poll tax which relatively advantaged richer taxpayers. Rich Hanoverians were not necessarily members of the nobility, the social group exempted from paying for the illegal loan. But for Berlepsch, the two categories were virtually interchangeable.

British empire even disturbed Hanoverians' repayment of the debts it had occasioned, by prompting Hanover's mercenary service in Britain's war against revolutionary France. Berlepsch wrote in the *Gedanken* that Hanoverians 'owe it entirely to the English union that they lost ten thousand men during the war against revolutionary France, and thereby ten million Taler in tax revenue according to the customary value of a person'.[131] This figure was, of course, a guestimate of the Hanoverian casualties' lifetime contributions. But Berlepsch did present harder numbers in the *Pragmatische Geschichte*, where he noted that excise returns fell by over 40,000 Reichstaler between fiscal year 1792 and fiscal year 1795.[132] These

127 [Berlepsch], *Gedanken eines teutschen Patrioten*, p. 17.
128 [Berlepsch], *Gedanken eines teutschen Patrioten*, p. 14.
129 [Berlepsch], *Gedanken eines teutschen Patrioten*, p. 14.
130 [Berlepsch], *Gedanken eines teutschen Patrioten*, p. 50.
131 [Berlepsch], *Gedanken eines teutschen Patrioten*, p. 50.
132 [Berlepsch], *Gedanken eines teutschen Patrioten*, p. 188 (text and note).

costs were ordinarily offset by subsidies, but dynastic union functioned to forgive Britain this expense.[133] Berlepsch was not merely economically, but morally, opposed to the trade in mercenaries. He likened it to the slave trade, and called for the abolition of both.[134]

Soldiers were not the only taxpayers Britain removed from Hanover. There was also the elector himself, who was something of a tax exile in Berlepsch's eyes. Berlepsch contrasted Hanover's present revenues with those at the introduction of the excise, in 1686. 'Then there was a *real* court in Hanover', he acidly observed, 'which generated more tax revenue in a day during the ruler's presence than the court kitchen does now in a quarter of a year.'[135] Berlepsch's economic case against the elector's absence contrasted with the government's argument, as stated by Rehberg and Martens, that dynastic union spared Hanover the cost of a full court.

A tax shortfall was hardly the gravest consequence of the electoral absence. Berlepsch revived the familiar paradox of a princely constitution without a prince, albeit in unprecedentedly provocative terms. He asked 'Does this connection not go against every concept of a monarchical constitution? Does the shepherd not belong by the flock? Is that not obviously in the contract of subjection? May the shepherd (the ruler) entrust the flock (the subjects) to hirelings?'[136] Berlepsch returned to the idea, first advanced in his *Mémoire*, that George III's absence made him the unwitting dupe of his Hanoverian ministers. He wrote that

> this [government], and a certain brotherhood of some government secretaries which is the principal mainspring of the Hanoverian machine of state, constitutes the true ruler in Hanover, because His Royal Majesty never finds himself in the country with the flock; therefore, he must always see through strange eyes, and no one can get admitted to him.[137]

The secretaries to whom Berlepsch referred were government officials (such as Rehberg and Brandes) of bourgeois origin, who were acknowledged to have acquired the dominant influence in government which noblemen had wielded before the death of Münchhausen. But far from governing in the interest of their fellow commoners, Berlepsch accused the secretaries of collaborating in an 'aristocratic nepotist-, minister- and secretary-government'.[138] Berlepsch was once again able to associate Britain (as the place of George III's residence) with Hanoverian social inequality.

Berlepsch believed the secretaries' pronounced anglophilia served their

---

133 [Berlepsch], *Gedanken eines teutschen Patrioten*, p. 21.
134 [Berlepsch], *Gedanken eines teutschen Patrioten*, pp. 20–1.
135 Berlepsch, *Pragmatische Geschichte*, p. 169 (note).
136 Berlepsch, *Pragmatische Geschichte*, p. 87 (note).
137 Berlepsch, *Pragmatische Geschichte*, pp. 6–7 (note).
138 [Berlepsch], *Gedanken eines teutschen Patrioten*, p. 47.

political ambition. He alleged that 'Herr Rehberg and his party would like to inculcate the territorial public law of Calenberg with English principles because it is easier to introduce something from newspapers which one writes oneself than from files and documents', the true sources of Hanoverian constitutional law. Berlepsch implied that journalistic accounts of the British constitution, such as Brandes had written, were more conducive to princely despotism than native precedent. Referring obliquely to the war against revolutionary France, he furthermore taunted the anglophiles that they had neglected one British constitutional principle which was clearly relevant to Hanover's predicament: the article of the Act of Settlement prohibiting war on behalf of foreign dominions without parliamentary consent.[139] Berlepsch also commended William Pitt the younger upon his introduction of an income tax, which he considered fairer than any Hanoverian tax.[140] He skillfully revealed Rehberg's hypocritical selectivity in applying British constitutional precepts to Hanover. But he also effectively conceded the superiority of the British constitution, writing that 'at a certain time, the Calenberg estates behaved better than the English parliament. But these times of true dignity and energy are over.'[141] Whereas Spittler believed that the 'British sense of freedom' had restored the defunct Hanoverian constitution to its rightful superiority, Berlepsch believed British empire had reduced the Hanoverian constitution to a corrupt lowest common denominator.

These attacks upon Hanoverian officialdom only partly exonerated George III of imperial abuses.[142] Berlepsch paraphrased Häberlin in his *Gedanken*, where he wrote that 'in accordance with his personal character, George III . . . believes himself to be more unfettered in Hanover than in England, and *unlimited monarchy* is therefore the tendency of all his actions'.[143] This was, of course, but one element of Häberlin's indictment of George III. Berlepsch added the other in the *Pragmatische Geschichte*, writing that 'Pitt and others . . . have built upon this prejudice . . . because when George III is an unlimited monarch those who rule under him are unlimited masters.'[144] Where Häberlin held British culture responsible for George III's exaggerated view of his power as elector, Berlepsch laid the blame squarely at the ambitious feet of William Pitt the younger.

Berlepsch finally supported dissolution of union in his *Gedanken*, which he considered would be a 'precaution against all revolution, against all dissatisfaction in Hanover'.[145] He forecast a natural end for union, which

---

139 Berlepsch, *Pragmatische Geschichte*, p. 94.
140 Berlepsch, *Pragmatische Geschichte*, p. 233.
141 Berlepsch, *Pragmatische Geschichte*, p. 91.
142 See, for example, Berlepsch, *Pragmatische Geschichte*, p. 232 (note).
143 [Berlepsch], *Gedanken eines teutschen Patrioten*, p. 24.
144 Berlepsch, *Pragmatische Geschichte*, p. 286 (note).
145 [Berlepsch], *Gedanken eines teutschen Patrioten*, p. 50.

would happen if Princess Charlotte ever ascended the British throne. Hanover's succession privileged male inheritance to a greater degree than Britain, and would pass to one of Charlotte's uncles.[146] But this eventuality was far too remote for Berlepsch, who demanded an expeditious end to union. He suggested replacing George III with his youngest son, Prince Adolphus, who already resided in the electorate.[147]

Despite his persistence, Berlepsch failed to win back his offices. His hero Bonaparte attacked Britain in Egypt rather than Hanover, precluding French aid.[148] Prussia regarded the matter as closed after its diplomatic intervention on Berlepsch's behalf failed to move the electoral government,[149] and did nothing for him during its brief occupation of Hanover in 1801. Finally, Berlepsch failed to rouse the Hanoverian people on his behalf. In this, he was partly a victim of his own success in procuring Hanoverian adherence to the neutrality of Basel. Hanoverians may have sympathized with Berlepsch's arguments, but saw no reason to risk their precious peace for his cause.

Imperial interpretations of the British-Hanoverian relationship rebounded during the French Revolution. Tom Paine revived the bogey of Hanoverian empire over Britain. But British arguments about Hanover were largely those which had prevailed before 1789. For the first time, the Hanoverian debate about British empire was more sophisticated and sustained that its British equivalent. Where they had once preferred innuendo, Hanoverian anglophobes explicitly denounced British empire over the electorate. Moreover, they connected British empire to Hanoverian social inequality. For the moment, this campaign was very much that of one person – Friedrich Ludwig Berlepsch – and his immediate collaborators. But their ideas later nurtured a wider constituency. Changing criticisms of British empire were matched by innovations in the personal union thesis, which became associative where it had once been dissociative.

---

146 [Berlepsch], *Gedanken eines teutschen Patrioten*, pp. 51–2.
147 [Berlepsch], *Gedanken eines teutschen Patrioten*, pp. 55–7.
148 For Berlepsch's praise of Bonaparte, see [Berlepsch], *Gedanken eines teutschen Patrioten*, p. 61.
149 Leerhoff, *Friedrich Ludwig v. Berlepsch*, pp. 176–7.

# 8

# *Napoleon*

Britain tremendously expanded its extra-European empire during the
Napoleonic period, acquiring Malta, the Cape of Good Hope, Ceylon, and
parts of India. It also consolidated its hold over Ireland with a parliamentary
union in 1800–1; the relationship with Hanover was the last remaining
dynastic tie of the early modern variety. Even this seemed over, as successive
occupations of that country by foreign powers effectively interrupted the two
countries' political relationship. In so far as Hanover's dilemma indirectly
resulted from British policy (the failure to evacuate Malta as promised in the
Treaty of Amiens), dynastic union continued to attract attention during its
hiatus. The ensuing debate in Hanover was unprecedented in scope.
Berlepsch's heirs built upon his charge that British empire over Hanover had
exacerbated social inequality, while ministerial authors argued that personal
union had rendered the French invasion illegal under international law.
British interest in Hanover only picked up after France briefly yielded the
electorate to Prussia in 1806. Britain's consequent declaration of war against
Prussia registered unhappiness with permanent exclusion from the continent, although it prompted howls of protest from opponents of dynastic
union. Had Hanover remained under foreign domination, these discussions
might have constituted nothing more than an interesting postmortem for
dynastic union. But because Hanover returned to the British monarchy in
1813, they greatly influenced the two countries' future relationship.

As the nineteenth century opened, Britain was reminded of Hanover's
vulnerability. Prussia occupied the electorate in the spring of 1801 at the
instigation of Russia's tsar, who hoped thereby to forestall British attacks
upon neutral shipping in the Baltic.[1] For a second time, British policy had
exposed Hanover to a foreign occupation. Charles James Fox reversed his
earlier opinion of the Fürstenbund era, observing that though 'in this
instance Hanover has suffered on account of her being under the same

---

[1] For the Prussian occupation of 1801, see Guy Stanton Ford, *Hanover and Prussia
1795–1803: A Study in Neutrality* (New York, 1903), pp. 192–268; Philip G. Dwyer,
'Prussia and the Armed Neutrality: The Invasion of Hanover in 1801', *International
History Review* 15 (1993), pp. 661–87; Torsten Riotte, 'Hanover in British Policy,
1792–1815' (Ph. D. dissertation, Cambridge, 2003), pp. 100–14.

sovereign as Great Britain . . . she is not in any way an ally of ours and much less a part of us'.[2] Nevertheless, the government of Henry Addington did everything short of calling off its blockade to procure Prussia's evacuation of the electorate. This eventuality was hastened by the assassination of the tsar, which left Prussia increasingly isolated. The final straw was Franco-British détente, which led to the Treaty of Amiens in 1802. Prussia reluctantly withdrew from Hanover in 1801.

But Prussia remained a threat to Hanover; it threatened to gain a strategic stranglehold over the electorate at the Reichshauptdeputationsschluß, in which German ecclesiastical territories were absorbed by their secular neighbors. George III feared that Prussia might win Osnabrück, currently ruled by the duke of York, or Hildesheim, which separated the principality of Göttingen from the main body of the electorate.[3] The king stopped short of advocating Hanoverian acquisition of the two bishoprics, although Prince Adolphus (now the duke of Cambridge) was attempting to enlist British support for such an outcome.[4] Hanover eventually gained Osnabrück, but watched helplessly as Hildesheim fell to Prussia in 1802.

Prussia's acquisition of Hildesheim occasioned a panicked letter from Ernst Brandes to the prince of Wales, in which the Hanoverian official pleaded the electorate's value to Britain. Brandes paid lip service to the idea of personal union, admitting that 'the two countries, tho' united under the dominion of one sovereign, may have their separate interests, and it is certainly not my wish to have the real interests of any one of the two sacrificed to those of the other'. But he claimed that 'the interests of Great Britain can clash but very seldom with those of Hanover', and recalled that electoral possession of Bremen and Verden had given Britain influence over the mouths of the Weser and Elbe.[5] This position was also represented by the British journalist William Cobbett. In an open letter to Lord Hawkesbury, the foreign secretary (later prime minister as Lord Liverpool), he wrote that 'to get Bremen . . . was one great object of the German and English politics of George I . . . Bremen and Hamburg are important places because by our influence through Hanover on them . . . they are the surest, though not the most convenient, inlets for our commerce into Germany.'[6] This was the maritime case for empire over Hanover which dated from the very period Cobbett cited.

Nevertheless, Cobbett displayed a sensitivity to the old republican case

---

2   Fox to Lauderdale, 17 Apr. 1801, published in Lord John Russell, ed., *Memorials and Correspondence of Charles James Fox* (4 vols., London, 1853–7), iii, p. 337.

3   George III to Cornwallis, 1 Nov. 1801, published in Charles Ross, ed., *Correspondence of Charles, First Marquis Cornwallis* (3 vols., London, 1859), iii, pp. 384–5.

4   Riotte, 'Hanover in British Policy', p. 204.

5   Brandes to prince of Wales, 4 Nov. 1802, Hannover, published in A. Aspinall, ed., *The Correspondence of George, Prince of Wales 1770–1812* (8 vols., Oxford, 1963–71), iv, p. 338.

6   *Cobbett's Annual Register* 2 (1802), col. 176.

against Hanoverian empire over Britain. Prussia's acquisition of Hildesheim, he wrote,

> will be far from appearing gloomy to those zealous patriots who think that the glory and liberty of their country consists in the humiliation of their sovereign. And it must be confessed that they will be most effectually relieved from the dread of seeing the Hanoverian troops in garrison at the Tower, which is doubtless a comforting reflection. But . . . if we have no longer to fear that the House of Hanover will enslave England by means of soldiers from the continent, we cannot but recollect that Prussia and France are absolute masters of all the shores of Europe.[7]

Cobbett's evocation of the old republican fear of Hanoverian empire was vivid enough to suggest an exercise in projection. Indeed, Cobbett's views on Hanover would owe more to republicanism as he himself became more radical. But for the moment, Cobbett opposed republicanism with a Burkean emphasis on Hanoverian civil liberty. A year before, he had written that the electorate's 'provinces . . . possess a considerable share of freedom, the people being represented in the assemblies of the states'.[8]

In early 1803, attention turned from Prussia to France. Although Britain had concluded peace with France the previous year at Amiens, war resumed when Britain refused to evacuate Malta. George III's enthusiasm for war surprised the marquess of Buckingham, who wrote that 'with the certain loss of Hanover, I cannot explain his eagerness'.[9] Buckingham's prediction came true later that spring, when France occupied the electorate.[10] The Hanoverian regency negotiated a cease-fire at Suhlingen, without first engaging the enemy. Britain's one substantive response was to blockade the Weser and Elbe rivers, which exacerbated rather than alleviated the electorate's distress.

The French occupation of Hanover provided William Cobbett with a fresh opportunity to embarrass the ministry. Detailing its omissions, he complained that it had not attempted to enlist Prussian protection for the electorate. But curiously, given his later views, he also complained that it had 'neglected to bring a Hanoverian army to Britain when it was in their power so to do'.[11] In fact, the British army was already recruiting Hanoverian

---

[7]  *Cobbett's Annual Register* 2 (1802), col. 176.
[8]  *The Porcupine* no. 93 (14 February 1801), p. 1.
[9]  Buckingham to Lord Grenville, 24 March 1803, published in Historical Manuscripts Commission (HMC), *Report on the Manuscripts of J. B. Fortescue, Esq., Preserved at Dropmore* (10 vols., London, Dublin, and Hereford, 1892–1927), vii, p. 151.
[10] See Ford, *Hanover and Prussia*, pp. 271–315; Philip G. Dwyer, 'Two Definitions of Neutrality: Prussia, the European States-System, and the French Invasion of Hanover in 1803', *International History Review* 19 (1997), pp. 522–40.
[11] *Cobbett's Annual Register* 4 (1803), col. 372.

volunteers for what would eventually be called the 'King's German Legion'.[12] But for the moment, Cobbett's eye for Hanoverian resources reflected his earlier imperialism. These transcended military manpower, as Cobbett reflected that Hanover was 'fresh and fat and a most delightful conquest, a conquest more valuable beyond all comparison than the prizes which we shall make at sea during the whole of the war'.[13] Cobbett had detailed Hanover's supposed bounty in an article two years earlier. [14]

Cobbett was, however, aware that 'the people of this country . . . think they have got rid of a burden'.[15] This critique of imperialism over Hanover was best illustrated in a caricture of 1803, which depicts Napoleon bearing a millstone representing Hanover. John Bull watches in Schadenfreude, hearkening back to the elder Pitt's historical attacks on British empire over Hanover.[16] And the old republican perspective which saw Hanover as a mechanism for royal corruption endured, at least in the person of Sir Francis Burdett. A radical member of parliament, Burdett opposed compensating the prince of Orange for the British seizure of the Cape of Good Hope on the grounds that it might set a precedent for similar indemnification of 'the elector of Hanover'.[17] It was nothing more than a snide aside, but one which reverberated in Hanover nonetheless.[18]

The Hanoverian responses to Burdett occurred in the context of the electorate's first pamphlet war. Berlepsch's ideas returned with a vengeance,[19] but with a much larger political and social constituency. The participants did not possess the social stature of the combatants in the Berlepsch affair, but that was in fact the pamphlet war's significance. Ironically critics of social inequality targeted barriers to government employment rather than taxation,

---

12 See N. Ludlow Beamish, *History of the King's German Legion* (2 vols., London, 1832–7); Bernhard Schwertfeger, *Geschichte der königlichen deutschen Legion* (2 vols., Hannover and Leipzig, 1907); Adolf Pfannkuche, *Die königlich deutsche Legion 1803–1816* (Hannover, 1926); Andreas Einsel, Dieter Kutschenreiter, and Wolfgang Seth, 'The King's German Legion: Hannoversche Soldaten unter britischer Flagge', in Heide N. Rohloff, ed., *Großbritannien und Hannover: Die Zeit der Personalunion 1714–1837* (Frankfurt, 1989), pp. 299–323.

13 *Cobbett's Annual Register* 3 (1803), col. 885.

14 *The Porcupine* no. 93 (14 Feb. 1801), p. 1.

15 *Cobbett's Annual Register* 4 (1803), col. 348.

16 See Frederic George Stephens and Mary Dorothy George, eds., *Catalogue of Political and Personal Satires Preserved in the Department of Prints and Drawings in the British Museum* (11 vols., London, 1870–1954), viii, pp. 162–3.

17 William Cobbett, ed., *The Parliamentary History of England* (36 vols., London, 1806–20), xxxvi, col. 1671.

18 *Beantwortung der Vertheidigung des Herrn Doctor Juris Seumnich* (n. p., 1803), p. 7; *Schreiben eines Hannoveraners zur Berichtigung mancher Urtheile* (n. p., 1803), p. 10.

19 For Berlepsch's influence in 1803, see Reinhard Oberschelp, 'Kurhannover im Spiegel von Flugschriften des Jahres 1803', *Niedersächsisches Jahrbuch für Landesgeschichte* 49 (1977), p. 240.

Boney in Possession of the Millstone (1803)
© Copyright the Trustees of the British Museum

an issue of greater moment to more people. Nevertheless debate about British empire was at its most widespread, despite (or perhaps because of) its apparent disappearance.

Opposition to British empire over the electorate was summarized best by the anonymous author of *Gedanken eines Hannoveraners* (Thoughts of a Hanoverian), who complained that 'Hanover was always sacrificed to England's interest and had to participate in all of its wars, ever since the country's elector unfortunately became king of England.'[20] But what was England's interest? Some observers echoed Berlepsch, who had blamed its alleged commercial hegemony for Hanoverian suffering. In Johann Matthäus Bauer's comic dialogue *Vetter Andres* (Cousin Andres), the eponymous character grumbled that Britain's wartime elimination of French competition had made coffee, sugar, and rice more expensive.[21] Although the economic dilemma was not uniquely Hanoverian, its military consequences were. Bauer wrote of the British, 'they wage war with our money, not for that dump Malta, but to maintain a trade monopoly ['Alleinhandel'] in which France wanted to share'.[22] 'Alleinhandel' clearly alluded to a German word for autocracy ('Alleinherrschaft'), saddling Britain with the rhetorical baggage of universal monarchy.

Commercial despotism not only furnished a motive for France's invasion, it complicated Hanover's defense. The private secretary of the electoral commander-in-chief excused his patron's passivity with reference to Hanover's diplomatic isolation. In *Historische Berichtigungen* (Historical Corrections), he wrote that 'England's policy of universal trade despotism, which grows more egotistical by the decade, finds the powers of the continent ever less inclined to alliances in cases where they have no prominent common interest. And . . . England believes its guineas to be better spent on any purpose other than the support of Hanover',[23] obviating the subsidies which might have conciliated the electorate's potential allies. Britain foisted its maritime foreign policy upon a state entirely unsuited for it. He wrote that 'while Hanover had no hope of preserving itself with an insular foreign policy, it nonetheless stood isolated from foreign connections and formed a sort of political island upon the continent'.[24] Hanover could not even rely upon Britain, although the electorate 'secures a point for its trade with the continent'. If it had wanted to, Britain, 'as impotent on the continent as it is

---

20 *Gedanken eines Hannoveraners über die sein Vaterland in den Monaten Junius und Julius 1803 betroffenen Unfälle, nebst wahrhafter Erzählung einiger derselben* (n. p., 1803), p. 15.
21 Johann Matthäus Bauer, *Vetter Andres, Kanter und Kunz. Ein politisch-komischer Dialog gehalten in einem Wirthshause zu Lüneburg* (Lüneburg, 1803), p. 7.
22 Bauer, *Vetter Andres, Kanter und Kunz*, p. 9.
23 [Karl Wilhelm Koppe], *Historische Berichtigungen des öffentlichen Urtheils über die durch die französische Okkupation des Kurfürstenthums Hannover daselbst veranlaßten militairischen Maaßregeln* (n. p., 1803), p. 2.
24 [Koppe], *Historische Berichtigungen*, pp. 8–9.

omnipotent at sea, would not be able to support Hanover – even if it were a British province in the real sense of the word'.[25] In other words, Hanover had all the drawbacks of a colony with none of the advantages. The author summarized its position by calling it 'Britain's stepdaughter'.[26]

Opponents of British empire had to argue that it was surreptitious, preserving the appearance of Hanoverian independence. A Hamburg anglophobe of Hanoverian origin, Carl Anton Johann Seumnich, wrote that

> Holstein is a part of Denmark, as is Pomerania of Sweden; both countries are under the governments of Copenhagen and Stockholm. The situation is totally different in Hanover, which is not part of the United Kingdom of Great Britain and Ireland. It is not under the English ministry, but has its own, entirely independent government. Its army is entirely different from England's, it maintains its own ambassadors at assorted foreign courts, and the Hanoverian minister in London is even listed as a foreign ambassador in English almanacs. It can be compared to the relationships which once prevailed between Saxony and Poland and, for a short time, Hesse-Cassel and Sweden, as well as the current one which unifies the French and Italian republics through the person of First Consul and President Bonaparte.[27]

If the last of Seumnich's comparisons was ominously imperial, he admitted that Hanover was, at least formally, what we might recognize to be a personal union.

Although Seumnich's opponents objected to the comparison with France and Italy, on the grounds that no British troops occupied Hanover,[28] they took up the personal union thesis. The anonymous author of a *Beantwortung* (Answer) to Seumnich argued that 'Hanover is separated from England, otherwise it could not be a part of the German state. The only thing it has in common with Great Britain is that the king of this empire is also elector of Hanover.'[29] Even in its dotage, the Holy Roman Empire served the proponents of personal union – as did Britain's Act of Settlement, which the author also cited. These were elements of positive law which appeared to bear out the personal union thesis. Its advocates also made reference to history, often distorting detail in the process. They were, however, certainly correct to highlight the Treaty of Basel, in which Hanover had joined Prussia in a separate peace while Britain continued to fight.[30] France had moved the goalposts when it suited Napoleon.

---

[25] Koppe, *Historische Berichtigungen*, p. 2.

[26] Koppe, *Historische Berichtigungen*, p. 7.

[27] Carl Anton Johann Seumnich, *Ueber die Verbindung des Churfürstenthums Hannover mit England und deren Folgen, über die hannöversche Verfassung, und über das Verhalten der Hannoveraner bey der jetzigen Besetzung des Landes* (Hamburg, 1803), pp. 8–9.

[28] *Einiges zur Vertheidigung des Churfürstenthums Hannover* (n. p., 1803), p. 19.

[29] *Beantwortung der Vertheidigung des Herrn Doctor Juris Seumnich*, p. 6.

[30] *Freimüthige Betrachtungen über die französische Besetzung der Kurbraunschweigischen Staaten* (n. p., 1803), p. 18; *Schreiben eines Hannoveraners zur Berichtigung mancher Urtheile*, p. 9.

One problem with the concept of 'personal union' was the inconsistency of the one commentator who actually used it. This was the anonymous author of *Müssen wir nicht von England getrennt werden?* (Should We not Be Separated from England?), which answered its own question in the negative. It made frequent use of the phrase 'personal union' (*persönliche Verbindung*),[31] and termed the appearance of any more intimate connection between Hanover and Britain an 'optical illusion'.[32] *Müssen wir nicht von England getrennt werden* denied that Hanover was a colony of London, or even a satellite such as Scotland and Ireland had supposedly been before their respective acts of union.[33] The author added that Westminster had never legislated for Hanover in the manner it occasionally had for the Channel Islands and the Isle of Man.[34] Yet he appeared to contradict himself, writing that 'when their political interests converged, Hanover had more advantage than disadvantage when it could attach itself as a satellite to powerful, influential England'.[35]

Personal union was more than a reproach against France for having invaded a supposedly neutral country, it was also an apology for Britain's backwardness in rendering assistance to Hanover. The anonymous author of *Schreiben eines Hannoveraners* (Letter of a Hanoverian) considered that the Act of Settlement 'had changed the [English] government, converting crown and scepter into mere decorations . . . so it is obvious how powerless the king is to follow his own inclination', which was presumably to help Hanover with British resources.[36] In this case, whiggish constitutionalism and personal union conspired to leave Hanover helpless. Common sense led *Einiges zur Vertheidigung des Churfürstenthums Hannover* (Something in Defense of the Electorate of Hanover) to concur, warning that

> if the French occupation of our land had provoked a reaction from England, then our perpetual fate might have been to be attacked in every quarrel between the two powers. But now we need not fear a similar action from an enlightened, just nation, since it could be sure that its strategy . . . would fail.[37]

Although this argument seemed reasonable in the aftermath of 1757, it was now utterly fatuous. Worse, some exponents of personal union went off-message while straining to condone British passivity. H. L. Villaume argued that 'to complain that [George III] has abandoned us would be just as unfair as the French in Saint-Domingue or other French islands and possessions

---

31 *Müssen wir nicht von England getrennt werden?* (n. p., 1803), pp. 56, 72–3, 76–7, 80, 89, 94.
32 *Müssen wir nicht von England getrennt werden?*, p. 5.
33 *Müssen wir nicht von England getrennt werden?*, p. 22.
34 *Müssen wir nicht von England getrennt werden?*, p. 23.
35 *Müssen wir nicht von England getrennt werden?*, pp. 75–6.
36 *Schreiben eines Hannoveraners zur Berichtigung mancher Urtheile*, pp. 5–6.
37 *Einiges zur Vertheidigung des Churfürstenthums Hannover*, p. 22.

complaining that Bonaparte does not protect them. Neither is omnipotent.'[38] This comparison placed Hanover somewhat closer to the status of a British colony, an assertion which sat uneasily with Villaume's otherwise consistent use of the personal union thesis.

This equivocation allowed Britain's apologists to envision future assistance, while excusing its absence in the past. The anonymous author of *Einiges zur Vertheidigung des Churfürstenthums Hannover* considered that a country 'whose ruler is king of a greater and richer nation' would be better able 'to recover better after such hardships' than one 'whose ruling house is impoverished along with the land'.[39] The author admitted that Britain had never paid reparations to Hanover after the Seven Years' War. But he added that this was 'no necessary consequence of these relationships' with Britain (i.e. dynastic union).[40] *Müssen wir nicht von England getrennt werden* argued further that this was not 'a fair reason to hate a nation thoroughly, or to entertain the wish to break with it'.[41]

*Einiges zur Vertheidigung des Churfürstenthums Hannover* was similarly equivocal on the subject of dynastic union's inadvertent benefits to Hanover. It added the new political consideration that as long as 'our ruler maintains his palace and household among us so that he can come and live with us at any time . . . we shall by no means become a province of England'.[42] The author also voiced the venerable argument that court expenditures helped the Hanoverian economy, observing that 'increased circulation of money promotes the wealth, and therefore the welfare, of a state'.[43] Yet he wanted to have both sides of the argument for dynastic union, in that he also revisited the argument that the king's absence reduced expenditure. Imagining the court of a resident elector, he wrote that 'the land would . . . have to make extraordinary contributions to it' and that 'sums would . . . leave the land for expenditure on luxuries'.[44]

Supporters of union also argued that the elector's absence in London hindered, rather than facilitated, British exploitation of Hanover. Recalling Spittler's paean to the patchwork of Hanoverian estates and rights, *Müssen wir nicht von England getrennt werden* wrote that 'it would be particularly difficult for an absent ruler of Hanover to abuse the electorate for Great Britain's advantage'.[45] Unsurprisingly, the anonymous author made no reference to the Berlepsch affair. Instead, he extended his argument from the estates to the government, recalling that George I had invested his electoral govern-

---

[38] H. L. Villaume, *Beyträge zur Geschichte Hannovers im Jahr 1803* (Hamburg, 1803), p. 29.

[39] *Einiges zur Vertheidigung des Churfürstenthums Hannover*, p. 11.

[40] *Einiges zur Vertheidigung des Churfürstenthums Hannover*, p. 12.

[41] *Müssen wir nicht von England getrennt werden?*, p. 87.

[42] *Einiges zur Vertheidigung des Churfürstenthums Hannover*, p. 52.

[43] *Einiges zur Vertheidigung des Churfürstenthums Hannover*, p. 54.

[44] *Einiges zur Vertheidigung des Churfürstenthums Hannover*, p. 36.

[45] *Müssen wir nicht von England getrennt werden?*, p. 46.

ment with substantial aspects of his sovereignty before departing for Britain in 1714. The anonymous author added that subsequent history had further expanded the government's authority.[46] He concluded that the electoral government's power prevented Britain from suborning Hanover to its foreign policy.[47] Although *Müssen wir nicht von England getrennt werden* echoed Spittler's skepticism about British civil liberties relative to those of Hanover, its argument was functionally anglophilic.

This argument countered renewed complaints that the elector's absence vitiated princely government. This was the view of a government official, Burchard Christian von Spilcker, in his *Noch Etwas über das Churfürstenthum Hannover* (Something Further on the Electorate of Hanover). He reflected that 'the less the ruler knows his subjects and servants personally, the greater the ministers' influence. Even if the latter are honest, their increasing power cannot help but hurt the constitution.' Spilcker considered this to be a perversion of princely government, whereby 'the ministry became plainly sovereign' in the place of the absent elector.[48] He took the latter charge from Seumnich. Seumnich referenced the prohibitions on remonstrating with the king in London, writing 'he to whom I can solely apply is a lot more likely to be considered the sovereign than is he to whom I am forbidden all admittance'.[49] To the edicts of 1763 and 1778 already highlighted by Berlepsch, Seumnich added a precedent dating from 1734.[50] He claimed that the government thereby made itself the only legitimate channel for the expression of grievances to the elector, ensuring its view would prevail.

So far, Spilcker's and Seumnich's perspective was broadly within an old tradition which had regretted the elector's absence. But they also blamed it for Hanover's aristocratic monopoly on jobs, which Berlepsch himself had not openly argued. Spilcker considered that 'this sort of aristocracy . . . has certainly been promoted and augmented by the absence of the prince',[51] although he admitted that a resident elector could be just as sheltered.[52] Seumnich had no such doubts. Claiming that George III was 'constantly surrounded by nobles', he added that 'the persons around him will probably influence him to choose nobles' for electoral posts.[53]

Critics of union also argued that the elector's absence had encouraged

---

46 *Müssen wir nicht von England getrennt werden?*, p. 37.
47 *Müssen wir nicht von England getrennt werden?*, p. 36.
48 [Burchard Christian von Spilcker], *Noch Etwas über das Churfürstenthum Hannover* (n. p., 1803), p. 7.
49 Carl Anton Johann Seumnich, *Vertheidigung des Dr. jur. Seumnich wider die Bemerkungen eines ungenannten Hannoveraners* (Hamburg, 1803), p. 11.
50 Seumnich, *Vertheidigung des Dr. jur. Seumnich*, pp. 8–9.
51 [Spilcker], *Noch Etwas über das Churfürstenthum Hannover*, p. 14.
52 [Spilcker], *Noch Etwas über das Churfürstenthum Hannover*, pp. 15–16.
53 Seumnich, *Vertheidigung des Dr. jur. Seumnich*, p. 24.

electoral officials in promoting members of their family as well as of their estate. Again, this had remained underdeveloped in Berlepsch's publicity. The clearest accusations of nepotism came from the author of *Gedanken eines Hannoveraners*, who wrote that

> the king of England is our elector . . . but was never here and only knows the country from descriptions which are made to him. This absence and ignorance is the misfortune of the land, because even with the best intentions, the king can only see through others and follow their recommendations. An even greater misfortune is that the land's ruler is king of England, to which its interest has always been sacrificed without the slightest advantages in return. Admittedly idle courtiers and other individuals have used their autonomy to draw large incomes and . . . to secure the best positions for their sons and relatives. The consequence was that mostly incompetent people came to the head of administration. Our poor land never suffered for this more than at this moment, when men of intelligence, heart, and patriotism were most necessary[54]

In this analysis dynastic union had facilitated the French occupation directly, by inculcating corruption of the sort that precluded a vigorous defense, as well as directly.

For some, Hanoverian corruption coexisted uneasily with Britain's eighteenth-century reputation for upward mobility. One author was perplexed, despite his opposition to British empire. He wrote that 'no talent could qualify the bourgeois . . . for an important post, because many of the first offices of the land were given in partisan fashion to the hereditary noble, which never should have been the case in a land which is almost the closest relative of free England'.[55] This cliché had only just been reiterated in Johann Friedrich von der Decken's 1802 *Versuch über den englischen National-Character* (Essay on English National Character), which held that 'the English constitution . . . furnishes a wide field to industry and genius' compared with those of the European continent.[56]

Others demolished this paradox with an equally durable stereotype about England, that of its political corruption. Seumnich wrote that for George III, 'Hanover is a true sinecure, of which there are so many in England.'[57] If George III was following the prevailing ethos of his birthland, then he was implicitly setting the tone for its adoption in Hanover. Seumnich further charged that George III brought one million Reichstaler from the Hanoverian revenues to London annually, some of which was used to

---

[54] *Gedanken eines Hannoveraners*, pp. 5–6.
[55] *Ueber das Benehmen Preussens bey der ungestörten Besetzhaltung des hannöverschen durch die Franzosen* (n. p., 1804), p. 9.
[56] Johann Friedrich von der Decken, *Versuch über den englischen National-Character* (Hannover, 1802), p. 47.
[57] Seumnich, *Ueber die Verbindung des Churfürstenthums Hannover mit England*, p. 9.

finance parliamentary elections. 'For Hanover', he observed, 'such [money] is as good as lost.'[58] The idea that Hanover might fuel even a part of Britain's exorbitant electoral campaigns struck many Hanoverians as deliciously absurd. The author of one *Sendschreiben* (Letter) asked if Seumnich 'would show us the gold mine from which the ministers got the money' purportedly sent to George III.[59] But given the general belief that the loan of 1700 had financed similar political corruption in Britain, Seumnich's fanciful charge seemed plausible.

Corruption was merely one of many British characteristics which threatened to overwhelm indigenous values. One self-described artisan complained that 'Our laughable anglomanie contributed to our present troubles and allowed our national character and practically our outward appearance to decay. It was a certain mixture of base fear and groveling respect which greeted Englishmen who came to Hanover or those who had spent some time in England.'[60] The vivid language anticipated later diagnoses of a 'cultural cringe' in Britain's imperial periphery.

Sensitivity to British empire contributed to a renewed campaign to separate from it in any eventual peace settlement. Seumnich suggested that he devolve Hanover upon one of his numerous sons, for whom 'Hanover would be a considerable establishment'.[61] This recalled Berlepsch's scheme to set up the duke of Cambridge, as elector. Indeed, a *Berichtigung* (Correction) of the *Gedanken* contemplated this openly.[62] Supporters of union retorted that union's dissolution was already preordained, by Princess Charlotte's presumptive inheritance of the British throne. Some supporters of union argued that its future dissolution obviated one in the present.[63] Another anglophilic pamphlet, *Ich kann nicht schweigen!* (I Cannot Keep Quiet!), regretted any dissolution and prayed that the prince of Wales might father a son, 'which would indisputably strengthen our union with England, and would make our land's happiness permanent'.[64] Its author worried that the dissolution of personal union would push Hanover into Prussia's orbit.[65]

The next Hanoverian debate over the relationship with Britain took place out of publicity's glare, in the German Chancery attached to the elector in London. Shortly before taking charge of it in 1805, Ernst Friedrich Herbert

---

58 Seumnich, *Ueber die Verbindung des Churfürstenthums Hannover mit England*, p. 11.
59 *Sendschreiben des Oberbürgermeisters des Alten-Landes an den herrn Doctor Seumnich in Hamburg* (n. p., 1803), p. 15.
60 *Schreiben des Churhannöverischen Kunstdrechslers C . . . an den Verfasser der Gedanken eines Hannoveraners* (n. p., 1803), p. 6.
61 Seumnich, *Ueber die Verbindung des Churfürstenthums Hannover mit England*, p. 23.
62 *Berichtigung der Broschüre, Gedanken eines Hannoveraners* (n. p., 1803), p. 40.
63 *Müssen wir nicht von England getrennt werden?*, p. 26; [Brester], *Ueber das Churfürstenthum Hannover* (n. p., 1803), p. 13.
64 *Ich kann nicht schweigen!* (n. p., 1803), p. 12.
65 *Ich kann nicht schweigen!*, p. 10.

Count Münster paused to take stock of Hanover's present and future. He asked the chancery's secretary, Georg Best, to anticipate what a restored Hanover might look like. Best observed that 'the electorate must suffer for each of England's feuds as long as both lands share one ruler, and I will neither think nor speak of another case'. Unwilling to imagine dynastic separation from Britain, Best resigned himself to its enemies' perception of Hanoverian status. He recommended 'gradually wiping from paper the principle which is claimed by pen – that Great Britain and Hanover, the king and elector, are completely different things and persons – but knocked down by sword and deed'.[66] Best condemned the personal union thesis as a legalistic fetish, but declined to specify an alternative.[67]

Münster understandably assumed Best was advocating some sort of British empire over Hanover, and countered with a defense of personal union. Münster replied, 'if we could become part of the British empire, we would enjoy some advantages. But I doubt whether our security would profit much, in so far as the sea which protects England doesn't surround us.' Of course this was already true of personal union, although rhetorical independence had occasionally spared Hanover the attentions of British enemies. What would change, if personal union were abandoned, was Hanover's position at peace conferences. 'Considered an English province', Münster observed, 'we could be sacrificed at a future peace, as has happened to other provinces. At least now England has no right to give up the patrimony of its king' and might even 'give back one of its conquests for the possession of Hanover, as it relinquished colonies in previous peace treaties to free Naples, Holland, and other countries from French troops.' Münster not only criticized what he took to be Best's opinion from a Hanoverian position, but in British terms as well. He thought that 'if England takes on the responsibility of defending a continental possession, all European powers will have a certain interest in paralyzing England's colonial enterprises by diverting its energies to Germany'.[68] This was, of course, the British case against imperialism in Hanover. Münster was to use his exquisite sensitivity to British interests in Hanover's favor during years to come.

His first opportunity came later the same year, when Napoleon evacuated the electorate to meet the challenge of an Austro-Russian army. Afraid that Prussia might occupy Hanover, Münster wrote to Prime Minister Pitt urging a British expedition (which would include the King's German Legion) to the

---

[66] [Georg Best], 'Meine Ansicht im Februar 1805', Niedersächsisches Hauptstaatsarchiv (NHStA), Dep. 110, A, Nr. 49.
[67] Later, in response to Münster's criticisms, Best answered that 'I certainly do not intend incorporation [and] provincial dependence.' Georg Best, 'Ein Paar Bemerkungen über des Herrn Grafen von Münster geneigte Beurtheilung meiner Ansicht', 11 Mar. 1805, NHStA, Dep. 110, A, Nr. 69.
[68] Ernst Friedrich Herbert, Graf Münster, 'Antwort auf des Herrn Geheimen Cabinets-Raths Best Ansicht im Februar', 7 Mar. 1805, NHStA, Dep. 110, A, Nr. 69.

electorate. His letter emphasized Hanover's strategic position astride important shipping lanes, including the Elbe river.[69] Although he had resisted British empire in private, he was not above hinting at it for a British audience. Hanover's dependence upon Britain was further evident in Münster's request that the foreign secretary, Lord Mulgrave, support the electorate's designs upon Hildesheim. Although the principality was ostensibly an 'indemnity' for Hanover's wrongful occupation – a reference to personal union – Münster realized that it was only available through British offices.[70] Pitt agreed to the expedition, and sent a small British army (including the King's German Legion) to the electorate in November of 1805.

This interval occasioned some of the most fulsome anglophilia ever expressed in Hanover, epitomized by the anonymously published pamphlet *Alt Hannover immerdar* (Old Hanover Forever). Echoing Spittler, it informed its readers that 'the spirit of English thinking and acting . . . had insinuated itself imperceptibly and was spread over the general and particular of your existence, so that even the traces of its errors became visible'.[71] The underhanded criticism demonstrated that disillusionment with Britain had reached such a pitch that even anglophiles had to pay it tribute. But mostly, *Alt Hannover immerdar* celebrated Britain. Its author posited two mechanisms for the transmission of British culture to Hanover, both of them royal. Speaking of the first two Georges, he remarked that 'the rare spirit of these rulers was further ennobled and expanded by mixture with the English form, and . . . flowed to you, into the smallest arteries of the state'.[72] The second engine of Hanoverian anglophilia were those of George III's sons who had visited, or lived in, the electorate.[73] There were, the pamphlet argued, 'always princes there, who . . . are to thank for the reception and elevation of that English sense which certainly would not suit a German people when unilaterally and inappropriately imitated (heaven forbid!), . . . but spreads a liberal and honest existence when introduced in an unforced and characteristic manner'.[74] The idea that dynastic union made anglophilia more 'natural' in Hanover than in other states seemed to bespeak a traditional monarchism.

---

[69] Münster to Pitt, 3 Oct. 1805, Weymouth, The National Archives (NA), PRO 30/8/338, f. 238.

[70] Münster to Mulgrave, 10 Nov. 1805, London, NA, FO 97/243.

[71] *Alt Hannover immerdar, oder Hannovers Errettung* (n. p., 1805), p. 13.

[72] *Alt Hannover immerdar*, p. 14.

[73] Prince Frederick resided in Hannover from 1781 to 1787, where he was visited by Prince William from 1783 to 1785. Prince Edward trained as a soldier in Lüneburg from 1785 to 1787. Princes Ernest, Adolphus, and Augustus studied at Göttingen from 1786 to 1790, when the former two received commissions in the Hanoverian army. Prince Ernest returned to Britain in 1799, and was followed by Adolphus in 1803.

[74] *Alt Hannover immerdar*, pp. 15–16.

But the author of *Alt Hannover immerdar* could dispense with monarchism, if doing so shored up the relationship with Britain. He informed his readers, 'you are more or less ruled in republican fashion, or at least in such a way that your constitution pragmatically and felicitously hangs together in ways similar to the exalted English monarchy'.[75] Republicanism could be acceptable to Hanoverians, so long as it meant a mixed monarchy on the British model. Nevertheless, this instance of republicanism was to remain singular in Hanovarian discourse.

The British position in Hanover became untenable after Napoleon's decisive victory over Austria and Russia at Austerlitz. The resulting vacuum was filled by Prussia, which occupied Hanover.[76] For the first time, there was no discernible British provocation behind an occupation of Hanover. But Prussia acted with the approval of Britain's enemy France, and justified its action with reference to British empire over Hanover. Some Hanoverians naturally took refuge in the personal union thesis. Baron von Rhaden denied that 'a real union existed between the states, Great Britain and Hanover'.[77] Another pamphlet, the *Erklärung der Hannoveraner über die Preußische Besetzung* (The Hanoverians' Declaration on the Prussian Occupation) argued that 'no British law was observed in Hanover. No Briton was employed here. The English parliament never attempted to spread and apply its ordinances to Hanover, let alone trouble itself with Hanover at all. The king of England remained elector of Brunswick-Lüneburg and, as such, an estate of the German Empire.'[78] Rhaden advanced the Peace of Basel, in which Hanover had acquiesced in neutrality while Britain continued its war against France, as an example of the personal union in action.[79]

Personal union not only preserved divergent foreign policies, but constitutions as well. The *Erklärung* wrote of the elector-king that 'both states hang on his orders, Hanover more than the other'.[80] Here was a rare acknowledgement that the electorate was more monarchical than Britain. But it simultaneously raised the question of the elector's absence. Rhaden wrote that 'if Hanover's ruler wants to make his country happy . . . no sea hinders his wise, paternal intentions'.[81] This was the old monarchical argument that the elector's absence would not affect Hanoverian government.

---

75 *Alt Hannover immerdar*, p. 20.
76 For the Prussian occupation of 1806, see Brendan Simms, ' "An Odd Question Enough": Charles James Fox, the Crown, and British Policy during the Hanoverian Crisis of 1806', *The Historical Journal* 38 (1995), pp. 567–96.
77 [Rhaden, Freiherr von], *Zufällige Gedanken eines Hannoveraners beym Lesen des IV. Heftes der Schrift von den höchsten Interessen des teutschen Reichs* (Regensburg, 1806), pp. 43–4.
78 *Erklärung der Hannover über die Preußische Besetzung und Verwahrung der Kurbraunschweig-Lüneburgischen Staaten im Jahre 1806* (Stralsund, 1806), p. 23 (note).
79 [Rhaden], *Zufällige Gedanken eines Hannoveraners*, p. 43.
80 *Erklärung der Hannover*, p. 44 (note).
81 [Rhaden], *Zufällige Gedanken eines Hannoveraners*, pp. 49–50.

Of course, personal union never ruled out British assistance to Hanover, indeed this became morally necessary if the electorate was attacked on account of the former's policies. L. H. Schelver considered that 'Hanover became the victim of this war, and all that it suffered, it suffered for the sake of the English nation. The latter gives so many subsidies to foreign powers. Should it not give a subsidy to the reconstruction of its sister-land Hanover, which it has made so unhappy?'[82] Here, Schelver reprised the argument of *Einiges zur Vertheidigung des Churfürstenthums Hannover*.

But the personal union theorists were willing to describe British empire over Hanover, if only to highlight the inconsistency of Prussian claims that George III would readily part with his Hanoverian dominions. The *Erklärung* wrote that if one has 'accepted the opinion that Hanover is an English dependency, can he . . . then imagine that England would allow such a dependency to be ripped from it?'[83] Making a more concrete comparison, the same pamphlet asked 'should England allow its American colonies to be taken from it with good will and without resistance?'[84]

Other Hanoverians were even readier to conceive of British empire over Hanover; France had created this situation regardless of opinions in Britain and the electorate. Schelver suggested that George III 'abdicate the electorate in favor of an English prince, for example the duke of Cambridge . . . If he never takes part in English affairs, then his country can never again be attacked by the French out of revenge against England.'[85] Another pamphleteer agreed, although he also noted that 'the separation from England looms anyway. Because the prince of Wales only has a daughter, who will succeed in England but not in the electorate because of imperial laws' against female succession.[86] This had been one of Berlepsch's solutions to the problem of Britain, and had been taken up again by the pamphlets of 1803.

Britain's response to Prussia's occupation of Hanover remained muted until Friedrich Wilhelm III annexed the electorate in the spring of 1806. George III launched a charm offensive in which British diplomats attempted to reverse Prussian policy. When that did not succeed, Britain declared war on Prussia and took up negotiations with Napoleon. In the context of the talks with France, Münster (with George III's foreknowledge) reiterated the case for Hanover to the foreign secretary Charles James Fox. He invoked the rhetorical tradition of maritime imperialism over the electorate, writing that it

---

82  [L. H. Schelver], *Das Kurfürstenthum Hannover unter den Franzosen in den Jahren 1803, 1804, 1805, und dessen fernere Schicksale* (n. p., 1806), p. 80.

83  *Erklärung der Hannover*, p. 189 (note).

84  *Erklärung der Hannover*, p. 188 (note).

85  [Schelver], *Das Kurfürstenthum Hannover*, p. 79.

86  *Gedanken und Wünsche eines patriotischen Hannoveraners für das Jahr 1807* (Pattensen, 1806), p. 11.

commands the only two considerable navigable rivers on the North Sea, the Elbe and the Weser . . . The channel of the Strecklitz running from Lübeck to the town of Lauenburg unites the navigation of the Baltic with that of the Elbe and North Sea and it is liable to become of high importance if ever the passage of the Sound should be shut up.

Part of this particular commercial argument for empire over Hanover had always been military, so Münster added that 'Hanover is the most conve-nient point for England in case this power should intend in future to coop-erate with the continental powers, which has been proved by the operations of the Seven Years' War.' But the Hanoverian minister noted that any coor-dination with Britain would expose the electorate to retaliation by that country's enemies. As a deterrent to this, he once again promoted Hanover's pretensions to the principality of Hildesheim.[87]

It is hard to gauge Münster's effect on Fox, whose view of Hanover changed according to the audience he was addressing. He pressed the personal union thesis on the French, refusing to exchange British conquests for Hanover on the grounds that 'it had been taken from the elector, not from the king of Great Britain'.[88] But in an anonymously published pamphlet, he extolled the advantages of British empire over the electorate. 'Hanover', wrote Fox, 'is the first and connecting link in the chain of our continental system.'[89] The electorate advantaged Britain in two senses, military and diplomatic. Speaking of Hanover, Fox wrote that 'it was here that we sent our continental armies, here they found a home and all the conveniences of being in their own country'. Fox further blurred the distinc-tion between Britain and Hanover when describing how the latter helped attract continental allies for the former. Inverting Spittler, he considered that 'England in possession, and in the friendly use, of Hanover was more than half German, a point . . . of no inconsiderable importance when we considered the necessity of German alliance.'[90] Possession of Hanover left no doubt about the seat of empire, which describing Britain as German might otherwise have left unclear.

That Münster and Fox had to spell out Hanover's advantages to Britain indicated that they were not obvious. Indeed, one caricature had ridiculed Prussia's annexation of Hanover by depicting the royal eagle eating excre-ment just 'evacuated' by Napoleon.[91] So the government's sponsorship of Hanover revived opposition to British empire over that electorate. This was the maritime devaluation of empire on the European continent, as opposed

87 Münster to Fox, 16 July 1806, Windsor, NA, FO 97/243.
88 [Charles James Fox], *The State of the Negotiation with Details of Its Progress and Causes of Its Termination in the Recall of the Earl of Lauderdale* (London, 1806), p. 77.
89 [Fox], *The State of the Negotiation*, p. 69.
90 [Fox], *The State of the Negotiation*, p. 71.
91 See Stephens and George, eds., *Catalogue of Political and Personal Satires*, viii, p. 436.

The Evacuation of Hanover (1806)
© Copyright the Trustees of the British Museum

to fortified possessions astride important shipping lanes. *The Courier*, a tory paper in temporary opposition, encapsulated this position when it observed that

> by consenting to purchase the surrender of it by some valuable colony, we hold out an encouragement and temptation to BONAPARTE in all future wars to overrun it and drain the inhabitants – making it the source of maintaining his troops in war and selling it to us at every peace for some island or colony he may wish to possess. We shall only be permitted to possess it during peace in order that we may give it up to him in time of war in a more improved state. We shall only be in the nature of leaseholders whose lease will expire whenever the good pleasure of the granter wills it.[92]

One of Cobbett's correspondents worried that Malta or the Cape of Good Hope would constitute Hanover's ransom.[93] Cobbett's maritime protests over British assistance to Hanover represented a volte face from his position of 1803. Cobbett's criticism of empire over Hanover progressed alongside his political radicalism, which nevertheless remained constitutional.[94] Indeed, he published a letter from another correspondent, who quoted Blackstone's maritime interpretation of the Act of Settlement.[95]

This selfsame correspondent continued to discuss the Act of Settlement, moving from maritime criticism of British empire over Hanover to the republican fear of the opposite scenario. He claimed that parliament had not been consulted about Hanover's defense, in contravention of the Act of Settlement[96] and the republican preference for balanced government. The correspondent even wished that parliament had stipulated to George I

> that unless you consent to part with dominions where political liberty is unknown and the people are in a condition . . . of political servitude, we cannot think you qualified to rule over us, the people of England. How could we contemplate him as the guardian of our freedom, who we should behold elsewhere swaying an arbitrary scepter?[97]

1806, it seems, was a time for regrets. Another author regretted that the electorate had never been ceded to the pretender, as suggested in *The Peace*

92 *The Courier* no. 4382 (1 Sept. 1806), p. 3.
93 *Cobbett's Political Register* 10 (1806), col. 146.
94 For popular constitutionalism, see John Belchem, 'Republicanism, Popular Constitutionalism and the Radical Platform in Early Nineteenth-Century England', *Social History* 6 (1981), pp. 1–32; James A. Epstein, 'The Constitutional Idiom: Radical Reasoning, Rhetoric, and Action in Early Nineteenth-Century England', *Journal of Social History* 23 (1990), pp. 533–74; James Vernon, *Politics and the People: A Study in English Political Culture, c. 1815–1867* (Cambridge, 1993), pp. 295–330.
95 *Cobbett's Political Register* 10 (1806), col. 277.
96 *Cobbett's Political Register* 10 (1806), col. 276.
97 *Cobbett's Political Register* 10 (1806), col. 277.

*Offering* (1746).[98] Although the latter did not explain why, Cobbett's correspondent clearly feared Hanoverian empire over Britain. The electorate was currently under Prussian dominion, but he insinuated its liberation might imperil British freedom. This was a far cry from Cobbett's Burkean praise for Hanover's provincial estates, published in 1801.

Corruption was an essential ingredient to republican fears of Hanoverian empire, and was soon detected. A third correspondent of Cobbett initially excused this, writing 'that His Majesty must feel a fond attachment to the dominions of his ancestors is naturally to be expected'. Here was the old republican admiration for patriotism, even that of another country. But Cobbett's correspondent added that

> true British interests must ever be the primary object of a British sovereign, and it were almost treason to suppose it possible that His Majesty could wish, his cabinet advise, or his people acquiesce in the protraction of a hopeless contest or the sacrifice of any great national object for the redemption of continental dominions.[99]

So George III was corrupt if he did not put aside his Hanoverian resentments as king of Britain. Also corrupt were any politicians who indulged the king's nostalgia for his ancestral homeland.

Along with corruption, professional soldiers substantiated an account of Hanoverian empire over Britain. Radicals influenced by classical republicanism focused their attention on the King's German Legion. Most histories of the Hanoverian legion have been elegiac, ignoring the substantial opposition to their presence in Britain. Cobbett ridiculed their practice of 'singing psalms in battalion and in the open streets to the . . . petrification of the hardened sinners',[100] but he saw a more sinister potential. He complained that

> amongst all the regiments . . . upon the embarkation list, I have not seen any of the Hanoverians, of whom we have, according to the lowest account, thirteen thousand in this country! That these heroes might not relish the East or West Indies or the Mediterranean or North America, that they might prefer the mild climate of England to the scorching of the South or the freezing of the North, I could easily conceive. But supposing . . . that they must burn . . . with impatience to join in the 'deliverance of Europe' and particularly of their own dear country I am . . . filled with astonishment . . . to see such a long embarkation list and not a single man of them upon it.[101]

---

98   W. P. R., *A Few Valuable Hints for the New Ministry Shewing that Peace with France Is Possibly Attainable without Degrading the Honour of Great Britain* (London, 1806), pp. 17–18.
99   *Cobbett's Political Register* 9 (1806), col. 668.
100   *Cobbett's Political Register* 10 (1806), cols. 583–4.
101   *Cobbett's Political Register* 10 (1806), col. 583.

This was not merely a question of favoritism. Republicans had long feared that England's mild climate would attract invaders, as it supposedly had during antiquity. Cobbett presented a cautionary tale by which British regulars were shipped to the colonies and replaced by less trustworthy Hanoverians. Even the imprecation of cowardice did not alleviate anxiety, for individual timidity went hand in hand with the power of a standing army in the aggregate. If the King's German Legion became an instrument for subverting British liberty, it would be a case of Hanoverian empire without a metropolis.

Hanover did not remain Prussian for long. The court of Friedrich Wilhelm III went to war with France upon discovering that Napoleon had considered returning Hanover to George III during abortive negotiations with Britain. Cobbett wryly observed that the French emperor 'was thereby securely refixing a millstone about the neck of England'.[102] Instead, Napoleon seized the electorate for a second time, in the course of a brilliant campaign which gravely humiliated Prussia. Britain ended its war with Prussia at Memel in January 1807.

Many Britons, desperate for continental allies, were appalled that France had used Hanover to hinder Prusso-British rapprochement.[103] The opposition member of parliament George Canning wondered 'if the restoration of Hanover were the sole object, it was worthwhile to make war against Prussia?'[104] Here was the old criticism of British empire over Hanover, articulated by a politician later associated with relative disengagement from the European continent. In answer to Canning, the foreign secretary Viscount Howick (later prime minister as Earl Grey) denied that Hanover had been the sole casus belli with Prussia. But he also wondered 'whether it could be reconciled with any sentiment of magnanimity, honor, or justice to allow its lawful sovereign to be deprived of Hanover in consequence of a war between Great Britain and France'.[105] This argument, the familiar case for assistance to Hanover on the basis of personal union, won over the majority of British politicians. Addington (now President of the Council as Lord Sidmouth) believed that the 1726 parliamentary guarantee, which pledged to protect Hanover from Britain's enemies, still applied.[106] The prime minister Lord Grenville concurred, but subverted his own position by paraphrasing George Bubb Dodington to the effect that 'if Hanover was invaded on account of its connection with this country, he would as soon fight for Hanover as for Hampshire'.[107] This could be confused with an imperialist obligation to defend Hanover.

[102] *Cobbett's Political Register* 10 (1806), col. 644.
[103] See the remarks of George Canning in T. C. Hansard, ed., *The Parliamentary Debates* (41 vols., London, 1812–20), viii, cols. 50–1.
[104] Hansard, ed., *The Parliamentary Debates*, viii, col. 49.
[105] Hansard, ed., *The Parliamentary Debates*, viii, col. 66.
[106] Hansard, ed., *The Parliamentary Debates*, viii, col. 282.
[107] Hansard, ed., *The Parliamentary Debates*, viii, col. 265.

Grenville's flourish particularly offended one resident of Hampshire, namely William Cobbett. Cobbett's first response to was to criticize British empire over Hanover, as it appeared that the electorate's restoration remained a sine qua non for peace. Observing that parliament had not authorized this policy,[108] Cobbett alleged the government was in violation of the Act of Settlement. He dismissed the argument that Britain owed assistance to the electorate invaded for its sake. Cobbett wrote,

> this is the very case provided for in the Act of Settlement. It was foreseen . . . that France would, when at war with our sovereign and his dominions, make war upon his other dominions as well as these. And therefore such a law was passed as was thought sufficient to guard this country against the expense and blood attending the defense of those other dominions . . . It was in the power of the king's ancestors to refuse to accept of the crown of England upon the conditions contained in the Act of Settlement.[109]

Here, counterfactual history of a wistful sort accompanied attacks on British empire over Hanover.

But Cobbett had not forgotten that the Act of Settlement also protected Britain from the reverse scenario, of Hanoverian empire over it. He believed the presence of the King's German Legion was illegal, writing

> the Act of Settlement provides that no foreigner shall hold in this kingdom any place of *trust*, civil or military. And to suppose that this meant to exclude foreign officers from our army while it left room for the introducing of both foreign officers and foreign troops into the nation . . . to remain established is an absurdity not for one moment to be tolerated.[110]

Although Cobbett complained that the Hanoverians were more expensive to maintain than an equivalent number of British regulars,[111] he reiterated that he would be less troubled 'if these Hanoverians were . . . hired by us to be sent to the *West* or the *East Indies* or to *Gibraltar* in order to spare the lives of our native troops'. He playfully argued that the King's German Legion exacerbated the overpopulation recently diagnosed by Thomas Malthus,[112] but Cobbett's real concern – left unstated – was that it could subvert Britain's liberties from within. Because Hanover was occupied by Napoleon, its role in the republican imagination changed from that of launching pad for invasion to that of recruiting ground for a Praetorian guard.[113]

Cobbett felt vindicated in 1809, when the King's German Legion helped

---

108 *Cobbett's Political Register* 11 (1807), col. 42.
109 *Cobbett's Political Register* 11 (1807), col. 43.
110 *Cobbett's Political Register* 11 (1807), col. 428.
111 *Cobbett's Political Register* 11 (1807), cols. 429–30.
112 *Cobbett's Political Register* 11 (1807), cols. 430–1.
113 I thank Christopher Thompson for this insight.

to suppress and flog militamen protesting the price of knapsacks in the Cambridgeshire town of Ely.[114] Unaware of the fatal clash between Hanoverian legionnaires and Irish militiamen in Tullamore three years earlier,[115] Cobbett sensationalized the scarcely less violent incident in East Anglia. It would have been bad enough if foreign regulars had flogged British enlisted men,[116] but it was far worse for them to discipline the citizen soldiers who had always represented the republican alternative to standing armies. For his breathless account of what had happened at Ely, Cobbett was convicted of seditious libel at King's Bench and consigned to Newgate prison for two years. The attorney general, Sir Vicary Gibbs, complained that Cobbett was impeding the government's ability to hire foreign auxiliaries.[117] After his release in 1812, Cobbett was on probation. But after it ran out, he never failed to remind British taxpayers that they were paying pensions to former legionnaires and their dependents. On one occasion, he compared the annual payment to Hanover to the total poor rates collected in Northumberland.[118] Of course, one key index of Hanoverian empire over Britain had always been the export of currency.

During the last few years of war with Napoleon, Count Münster laid the foundation for the post-war relationship between Britain and Hanover. He buried successive British foreign secretaries with correspondence, pleading Hanover's case. In 1811, he lobbied the foreign secretary for a declaration condemning Napoleon's incorporation of northern Hanover into the French empire. He argued that Hanover

> is doubly connected with the interest of Great Britain not merely as belonging to the king and from the consideration of its having been invaded by the enemy on the sole pretence of hostility against His Majesty's crown, but also on account of its great importance in a commercial point of view. The Hanoverian territory . . . contains the whole of the coast between the great navigable rivers of the north of Germany, and a canal which unites the Elbe with the Baltic, and . . . reaches to the very gates of the three Hanseatic towns.[119]

Here was the familiar maritime argument for British influence over Hanover, which dated back to the electoral seizure of Bremen and Verden in the early eighteenth century. It represented something of a climbdown from Münster's

---

114 *Cobbett's Political Register* 15 (1809), cols. 993–4.
115 Beamish, *History of the King's German Legion*, i, pp. 95–100.
116 See J. R. Dinwiddy, 'The Early Nineteenth-Century Campaign against Flogging in the Army', *The English Historical Review* 97 (1982), pp. 308–31; Linda Colley, *Captives* (New York, 2002), pp. 328–41.
117 *Cobbett's Political Register* 18 (1810), cols. 5–6.
118 *Cobbett's Political Register* 73 (1831), cols. 521–2.
119 Münster to Wellesley, 6 Feb. 1811, NA, FO 34/3.

emphasis on independence six years earlier. But had Hanover been the equivalent of a British possession, Münster could not have implied the injustice of its occupation on account of British policy. This position amounted to the personal union thesis; Münster wanted to have his cake and eat it too.

Münster elaborated upon this point in a letter to another foreign secretary, Lord Castlereagh, late the following year during Napoleon's retreat from Russia. He wrote that

> it may be foreseen that according to the law of succession, the crown of Great Britain is likely to be transferred to another family. The House of Brunswick possessing no real estate in this country and having been deprived of their dominions in Germany for the avowed purpose of the enemy of avenging his grievances against England, would be reduced to a situation far beneath that of many private families in this country. And it cannot be denied that this humiliation would be the unfortunate consequence of their having been called to fill the throne of Great Britain.[120]

Münster referred to the eventual succession of Princess Charlotte, the only daughter of the prince regent.[121] As Berlepsch had earlier noticed, this would have ended the dynastic union of Hanover and Britain under normal circumstances. Münster worried that the male line, which would have inherited the electorate, would be left with less so long as Napoleon occupied it.

As Hanover's eventual restoration seemed more assured in light of French defeats, Münster's attentions shifted to procuring British support for Hanoverian enlargement at an eventual peace conference.[122] In early 1813, Münster submitted a memorandum to Castlereagh (again with the knowledge of the prince regent) specifying the Prussian territories of Hildesheim, Minden, and Ravensberg as possible Hanoverian acquisitions. He added,

> Great Britain may surely claim some advantages in favor of the German possessions of the royal family, to which possessions the illustrious House of Brunswick Lüneburg will be reduced if in the course of time the crown should be transferred to another family. These acquisitions will not increase the sacrifices England is to make at present, and her real interest would certainly be promoted by establishing a country on a more solid basis, which from its geographical situation is very interesting in a commercial point of view.[123]

---

120 Münster to Castlereagh, Dec. 1812, NA, FO 34/4.

121 Münster had first anticipated the end of dynastic union in a letter to George Canning, 30 June 1807, London, NA, FO 34/1.

122 See Günther Lange, 'Die Rolle Englands bei der Wiederherstellung und Vergrößerung Hannovers 1813–1815', *Niedersächsisches Jahrbuch für Landesgeschichte* 28 (1956), pp. 73–178.

123 Ernst Friedrich Herbert, Graf Münster, 'Memoire Concerning the Question: How the interest of the King's German Dominions Might Be Best Secured under the Present Circumstances', 30 Mar. 1813, NA, FO 34/6.

Here again, Münster sugar-coated Hanover's independence for a British audience by emphasizing its strategic maritime location, and implying a degree of electoral deference. George Cruikshank later simplified this position in a caricature which depicted an eventual peace with Napoleon. Napoleon's toadies carry off John Bull's arm, which is labeled 'Hanover', while his other limbs are 'Ireland', the 'West Indies', and the 'East Indies'. This is the most vivid illustration of the argument which incorporated Hanover into the British empire.[124]

Unsurprisingly, this unprecedented diplomatic cooperation ran alongside a familiar chorus of misgivings. *The Times* warned in 1812 that 'the reunion of Hanover to the crown of England is a consummation by no means to be wished . . . the fate of Hanover is that of the continent. We can only feel for her as we feel for Saxons, Hessians, or Dutchmen.'[125] Here was the familiar maritime critique of empire on the continent. Earl Grey echoed this vein of argument the following year, when he told the house of lords that 'it would have been better for this country had Hanover been at the bottom of the sea'.[126]

The first specific issue to raise the hackles of the British opposition was the elevation of Hanover into a kingdom, which Münster persuaded the prince regent to announce in October 1814. Referring to the simultaneous employment of 15,000 Hanoverian auxiliaries, the whig leader George Tierney complained to the house of commons that 'in order that Hanover should be made a kingdom and gain an accession of territory England was to pay for it'.[127] In response, Nicholas Vansittart (the chancellor of the exchequer) informed Tierney that 'the titles of electors could not longer be retained with any degree of propriety. Surely when there was no longer any emperor to elect there could be no use for electors! Whether the powers of Germany chose to be called grand dukes or kings . . . this country had no concern with it.'[128] Once again, the personal union theory quelled the imperial interpretations that fuelled scrutiny of Hanover.

If Hanover's regal status did not concern Britain, the whig member of parliament Samuel Whitbread answered, then its territorial expansion certainly did. He reasoned that 'the more extensive that kingdom should become the more likely it was to draw this country at some future period into a new continental war'.[129] Here again was the maritime critique of empire over Hanover. But it did not prevent Castlereagh from making the opposite

---

124 See Stephens and George, eds., *Catalogue of Political and Personal Satires*, ix, pp. 264–5.
125 *The Times* no. 8709 (18 Sept. 1812), p. 2.
126 Hansard, ed., *The Parliamentary Debates*, xxvi, col. 739.
127 Hansard, ed., *The Parliamentary Debates*, xxix, col. 348.
128 Hansard, ed., *The Parliamentary Debates*, xxix, col. 350.
129 Hansard, ed., *The Parliamentary Debates*, xxix, col. 363.

*Preparing John Bull for General Congress* (1813), George Cruikshank

case a few months later. Returning from the Congress of Vienna, Castle-reagh referred the house of commons to Hanover's acquisition of Hildesheim and East Friesland. Although the price for East Friesland was the pivotal duchy of Lauenburg (located as it was between the Elbe and the Baltic), the new accession gave Hanover control over a third major German river – the Ems. Castlereagh concluded 'that the increase of territory she had received tended to consolidate her connection with this country by the extent of seacoast which it gave her. While liable to be intercepted from this country, her efficiency was less considerable.' Here again was the maritime argument for empire over Hanover, which had always emphasized the electorate's stra-tegic location astride shipping lanes. Attempting to preempt criticism, Castlereagh conceded that 'on this point there had always been some degree of jealousy in this country. But he was rather inclined to think that Hanover had, generally speaking, suffered more than she had gained from the connec-tion.'[130] Of course, Castlereagh glossed over the fact that Hanover's suffering might entail British suffering – the heart of the position which opposed im-perialism over that country.

The response to Castlereagh's speech was muted, both in the house of commons and in public. The Cornish-born doctor and satirist John Wolcot captured the atmosphere of critical levity in addressing Castlereagh's return from Vienna.

> 'Tis said he's work'd with glorious aim,
> To elevate *Britannia's* name,
> Which we may readily infer
> Since he has made of *Hanover*
>
> A *kingdom*. Matchless patriot! Who
> Such tow'ring genius ever knew?
> And it is said (though heav'n give
> Our king and regent long to live)
>
> Should Charlotte mount the British throne
> That kingdom must her sway disown
> Because ('tis thus report doth speak)
> It's subject to the law salique
>
> Which (ungallantly, I must own)
> Will let no lady mount a throne
> Not deeming *female* competent
> To hold the reins of government,

---

[130] Hansard, ed., *The Parliamentary Debates*, xxx, col. 301.

*Gen'rals* or *captains* to create
Or to appoint in *church* or *state*
Therefore Hanover (matchless work!)
Will have for king THE D--- OF YORK.[131]

Here was the most accessible and public prophecy of the eventual end of Britain's dynastic relationship with Hanover, although it would be Victoria rather than Charlotte whose succession was the catalyst.

The Napoleonic period witnessed the consummation of maritime dreams: the extended excision of Hanover, and thereby the European continent, from the British monarchy. But the reality of ostracism from Europe was unpleasant enough that Britain fought to restore the status quo ante, finally doing so between 1813 and 1815. This was a victory not only for Britons who envisioned a kind of empire over Hanover, but for Hanoverians who had upheld personal union during its darkest days in 1803. But as they reestablished dynastic union, Britons and Hanoverians simultaneously anticipated its eventual demise. Princess Charlotte looked poised to inherit the British crown from her father the prince regent, later George IV. But she could not rule in Hanover, which privileged male succession. Her premature death in 1817 only delayed dynastic union's end, which came with Victoria's succession to the British throne in 1837. But dynastic union's imminent end never dampened interest in it. The years between 1815 and 1837 were controversial, containing as they did the throes of religious and political modernization in both Britain and Hanover. Britons and Hanoverians perceived that both countries were confronting similar issues (for example, Catholic emancipation and parliamentary reform), and wondered whether their countries' dynastic connection might play a role in them. In its final years, dynastic union was anything but a lame duck.

131 [John Wolcot], *Bonaparte in Paris, or the Flight of the Bourbons* (London, [1815]), pp. 10–11.

# 9

# Reform

The period after 1815 is the least studied period in the history of Britain's relationship with Hanover.[1] Historians seem to have assumed that knowledge of the impending end of union, issuing from different laws respecting female succession, reduced the relevance of dynastic union. But this eventuality could appear remote, and observers usually focused upon dynastic union's contemporary influence. This was most often detected in liberalism, the expansion of the right to participate in formal politics or the economy. George IV's extension of civil and political rights to Hanoverian Catholics in 1824 made it harder for him to resist similar measures in Britain; Hanoverian Catholics apparently benefited from the same double standard established for Quebec in 1774. Both precedents were of great interest to the activists who managed to procure equality for Catholic laymen in 1829. Just as Hanoverian developments influenced Catholic emancipation in Britain, Britain's reform act of 1832 influenced Hanover's constitution of the following year; both enfranchised middle-class men. Finally, Britain and Hanover reduced the legacy of coerced labor in 1833. Britain provided for the eventual abolition of slavery in its Caribbean colonies by a combination of compensation and apprenticeship, while Hanover abolished the last remnants of such commutation – seigneurial dues.[2] Finally, Hanoverian reform occurred in the context of rule by the duke of Cambridge – especially

---

[1] For exceptions, see Wolf D. Gruner, 'England, Hannover, und der deutsche Bund 1814–1837', in Adolf M. Birke and Kurt Kluxen, eds., *England und Hannover* (München, 1986), pp. 81–126; Philip Konigs, *The Hanoverian Kings and Their Homeland: A Study of the Personal Union 1714–1837* (Sussex, 1993), pp. 161–71; Michael John, 'National and Regional Identities and the Dilemmas of Reform in Britain's "Other Province": Hanover, c. 1800 – c. 1850', in Laurence Brockliss and David Eastwood, eds., *A Union of Multiple Identities: The British Isles, c. 1750 – c. 1850* (Manchester, 1997), pp. 179–92; Nicholas B. Harding, 'North African Piracy, the Hanoverian Carrying Trade, and the British State, 1728–1828', *The Historical Journal* 43 (2000), pp. 25–47; Mijndert Bertram, 'The End of the Dynastic Union, 1820–1837', in Brendan Simms and Torsten Riotte, eds., *The Hanoverian Dimension in British History, 1714–1837* (Cambridge, 2007).

[2] For Hanover's abolition of seigneurial dues, see Reinhard Oberschelp, *Politische Geschichte Niedersachsens 1803–1866* (Hildesheim, 1988), p. 130; Mijndert Bertram, *Das Königreich Hannover: Kleine Geschichte eines vergangenen deutschen Staates* (Hannover, 2003), p. 48.

after his promotion to viceroy in 1831. The formal supercession of collegial by viceregal rule brought Hanover closer to British colonial forms. All of these developments informed imperial interpretations of the dynastic union during its latter days.

Yet liberalism was not limited to the British empire; indeed, it was spreading throughout the Atlantic world. Although the British reform act of 1832 attempted to avoid the means of France's 1830 revolution, it had similar ends. Liberalism would have advanced in Hanover and Britain, even had they not been joined in dynastic union. In conferring civil and political equality upon Hanoverian Catholics, George IV was simply bringing Hanoverian law into conformity with the constitution of the German confederation as established at the Congress of Vienna. Furthermore, Britain's reform act of 1832 and the Hanoverian constitution of 1833 functioned rather differently. While the Hanoverian constitution mandated elections for urban representatives to the estates (these had previously been selected by magistrates only),[3] elections were a familiar ritual of British politics. Accordingly, the reform act instead targeted constituencies and qualifications for the franchise. And while Münster's 1831 resignation reduced the appearance of rule from Britain, Hanover's resulting autonomy was different from the 'responsible government' won by British colonies of settlement after the 1840s. While the latter required governors to draw their officials from colonial assembly, there was no comparable provision in the Hanoverian constitution of 1833. These disparities promoted the personal union thesis.

British reformers initially took a dim view of Hanover. This was first apparent after the Prince Regent appointed his younger brother, the duke of Cambridge, to be first military governor (1813) and then governor general (1816) of Hanover. Although the appointments promised to mitigate the problem of the royal absence from Hanover, real power continued to rest with Münster in London. The real significance of Cambridge's promotion lay in Britain, where reformers opposed increasing the duke's civil list upon the occasion of his marriage in 1818 (itself a response to the succession crisis posed by the death of Princess Charlotte). The whig member of parliament Henry Brougham requested that the house of commons 'should be apprised of the revenue derived from Hanover by the duke of Cambridge' and hoped that 'a country which had so often been the cause of augmenting the expense of Great Britain should at length contribute something towards an alleviation of our burdens'.[4] Brougham's emphasis upon Hanoverian self-sufficiency might have indicated adhesion to the ideal of personal union. But a strict construction of personal union might preclude parliament from considering

---

3  Oberschelp, *Politische Geschichte Niedersachsens 1803–1866*, p. 120.
4  T. C. Hansard, ed., *The Parliamentary Debates* (41 vols., London, 1812–20), xxxviii, col. 12.

Cambridge's Hanoverian position at all. The abolitionist member of parliament William Wilberforce objected that 'he thought that the House had nothing to do with Hanover. It was never . . . the habit of parliament to meddle in the concerns of Hanover, and he believed that we should rather lose than gain by any connection with the affairs of that country.'[5]

Wilberforce was closest to the personal union thesis, while opposition figures used it to disguise what were actually imperial arguments. The member of parliament Thomas Brand agreed that 'the House ought not to inquire into the income of the royal duke in Hanover . . . but the House ought to inquire whether the sum demanded was to be expended in England or in Hanover'.[6] To Brand, British monies spent by the duke in Hanover looked like imperial tribute. George Tierney saw the issue in opposite terms. He announced that

> the viceroy or chief governor of Hanover had all the means under his own control that could be required to supply his wants or to maintain his dignity. There was in fact no civil list in Hanover to limit the wishes of the duke of Cambridge. His Royal Highness could therefore command whatever he desired . . . He also knew . . . that money was of much greater value in that country than here.[7]

This was the familiar suggestion that Britain exploit Hanoverian absolutism for its own benefit. In the end, parliament rejected imperial interpretations of the relationship with Hanover by awarding Cambridge an increased civil list. But imperial arguments continued to flourish in opposition (particularly radical) circles.

These resurfaced when George IV announced that he intended to visit his German kingdom after his coronation, the first time Hanover had enjoyed its ruler's presence since 1755. In the uproar over the king's attempt to divorce Queen Caroline,[8] the radical journalist Richard Carlile playfully observed that

> the best way to settle this dispute will be for the king to sit on the Hanoverian throne, and the queen on that of Great Britain and Ireland . . . The queen has shown much more of the spirit which characterizes the English nation than the king has ever done. He will be much better adapted for a German climate.[9]

Facetious or not, Carlile effectively proposed an end to dynastic union. On the face of it, his assertion that a German was better suited to rule Britain

---

5   Hansard, ed., *The Parliamentary Debates*, xxxviii, col. 131.
6   Hansard, ed., *The Parliamentary Debates*, xxxviii, col. 134.
7   Hansard, ed., *The Parliamentary Debates*, xxxviii, col. 135.
8   See Thomas W. Laqueur, 'The Queen Caroline Affair: Politics as Art in the Reign of George IV', *Journal of Modern History* 54 (1982), pp. 417–66.
9   *The Republican* 3 (1820), p. 336.

and that a Briton better suited to govern Hanover was peculiar. But Caroline was popular with constitutional radicals, while George IV's authoritarian manner evoked continental European associations.

Caroline died in the summer of 1821, but Hanover remained in the news because George IV visited it immediately after his trip to Ireland in the autumn. If the visit itself were not enough to confirm George IV's Hanoverian loyalties to his skeptical British subjects, his behavior there was. The king informed a jubilant Hanoverian crowd that 'I have always been a Hanoverian. I will live and die a Hanoverian!' The flourish ingratiated Hanoverians, but put off English observers. James Leigh Hunt's *Examiner* observed that when in Dublin, the 'king had an "Irish heart" and we now learn that he always has been an Hanoverian. Whether any part of the sacred body is peculiarly British, or whether like Christ Jesus His Majesty has more than one nature, may perhaps be announced some day by those in the secret.'[10]

Apart from George IV's attempt to be all things to all people, British radicals also scrutinized Hanoverian ceremonial. Much like the tour of Ireland which preceded it, the visit was a whirlwind of pageantry worthy of its royal impresario. In his radical newspaper *The Black Dwarf*, Thomas Jonathan Wooler remarked that ' "*the humblest inhabitants*" displayed the letters G. R. IV. decorated with various ornaments. Now if the humblest inhabitants of England were to do this they must *steal* the lamps and the oil and the ornaments, for it is certain they *cannot afford* to buy them.' Not that Hanoverians were any better off; Wooler could not 'conceive where the Hanoverians contrived to find *the means*. Hanover was never rich, and when the French took a fancy to the ancient electorate they made it still poorer than it used to be. It has little trade, and but few resources.' This was one of the few instances where an observer posited economic parity between the two countries, or at least the majority of their respective populations. Ultimately, Wooler ascribed any apparent discrepancy to public assistance.[11]

If British money had underwritten Hanoverian display, then it represented a transfer of wealth to Hanover. Indeed, fears of Hanoverian empire over Britain revived during the king's visit. Wooler reported that

> while *arms* are interdicted to the mass of the people of Ireland, and while whole counties in Great Britain are under statutory restrictions with respect to the possession of arms, it is said the *citizens* of Hanover who lined the streets in numerous bodies to receive His Majesty had '*each of them a musket in his hands*'!

Wooler referred to the Seizure of Arms Act, one of the notorious Six Acts passed in 1819 to quell popular radicalism. From this, Wooler extrapolated that

[10] *The Examiner: A Sunday Paper on Politics, Domestic Economy, and Theatricals for the Year 1821* (London, 1822), p. 696.
[11] *The Black Dwarf* 7 (1821), p. 569.

the conqueror of Great Britain and Ireland had returned to the capital of his native country and was received by a nation of *armed men* in triumph from the conquest of the countries which have been *disarmed* by act of parliament. It is a singular contrast at any rate that a free nation should be forbidden the possession of arms, and that a state notoriously despotic should bring forth its citizens with arms in their hands to receive their sovereign![12]

Focusing on possession of firearms, a precondition for resistance to tyranny, Wooler reprised the republican case against Hanoverian empire.

*The Morning Chronicle* countered that Britain was insulated from Hanoverian influence, the royal visit notwithstanding. It considered that 'we can take no cognizance of what passes there any more than the Hanoverians can of what passes here'. This sounded very much like the personal union thesis. The *Chronicle* continued, writing

parliament having allowed a foreign sovereign to ascend our throne and to retain dominions independent of this country, all the rest follows a matter of course. Indeed, previous to the dissolution of the German empire His MAJESTY, as a state of that empire, might according to its constitution have been obliged to contribute his share to a war against England. The wisdom of our forefathers was no doubt very great, but they overlooked occasionally very important matters.[13]

Although personal union seemed to provide Britain with a measure of security, many Britons still wished that it had been nipped in the bud – by the Act of Settlement. Anxieties subsided after the king had returned to Britain, but showed how easily the grievances of the eighteenth century might resurface.

The next German development to resonate in Britain was a proclamation of 18 December 1824, in which the Hanoverian government recognized the civil and political equality of Catholics. In a German context, this was merely confirmation of the Vienna settlement, which had mandated religious toleration on the regional as well as national level. It was also an attempt to facilitate the integration of new acquisitions such as Hildesheim and Osnabrück, which had Catholic majorities, into the kingdom of Hanover. George IV later disclaimed any advance knowledge of the proclamation, which could have ominous repercussion in Britain.[14] There, the king refused to legalize Catholic officeholding in Britain even if it might appease another majority-Catholic jurisdiction – Ireland. He believed

12 *The Black Dwarf* 7 (1821), p. 565.
13 *The Morning Chronicle* no. 16397 (7 Nov. 1821), p. 2.
14 George IV to Liverpool, 25 Feb. 1825, King's Lodge, in Arthur Richard Wellesley, 2nd duke of Wellington, ed., *Despatches, Correspondence, and Memoranda of Field Marshal Arthur, Duke of Wellington K. G.* (8 vols., London, 1867–80), ii, p. 418.

Catholic emancipation would contradict his British coronation oath. So Hanover joined Quebec among possessions which apparently profited from a double standard.

The Hanoverian proclamation could not have come sooner for Daniel O'Connell, the Dublin barrister who was coming to personify the campaign for Catholic emancipation. Not only was the parliament expected to consider the measure during its coming session, but it also looked ready to outlaw his political organization – the Catholic Association. At one of its meetings, O'Connell praised George IV as a 'king that by his Hanoverian proclamation has proved that . . . if left to the exercise of his genuine sentiments he would long since have smitten the foul demon of intolerance . . . But the beneficent intentions of his sovereign had been counteracted . . . by the intolerance of a bigoted and base borough-mongering oligarchy.'[15] The proclamation gave O'Connell an opportunity to flaunt his loyalty, and thereby appeal to traditionalists otherwise skeptical about his reformist agenda. He even avoided accusing the king of hypocrisy by alluding to personal union; while supposedly absolute in Hanover, the king was limited in Britain. He later underscored this point by proposing separate toasts to George IV in each of his royal capacities.[16] O'Connell had a vested interest in personal union, as it would have resulted from his proposed repeal of Anglo-Irish union.

Nevertheless other Catholic nationalists repined at personal union, at least between Hanover and Britain. Nicholas Purcell O'Gorman, the secretary of O'Connell's Catholic Association, informed one meeting that

> George the fourth was the king of Hanover as well as of Great Britain, and that in the former state his power was absolute. He (Mr. O'Gorman) almost wished that his absolute authority extended over these realms because it was seen that where that authority did prevail it was exerted in the abolition of all religious distinctions.[17]

To some Catholics and their sympathizers, Hanoverian absolutism – or even empire – seemed appealing in early 1825.

The Catholic Association was echoed within the house of commons itself by Brougham. Damning Hanover with faint praise, he observed that

> England has had frequent occasion to lament her connection with Hanover. It is an ill wind, however, that blows nobody any good. That connection has proved highly serviceable to the cause of Ireland by showing the sentiments entertained by the king on the subject which now agitates Ireland. I allude to . . . the proclamation of George the 4th, king of Hanover. It is his proclamation

15 *The Dublin Evening Post* no. 9300 (11 Jan. 1825), p. 4.
16 *The Dublin Evening Post* no. 9305 (22 Jan. 1825), p. 4.
17 *Supplement to the Dublin Evening Post* (17 Feb. 1825), p. 3.

individually. It does not proceed from responsible advisers . . . It was, therefore, with no small delight that I read this, which I consider as a test of His Majesty's real opinion.[18]

Hanover's monarchy still appeared absolute to Britons, but supporters of Catholic emancipation found this was preferable to responsible government. Brougham continued, saying 'our government has too frequently been in the habit of imitating the governments of the continent . . . I hope they will take this whole leaf out of the volume of the practice of Hanover'.[19] Brougham could be said to support a form of Hanoverian empire, in this one case.

Opponents of emancipation were in a bind. They dared not openly criticize the king as ruler of Hanover, for fear of alienating an important ally. But they were relatively free to vent in private correspondence. This was William Wordswoth's response. In a letter, the conservative poet observed that

> Mr. Brougham exults in the late application of his liberal notions to Hanover, but in Hanover the Protestants are more than ten to one and the government is military . . . Hanover indeed possesses a legislative assembly, but its powers are so ill defined that it could not attempt to do anything important without bringing on immediately its own dissolution from the military force. It has on the other hand a censorship of the press.[20]

In other words, religious liberalism was only possible in an absolute monarchy. Wordsworth was in the familiar tradition of resisting Hanoverian influence (even empire) in Britain. This was the tradition which won in 1825, when parliament rejected Catholic emancipation and outlawed the Catholic Association. Nevertheless, O'Connell still hoped that the Hanoverian proclamation had made Catholic emancipation more likely in the long term. In a speech at Freemason's Hall, he informed his audience that he had 'pasted the Hanoverian proclamation in my parlor'.[21] How long the proclamation remained there is uncertain, but it remained an arrow in the quiver of emancipists until their eventual success in 1829.

Hanover's connection to Britain looked strong during the Restoration period; given the lengthy Napoleonic interlude it could hardly have seemed otherwise. In certain respects, the connection was even stronger than that which had prevailed before 1803. Never before had a member of the British

---

[18] T. C. Hansard, ed., *The Parliamentary Debates* second series (25 vols., London, 1820–30), xii, col. 61.

[19] Hansard, ed., *The Parliamentary Debates* second series, xii, cols. 61–2.

[20] Wordsworth to Lowther, 12 Feb. 1825, Rydal Mount, published in *The Letters of William and Dorothy Wordsworth: The Later Years*, Alan G. Hill, Mary Moorman, Ernest de Selincourt, and Chester L. Shaver, eds. (8 vols., Oxford, 1967–93), iv, p. 311.

[21] *Supplement to the Dublin Evening Post* (3 Mar. 1825), p. 2.

royal family served as governor, as Cambridge did after 1813. Cambridge's promotion inspired identification with Britain, exemplified by his appearance before Hanover's unprecedented estates general in 1814. In a speech drafted by Rehberg,[22] the duke admonished deputies 'to be to [the prince regent] here what the parliament is in the sister kingdom Great Britain, the high council of the nation'.[23] Use of the word 'sister' notwithstanding, Cambridge and Rehberg assumed British constitutional superiority. But, at least, he left open the possibility of future equality.

But identification was not submission, and the estates had no intention of allowing Britain to exploit Hanover as it had done in the eighteenth century. When the Hanoverian government was organizing the kingdom's militia, the estates asked for a promise that the force would not be deployed overseas. While the prince regent rejected this request, he informed Cambridge that he would not use it 'for an interest foreign to the kingdom of Hanover'.[24] The estates asked for, and received, the same assurance when the militia and army were amalgamated in 1820.[25] It is difficult to ascertain whether the word 'foreign' was meant to apply to Britain in 1820. But that was certainly how it was interpreted in 1824, when Hanover refused to sell auxiliaries to Britain for use in Portugal.[26] Münster cautioned George IV that protests would attend a broken promise, adding that the king's 'states in Germany have suffered from their supposed identity with England'.[27] Here was the implicit equivalent of the Act of Settlement's war clause which, if it had existed at all during the eighteenth century, had been more often honored in the breach.

But other grievances against Britain remained. A Hanoverian correspondent of the Saxon publicist Christian Daniel Voß complained in 1816 that

> what promotes England's happiness disturbs our own . . . The government of a great empire with provinces in all regions of the world deprives the smaller state of [the prince's] vigilance. The great remove and eternal absence of the prince . . . estranges. Herein lies the origin of our aristocracy, which has nearly grown into an oligarchy.[28]

This author echoed those critics of 1803, such as Spilcker and Seumnich, who depicted British empire and Hanoverian aristocracy in a symbiotic

---

[22] See Bertram, *Das Königreich Hannover*, p. 34.

[23] *The Times* no. 9402 (27 Dec. 1814), p. 2.

[24] *Acten-Stücke der provisorischen oder ersten allgemeinen Stände-Versammlung des Königreichs Hannover* (4 vols., Hannover, 1822), i, p. 182.

[25] *Acten-Stücke der zweiten allgemeinen Stände-Versammlung des Königreichs Hannover* (6 vols., Hannover, 1820–5), i, p. 200.

[26] Oberschelp, *Politische Geschichte Niedersachsens 1803–1866*, p. 89; Bertram, *Das Königreich Hannover*, p. 39.

[27] Münster to George IV, 19 July 1824, Hannover, Niedersächsisches Hauptstaatsarchiv (NHStA), Dep. 110, A, Nr. 185.

[28] *Die Zeiten, oder Archiv für die neueste Staatengeschichte und Politik* 47 (1816), p. 27.

relationship. He only parted company with the anglophobic tradition in his admission that the prince regent did not transport Hanoverian revenues to Britain.[29] The king's absence remained an issue despite George IV's visit in 1821.

Much as it had in the 1790s, a French Revolution loosed the tongues of Hanoverian anglophobes. The July Revolution of 1830 was an occasion to criticize Restoration Europe, including Hanoverian dynastic union with Britain. The opportunity was compounded by the death, in June, of George IV. His successor, William IV, was open to change in Britain, where his new whig ministry began to explore parliamentary reform. But in Hanover, he seemed content to preside over the status quo. The time seemed ripe to demand change.

In January 1831, the Osterode lawyer Georg Friedrich König published a blistering assault on Count Münster's government of Hanover entitled *Anklage des Ministeriums Münster vor der öffentlich Meinung* (Indictment of the Münster Ministry before Public Opinion). Unsurprisingly, König faulted the king's absence, writing 'William our citizen king is ignorant of the state of things. How indeed should he know anything of it? The name of the king – to Hanoverians a mere phantom in consequence of his eternal absence – only affords protection to the boundless exercise of ministerial despotism.' As the royal residence, Britain had, at the very least, inadvertently occasioned misrule in Hanover. But had it knowingly exploited Hanover? König was equivocal. Noting the restoration of serfdom to Osnabrück in 1814, he highlighted the irony that this happened at 'the arbitrary hands of the ministers of a king reigning over the freest nation of the earth'. By highlighting an apparent double standard, König appeared to assume the existence of a personal union. But elsewhere he hinted at British empire over Hanover, an allegation given credence by Münster's continued residence in London. König complained, for instance, that 'Wellington and Münster have taken care that we Hanoverians should not receive a farthing for the ten years' occupation of our country.' This recalled Hanoverian resentment that similar aid had never materialized after the Seven Years' War. König also complained that 'sinecures, those parasite plants of which we knew nothing before 1814, have been introduced into our soil where they spread and thrive wonderfully. But the minister will in due time have to answer for transplanting this English abuse to Hanover.'[30] König might have owed this observation to Seumnich, but the latter had made it long before 1814. Nevertheless, both saw political corruption as evidence for cultural imperialism from Britain. Before König could publish the *Anklage*, he was imprisoned. But the news of his incarceration inspired civil unrest in nearby Göttingen, where the *Anklage* circulated widely. A number of residents

---

[29] *Die Zeiten, oder Archiv für die neueste Staatengeschichte und Politik* 47 (1816), p. 37.
[30] [Georg Friedrich König], 'Charges against Count Münster's Administration Preferred before the Tribunal of Public Opinion', *The Times* no. 14474 (28 Feb. 1831), p. 3.

founded a national guard, while the military fled. Although it soon returned and suppressed the revolt,[31] the Restoration regime's days were numbered.

Perhaps the only figure not to realize this was Münster himself. Münster responded to König with two pamphlets, the anonymously published *Acten-mäßige Würdigung einer Schmähschrift* (Documentary Estimate of a Libel) and the *Erklärung des Ministers Grafen von Münster* (Declaration of the Minister, Count Münster). Münster seized upon the question of William IV's absence, asking 'were not George I, George II, and George III also absent? Did these princes, who are still remembered with grateful love, have better ways of acquiring information about the country's condition than George IV and William IV, who sent their noble brother here as lieutenant?'[32] Recounting the generosity of absent rulers, Münster added that 'only kings whose throne is situated in a separate empire can be so openhanded'. This was, of course, the old argument that the ruler's absence spared Hanoverian taxpayers certain expenses. As for the complaint that the monarch's absence encouraged oligarchy, Münster claimed that 'our nobility is what the gentry is in England – landed freeholders'.[33] By the time Münster composed his *Erklärung*, he had already resigned under pressure from William IV. The king had acted upon the request of Cambridge, who was subsequently promoted to viceroy. These two events not only left Cambridge unrivalled in Hanoverian politics, but cleared the deck for reform in the kingdom.

Hanoverian reform culminated in the constitution of 1833, which was initially drafted by the anglophilic Göttingen professor Friedrich Christoph Dahlmann. How similar were Hanoverian reformers to their British counterparts? The Celle lawyer and publisher Salomon Philipp Gans claimed they shared the same opponent, a force 'which until now stubbornly opposed every urgent reform in England; it was an aristocracy which ruled in Hanover as in England. But in Hanover, as in England, the power of circumstances finally triumphed.'[34] August Wilhelm Rehberg argued against comparison, writing that 'whatever might happen in England, the secluded island empire, cannot be applied to German countries'.[35] This represented a retreat from the more nuanced position he had represented against Berlepsch

---

31 Oberschelp, *Politische Geschichte Niedersachsens 1803–1866*, pp. 100–1.

32 [Ernst Friedrich Herbert Graf von Münster], *Actenmäßige Würdigung einer Schmäh-schrift welche unter dem Titel 'Anklage des Ministeriums Münster vor der öffentlichen Meinung' in dem Königreich Hannover verbreitet worden ist* (Hannover, 1831), p. 5.

33 Ernst Friedrich Herbert Graf von Münster, *Erklärung des Ministers Grafen von Münster über einige in der Schmähschrift 'Anklage des Ministeriums Münster' ihm persönlich gemachte Vorwürfe so wie über seinen Austritt aus dem Königlich-Hannöverschen Staatsdienst* (Hannover, 1831), p. 14.

34 *Verhandlungen über die öffentlichen Angelegenheiten des Königreichs Hannover und des Herzogthums Braunschweig* 1 (1831), p. 146.

35 [August Wilhelm Rehberg], *Constitutionelle Phantasien eines alten Steuermannes im Sturme des Jahrs 1832* (Hamburg, 1832), p. 89.

and Häberlin in 1797. Rehberg also believed that the two countries' reform projects differed in so far as Hanoverians contemplated a 'fundamental law which will order all branches of the constitution – and perhaps also the government',[36] while the British 'parliamentary reform only involves a change in the franchise'.[37] In so doing, Rehberg both exaggerated the radicalism of Hanoverian reform and underestimated its importance in Britain. In contrast to Rehberg, Hanoverian liberals tended to associate their cause with British reform.

Implicit in Rehberg's treatment, the personal union theory was explicitly endorsed by the conservative anglophobe Hermann Grote. Writing in 1832, Grote considered that

> it is immaterial whether the prince of East Friesland lives in Aurich, Hannover, or London; East Frieslanders need not be hanoverianized or anglicized. England and Hanover were unified under a ruler by Ernst August's marriage with a princess of the Palatinate. But this bond has been a blessing for both, because both exist independently of one another, because the interests of one are never sacrificed to those of the other.[38]

Such diffidence about the residence of the monarch was rare, and probably had something to do with its East Frisian context. East Friesland, with its relatively egalitarian history, never fit comfortably into the kingdom of Hanover. In his attempt to defuse East Frisian resentment at being ruled from Hannover, Grote likewise had to downplay the possibility of control from London.

Of course, a purely Hanoverian context conferred greater latitude in diagnosing effects of the monarch's residence in Britain. Usually, some sort of British primacy over Hanover was ascribed to this fact. Some observers construed this to be salutary. The syndic of Soltau, Eduard Weinlig, rhapsodized that

> free Albion's rulers are accustomed from the cradle to truth and liberty, which otherwise flee before the luster of the throne. Their spirit's first breath inhales the principle that the power of their scepter rests solely in the freedom, strength, and love of their people. And these noble rulers of the freest people under the sun are . . . also your kings.[39]

This was the argument, initially articulated by Spittler, that British freedom was transferred to Hanover through the person of the monarch.

---

36 [Rehberg], *Constitutionelle Phantasien*, p. 11.
37 [Rehberg], *Constitutionelle Phantasien*, p. 10.
38 *Beiträge zur Kenntniß der Verfassung, Gesetzgebung und Verwaltung des Königreichs Hannover* 1 (1831–2), p. 181.
39 Eduard Weinlig, *Was drückt das hannoversche Volk und wie könnte ihm vielleicht geholfen werden?* (Hamburg, 1832), p. 100.

Another silver lining in the monarch's absence was the fact that court expenditures were not as high as they otherwise would have been; indeed, the leftover money was not (as anglophobes feared) shipped to Britain but spent on philanthropy. Addressing a British-inspired proposal – the introduction of a civil list in Hanover – before the second chamber of the estates, the government officer Justus Philipp Rose observed that

> no English prince has helped himself to the country's money except for that which has been spent within Hanover for His Royal Highness the duke of Cambridge. By this means the royal house has, with admirable generosity, sacrificed an immense private income to the country. But we must anticipate that, God forbid, . . . this land may be separated from the English crown. We must ensure that insoluble difficulties do not arise from the sacrifices which that connection has made possible.[40]

The fear was that the court of a resident monarch would eat into the income previously devoted to charity, and might even necessitate higher taxes.

Other observers were less sanguine than Rose. A deputy to the estates from Osnabrück, Johann Carl Bertram Stüve, noted that 'the preservation of the court admittedly served to keep a part of the royal domain's income in the country. But the court offices were now lucrative sinecures for the nobility.' Unsurprisingly, he connected the rise of Hanover's aristocracy to the monarch's absence, writing that

> since Elector Georg Ludwig ascended the English throne as George I, the nobility gained influence everywhere. The prince was no longer in the country and his servants, furnished with unbelievably expanded authority, took his place. With them rose the nobility to which they belonged, and which had previously been easily repressed by princely power.[41]

Stüve managed to keep open the possibility that Hanoverian funds went to Britain while nevertheless weakening Rose's argument. While favoring a civil list, Stüve argued (in vain, as it turned out) against another British import – the upper chamber of the estates, introduced by Münster in 1819. Agreeing from prison, König argued against retaining the first chamber in any new constitution on the grounds that

> materially speaking, there is no aristocracy on hand, and therefore it cannot be represented. As for the form, an aristocracy has evolved in Hanover over many years. But this has no aristocratic elements in it, but rather artificially produces a surrogate in bureaucrats. Such an aristocracy cannot exist on its own, as in

---

40 *Hannoversche Zeitung* no. 157 (3 July 1832), p. 1012.
41 Johann Carl Bertram Stüve, *Ueber die gegenwärtige Lage des Königreichs Hannover* (Jena, 1832), p. 24.

England, France, and the southern German states, but only at the cost of the people.[42]

Having attempted to defeat Hanoverian aristocracy by decrying it, Hanoverian reformers now tried to do so by denying it. Unlike Münster had done in his *Erklärung*, König radically differentiated between the Hanoverian and British aristocracies. In so doing, he represented a long tradition; this distinction had first been made by the anglophilic pastor of 1790, who had modeled his estates upon the house of commons rather than Britain's bicameral parliament. Liberals still argued against the extension of some British models to Hanover.

On balance, the monarchical absence remained unpopular. Stüve complained that

> it certainly is difficult to structure the government well, when the prince does not live in the country. It is fair – indeed essential – that the subject who is inconvenienced by a decision of the minister bring his complaint to the ear of the ruler. But the latter, born and raised in a foreign land and ignorant of affairs, will always need the reports of his advisers. If these are the same whose decision is questioned, the complaint is useless.

This was obviously in the tradition of Berlepsch and Seumnich, who had similarly emphasized Hanoverians' difficulty in reaching their absent king. And like Berlepsch, Stüve saw the consequences of the ruler's absence deteriorating with time. The visits of George I and George II had compensated for their long absences, but 'George III never came to Germany'.[43] While Stüve presented the most detailed case against the royal absence, a colleague from the county of Hoya – Karl Rudolf Ferdinand Christiani – added the novel observation that 'the estates had not approved' the 'absence of the king'.[44] Even strong partisans of the estates, such as Spittler and Berlepsch, had avoided arguing the estates' right to veto princely absences. This position informed Christiani's proposal that the estates invite William IV to visit his German kingdom.[45]

The king's absence also had an effect upon the Hanoverian resident in London. The obvious illustration was Münster, whose long absences in London had earned him the sobriquet of Mondminister (minister on the

---

[42] Georg Friedrich König, *Ueber die politischen und bürgerlichen Reformen und den Entwurf eines Staatsgrundgesetzes für Hannover* (Leipzig, 1832), p. 187.

[43] Johann Carl Bertram Stüve, *Ueber die gegenwärtige Lage des Königreichs Hannover* (Jena, 1832), p. 63.

[44] *Verhandlungen über die öffentlichen Angelegenheiten des Königreichs Hannover und des Herzogthums Braunschweig* 1 (1831), p. 74.

[45] See *Verhandlungen über die öffentlichen Angelegenheiten des Königreichs Hannover und des Herzogthums Braunschweig* 1 (1831), pp. 131–2.

moon).[46] Stüve considered that 'proximity to the king can promote this minister over the others . . . But . . . the ignorance about the country of this highly placed but long distant statesman . . . has led to countless mistakes.'[47] This was actually generous, as other liberals tended to blame Münster for witting, rather than inadvertent, misrule. Regardless, the constitution of 1833 required future governments to reside in Hanover.[48]

The events which led to Münster's fall quickly drew British attention. *The Times* regretted that 'the Hanoverian dominions of HIS MAJESTY have been the worst governed state in Germany'. This was because

> the system of absentee kings is as injurious to a country as that of absentee landlords, and for more than a century Hanover has seen less of her English sovereigns than Ireland of her English proprietors. As the attorneys and the land agents of the latter are often a bad substitute for their own presence and superintendence so are viceroys, ministers, and commanders-in-chief of the former.

Comparisons to Ireland were nothing new, but an additional charge was – at least in Britain. *The Times* finally updated the old republican definition of absolute rule, which had rested on the professional military, to one which depended upon aristocratic hegemony. 'The ascendancy', it explained, 'of the aristocracy over the people was nowhere asserted with more insolence or exercised with greater oppression.' *The Times* was aware, of course, that the same could be said of Britain; it concluded by observing that 'a liberal and humane monarch who gives his willing sanction to reform in this country cannot be inattentive to a call upon him for a similar boon from a state which was the cradle of his ancestors'.[49] But while urban unrest caught the attention of the press, its vigilance flagged during the next two years of Hanoverian constitutional reform.

If *The Times* had introduced new perspectives on Hanover, other newspapers reheated old ones. As Britain moved to support an independent Belgium in 1831, William Cobbett returned to grind a familiar axe. He fulminated that

> all this uncertainty and this deadening of trade and commerce has arisen from a desire to keep the French out of Belgium . . . for the protection of the *north of Germany!* Why do they not say Hanover, Brunswick, and the rest of it at once?

---

[46] Richard W. Fox, 'Konservative Anpassung an die Revolution: Friedrich von der Decken und die hannoversche Militärreform 1789–1820', *Niedersächsisches Jahrbuch für Landesgeschichte* 45 (1973), p. 216.

[47] Stüve, *Ueber die gegenwärtigen Lage*, p. 64.

[48] § 4.

[49] *The Times*, no. 14447 (27 Jan. 1831), p. 2.

And why do they not say, as Lord GRENVILLE said in 1806, that Hanover ought to be *as dear to us as Hampshire?* . . . If I were minister and found Hanover to be the property of England, as Canada and Nova Scotia and Prince Edward Island (unhappily for us) are our property, I should be selling it to the highest bidder and bringing the florins to help pay off the debt that has been contracted in the German wars.[50]

Although Cobbett distinguished between Canada and Hanover, he implied that the latter functioned as an imperial responsibility of Britain. This did nothing for his opinion of the country, for Cobbett had extended his skepticism about the European continent to transoceanic empire more generally.

The next time Hanover came before the attention of the British public was in 1832, when its government concurred in a decree of the German federal diet which reduced the powers of local estates and expanded censorship on the national level. News of this action punctured the euphoria of British liberals, who had only just secured parliamentary reform with the assistance of William IV. As *The Morning Chronicle* put it, 'it is difficult to believe that the individual who was a constitutional reformer in England could be an enemy of constitutional liberty in Hanover'. Conspiracy theorists found it peculiarly ominous that the king had approved the measure during the duke of Wellington's brief, anti-reform government earlier that same year.[51] The matter reached a head when members of the National Political Union declined to drink the king's health at a festival celebrating the passage of parliamentary reform.[52]

The Frankfurt diet's decree revived the older understanding of Hanoverian conservatism, which had focused on monarchy rather than aristocracy. This was evident in William's supporters as well as detractors. During an assembly of reformers at London's Crown and Anchor Tavern, one George Yorke attempted to 'defend the king from the attacks that had been made upon him relative to Hanover. That kingdom was his property just as much as this room was the property of the proprietor of the tavern, and therefore he might deal with it just as he pleased.'[53] The theory which accounted for the coexistence of two different constitutions under one monarch was, of course, that of personal union.

This foremost representative of this position was the foreign secretary, Lord Palmerston. Palmerston reassured William IV that 'Great Britain and Hanover have little in common except the sovereign whom both have the happiness to obey . . . Placed geographically in situations essentially different, they must frequently have interests and engagements differing no

---

[50] *Cobbett's Political Register* 73 (1831), col. 338.
[51] *The Morning Chronicle* no. 14914 (26 July 1832), p. 3.
[52] *The Morning Chronicle* no. 19646 (14 Aug. 1832), p. 3.
[53] *The Morning Chronicle* no. 19640 (7 Aug. 1832), p. 2.

less.'[54] But Palmerston also found it necessary to inform parliament that soon after William IV had ratified the Frankfurt Diet's action, he had confirmed the rights of his Hanoverian estates.[55] It was still necessary to reassure parliament that Hanover was governed constitutionally, personal union notwithstanding. And Palmerston confided doubts about personal union to Earl Grey, writing

> that if the politics of the two countries are to be . . . bound together, England, being the most powerful and important, is entitled to lead Hanover and not Hanover to lead England . . . If the English government is to be tied by that which the Hanoverian has done, they ought to be previously consulted and to have a voice in the deliberation.[56]

The personal union theory's most prominent advocate was privately considering British empire over Hanover.

The parliamentary radical Joseph Hume expressed the same ambivalence about personal union. 'Considering Hanover as separate and apart from this country', he observed, 'there was a great distinction to be drawn between the acts of the king of Hanover and the acts of the king of England. But the majority of persons would not be able to appreciate the justice of such a distinction.'[57] For this reason, Hume

> had always regretted the connection of England with Hanover for that connection had been an unceasing source of evils to this country. He was sorry to see the government of England about to lose its reputation in Europe as a liberal government and as the protector of liberal institutions . . . at a moment when the people of England had just secured for themselves the maintenance of their own rights and privileges.[58]

Given his belief in personal union, Hume was mostly concerned about guilt by association.

The liberal member of parliament Henry Lytton Bulwer concurred in Hume's pessimistic assessment of Hanover's role in British history. He contended that 'one of the misfortunes which accompanied the otherwise happy event of the accession of the present family to the British throne was that by which George the 1st remained elector'. But he parted company from Hume in the question of personal union. Bulwer asserted that

---

[54] Palmerston to William IV, 5 Aug. 1832, London, published in Sir Charles Webster, *The Foreign Policy of Palmerston 1830–1841* (2 vols., London, 1951), ii, p. 799.

[55] *Hansard's Parliamentary Debates* third series (361 vols., London, 1830–91), xiv, col. 1067.

[56] Palmerston to Grey, 3 Aug. 1832, London, published in Webster, *The Foreign Policy of Palmerston*, ii, p. 800.

[57] *Hansard's Parliamentary Debates* third series, xiv, col. 1062.

[58] *Hansard's Parliamentary Debates* third series, xiv, col. 1063.

it might be very well to say that Hanover and England were two separate kingdoms, that the one had nothing to do with the other. This might be the case
theoretically, but it never had been – it could not be so – practically . . .
Besides, was it possible to contend that an individual could be so little identified with himself as to have his troops as king of Hanover fighting on one side
of a question and his troops as king of England on another? The policy pursued
by the king of Hanover must, without strong proofs to the contrary, be considered as the probable policy of the king of England.[59]

Bulwer believed Hanover and Britain formed a more unitary (and unwhole-
some) entity.

Inevitably, there were calls for an end to union. Complaining about the
king's civil list to a meeting of the National Union of the Working Classes,
Julian Hibbert suggested that William IV 'go back to Hanover and get better
paid there'.[60] Hibbert strategically ignored Hanover's relative poverty. But
cooler heads argued that personal union was already over in all but name.
The Morning Chronicle wondered

whether King WILLIAM, though nominally master of Hanover, at all inter-
feres in Hanoverian politics. As Hanover must soon pass from the sovereign of
England, it is by no means impossible that His MAJESTY has resigned to the
individual who will succeed to it the management of its affairs. And there
would be nothing singular in the duke of CUMBERLAND's concurrence
heartily in the decree of Frankfurt.[61]

The Chronicle overestimated Cumberland's influence over contemporary
Hanover, but it was certainly right that he would eventually inherit Hanover
upon his niece Victoria's succession to the British throne. Indeed, Cumberland was already burnishing his Hanoverian credentials. During a visit to
Hanover in 1836, the duke informed his hosts that 'Hanoverian blood flows
in my veins. From my fifteenth year I received my education in this country,
and cannot but look on Hanover as my native land.'[62]

As it happened, Cumberland inherited the Hanoverian crown upon William
IV's death in 1837. German law, which did not recognize female succession,
ruled out his niece Victoria. Union with Britain ended as it had begun, via
dynastic mechanism. This solidified the conviction of certain contemporaries that the relationship had always been a personal union. Hanover's
daily paper observed that

---

59 *Hansard's Parliamentary Debates* third series, xiv, col. 1039.
60 *The Poor Man's Guardian* no. 60 (4 Aug. 1832), p. 483.
61 *The Morning Chronicle* no. 19634 (31 July 1832), p. 3
62 *The Times* no. 16007 (23 Jan. 1836), p. 3.

the union of both kingdoms was personal rather than real, the constitutions and administrations of both countries different from each other. Both countries drew from this union all the advantages which corresponded to their respective interests, without being sacrificed to that of the other. While England has recently belonged to the system of western European powers, Hanover has – as a member of the German federation – remained in that of the eastern Europeans.[63]

Here was a familiar – almost canned – rendition of the personal union thesis, already demonstrating its capacity to thwart anything more than a superficial history of Hanover's relationship with Britain.

One might have expected a similar response from the journalist Hermann Grote, who had upheld the personal union thesis since 1832. In 1835, he had even proposed renumbering the Hanoverian rulers to reflect the adoption of the royal dignity in 1814 – and to reject the British usage which had prevailed since 1714.[64] But because of this anglophobia, Grote greeted the end of union with a jubilant 'hurrah!'[65] Explaining himself, he wrote that

the princes who ruled Hanover during this period [of union with Britain] were all highly distinguished rulers, and would have improved Hanover even more than they did had they been present. But the princes had to leave their government to officials, and their autonomous will no longer had any opportunity to show itself. The administration, which no longer felt the immediate influence of the monarch . . . sank . . . into the worst slothocracy.[66]

Gone was Grote's insouciance about the king's location. Indeed, he appeared to resurrect the monarchical ethos which had been declining ever since George I had departed to claim the British crown. He considered that

a prince is necessary not merely to ascend the throne, but . . . to assume control of the administration. A king who reigns, but governs as well! . . . A prince with political experience and certain principles . . . who lived the first half of his life under the most enlightened of all constitutional monarchies and the other under the most enlightened of all absolute monarchies.[67]

Grote rarely complimented Great Britain; his praise of Prussia was far less perfunctory. This, of course, had been Cumberland's primary residence after the Napoleonic wars. Grote hoped that Cumberland would provide the monarchical leadership which Hanover had lacked ever since the inception of union with Britain. His expectations would be exceeded.

63  *Hannoversche Zeitung* (29 June 1837), p. 1786.
64  *Hannoversche Landesblätter* 5 (1835), p. 59.
65  *Hannoversche Landesblätter* 6 (1837), p. 88.
66  *Hannoversche Landesblätter* 6 (1837), p. 87.
67  *Hannoversche Landesblätter* 6 (1837), p. 88.

Grote's happiness at the end of union was matched by that of at least one British paper. *The Globe* cheered that

> the interests of Great Britain will therefore be no longer involved with those of a continental state, and its rulers will for the future be freed from a necessity, which has often proved both costly and perilous, of interfering with affairs in which the people of this country had no immediate concern . . . We have also lost the right of intermeddling with matters that do not belong to us.[68]

This was, of course, the traditional maritime argument against British empire over Hanover.

*The Globe* was practically the only British paper to analyze the end of union. Indeed, the end of dynastic union was strangely anti-climactic. One reason the end of union did not attract much press attention was the fact that it might have proved to be a false cadence. Cumberland (or King Ernst August, as he was now known) was Britain's heir presumptive until the birth of Princess Victoria in 1840. The first three years of Queen Victoria's reign resembled the period between 1701 and 1714, when a Hanoverian succession appeared imminent. Of course, the teenaged queen was more likely to live and reproduce than Anne, who was middle-aged and infirm upon her succession. Knowing that Ernst August did not succeed to the British throne, 1837 looks more like 1714 in reverse. *The Morning Chronicle* published a letter from Britannia to Hanover, which began 'some hundred years ago I borrowed a sovereign from you. I have now the satisfaction of repaying the loan.'[69]

'Satisfaction' was the prevailing sentiment at Cumberland's departure. Ernst August had been something of a press sensation in Britain, where allegations of incest and murder dogged him. Liberals despised the duke's politics, which had brought him back from Berlin to oppose Catholic emancipation and parliamentary reform. Even political allies mistrusted his ambition and regretted his indiscretion. Both groups were horrified to see him overturn the constitution Hanover had adopted in 1833, which led to the protest and dismissal of the 'Göttingen 7' from their professorships. Focus upon these events, and Ernst August's personality, helps to explain the relative scarcity of structural commentaries upon the end of union. And while Ernst August's coup necessitated greater knowledge in Britain and Hanover of each other's affairs, the resulting debates were fundamentally different from those which had characterized the union before 1837. For one, Ernst August's British background reversed the asymmetry in freedom which had been perceived earlier; now, Hanoverian liberalism was threatened by British autocracy. If the coincidence of reform in Britain and Hanover had

---

68 *The Globe and Traveller* no. 10802 (21 June 1837), p. 2.
69 *The Morning Chronicle* no. 21095 (23 June 1837), p. 3.

not depended upon dynastic union, the end of the latter nevertheless ended the former at a stroke.

In an ironic symmetry, dynastic union – which had begun with a death (the duke of Gloucester's) – ended with a birth (the princess royal's). Metropolitan Britain evolved into a nation state, while Hanover itself became part of a larger German nation state. The nation-state preoccupied the new 'profession' of history, which was of the same vintage. But historians' search for the origins of the nation-state led them, in the case of Hanover and Britain, to valorize one historical interpretation of their relationship (the personal union) over others which had emphasized political convergence. Now that historians find themselves explaining the decline of the nation state rather than its rise, it makes sense to rehabilitate the discourses of transnational integration. These, in turn, introduce the European continent to the history of the British empire, and the empire to the history of European Union.

# Index